Getting Started with Python for the Internet of Things

Leverage the full potential of Python to prototype and build IoT projects using the Raspberry Pi

Tim Cox
Dr. Steven Lawrence Fernandes
Sai Yamanoor
Srihari Yamanoor
Prof. Diwakar Vaish

BIRMINGHAM - MUMBAI

Getting Started with Python for the Internet of Things

First published: February 2019

Production reference: 1250219

Published by Packt Publishing Ltd.
Livery Place
35 Livery Street
Birmingham
B3 2PB, UK.

ISBN 978-1-83855-579-5

www.packtpub.com

`mapt.io`

Mapt is an online digital library that gives you full access to over 5,000 books and videos, as well as industry leading tools to help you plan your personal development and advance your career. For more information, please visit our website.

Why subscribe?

- Spend less time learning and more time coding with practical eBooks and Videos from over 4,000 industry professionals

- Improve your learning with Skill Plans built especially for you

- Get a free eBook or video every month

- Mapt is fully searchable

- Copy and paste, print, and bookmark content

Packt.com

Did you know that Packt offers eBook versions of every book published, with PDF and ePub files available? You can upgrade to the eBook version at `www.packt.com` and as a print book customer, you are entitled to a discount on the eBook copy. Get in touch with us at `customercare@packtpub.com` for more details.

At `www.packt.com`, you can also read a collection of free technical articles, sign up for a range of free newsletters, and receive exclusive discounts and offers on Packt books and eBooks.

Contributors

About the authors

Tim Cox works as a software engineer and is passionate about programming. He holds a bachelor's degree in electronics and electrical engineering and has a rich career in developing embedded software for a range of industries. To support the vision behind the Raspberry Pi and to encourage a new generation of engineers, Tim co-founded the MagPi magazine (the official magazine for the Raspberry Pi). He also produces electronic kits through his site PiHardware.

Dr. Steven Lawrence Fernandes holds a bachelor's degree in electronics and communication engineering, a master's degree in microelectronics, and a Ph.D. in computer vision and machine learning. His Ph.D work "Match composite sketch with drone images" has received patent notification (Patent Application Number: 2983/CHE/2015). has post the doctoral research experience working in deep learning at the University of Alabama at Birmingham, USA. He received the prestigious US award from the Society for Design and Process Science for his outstanding service contributions in 2017 and Young Scientist Award by Vision Group on Science and Technology in 2014. He has also received a research grant from the Institution of Engineers.

Sai Yamanoor is an embedded systems engineer working for a private startup school in the San Francisco Bay Area, where he builds devices that help students achieve their full potential. He completed his undergraduate work in mechatronics engineering from Sri Krishna College of Engineering and Technology, Coimbatore, India and his graduate studies in mechanical engineering at Carnegie Mellon University, Pittsburgh PA. His interests, deeply rooted in DIY and open software and hardware cultures, include developing gadgets and apps that improve the quality of life, Internet of Things, crowdfunding, education, and new technologies. In his spare time, he plays with various devices and architectures, such as the Raspberry Pi, Arduino, Galileo, Android devices and others. Sai has earlier published a book titled Raspberry Pi Mechatronics Projects.

Srihari Yamanoor is a mechanical engineer, working on medical devices, sustainability, and robotics in the San Francisco Bay Area. He completed his undergraduate studies in mechanical engineering from PSG College of Technology, Coimbatore, India and graduate studies in mechanical engineering at Stanford University. He is certified in SolidWorks, simulation, sustainable design, PDM as well as in quality and reliability engineering and auditing. His has a wide range of interests, from DIY, crowdfunding, AI, travelling, photography to gardening and ecology.

Prof. Diwakar Vaish is a robotics scientist and the inventor of Manav, India's first indigenous humanoid robot. He has invented the world's first mind-controlled wheelchair, brain cloning, and the world's cheapest ventilator. He has also been a guest lecturer at over 13 IITs and various other institutions. He is the founder of A-SET Robotics, a leading robotics research company based in New Delhi.

Packt is searching for authors like you

If you're interested in becoming an author for Packt, please visit `authors.packtpub.com` and apply today. We have worked with thousands of developers and tech professionals, just like you, to help them share their insight with the global tech community. You can make a general application, apply for a specific hot topic that we are recruiting an author for, or submit your own idea.

Table of Contents

Preface

This Learning Path takes you on a journey in the world of robotics and teaches you all that you can achieve with Raspberry Pi and Python.

It teaches you to harness the power of Python with the Raspberry Pi 3 and the Raspberry Pi zero to build superlative automation systems that can transform your business. You will learn to create text classifiers, predict sentiment in words, and develop applications with the Tkinter library. Things will get more interesting when you build a human face detection and recognition system and a home automation system in Python, where different appliances are controlled using the Raspberry Pi. With such diverse robotics projects, you'll grasp the basics of robotics and its functions, and understand the integration of robotics with the IoT environment.

By the end of this Learning Path, you will have covered everything from configuring a robotic controller, to creating a self-driven robotic vehicle using Python.

This Learning Path includes content from the following Packt products:

- Raspberry Pi 3 Cookbook for Python Programmers - Third Edition by Tim Cox, Dr. Steven Lawrence Fernandes
- Python Programming with Raspberry Pi by Sai Yamanoor, Srihari Yamanoor
- Python Robotics Projects by Prof. Diwakar Vaish

Who this book is for

This book is specially designed for Python developers who want to take their skills to the next level by creating robots that can enhance people's lives. Familiarity with Python and electronics will aid understanding the concepts in this Learning Path.

What this book covers

Chapter 1, Getting Started with a Raspberry Pi 3 Computer, introduces the Raspberry Pi and explores the various ways in which it can be set up and used.

Chapter 2, Dividing Text Data and Building Text Classifiers, guides us to build a text classifier; it can classify text using the bag-of-words model.

Chapter 3, Using Python for Automation and Productivity, explains how to use graphical user interfaces to create your own applications and utilities.

Chapter 4, Predicting Sentiments in Words, explains how Naive Bayes classifiers and logistic regression classifiers are constructed to analyze the sentiment in words

Chapter 5, Detecting Edges and Contours in Images, describes in detail how images are loaded, displayed, and saved. It provides detailed implementations of erosion and dilation, image segmentation, histogram equalization, edge detection, detecting corners in images, and more.

Chapter 6, Building Face Detector and Face Recognition Applications, explains how human faces can be detected from webcams and recognized using images stored in a database.

Chapter 7, Using Python to Drive Hardware, establishes the fact that to experience the Raspberry Pi at its best, we really have to use it with our own electronics. This chapter discusses how to create circuits with LEDs and switches, and how to use them to indicate the status of a system and provide control. Finally, it shows us how to create our own game controller, light display, and a persistence-of-vision text display.

Chapter 8, Sensing and Displaying Real-World Data, explains how to use an analog-todigital converter to provide sensor readings to the Raspberry Pi. We discover how to store and graph the data in real time, as well as display it on an LCD text display. Next, we record the data in a SQL database and display it in our own web server. Finally, we transfer the data to the internet, which will allow us to view and share the captured data anywhere in the world.

Chapter 9, Building a Neural Network Module for Optical Character Recognition, introduces neural network implementation on Raspberry Pi 3. Optical characters are detected, displayed, and recognized using neural networks

Chapter 10, Arithmetic Operations, Loops, and Blinky Lights, walks through the arithmetic operations in Python and loops in Python. In the second half of the chapter, we will discuss the Raspberry Pi Zero's GPIO interface and then learn to blink an LED using a GPIO pin.

Chapter 11, Conditional Statements, Functions, and Lists, discusses the types of conditional statements, variables, and logical operators in Python. We will also discuss functions in Python. Then, we will learn to write a function that is used to control DC motors using the Raspberry Pi Zero.

Chapter 12, Communication Interfaces, covers all the communication interfaces available on the Raspberry Pi Zero. This includes the I2C, UART, and the SPI interface. These communication interfaces are widely used to interface sensors. Hence, we will demonstrate the operation of each interface using a sensor as an example.

Chapter 13, Data Types and Object-Oriented Programming in Python, discusses object-oriented programming in Python and the advantages of object-oriented programming. We will discuss this using a practical example.

Chapter 14, File I/O and Python Utilities, discusses reading and writing to files. We discuss creating and updating config files. We will also discuss some utilities available in Python.

Chapter 15, Requests and Web Frameworks, discusses libraries and frameworks that enable retrieving data from the Web. We will discuss an example, fetching local weather information. We will also discuss running a web server on the Raspberry Pi Zero.

Chapter 16, Awesome Things You Could Develop Using Python, discusses libraries and frameworks that enable retrieving data from the web. We will discuss examples such as fetching the local weather information. We will also discuss running a web server on the Raspberry Pi Zero

Chapter 17, Robotics 101, will make you understand the basics of our hardware and Python. Using simple LEDs, we will start to make simple programs in Python.

Chapter 18, Using GPIOs as Input, will discuss how to connect various sensors, starting with interfacing a switch through an ultrasonic range finder and finally to a light sensor (LDR) using an analog-to-digital converter.

Chapter 19, Making a Gardener Robot, will use various sensors, such as a soil humidity sensor, and a temperature sensor to sense the climate, and using a solenoid valve controlled by a relay, we will be making a robot that waters the garden whenever required.

Chapter 20, Basics of Motors, will discuss the working of motor and how it can be driven by a motor driver, how a full H bridge motor driver works, and also how the speed control mechanism works in the motor driver. While doing all this, we will control a motor and make it move in a different direction at different speeds.

Chapter 21, Bluetooth-Controlled Robotic Car, will teach more about steering and controlling a robotic vehicle, and the concepts of a skid-steer mechanism will be implemented. You will also learn how to use the Bluetooth onboard our Raspberry Pi and connect it to your mobile phone. Finally, using an app, we will control our robotic vehicle using our mobile phone.

Chapter 22, Sensor Interface for Obstacle Avoidance, will provide an insight into how we can use IR proximity sensors to determine distances. Also, we will make smart algorithms to sense distance on all sides and then move in the direction where the distance is greatest.

Chapter 23, Making Your Own Area Scanner, will teach you the basics of servo motors and how they can be controlled. Using servo motor, we will make an area scanner, in other words, a homemade LIDAR. Using this home-built sensor, we would make a self navigating car.

Chapter 24, Basic Switching, will control the equipment at your home with simple logic. Finally, we will make an alarm that will wake you up in the natural way by lights. This will have a smart automatic snooze.

Chapter 25, Recognizing Humans with Jarvis, will teach you how to control devices at your home with a room occupancy sensor that we will build at home using an IR proximity sensor. We will then make this occupancy sensor smart and ready to count the number of people in the room and only switch off the lights or other equipment once no one is left in the room.

Chapter 26, Making Jarvis IoT Enabled, will provide you with insights into the concepts of IoT and MQTT server through which we will be able to monitor our home based on events. Also, you will learn how to control the devices in our home while sitting anywhere in the world.

Chapter 27, Giving Voice to Jarvis, will teach you how the system can be made capable of synthesizing speech. Also, you will learn how you can make the system recognize our speech, and based on it, everything in the home can be controlled.

Chapter 28, Gesture Recognition, will make you identify the gestures made on the board using electric waves, and based on those gestures, the smart home will be controlled.

`Chapter 29`, Machine Learning, will make you understand the concepts of machine learning and especially the k-nearest algorithm. Using this algorithm, you will understand how data can be given to the system and predictions can be made based on it . Finally, you will execute a program to generate its own data by the inputs of the users over the course of time, and based on that data, it will start automatically controlling the home without any human intervention.

`Chapter 30`, Making a Robotic Arm, will help you make a robotic hand. You will understand how to set the physical limits of the servos for protection purposes, and we will then make a program in which you will control the robot will be controlled based on different frames. Finally, you will go ahead and understand how to control speed of motion of the robot.

To get the most out of this book

To start using this book, Readers are expected to know the basics of Python programming. It would be beneficial for readers to have a basic understanding of machine learning, computer vision, and neural networks.
The following hardware is recommended as well:

- A laptop computer, with any OS
- Raspberry Pi
- A microSD card, either 8 GB or 16 GB
- A USB keyboard, mouse and a WiFi card
- A display with HDMI input
- Power supply, minimum 500 mA
- Display cables and other accessories

Readers will have to download and install RASPBIAN STRETCH WITH DESKTOP; this will give us the GUI interface for Raspberry Pi

Download the example code files

You can download the example code files for this book from your account at `www.packt.com`. If you purchased this book elsewhere, you can visit `www.packt.com/support` and register to have the files emailed directly to you.

You can download the code files by following these steps:

1. Log in or register at www.packt.com.
2. Select the **SUPPORT** tab.
3. Click on **Code Downloads & Errata**.
4. Enter the name of the book in the **Search** box and follow the onscreen instructions.

Once the file is downloaded, please make sure that you unzip or extract the folder using the latest version of:

- WinRAR/7-Zip for Windows
- Zipeg/iZip/UnRarX for Mac
- 7-Zip/PeaZip for Linux

The code bundle for the book is also hosted on GitHub at https://github.com/ PacktPublishing/GettingStartedwithPythonfortheInternetofThings. In case there's an update to the code, it will be updated on the existing GitHub repository.

We also have other code bundles from our rich catalogue of books and videos available at https://github.com/PacktPublishing/. Check them out!

Conventions used

There are a number of text conventions used throughout this book.

CodeInText: Indicates code words in text, database table names, folder names, filenames, file extensions, pathnames, dummy URLs, user input, and Twitter handles. Here is an example: "The input() method is used to get an input from the user."

A block of code is set as follows:

```
try:
    input_value = int(value)
except ValueError as error:
    print("The value is invalid %s" % error)
```

Any command-line input or output is written as follows:

```
sudo pip3 install schedule
```

Bold: Indicates a new term, an important word, or words that you see onscreen. For example, words in menus or dialog boxes appear in the text like this. Here is an example: "If you need something different, click on the **DOWNLOADS** link in the header for all possible downloads: "

Warnings or important notes appear like this.

Tips and tricks appear like this.

Get in touch

Feedback from our readers is always welcome.

General feedback: If you have questions about any aspect of this book, mention the book title in the subject of your message and email us at customercare@packtpub.com.

Errata: Although we have taken every care to ensure the accuracy of our content, mistakes do happen. If you have found a mistake in this book, we would be grateful if you would report this to us. Please visit www.packt.com/submit-errata, selecting your book, clicking on the Errata Submission Form link, and entering the details.

Piracy: If you come across any illegal copies of our works in any form on the Internet, we would be grateful if you would provide us with the location address or website name. Please contact us at copyright@packt.com with a link to the material.

If you are interested in becoming an author: If there is a topic that you have expertise in and you are interested in either writing or contributing to a book, please visit authors.packtpub.com.

Reviews

Please leave a review. Once you have read and used this book, why not leave a review on the site that you purchased it from? Potential readers can then see and use your unbiased opinion to make purchase decisions, we at Packt can understand what you think about our products, and our authors can see your feedback on their book. Thank you!

For more information about Packt, please visit packt.com.

1
Getting Started with a Raspberry Pi 3 Computer

In this chapter, we will cover the following topics:

- Connecting peripherals to Raspberry Pi
- Using NOOBS to set up your Raspberry Pi SD card
- Networking and connecting your Raspberry Pi to the internet via the LAN connector
- Using built-in Wi-Fi and Bluetooth on Raspberry Pi
- Configuring your network manually
- Networking directly to a laptop or computer
- Networking and connecting your Raspberry Pi to the internet via a USB Wi-Fi dongle
- Connecting to the internet through a proxy server
- Connecting remotely to Raspberry Pi over the network using VNC
- Connecting remotely to Raspberry Pi over the network using SSH (and X11 forwarding)
- Sharing the home folder of Raspberry Pi with SMB
- Keeping Raspberry Pi up to date

Introduction

This chapter introduces Raspberry Pi 3 and the process of setting it up for the first time. We will connect Raspberry Pi to a suitable display, power, and peripherals. We will install an operating system on an SD card. This is required for the system to boot. Next, we will ensure that we can connect successfully to the internet through a local network.

Finally, we will make use of the network to provide ways to remotely connect to and/or control Raspberry Pi from other computers and devices, as well as to ensure that the system is kept up to date.

Once you have completed the steps within this chapter, your Raspberry Pi will be ready for you to use for programming. If you already have your Raspberry Pi set up and running, ensure that you take a look through the following sections, as there are many helpful tips.

Introducing Raspberry Pi

The Raspberry Pi is a single-board computer created by the **Raspberry Pi Foundation**, a charity formed with the primary purpose of re-introducing low-level computer skills to children in the UK. The aim was to rekindle the microcomputer revolution of the 1980s, which produced a whole generation of skilled programmers.

Even before the computer was released at the end of February 2012, it was clear that Raspberry Pi had gained a huge following worldwide and, at the time of writing this book, has sold over 10 million units. The following image shows several different Raspberry Pi models:

The Raspberry Pi Model 3B, Model A+, and Pi Zero

What's with the name?

The name, Raspberry Pi, was a combination of the desire to create an alternative computer with a fruit-based name (such as Apple, BlackBerry, and Apricot) and a nod to the original concept of a simple computer that could be programmed using **Python** (shortened to **Pi**).

In this book, we will take this little computer, find out how to set it up, and then explore its capabilities chapter by chapter, using the Python programming language.

Why Python?

It is often asked, "Why has Python been selected as the language to use on Raspberry Pi?" The fact is that Python is just one of the many programming languages that can be used on Raspberry Pi.

There are many programming languages that you can choose, from high-level graphical block programming, such as **Scratch**, to traditional **C**, right down to **BASIC**, and even the raw **machine code assembler**. A good programmer often has to be code multilingual to be able to play to the strengths and weaknesses of each language to best meet the needs of their desired application. It is useful to understand how different languages (and programming techniques) try to overcome the challenge of converting *what you want* into *what you get*, as this is what you are trying to do as well while you program.

Python has been selected as a good place to start when learning about programming, as it provides a rich set of coding tools while still allowing simple programs to be written without fuss. This allows beginners to gradually be introduced to the concepts and methods on which modern programming languages are based without requiring them to know it all from the start. It is very modular with lots of additional libraries that can be imported to quickly extend the functionality. You will find that, over time, this encourages you to do the same, and you will want to create your own modules that you can plug into your own programs, thus taking your first steps into structured programming.

Python addresses formatting and presentation concerns. As indentation will add better readability, indents matter a lot in Python. They define how blocks of code are grouped together. Generally, Python is slow; since it is interpreted, it takes time to create a module while it is running the program. This can be a problem if you need to respond to time-critical events. However, you can precompile Python or use modules written in other languages to overcome this.

It hides the details; this is both an advantage and a disadvantage. It is excellent for beginners but can be difficult when you have to second-guess aspects such as datatypes. However, this in turn forces you to consider all the possibilities, which can be a good thing.

Python 2 and Python 3

A massive source of confusion for beginners is that there are two versions of Python on Raspberry Pi (**Version 2.7** and **Version 3.6**), which are not compatible with each other, so code written for Python 2.7 may not run with Python 3.6 (and vice versa).

The **Python Software Foundation** is continuously working to improve and move forward with the language, which sometimes means they have to sacrifice backward compatibility to embrace new improvements (and, importantly, remove redundant and legacy ways of doing things).

Supporting Python 2 and Python 3

There are many tools that will ease the transition from Python 2 to Python 3, including converters such as 2to3, which will parse and update your code to use Python 3 methods. This process is not perfect, and in some cases you'll need to manually rewrite sections and fully retest everything. You can write the code and libraries that will support both. The import __future__ statement allows you to import the friendly methods of Python 3 and run them using Python 2.7.

Which version of Python should you use?

Essentially, the selection of which version to use will depend on what you intend to do. For instance, you may require Python 2.7 libraries, which are not yet available for Python 3.6. Python 3 has been available since 2008, so these tend to be older or larger libraries that have not been translated. In many cases, there are new alternatives to legacy libraries; however, their support can vary.

In this book, we have used Python 3.6, which is also compatible with Python 3.5 and 3.3.

The Raspberry Pi family – a brief history of Pi

Since its release, Raspberry Pi has come in various iterations, featuring both small and large updates and improvements to the original Raspberry Pi Model B unit. Although it can be confusing at first, there are three basic types of Raspberry Pi available (and one special model).

The main flagship model is called **Model B**. This has all the connections and features, as well as the maximum RAM and the latest processor. Over the years, there have been several versions, most notably Model B (which had 256 MB and then 512 MB RAM) and then Model B+ (which increased the 26-pin GPIO to 40 pins, switched to using a microSD card slot, and had four USB ports instead of two). These original models all used the Broadcom BCM2835 **system on chip** (**SOC**), consisting of a single core 700 MHz ARM11 and VideoCore IV **graphical processing unit** (**GPU**).

The release of Raspberry Pi 2 Model B (also referred to as 2B) in 2015 introduced a new Broadcom BCM2836 SOC, providing a quad-core 32-bit ARM Cortex A7 1.2 GHz processor and GPU, with 1 GB of RAM. The improved SOC added support for Ubuntu and Windows 10 IoT. Finally, we had the latest Raspberry Pi 3 Model B, using another new Broadcom BCM2837 SOC, which provides a quad-core 64-bit ARM Cortex-A53 and GPU, alongside on-board Wi-Fi and Bluetooth.

Model A has always been targeted as a cut-down version. While having the same SOC as Model B, there are limited connections consisting of a single USB port and no wired network (LAN). Model A+ again added more GPIO pins and a microSD slot. However, the RAM was later upgraded to 512 MB of RAM and again there was only a single USB port/no LAN. The Broadcom BCM2835 SOC on Model A has not been updated so far (so is still a single core ARM11); however, a Model 3A (most likely using the BCM2837).

The **Pi Zero** is an ultra-compact version of Raspberry Pi intended for embedded applications where cost and space are a premium. It has the same 40-pin GPIO and microSD card slot as the other models, but lacks the on-board display (CSI and DSI) connection. It does still have HDMI (via a mini-HDMI) and a single micro USB **on-the-go** (**OTG**) connection. Although not present in the first revision of the Pi Zero, the most recent model also includes a CSI connection for the on-board camera.

Pi Zero was famously released in 2015 and was given away with Raspberry Pi foundation's magazine *The MagPi*, giving the magazine the benefit of being the first magazine to give away a computer on its cover! This did make me rather proud since (as you may have read in my biography at the start of this book) I was one of the founders of the magazine.

The special model is known as the **compute module**. This takes the form of a 200-pin SODIMM card. It is intended for industrial use or within commercial products, where all the external interfaces would be provided by a host/motherboard, into which the module would be inserted. Example products include the Slice Media Player (`http://fiveninjas.com`) and the OTTO camera. The current module uses the BCM2835, although an updated compute module (CM3).

The Raspberry Pi Wikipedia page provides a full list of the all different variants and their specifications:
`https://en.wikipedia.org/wiki/Raspberry_Pi#Specifications`

Also, the Raspberry Pi product page gives you the details about the models available and the accessories' specifications:
`https://www.raspberrypi.org/products/`

Which Pi to choose?

All sections of this book are compatible will all current versions of Raspberry Pi, but Model 3B is recommended as the best model to start with. This offers the best performance (particularly useful for the GPU examples in OpenCV examples used in `Chapter 5`, *Detecting Edges and Contours in Images*), lots of connections, and built-in Wi-Fi, which can be very convenient.

Pi Zero is recommended for projects where you want low power usage or reduced weight/size but do not need the full processing power of Model 3B. However, due to its ultra-low cost, Pi Zero is ideal for deploying a completed project after you have developed it.

Connecting to Raspberry Pi

There are many ways to wire up Raspberry Pi and use the various interfaces to view and control content. For typical use, most users will require power, display (with audio), and a method of input such as a keyboard and mouse. To access the internet, refer to the *Networking and connecting your Raspberry Pi to the internet via the LAN connector* or *Using built-in Wi-Fi and Bluetooth on Raspberry Pi* recipes.

Getting ready

Before you can use your Raspberry Pi, you will need an SD card with an operating system installed or with the **New Out Of Box System** (**NOOBS**) on it, as discussed in the *Using NOOBS to set up your Raspberry Pi SD card* recipe.

The following section will detail the types of devices you can connect to Raspberry Pi and, importantly, how and where to plug them in.

As you will discover later, once you have your Raspberry Pi set up, you may decide to connect remotely and use it through a network link, in which case you only need power and a network connection. Refer to the following sections: *Connecting remotely to Raspberry Pi over the Network using VNC* and *Connecting Remotely to Raspberry Pi over the Network using SSH (and X11 Forwarding)*.

How to do it...

The layout of Raspberry Pi is shown in the following diagram:

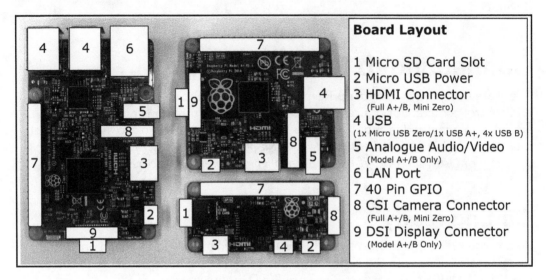

The Raspberry Pi connection layout (Model 3 B, Model A+, and Pi Zero)

More information about the preceding figure is listed as follows:

- **Display**: The Raspberry Pi supports the following three main display connections; if both HDMI and composite video are connected, it will default to HDMI only:
    - **HDMI**: For best results, use a TV or monitor that has an HDMI connection, thus allowing the best resolution display (1080p) and also digital audio output. If your display has a DVI connection, you may be able to use an adapter to connect through the HDMI. There are several types of DVI connection; some support analogue (DVI-A), some digital (DVI-D), and some both (DVI-I). Raspberry Pi is only able to provide a digital signal through the HDMI, so an HDMI-to-DVI-D adapter is recommended (shown with a tick mark in the following screenshot). This lacks the four extra analogue pins (shown with a cross mark in the following screenshot), thus allowing it to fit into both DVI-D and DVI-I type sockets:

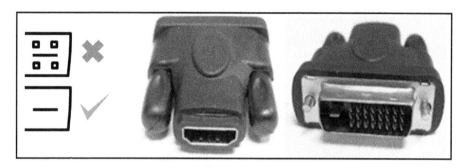

HDMI-to-DVI connection (DVI-D adaptor)

If you wish to use an older monitor (with a VGA connection), an additional HDMI-to-VGA converter is required. Raspberry Pi also supports a rudimentary VGA adaptor (VGA Gert666 Adaptor), which is driven directly off of the GPIO pins. However, this does use up all but four pins of the 40-pin header (older 26-pin models will not support the VGA output):

HDMI-to-VGA adapter

- **Analogue**: An alternative display method is to use the analogue composite video connection (via the phono socket); this can also be attached to an S-Video or European SCART adapter. However, the analogue video output has a maximum resolution of 640 x 480 pixels, so it is not ideal for general use:

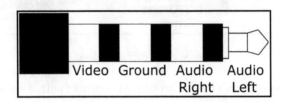

3.5 mm phono analogue connections

When using the RCA connection or a DVI input, audio has to be provided separately by the analogue audio connection. To simplify the manufacturing process (by avoiding through-hole components), the Pi Zero does not have analogue audio or an RCA socket for analogue video (although they can be added with some modifications):

- **Direct Display DSI**: A touch display produced by Raspberry Pi Foundation will connect directly into the DSI socket. This can be connected and used at the same time as the HDMI or analogue video output to create a dual display setup.

- **Stereo analogue audio (all except Pi Zero)**: This provides an analogue audio output for headphones or amplified speakers. The audio can be switched via Raspberry Pi configuration tool on the desktop between analog (stereo socket) and digital (HDMI), or via the command line using `amixer` or `alsamixer`.

To find out more information about a particular command in the Terminal, you can use the following `man` command before the terminal reads the manual (most commands should have one):

```
man amixer
```

Some commands also support the `--help` option for more concise help, shown as follows:

```
amixer --help
```

- **Network (excluding models A and Pi Zero)**: The network connection is discussed in the *Networking and connecting your Raspberry Pi to the internet via the LAN connector* recipe later in this chapter. If we use the Model A Raspberry Pi, it is possible to add a USB network adapter to add wired or even wireless networking (refer to the *Networking and connecting your Raspberry Pi to the internet via a USB Wi-Fi dongle* recipe).
- **Onboard Wi-Fi and Bluetooth (Model 3 B only)**: The Model 3 B has built-in 802.11n Wi-Fi and Bluetooth 4.1; see the *Using the built-in Wi-Fi and Bluetooth on Raspberry Pi* recipe.
- **USB (1x Model A/Zero, 2x Model 1 B, 4x Model 2 B and 3 B)**: Using a keyboard and mouse:
    - Raspberry Pi should work with most USB keyboards and mice. You can also use wireless mice and keyboards, which use RF dongles. However, additional configuration is required for items that use the Bluetooth dongles.
    - If there is a lack of power supplied by your power supply or the devices are drawing too much current, you may experience the keyboard keys appearing to stick, and, in severe cases, corruption of the SD card.

USB power can be more of an issue with the early Model B revision 1 boards that were available prior to October 2012. They included additional **Polyfuses** on the USB output and tripped if an excess of 140 mA was drawn. The Polyfuses can take several hours or days to recover completely, thus causing unpredictable behavior to remain even when the power is improved.

You can identify a revision 1 board, as it lacks the four mounting holes that are present in the later models.

- Debian Linux (upon which Raspbian is based) supports many common USB devices, such as flash storage drives, hard-disk drives (external power may be required), cameras, printers, Bluetooth, and Wi-Fi adapters. Some devices will be detected automatically, while others will require drivers to be installed.

- **Micro USB power**: The Raspberry Pi requires a 5V power supply that can comfortably supply at least 1,000 mA (1,500 mA or more is recommended, particularly with the more power-hungry Model 2 and Model 3) with a micro USB connection. It is possible to power the unit using portable battery packs, such as the ones suitable for powering or recharging tablets. Again, ensure that they can supply 5V at 1,000 mA or over.

You should aim to make all other connections to Raspberry Pi before connecting the power. However, USB devices, audio, and networks may be connected and removed while it is running, without problems.

There's more...

In addition to the standard primary connections you would expect to see on a computer, Raspberry Pi also has a number of other connections.

Secondary hardware connections

Each of the following connections provides additional interfaces for Raspberry Pi:

- **20 x 2 GPIO pin header (Model A+, B+, 2 B, 3 B, and Pi Zero)**: This is the main 40-pin GPIO header of Raspberry Pi used for interfacing directly with hardware components. The chapters in this book are also compatible with older models of Raspberry Pi that have a 13 x 2 GPIO pin header.
- **P5 8 x 2 GPIO pin header (Model 1 B revision 2.0 only)**: We do not use this in the book.
- **Reset connection**: This is present on later models (no pins fitted). A reset is triggered when Pin 1 (reset) and Pin 2 (GND) are connected together. We use this in the *A controlled shutdown button* concept in Chapter 7, *Using Python to Drive Hardware*.

- **GPU/LAN JTAG**: The **Joint Test Action Group** (**JTAG**) is a programming and debugging interface used to configure and test processors. These are present on newer models as surface pads. A specialist JTAG device is required to use this interface. We do not use this in the book.
- **Direct camera CSI**: This connection supports Raspberry Pi Camera Module. Note that the Pi Zero has a smaller CSI connector than the other models, so it requires a different ribbon connector.
- **Direct Display DSI**: This connection supports a directly connected display, such as a 7-inch 800 x 600 capacitive touch screen.

Using NOOBS to set up your Raspberry Pi SD card

The Raspberry Pi requires the operating system to be loaded onto an SD card before it starts up. The easiest way to set up the SD card is to use **NOOBS**; you may find that you can buy an SD card with NOOBS already loaded on it.

NOOBS provides an initial start menu that provides options to install several of the available operating systems on to your SD card.

Getting ready

Since NOOBS creates a **RECOVERY** partition to keep the original installation images, an 8 GB SD card or larger is recommended. You will also need an SD card reader (experience has shown that some built-in card readers can cause issues, so an external USB type reader is recommended).

If you are using an SD card that you have used previously, you may need to reformat it to remove any previous partitions and data. NOOBS expects the SD card to consist of a single FAT32 partition.

If using Windows or macOS X, you can use the SD Association's formatter, as shown in the following screenshot (available at
`https://www.sdcard.org/downloads/formatter_4/`):

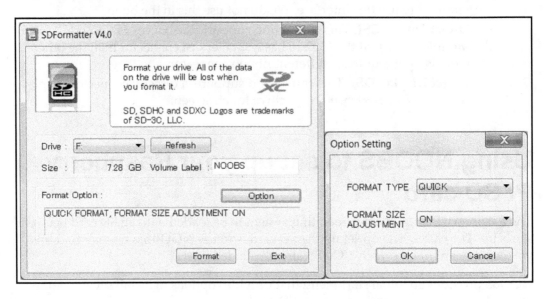

Getting rid of any partitions on the SD card, using SD formatter

From the **Option Setting** dialog box, set **FORMAT SIZE ADJUSTMENT**. This will remove all the SD card partitions that were created previously.

If using Linux, you can use `gparted` to clear any previous partitions and reformat it as a FAT32 partition.

The full NOOBS package (typically just over 1 GB) contains Raspbian, the most popular Raspberry Pi operating system image built in. A lite version of NOOBS is also available that has no preloaded operating systems (although a smaller initial download of 20 MB and a network connection on Raspberry Pi are required to directly download the operating system you intend to use).

NOOBS is available at `http://www.raspberrypi.org/downloads`, with the documentation available at `https://github.com/raspberrypi/noobs`.

How to do it...

By performing the following steps, we will prepare the SD card to run NOOBS. This will then allow us to select and install the operating system we want to use:

1. Get your SD card ready.
2. On a freshly formatted or new SD card, copy the contents of the NOOBS_vX.zip file. When it has finished copying, you should end up with something like the following screenshot of the SD card:

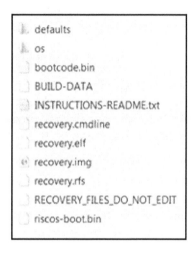

NOOBS files extracted onto the SD card

 The files may vary slightly with different versions of NOOBS, and the icons displayed may be different on your computer.

3. You can now put the card into your Raspberry Pi, connect it to a keyboard and display, and turn the power on. Refer to the *Connecting to Raspberry Pi* recipe for details on what you need, and how to do this.

By default, NOOBS will display via the HDMI connection. If you have another type of screen (or you don't see anything), you will need to manually select the output type by pressing 1, 2, 3, or 4, according to the following functions:

- Key 1 stands for the **Standard HDMI** mode (the default mode)
- Key 2 stands for the **Safe HDMI** mode (alternative HDMI settings if the output has not been detected)
- Key 3 stands for **Composite PAL** (for connections made via the RCA analogue video connection)
- Key 4 stands for **Composite NTSC** (again, for connections via the RCA connector)

This display setting will also be set for the installed operating system.

After a short while, you will see the NOOBS selection screen that lists the available distributions (the offline version only includes Raspbian). There are many more distributions that are available, but only the selected ones are available directly through the NOOBS system. Click on **Raspbian**, as this is the operating system being used in this book.

Press *Enter* or click on **Install OS**, and confirm that you wish to overwrite all the data on
the card. This will overwrite any distributions previously installed using NOOBS but will not remove the NOOBS system; you can return to it at any time by pressing *Shift* when you turn the power on.

It will take around 20 to 40 minutes to write the data to the card depending on its speed. When it completes and the **Image Applied Successfully** message appears, click on **OK**, and Raspberry Pi will start to boot into `Raspberry Pi Desktop`.

How it works...

The purpose of writing the image file to the SD card in this manner is to ensure that the SD card is formatted with the expected filesystem partitions and files required to correctly boot the operating system.

When Raspberry Pi powers up, it loads some special code contained within the GPU's internal memory (commonly referred to as **binary blob** by Raspberry Pi Foundation). The binary blob provides the instructions required to read the BOOT partition on the SD card, which (in the case of a NOOBS install) will load NOOBS from the RECOVERY partition. If at this point *Shift* is pressed, NOOBS will load the recovery and installation menu. Otherwise, NOOBS will begin loading the OS as specified by the preferences stored in the SETTINGS partition.

When loading the operating system, it will boot via the BOOT partition, using the settings defined in config.txt and options in cmdline.txt to finally load to the desktop on the root partition. Refer to the following diagram:

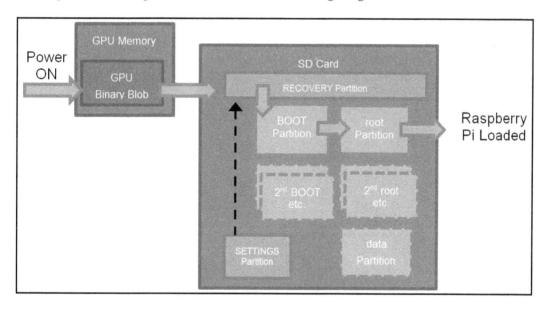

NOOBS creates several partitions on the SD card to allow the installation of multiple operating systems and to provide recovery

NOOBS allows the user to optionally install multiple operating systems on the same card and provides a boot menu to choose between them (with an option to set a default value in the event of a time-out period).

If you later add, remove, or re-install an operating system, ensure first that you make a copy of any files, including system settings you wish to keep, as NOOBS may overwrite everything on the SD card.

There's more...

When you power up Raspberry Pi for the first time directly, the desktop will be loaded. You can configure the system settings using the **Raspberry Pi Configuration** menu (under the **Preferences** menu on the Desktop or via the `sudo raspi-config` command). With this menu, you can make changes to your SD card or set up your general preferences:

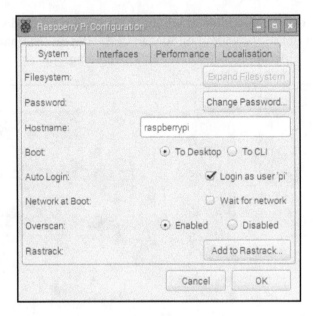

Changing the default user password

Ensure that you change the default password for the `pi` user account once you have logged in, as the default password is well known. This is particularly important if you connect to public networks. You can do this with the `passwd` command, as shown in the following screenshot:

```
pi@raspberrypi ~ $ passwd
Changing password for pi.
(current) UNIX password:
Enter new UNIX password:
Retype new UNIX password:
passwd: password updated successfully
```

Setting a new password for the Pi user

This provides greater confidence because if you later connect to another network, only you will be able to access your files and take control of your Raspberry Pi.

Ensuring that you shut down safely

To avoid any data corruption, you must ensure that you correctly shut down Raspberry Pi by issuing a `shutdown` command, as follows:

```
sudo shutdown -h now
```

Or, use this one:

```
sudo halt
```

You must wait until this command completes before you remove power from Raspberry Pi (wait for at least 10 seconds after the SD card access light has stopped flashing).

You can also restart the system with the `reboot` command, as follows:

```
sudo reboot
```

Preparing an SD card manually

An alternative to using NOOBS is to manually write the operating system image to the SD card. While this was originally the only way to install the operating system, some users still prefer it. It allows the SD cards to be prepared before they are used in Raspberry Pi. It can also provide easier access to startup and configuration files, and it leaves more space available for the user (unlike NOOBS, a RECOVERY partition isn't included).

The default Raspbian image actually consists of two partitions, BOOT and SYSTEM, which will fit into a 2 GB SD card (4 GB or more is recommended).

You need a computer running Windows/Mac OS X/Linux (although it is possible to use another Raspberry Pi to write your card; be prepared for a very long wait).

Download the latest version of the operating system you wish to use. For the purpose of this book, it is assumed you are using the latest version of Raspbian available at http://www.raspberrypi.org/downloads.

Perform the following steps depending on the type of computer you plan to use to write to the SD card (the .img file you need is sometimes compressed, so before you start, you will need to extract the file).

The following steps are for Windows:

1. Ensure that you have downloaded the Raspbian image, as previously detailed, and extracted it to a convenient folder to obtain an .img file.
2. Obtain the Win32DiskImager.exe file available at http://www.sourceforge.net/projects/win32diskimager.
3. Run Win32DiskImager.exe from your downloaded location.
4. Click on the folder icon and navigate to the location of the .img file and click on **Save**.
5. If you haven't already done so, insert your SD card into your card reader and plug it into your computer.
6. Select the **Device** drive letter that corresponds to your SD card from the small drop-down box. Double-check that this is the correct device (as the program will overwrite whatever is on the device when you write the image).

 The drive letter may not be listed until you select a source image file.

7. Finally, click on the **Write** button and wait for the program to write the image to the SD card, as shown in the following screenshot:

Manually writing operating system images to the SD card, using Disk Imager

8. Once completed, you can exit the program. Your SD card is ready.

The following steps should work for the most common Linux distributions, such as Ubuntu and Debian:

1. Using your preferred web browser, download the Raspbian image and save it in a suitable place.
2. Extract the file from the file manager or locate the folder in the terminal and unzip the `.img` file with the following command:

   ```
   unzip filename.zip
   ```

3. If you haven't already done so, insert your SD card into your card reader and plug it into your computer.
4. Use the `df -h` command and identify the **sdX** identifier for the SD card. Each partition will be displayed as **sdX1**, **sdX2**, and so on, where **X** will be a, b, c, d, and so on for the device ID.
5. Ensure that all the partitions on the SD card are unmounted using the `umount /dev/sdXn` command for each partition, where `sdXn` is the partition being unmounted.
6. Write the image file to the SD card, with the following command:

   ```
   sudo dd if=filename.img of=/dev/sdX bs=4M
   ```

7. The process will take some time to write to the SD card, returning to the Terminal prompt when complete.
8. Unmount the SD card before removing it from the computer, using the following command:

   ```
   umount /dev/sdX1
   ```

The following steps should work for most of the versions of OS X:

1. Using your preferred web browser, download the Raspbian image and save it somewhere suitable.
2. Extract the file from the file manager or locate the folder in the terminal and unzip the `.img` file, with the following command:

   ```
   unzip filename.zip
   ```

3. If you haven't already done so, insert your SD card into your card reader and plug it into your computer.

4. Use the `diskutil list` command and identify the **disk#** identifier for the SD card. Each partition will be displayed as **disk#s1**, **disk#s2**, and so on, where # will be 1, 2, 3, 4, and so on, for the device ID.

> If **rdisk#** is listed, use this for faster writing (this uses a raw path and skips data buffering).

5. Ensure that the SD card is unmounted using the `unmountdisk /dev/diskX` command, where `diskX` is the device being unmounted.

6. Write the image file to the SD card, with the following command:

```
sudo dd if=filename.img of=/dev/diskX bs=1M
```

7. The process will take some time to write to the SD card, returning to the Terminal prompt when complete.

8. Unmount the SD card before removing it from the computer, using the following command:

```
unmountdisk /dev/diskX
```

Refer to the following diagram:

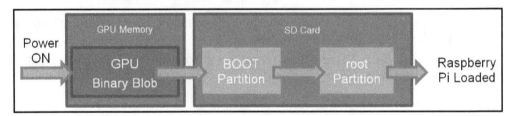

The boot process of a manually installed OS image

Expanding the system to fit in your SD card

A manually written image will be of a fixed size (usually made to fit the smallest-sized SD card possible). To make full use of the SD card, you will need to expand the system partition to fill the remainder of the SD card. This can be achieved using the **Raspberry Pi Configuration** tool.

Select `Expand Filesystem`, as shown in the following screenshot:

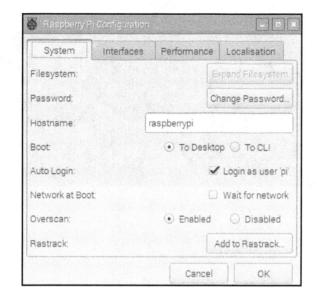

Raspberry Pi Configuration tool

Accessing the RECOVERY/BOOT partition

Windows and macOS X do not support the `ext4` format, so when you read the SD card, only the **File Allocation Table** (**FAT**) partitions will be accessible. In addition, Windows only supports the first partition on an SD card, so if you've installed NOOBS, only the `RECOVERY` partition will be visible. If you've written your card manually, you will be able to access the `BOOT` partition.

The `data` partition (if you installed one via NOOBS) and the `root` partition are in `ext4` format and won't usually be visible on non-Linux systems.

 If you do need to read files from the SD card using Windows, a freeware program, **Linux Reader** (available at `www.diskinternals.com/linux-reader`) can provide read-only access to all of the partitions on the SD card.

Access the partitions from Raspberry Pi. To view the currently mounted partitions, use df, as shown in the following screenshot:

```
pi@raspberrypi:~ $ df
Filesystem      1K-blocks     Used Available Use% Mounted on
/dev/root        5964864  3554020   2084804  64% /
devtmpfs          469544        0    469544   0% /dev
tmpfs             473880        0    473880   0% /dev/shm
tmpfs             473880     6460    467420   2% /run
tmpfs               5120        4      5116   1% /run/lock
tmpfs             473880        0    473880   0% /sys/fs/cgroup
/dev/mmcblk0p6     64366    20442     43924  32% /boot
tmpfs              94776        0     94776   0% /run/user/1000
/dev/mmcblk0p5     30701      398     28010   2% /media/pi/SETTINGS
pi@raspberrypi:~ $ █
```

The result of the df command

To access the BOOT partition from within Raspbian, use the following command:

```
cd /boot/
```

To access the RECOVERY or data partition, we have to mount it by performing the following steps:

1. Determine the name of the partition as the system refers to it by listing all the partitions, even the unmounted ones. The sudo fdisk −l command lists the partitions, as shown in the following screenshot:

```
Device         Boot   Start       End   Sectors  Size Id Type
/dev/mmcblk0p1         8192   2541015   2532824  1.2G  e W95 FAT16 (LBA)
/dev/mmcblk0p2      2541016  15130623  12589608   6G  5 Extended
/dev/mmcblk0p5      2547712   2613245     65534  32M 83 Linux
/dev/mmcblk0p6      2613248   2742271    129024  63M  c W95 FAT32 (LBA)
/dev/mmcblk0p7      2744320  15130623  12386304 5.9G 83 Linux
```

NOOBS installation and data partition

The following table shows the names of partitions and their meanings

Partition name	Meaning
mmcblk0p1	(VFAT) RECOVERY
mmcblk0p2	(Extended partition) contains (root, data, BOOT)
mmcblk0p5	(ext4) root
mmcblk0p6	(VFAT) BOOT
mmcblk0p7	(ext4) SETTINGS

If you have installed additional operating systems on the same card, the partition identifiers shown in the preceding table will be different.

2. Create a folder and set it as the mount point for the partition; for the RECOVERY partition, use the following command:

```
mkdir ~/recovery
sudo mount -t vfat /dev/mmcblk0p1 ~/recovery
```

To ensure that they are mounted each time the system is started, perform the following steps:

1. Add the sudo mount commands to /etc/rc.local before exit 0. If you have a different username, you will need to change pi to match:

```
sudo nano /etc/rc.local
sudo mount -t vfat /dev/mmcblk0p1 /home/pi/recovery
```

2. Save and exit by pressing *Ctrl + X, Y,* and *Enter.*

 Commands added to /etc/rc.local will be run for any user who logs on to Raspberry Pi. If you only want the drive to be mounted for the current user, the commands can be added to .bash_profile instead.

If you have to install additional operating systems on the same card, the partition identifiers shown here will be different.

Using the tools to back up your SD card in case of failure

You can use **Win32 Disk Imager** to make a full backup image of your SD card by inserting your SD card into your reader, starting the program, and creating a filename to store the image in. Simply click on the **Read** button instead to read the image from the SD card and write it to a new image file.

To make a backup of your system, or to clone to another SD card using Raspberry Pi, use the **SD Card Copier** (available from the desktop menu via the **Accessories | SD Card Copier**).

Insert an SD card into a card reader into a spare USB port of Raspberry Pi and select the new storage device, as shown in the following screenshot:

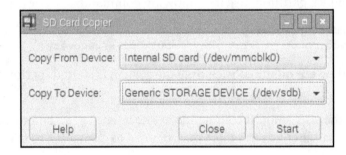

SD Card Copier program

Before continuing, the **SD Card Copier** will confirm that you wish to format and overwrite the target device and, if there is sufficient space, make a clone of your system.

The dd command can similarly be used to back up the card, as follows:

- For Linux, replacing sdX with your device ID, use this command:

    ```
    sudo dd if=/dev/sdX of=image.img.gz bs=1M
    ```

- For OS X, replacing diskX with your device ID, use the following command:

    ```
    sudo dd if=/dev/diskX of=image.img.gz bs=1M
    ```

- You can also use `gzip` and split to compress the contents of the card and split them into multiple files, if required, for easy archiving, as follows:

  ```
  sudo dd if=/dev/sdX bs=1M | gzip -c | split -d -b 2000m -
  image.img.gz
  ```

- To restore the split image, use the following command:

  ```
  sudo cat image.img.gz* | gzip -dc | dd of=/dev/sdX bs=1M
  ```

Networking and connecting your Raspberry Pi to the internet via an Ethernet port, using a CAT6 Ethernet cable

The simplest way to connect Raspberry Pi to the internet is by using the built-in LAN connection on the Model B. If you are using a Model A Raspberry Pi, a USB-to-LAN adapter can be used (refer to the *There's more...* section of the *Networking and connecting your Raspberry Pi to the internet via a USB Wi-Fi dongle* recipe for details of how to configure this).

Getting ready

You will need access to a suitable wired network, which will be connected to the internet, and a standard network cable (with an **RJ45** type connector for connecting to Raspberry Pi).

How to do it...

Many networks connect and configure themselves automatically using the **Dynamic Host Configuration Protocol** (**DHCP**), which is controlled by the router or switch. If this is the case, simply plug the network cable into a spare network port on your router or network switch (or wall network socket if applicable).

Alternatively, if a DHCP server is not available, you shall have to configure the settings manually (refer to the *There's more...* section for details).

You can confirm this is functioning successfully with the following steps:

1. Ensure that the two LEDs on either side of Raspberry Pi light up (the left orange LED indicates a connection and the green LED on the right shows activity by flashing). This will indicate that there is a physical connection to the router and that the equipment is powered and functioning.

2. Test the link to your local network using the `ping` command. First, find out the IP address of another computer on the network (or the address of your router, perhaps, often `192.168.0.1` or `192.168.1.254`). Now, on the Raspberry Pi Terminal, use the `ping` command (the `-c 4` parameter is used to send just four messages; otherwise, press *Ctrl* + *C* to stop) to ping the IP address, as follows:

   ```
   sudo ping 192.168.1.254 -c 4
   ```

3. Test the link to the internet (this will fail if you usually connect to the internet through a proxy server) as follows:

   ```
   sudo ping www.raspberrypi.org -c 4
   ```

4. Finally, you can test the link back to Raspberry Pi by discovering the IP address using `hostname -I` on Raspberry Pi. You can then use the ping command on another computer on the network to ensure it is accessible (using Raspberry Pi's IP address in place of `www.raspberrypi.org`). The Windows version of the `ping` command will perform five pings and stop automatically, and will not need the `-c 4` option.

If the aforementioned tests fail, you will need to check your connections and then confirm the correct configuration for your network.

There's more...

If you find yourself using your Raspberry Pi regularly on the network, you won't want to have to look up the IP address each time you want to connect to it.

On some networks, you may be able to use Raspberry Pi's hostname instead of its IP address (the default is `raspberrypi`). To assist with this, you may need some additional software, such as **Bonjour**, to ensure hostnames on the network are correctly registered. If you have macOS X, you will have Bonjour running already.

On Windows, you can either install iTunes (if you haven't got it), which also includes the service, or you can install it separately (via the Apple Bonjour Installer available from `https://support.apple.com/kb/DL999`). Then you can use the hostname, `raspberrypi` or `raspberrypi.local`, to connect to Raspberry Pi over the network. If you need to change the hostname, then you can do so with the Raspberry Pi configuration tool, shown previously.

Alternatively, you may find it helpful to fix the IP address to a known value by manually setting the IP address. However, remember to switch it back to use DHCP when connecting to another network.

Some routers will also have an option to set a **Static IP DHCP address**, so the same address is always given to Raspberry Pi (how this is set will vary depending on the router itself).

Knowing your Raspberry Pi's IP address or using the hostname is particularly useful if you intend to use one of the remote access solutions described later on, which avoids the need for a display.

Using built-in Wi-Fi and Bluetooth on Raspberry Pi

Many home networks provide a wireless network over Wi-Fi; if you have Raspberry Pi 3, then you can make use of the on-board Broadcom Wi-Fi to connect to it. Raspberry Pi 3 also supports Bluetooth, so you can connect most standard Bluetooth devices and use them like you would on any other computer.

This method should also work for any supported USB Wi-Fi and Bluetooth devices; see the *Networking and connecting your Raspberry Pi to the internet via a USB Wi-Fi dongle* recipe for extra help on identifying devices and installing firmware (if required).

Getting ready

The latest version of Raspbian includes helpful utilities to quickly and easily configure your Wi-Fi and Bluetooth through the graphical interface.

Note: If you need to configure the Wi-Fi via the command line, then see the *Networking and connecting your Raspberry Pi to the internet via a USB Wi-Fi dongle* recipe for details.

Wi-Fi and Bluetooth configuration applications

You can use the built-in Bluetooth to connect a wireless keyboard, a mouse, or even wireless speakers. This can be exceptionally helpful for projects where additional cables and wires are an issue, such as robotic projects, or when Raspberry Pi is installed in hard-to-reach locations (acting as a server or security camera).

How to do it...

Here are the various methods.

Connecting to your Wi-Fi network

To configure your Wi-Fi connection, click on the networking symbol to list the local available Wi-Fi networks:

Wi-Fi listing of the available access points in the area

Select the required network (for example, `Demo`) and, if required, enter your password (also known as a `Pre Shared Key`):

Providing the password for the access point

After a short while, you should see that you have connected to the network and the icon will change to a Wi-Fi symbol. If you encounter problems, ensure you have the correct password/key:

Successful connection to an access point

That is it; it's as easy as that!

You can now test your connection and ensure it is working by using the web browser to navigate to a website or by using the following command in the terminal:

```
sudo ping www.raspberrypi.com
```

Connecting to Bluetooth devices

To start, we need to put the Bluetooth device into discoverable mode by clicking on the Bluetooth icon and selecting **Make Discoverable**. You will also need to make the device you want to connect to discoverable and ready to pair; this may vary from device to device (such as pressing a pairing button):

Setting the Bluetooth up as discoverable

Next, select **Add Device...** and select the target device and **Pair**:

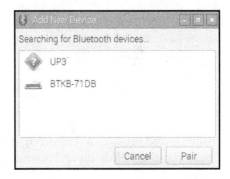

Selecting and pairing the required device

The pairing process will then start; for example, the **BTKB-71DB** keyboard will need the pairing code 467572 to be entered onto the keyboard for the pairing to complete. Other devices may use default pairing codes, often set to 0000, 1111, 1234, or similar:

Following the instructions to pair the device with the required pairing code

Once the process has completed, the device will be listed and will connect automatically each time the devices are present and booted.

Configuring your network manually

If your network does not include a DHCP server or it is disabled (typically, these are built into most modern ADSL/cable modems or routers), you may need to configure your network settings manually.

Getting ready

Before you start, you will need to determine the network settings for your network.

You will need to find out the following information from your router's settings or another computer connected to the network:

- **IPv4 address**: This address will need to be selected to be similar to other computers on the network (typically, the first three numbers should match, that is, 192.168.1.X if netmask is 255.255.255.0), but it should not already be used by another computer. However, avoid x.x.x.255 as the last address, since this is reserved as a broadcast address.
- **Subnet mask**: This number determines the range of addresses the computer will respond to (for a home network, it is typically 255.255.255.0, which allows up to 254 addresses). This is also sometimes referred to as the **netmask**.
- **Default gateway address**: This address is usually your router's IP address, through which the computers connect to the internet.
- **DNS servers**: The **Domain Name Service** (**DNS**) server converts names into IP addresses by looking them up. Usually, they will already be configured on your router, in which case you can use your router's address. Alternatively, your **Internet Service Provider** (**ISP**) may provide some addresses, or you can use Google's public DNS servers at the addresses 8.8.8.8 and 8.8.4.4. These are also called **nameservers** in some systems.

For Windows, you can obtain this information by connecting to the internet and running the following command:

```
ipconfig /all
```

Locate the active connection (usually called `Local Area Connection 1` or similar if you are using a wired connection, or if you are using Wi-Fi, it is called a wireless network connection) and find the information required, as follows:

The ipconfig/all command shows useful information about your network settings

For Linux and macOS X, you can obtain the required information with the following command (note that it is `ifconfig` rather than `ipconfig`):

```
ifconfig
```

The DNS servers are called nameservers and are usually listed in the `resolv.conf` file. You can use the `less` command as follows to view its contents (press Q to quit when you have finished viewing it):

```
less /etc/resolv.conf
```

How to do it...

To set the network interface settings, edit `/etc/network/interfaces` using the following code:

```
sudo nano /etc/network/interfaces
```

Now perform the following steps:

1. We can add the details for our particular network, the IP `address` number we want to allocate to it, the `netmask` address of the network, and the `gateway` address, as follows:

   ```
   iface eth0 inet static
       address 192.168.1.10
       netmask 255.255.255.0
       gateway 192.168.1.254
   ```

2. Save and exit by pressing *Ctrl + X, Y,* and *Enter.*
3. To set the name servers for DNS, edit `/etc/resolv.conf` using the following code:

   ```
   sudo nano /etc/resolv.conf
   ```

4. Add the addresses for your DNS servers as follows:

   ```
   nameserver 8.8.8.8
   nameserver 8.8.4.4
   ```

5. Save and exit by pressing *Ctrl + X, Y,* and *Enter.*

There's more...

You can configure the network settings by editing `cmdline.txt` in the BOOT partition and adding settings to the startup command line with `ip`.

The `ip` option takes the following form:

```
ip=client-ip:nfsserver-ip:gw-ip:netmask:hostname:device:autoconf
```

- The `client-ip` option is the IP address you want to allocate to Raspberry Pi
- The `gw-ip` option will set the gateway server address if you need to set it manually
- The `netmask` option will directly set the `netmask` of the network
- The `hostname` option will allow you to change the default `raspberrypi` hostname
- The `device` option allows you to specify a default network device if more than one network device is present
- The `autoconf` option allows the automatic configuration to be switched on or off

Networking directly to a laptop or computer

It is possible to connect Raspberry Pi LAN port directly to a laptop or computer using a single network cable. This will create a local network link between the computers, allowing all the things you can do if connected to a normal network without the need for a hub or a router, including connection to the internet, if **Internet Connection Sharing (ICS)** is used, as follows:

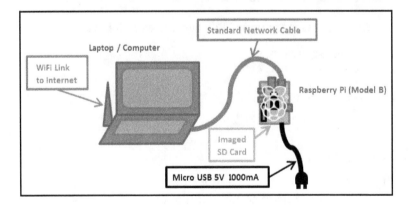

Make use of Raspberry Pi, with just a network cable, a standard imaged SD card, and power.

ICS allows Raspberry Pi to connect to the internet through another computer. However, some additional configuration is required for the computers to communicate across the link, as Raspberry Pi does not automatically allocate its own IP address.

We will use the ICS to share a connection from another network link, such as a built-in Wi-Fi on a laptop. Alternatively, we can use a direct network link (refer to the *Direct network link* section under the *There's more...* section) if the internet is not required or if the computer has only a single network adapter.

Although this setup should work for most computers, some setups are more difficult than the others. For additional information, see www.pihardware.com/guides/direct-network-connection.

Getting ready

You will need Raspberry Pi with power and a standard network cable.

Raspberry Pi Model B LAN chip includes **Auto-MDIX (Automatic Medium-Dependent Interface Crossover)**. Removing the need to use a special crossover cable (a special network cable wired so that the transmit lines connect to receive lines for direct network links), the chip will decide and change the setup as required automatically.

It may also be helpful to have a keyboard and monitor available to perform additional testing, particularly if this is the first time you have tried this.

To ensure that you can restore your network settings to their original values, you should check whether it has a fixed IP address or the network is configured automatically.

To check the network settings on Windows 10, perform these steps:

1. Open **Settings** from the start menu, then select **Network and Internet**, then **Ethernet,** and click on **Change adapter options** from the list of **Related Settings**.

To check the network settings on Windows 7 and Vista, perform the following steps:

1. Open **Network and Sharing Center** from the **Control Panel** and click on **Change adapter settings** on the left-hand side.
2. To check the network settings on Windows XP, open **Network Connections** from the **Control Panel**.
3. Find the item that relates to your wired network adapter (by default, this is usually called **Ethernet** or **Local Area Connection**, as shown in the following screenshot):

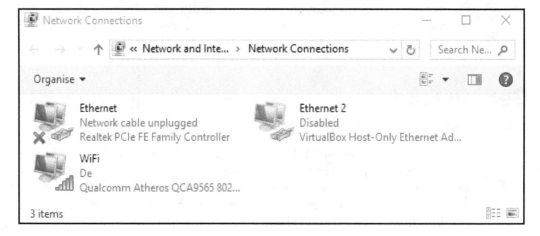

Locating your wired network connection

4. Right-click on its icon and click on **Properties**. A dialog box will appear, as shown in this screenshot:

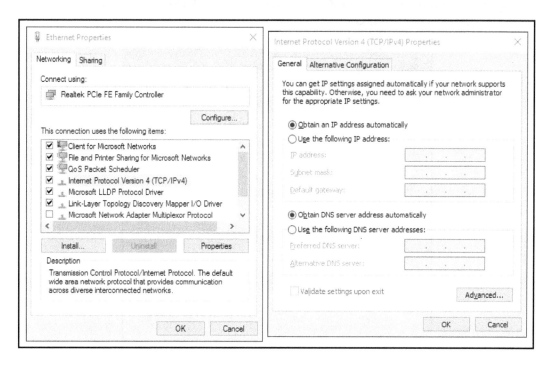

Selecting the TCP/IP properties and checking the settings

5. Select the item called **Internet Protocol (TCP/IP)** or **Internet Protocol Version 4 (TCP/IPv4)** if there are two versions (the other is Version 6), and click on the **Properties** button.

6. You can confirm that your network is set by using automatic settings or a specific IP address (if so, take note of this address and the remaining details as you may want to revert the settings at a later point).

To check the network settings on Linux, perform the following steps:

1. Open the **Network Settings** dialog box and select **Configure Interface**. Refer to the following screenshot:

Linux Network Settings dialog box

2. If any settings are manually set, ensure you take note of them so that you can restore them later if you want.

To check the network settings on macOS X, perform the following steps:

1. Open **System Preferences** and click on **Networks**. You can then confirm whether the IP address is allocated automatically (using DHCP) or not.

2. Ensure that if any settings are manually set you take note of them so you can restore them later if you want to. Refer to the following screenshot:

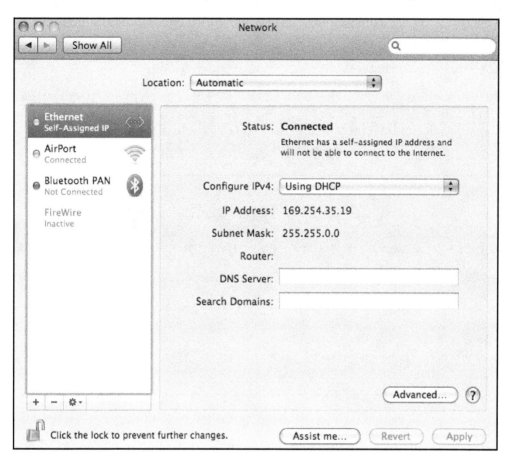

OS X Network Settings dialog box

If you just need to access or control Raspberry Pi without an internet connection, refer to the *Direct network link* section in the *There's more...*section.

How to do it...

First, we need to enable ICS on our network devices. In this case, we will be sharing the internet, which is available on **Wireless Network Connection** through the **Ethernet** connection to Raspberry Pi.

For Windows, perform these steps:

1. Return to the list of network adapters, right-click on the connection that links
to the internet (in this case, the **WiFi** or **Wireless Network Connection** device), and click on **Properties**:

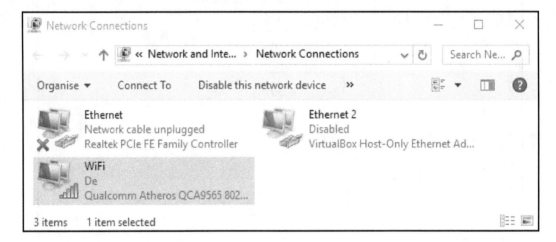

Locating your wired network connection

2. At the top of the window, select the second tab (in Windows XP, it is called **Advanced**; in Windows 7 and Windows 10, it is called **Sharing**), as shown in the following screenshot:

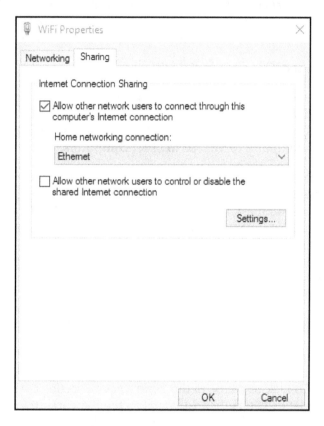

Selecting the TCP/IP properties and noting the allocated IP address

3. In the **Internet Connection Sharing** section, check the box for **Allow other network users to connect through this computer's Internet connection** (if present, use the drop-down box to select the **Home networking connection:** option as **Ethernet** or **Local Area Connection**). Click on **OK** and confirm whether you previously had a fixed IP address set for **Local Area Connection**.

For macOS X, to enable the ICS, perform the following steps:

1. Click on **System Preferences** and then click on **Sharing**.
2. Click on **Internet Sharing** and select the connection from which we want to share the internet (in this case, it will be the Wi-Fi **AirPort**). Then select the connection that we will connect Raspberry Pi to (in this case, **Ethernet**).

For Linux to enable the ICS, perform the following steps:

1. From the **System** menu, click on **Preferences** and then on **Network Connections**. Select the connection you want to share (in this case, **Wireless**) and click on **Edit** or **Configure**. In the **IPv4 Settings** tab, change the **Method** option to **Shared to other computers**.

The IP address of the network adapter will be the **Gateway IP** address to be used on Raspberry Pi, and will be assigned an IP address within the same range (it will all match, except the last number). For instance, if the computer's wired connection now has `192.168.137.1`, the Gateway IP of Raspberry Pi will be `192.168.137.1` and its own IP address might be set to `192.168.137.10`.

Fortunately, thanks to updates in the operating system, Raspbian will now automatically allocate a suitable IP address to join the network and set the gateway appropriately. However, unless we have a screen attached to Raspberry Pi or scan for devices on our network, we do not know what IP address Raspberry PI has given itself.

Fortunately (as mentioned in the *Networking and connecting your Raspberry Pi to the internet via the LAN connector* recipe in the *There's more...* section), Apple's **Bonjour** software will automatically ensure hostnames on the network are correctly registered. As stated previously, if you have a Mac OS X, you will have Bonjour running already. On Windows, you can either install iTunes, or you can install it separately (available from `https://support.apple.com/kb/DL999`). By default, the hostname **raspberrypi** can be used.

We are now ready to test the new connection, as follows:

1. Connect the network cable to Raspberry Pi and the computer's network port, and then power up Raspberry Pi, ensuring that you have re-inserted the SD card if you previously removed it. To reboot Raspberry Pi, if you edited the file there, use `sudo reboot` to restart it.
2. Allow a minute or two for Raspberry Pi to fully power up. We can now test the connection.

3. From the connected laptop or computer, test the connection by pinging with the hostname of Raspberry Pi, as shown in the following command (on Linux or OS X, add `-c 4` to limit to four messages or press Ctrl + C to exit):

```
ping raspberrypi
```

Hopefully, you will find you have a working connection and receive replies from the Raspberry Pi.

If you have a keyboard and a screen connected to Raspberry Pi, you can perform the following steps:

1. You can ping the computer in return (for example, `192.168.137.1`) from Raspberry Pi Terminal as follows:

```
sudo ping 192.168.137.1 -c 4
```

2. You can test the link to the internet by using `ping` to connect to a well-known website as follows, assuming you do not access the internet through a proxy server:

```
sudo ping www.raspberrypi.org -c 4
```

If all goes well, you will have full internet available through your computer to Raspberry Pi, allowing you to browse the web as well as update and install new software.

If the connection fails, perform the following steps:

1. Repeat the process, ensuring that the first three sets of numbers match with Raspberry Pi and the network adapter IP addresses.
2. You can also check that when Raspberry Pi powers up, the correct IP address is being set using the following command:

```
hostname -I
```

3. Check your firewall settings to ensure your firewall is not blocking internal network connections.

How it works...

When we enable ICS on the primary computer, the operating system will automatically allocate a new IP address to the computer. Once connected and powered up, Raspberry Pi will set itself to a compatible IP address and use the primary computer IP address as an Internet Gateway.

By using Apple Bonjour, we are able to use `raspberrypi` hostname to connect to Raspberry Pi from the connected computer.

Finally, we check whether the computer can communicate over the direct network link to Raspberry Pi, back the other way, and also through to the internet.

There's more...

If you do not require the internet on Raspberry Pi, or your computer has only a single network adapter, you can still connect the computers together through a direct network link. Refer to the following diagram:

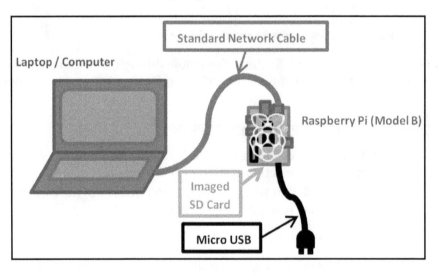

Connecting and using Raspberry Pi with just a network cable, a standard imaged SD card, and power

Direct network link

For a network link to work between two computers, they need to be using the same address range. The allowable address range is determined by the subnet mask (for example, `255.255.0.0` or `255.255.255.0` would mean all IP addresses should be the same except for the last two, or just the last number in the IP address; otherwise, they will be filtered).

To use a direct link without enabling ICS, check the IP settings of the adapter you are going to connect to and determine whether it is automatically allocated or fixed to a specific IP address.

Most PCs connected directly to another computer will allocate an IP address in the range `169.254.X.X` (with a subnet mask of `255.255.0.0`). However, we must ensure that the network adaptor is set to **Obtain an IP address automatically**.

For Raspberry Pi to be able to communicate through the direct link, it needs to have an IP address in the same address range, `169.254.X.X`. As mentioned before, Raspberry Pi will automatically give itself a suitable IP address and connect to the network.

Therefore, assuming we have **Apple Bonjour** (mentioned previously), we only need to know the hostname given to Raspberry Pi (`raspberrypi`).

See also

If you don't have a keyboard or screen connected to Raspberry Pi, you can use this network link to remotely access Raspberry Pi just as you would on a normal network (just use the new IP address you have set for the connection). Refer to the *Connecting remotely to Raspberry Pi over the network using VNC* and *Connecting remotely to Raspberry Pi over the network using SSH (and X11 Forwarding)* recipes.

There is lots of additional information available on my website, `https://pihw.wordpress.com/guides/direct-network-connection`, including additional troubleshooting tips and several other ways to connect to your Raspberry Pi without needing a dedicated screen and keyboard.

Networking and connecting your Raspberry Pi to the internet via a USB Wi-Fi dongle

By adding a **USB Wi-Fi dongle** to Raspberry Pi's USB port, even models without built-in Wi-Fi can connect to and use the Wi-Fi network.

Getting ready

You will need to obtain a suitable USB Wi-Fi dongle, and, in some cases, you may require a powered USB hub (this will depend on the hardware version of Raspberry Pi you have and the quality of your power supply). General suitability of USB Wi-Fi dongles will vary depending on the chipset that is used inside and the level of Linux support available. You may find that some USB Wi-Fi dongles will work without installing additional drivers (in which case you can jump to configuring it for the wireless network).

A list of supported Wi-Fi adapters is available at `http://elinux.org/RPi_USB_Wi-Fi_Adapters`.

You will need to ensure that your Wi-Fi adapter is also compatible with your intended network; for example, it supports the same types of signals **802.11bgn** and the encryptions **WEP**, **WPA**, and **WPA2** (although most networks are backward compatible).

You will also need the following details of your network:

- **Service set identifier (SSID)**: This is the name of your Wi-Fi network and should be visible if you use the following command:

    ```
    sudo iwlist scan | grep SSID
    ```

- **Encryption type and key**: This value will be **None**, **WEP**, **WPA**, or **WPA2**, and the key will be the code you normally enter when you connect your phone or laptop to the wireless network (sometimes, it is printed on the router).

You will require a working internet connection (that is, wired Ethernet) to download the required drivers. Otherwise, you may be able to locate the required firmware files (they will be the `.deb` files) and copy them to Raspberry Pi (that is, via a USB flash drive; the drive should be automatically mounted if you are running in desktop mode). Copy the file to a suitable location and install it, using the following command:

```
sudo apt-get install firmware_file.deb
```

How to do it...

This task has two stages: first, we identify and install firmware for the Wi-Fi adapter, and then we need to configure it for the wireless network.

We will try to identify the chipset of your Wi-Fi adapter (the part that handles the connection); this may not match the actual manufacturer of the device.

An approximate list of supported firmware can be found with this command:

```
sudo apt-cache search wireless firmware
```

This will produce results similar to the following output (disregarding any results without `firmware` in the package title):

```
atmel-firmware - Firmware for Atmel at76c50x wireless networking
chips.
firmware-atheros - Binary firmware for Atheros wireless cards
firmware-brcm80211 - Binary firmware for Broadcom 802.11 wireless
cards
firmware-ipw2x00 - Binary firmware for Intel Pro Wireless 2100, 2200
and 2915
firmware-iwlwifi - Binary firmware for Intel PRO/Wireless 3945 and
802.11n cards
firmware-libertas - Binary firmware for Marvell Libertas 8xxx wireless
cards
firmware-ralink - Binary firmware for Ralink wireless cards
firmware-realtek - Binary firmware for Realtek wired and wireless
network adapters
libertas-firmware - Firmware for Marvell's libertas wireless chip
series (dummy package)
zd1211-firmware - Firmware images for the zd1211rw wireless driver
```

To find out the chipset of your wireless adapter, plug the Wi-Fi-adapter into Raspberry Pi, and from the terminal, run the following command:

```
dmesg | grep 'Product:|Manufacturer:'
```

This command stitches together two commands into one. First, dmesg displays the message buffer of the kernel (this is an internal record of system events that have occurred since power on, such as detected USB devices). You can try the command on its own to observe the complete output.

The | (pipe) sends the output to the grep command; grep 'Product:|Manufacturer' checks it and only returns lines that contain Product or Manufacturer (so we should get a summary of any items that are listed as Product and Manufacturer). If you don't find anything or want to see all your USB devices, try the grep 'usb' command instead.

This should return something similar to the following output—in this case, I've got a ZyXEL device, which has a ZyDAS chipset (a quick Google search reveals that zd1211-firmware is for ZyDAS devices):

```
[    1.893367] usb usb1: Product: DWC OTG Controller
[    1.900217] usb usb1: Manufacturer: Linux 3.6.11+ dwc_otg_hcd
[    3.348259] usb 1-1.2: Product: ZyXEL G-202
[    3.355062] usb 1-1.2: Manufacturer: ZyDAS
```

Once you have identified your device and the correct firmware, you can install it as you would any other package available through apt-get (where zd1211-firmware can be replaced with your required firmware). This is shown in the following command:

```
sudo apt-get install zd1211-firmware
```

Remove and reinsert the USB Wi-Fi dongle to allow it to be detected and the drivers loaded. We can now test whether the new adapter is correctly installed with ifconfig. The output is shown as follows:

```
wlan0     IEEE 802.11bg  ESSID:off/any
          Mode:Managed  Access Point: Not-Associated   Tx-Power=20 dBm
          Retry  long limit:7   RTS thr:off   Fragment thr:off
          Power Management:off
```

The command will show the network adapters present on the system. For Wi-Fi, this is usually `wlan0` or `wlan1` and so on if you have installed more than one. If not, double-check the selected firmware and perhaps try an alternative or check on the site for troubleshooting tips.

Once we have the firmware installed for the Wi-Fi adapter, we will need to configure it for the network we wish to connect to. We can use the GUI as shown in the previous recipe, or we can manually configure it through the Terminal, as shown in the following steps:

1. We will need to add the wireless adapter to the list of network interfaces, which is set in `/etc/network/interfaces`, as follows:

   ```
   sudo nano -c /etc/network/interfaces
   ```

   Using the previous `wlan#` value in place of `wlan0` if required, add the following command:

   ```
   allow-hotplug wlan0
   iface wlan0 inet manual
   wpa-conf /etc/wpa_supplicant/wpa_supplicant.conf
   ```

   When the changes have been made, save and exit by pressing *Ctrl + X, Y,* and *Enter*.

2. We will now store the Wi-Fi network settings of our network in the `wpa_supplicant.conf` file (don't worry if your network doesn't use the `wpa` encryption; it is just the default name for the file):

   ```
   sudo nano -c /etc/wpa_supplicant/wpa_supplicant.conf
   ```

   It should include the following:

   ```
   ctrl_interface=DIR=/var/run/wpa_supplicant GROUP=netdev
   update_config=1
   country=GB
   ```

The network settings can be written within this file as follows (that is, if the SSID is set as theSSID):

- If no encryption is used, use this code:

```
network={
    ssid="theSSID"
    key_mgmt=NONE
}
```

- With the WEP encryption (that is, if the WEP key is set as theWEPkey), use the following code:

```
network={
    ssid="theSSID"
    key_mgmt=NONE
    wep_key0="theWEPkey"
}
```

- For the WPA or WPA2 encryption (that is, if the WPA key is set as theWPAkey), use the following code:

```
network={
    ssid="theSSID"
    key_mgmt=WPA-PSK
    psk="theWPAkey"
}
```

3. You can enable the adapter with the following command (again, replace wlan0 if required):

```
sudo ifup wlan0
```

Use the following command to list the wireless network connections:

```
iwconfig
```

You should see your wireless network connected with your SSID listed, as follows:

```
wlan0     IEEE 802.11bg  ESSID:"theSSID"
          Mode:Managed  Frequency:2.442 GHz  Access Point:
     00:24:BB:FF:FF:FF
          Bit Rate=48 Mb/s    Tx-Power=20 dBm
          Retry  long limit:7   RTS thr:off    Fragment thr:off
          Power Management:off
          Link Quality=32/100   Signal level=32/100
          Rx invalid nwid:0  Rx invalid crypt:0  Rx invalid
frag:0
          Tx excessive retries:0  Invalid misc:15   Missed
beacon:0
```

If not, adjust your settings and use `sudo ifdown wlan0` to switch off the network interface, and then `sudo ifup wlan0` to switch it back on. This will confirm that you have successfully connected to your Wi-Fi network.

4. Finally, we will need to check whether we have access to the internet. Here, we have assumed that the network is automatically configured with DHCP and no proxy server is used. If not, refer to the *Connecting to the internet through a proxy server* recipe.

Unplug the wired network cable, if still connected, and see whether you can ping the Raspberry Pi website, as follows:

`sudo ping www.raspberrypi.org`

If you want to quickly know the IP address currently in use by Raspberry Pi, you can use `hostname -I`, or to find out which adapter is connected to which IP address, use `ifconfig`.

There's more...

The Model A version of Raspberry Pi does not have a built-in network port, so to get a network connection, a USB network adapter will have to be added (either a Wi-Fi dongle, as explained in the preceding section, or a LAN-to-USB adapter, as described in the following section).

Using USB wired network adapters

Just like USB Wi-Fi, the adapter support will depend on the chipset used and the drivers available. Unless the device comes with Linux drivers, you may have to search the internet to obtain the suitable Debian Linux drivers.

If you find a suitable `.deb` file, you can install it with the following command:

```
sudo apt-get install firmware_file.deb
```

Also, check using `ifconfig`, as some devices will be supported automatically, appear as `eth1` (or `eth0` on Model A), and be ready for use immediately.

Connecting to the internet through a proxy server

Some networks, such as ones within workplaces or schools, often require you to connect to the internet through a proxy server.

Getting ready

You will need the address of the proxy server you are trying to connect to, including the username and password, if one is required.

You should confirm that Raspberry Pi is already connected to the network and that you can access the proxy server.

Use the `ping` command to check this, as follows:

```
ping proxy.address.com -c 4
```

If this fails (you get no responses), you will need to ensure your network settings are correct before continuing.

How to do it...

1. Create a new file using `nano` as follows (if there is already some content in the file, you can add the code at the end):

   ```
   sudo nano -c ~/.bash_profile
   ```

2. To allow basic web browsing through programs such as **Midori** while using a proxy server, you can use the following script:

   ```
   function proxyenable {
   # Define proxy settings
   PROXY_ADDR="proxy.address.com:port"
   # Login name (leave blank if not required):
   LOGIN_USER="login_name"
   # Login Password (leave blank to prompt):
   LOGIN_PWD=
   #If login specified - check for password
   if [[ -z $LOGIN_USER ]]; then
     #No login for proxy
     PROXY_FULL=$PROXY_ADDR
   else
     #Login needed for proxy Prompt for password -s option hides
   input
     if [[ -z $LOGIN_PWD ]]; then
       read -s -p "Provide proxy password (then Enter):"
   LOGIN_PWD
       echo
     fi
     PROXY_FULL=$LOGIN_USER:$LOGIN_PWD@$PROXY_ADDR
   fi
   #Web Proxy Enable: http_proxy or HTTP_PROXY environment
   variables
   export http_proxy="http://$PROXY_FULL/"
   export HTTP_PROXY=$http_proxy
   export https_proxy="https://$PROXY_FULL/"
   export HTTPS_PROXY=$https_proxy
   export ftp_proxy="ftp://$PROXY_FULL/"
   export FTP_PROXY=$ftp_proxy
   #Set proxy for apt-get
   sudo cat <<EOF | sudo tee /etc/apt/apt.conf.d/80proxy >
   /dev/null
   Acquire::http::proxy "http://$PROXY_FULL/";
   Acquire::ftp::proxy "ftp://$PROXY_FULL/";
   Acquire::https::proxy "https://$PROXY_FULL/";
   EOF
   #Remove info no longer needed from environment
   ```

```
unset LOGIN_USER LOGIN_PWD PROXY_ADDR PROXY_FULL
echo Proxy Enabled
}

function proxydisable {
#Disable proxy values, apt-get and git settings
unset http_proxy HTTP_PROXY https_proxy HTTPS_PROXY
unset ftp_proxy FTP_PROXY
sudo rm /etc/apt/apt.conf.d/80proxy
echo Proxy Disabled
}
```

3. Once done, save and exit by pressing *Ctrl* + *X*, *Y*, and *Enter*.

 The script is added to the user's own `.bash_profile` file, which is run when that particular user logs in. This will ensure that the proxy settings are kept separately for each user. If you want all users to use the same settings, you can add the code to `/etc/rc.local` instead (this file must have `exit 0` at the end).

How it works...

Many programs that make use of the internet will check for the `http_proxy` or `HTTP_PROXY` environment variables before connecting. If they are present, they will use the proxy settings to connect through. Some programs may also use the `HTTPS` and `FTP` protocols, so we can set the proxy setting for them here too.

 If a username is required for the proxy server, a password will be prompted for. It is generally not recommended to store your passwords inside scripts unless you are confident that no one else will have access to your device (either physically or through the internet).

The last part allows any programs that execute using the `sudo` command to use the proxy environment variables while acting as the super user (most programs will try accessing the network using normal privileges first, even if running as a super user, so it isn't always needed).

There's more...

We also need to allow the proxy settings to be used by some programs, which use superuser permissions while accessing the network (this will depend on the program; most don't need this). We need to add the commands into a file stored in /etc/sudoers.d/ by performing the following steps:

1. Use the following command to open a new sudoer file:

   ```
   sudo visudo -f /etc/sudoers.d/proxy
   ```

2. Enter the following text in the file (on a single line):

   ```
   Defaults env_keep += "http_proxy HTTP_PROXY https_proxy
   HTTPS_PROXY ftp_proxy FTP_PROXY"
   ```

3. Once done, save and exit by pressing *Ctrl + X, Y,* and *Enter;* don't change the proxy.tmp filename (this is normal for visudo; it will change it to proxy when finished).
4. If prompted What now?, there is an error in the command. Press *X* to exit without saving and retype the command.
5. After a reboot (using sudo reboot), you will be able to use the following commands to enable and disable the proxy respectively:

   ```
   proxyenable
   proxydisable
   ```

It is important to use visudo here, as it ensures the permissions of the file are created correctly for the sudoers directory (read only by the root user).

Connecting remotely to Raspberry Pi over the network using VNC

Often, it is preferable to remotely connect to and control Raspberry Pi across the network, for instance, using a laptop or desktop computer as a screen and keyboard, or while Raspberry Pi is connected elsewhere, perhaps even connected to some hardware it needs to be close to.

VNC is just one way in which you can remotely connect to Raspberry Pi. It will create a new desktop session that will be controlled and accessed remotely. The VNC session here is separate from the one that may be active on Raspberry Pi's display.

Getting ready

Ensure that your Raspberry Pi is powered up and connected to the internet. We will use the internet connection to install a program using `apt-get`. This is a program that allows us to find and install applications directly from the official repositories.

How to do it...

1. First, we need to install the TightVNC server on Raspberry Pi with the following commands. It is advisable to run an `update` command first to get the latest version of the package you want to install, as follows:

   ```
   sudo apt-get update
   sudo apt-get install tightvncserver
   ```

2. Accept the prompt to install and wait until it completes. To start a session, use the following command:

   ```
   vncserver :1
   ```

3. The first time you run this, it will ask you to enter a password (of no more than eight characters) to access the desktop (you will use this when you connect from your computer).

   The following message should confirm that a new desktop session has been started:

   ```
   New 'X' desktop is raspberrypi:1
   ```

If you do not already know the IP address of Raspberry Pi, use `hostname -I` and take note of it.

Next, we need to run a VNC client. **VNC Viewer** is suitable program, which is available at `http://www.realvnc.com/` and should work on Windows, Linux, and OS X.

When you run VNC Viewer, you will be prompted for the **Server** address and **Encryption** type. Use the IP address of your Raspberry Pi with :1. That is, for the IP address 192.168.1.69, use the 192.168.1.69:1 address.

You can leave the **Encryption type** as **Off** or **Automatic**.

Depending on your network, you may be able to use the hostname; the default is raspberrypi, that is raspberrypi:1.

You may have a warning about not having connected to the computer before or having no encryption. You should enable encryption if you are using a public network or if you are performing connections over the internet (to stop others from being able to intercept your data).

There's more...

You can add options to the command line to specify the resolution and also the color depth of the display. The higher the resolution and color depth (can be adjusted to use 8-bits to 32-bits per pixel to provide low or high color detail), the more data has to be transferred through the network link. If you find the refresh rate a little slow, try reducing these numbers as follows:

```
vncserver :1 -geometry 1280x780 -depth 24
```

To allow the VNC server to start automatically when you switch on, you can add the vncserver command to .bash_profile (this is executed each time Raspberry Pi starts).

Use the nano editor as follows (the -c option allows the line numbers to be displayed):

```
sudo nano -c ~/.bash_profile
```

Add the following line to the end of the file:

```
vncserver :1
```

The next time you power up, you should be able to remotely connect using VNC from another computer.

Connecting remotely to Raspberry Pi over the network using SSH (and X11 forwarding)

An **Secure Shell** (**SSH**) is often the preferred method for making remote connections, as it allows only the Terminal connections and typically requires fewer resources.

An extra feature of SSH is the ability to transfer the **X11** data to an **X Windows** server running on your machine. This allows you to start programs that would normally run on Raspberry Pi desktop, and they will appear in their own Windows on the local computer, as follows:

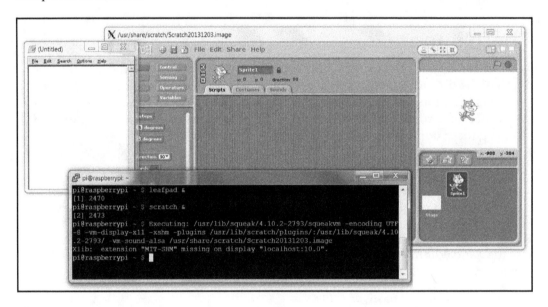

X11 forwarding on a local display

X11 forwarding can be used to display applications which are running on Raspberry Pi on a Windows computer.

Getting ready

If you are running the latest version of Raspbian, SSH, and X11 forwarding will be enabled by default (otherwise, double-check the settings explained in the *How it works...* section).

How to do it...

Linux and OS X have built-in support for X11 forwarding, but if you are using Windows, you will need to install and run the X Windows server on your computer.

Download and run `xming` from the **Xming** site (`http://sourceforge.net/projects/xming/`).

Install `xming`, following the installation steps, including the installation of **PuTTY** if you don't have it already. You can also download PuTTY separately from `http://www.putty.org/`.

Next, we need to ensure that the SSH program we use has X11 enabled when we connect.

For Windows, we shall use PuTTY to connect to Raspberry Pi.

In the **PuTTY Configuration** dialog box, navigate to **Connection** I **SSH** I **X11** and tick the checkbox for **Enable X11 forwarding**. If you leave the **X display location** option blank, it will assume the default `Server 0:0` as follows (you can confirm the server number by moving your mouse over the Xming icon in the system tray when it is running):

Enabling X11 forwarding within the PuTTY configuration

Enter the IP address of Raspberry Pi in the **Session** settings (you may also find that you can use Raspberry Pi's hostname here instead; the default hostname is `raspberrypi`).

Save the setting using a suitable name, `RaspberryPi`, and click on **Open** to connect to your Raspberry Pi.

You are likely to see a warning message pop up stating you haven't connected to the computer before (this allows you to check whether you have everything right before continuing):

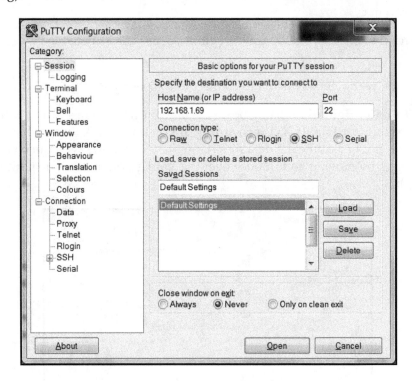

Opening an SSH connection to Raspberry Pi using PuTTY

For OS X or Linux, click on **Terminal** to open a connection to Raspberry Pi.

To connect with the default `pi` username, with an IP address of `192.168.1.69`, use the following command; the `-X` option enables X11 forwarding:

```
ssh -X pi@192.168.1.69
```

All being well, you should be greeted with a prompt for your password (remember the default value for the `pi` user is `raspberry`).

Ensure that you have Xming running by starting the Xming program from your computer's Start menu. Then, in the Terminal window, type a program that normally runs within Raspberry Pi desktop, such as `leafpad` or `scratch`. Wait a little while and the program should appear on your computer's desktop (if you get an error, you have probably forgotten to start Xming, so run it and try again).

How it works...

X Windows and X11 is what provides the method by which Raspberry Pi (and many other Linux-based computers) can display and control graphical Windows as part of a desktop.

For X11 forwarding to work over a network connection, we need both SSH and X11 forwarding enabled on Raspberry Pi. Perform the following steps:

1. To switch on (or off) SSH, you can access **Raspberry Pi Configuration** program under the **Preferences** menu on the **Desktop** and click on **SSH** within the **Interfaces** tab, as shown in the following screenshot (SSH is often enabled by default for most distributions to help allow remote connections without needing a monitor to configure it):

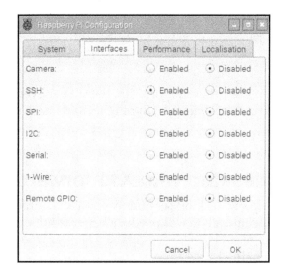

The advanced settings menu in the raspi-config tool

2. Ensure that X11 forwarding is enabled on Raspberry Pi (again, most distributions now have this enabled by default).

3. Use `nano` with the following command:

```
sudo nano /etc/ssh/sshd_config
```

4. Look for a line in the `/etc/ssh/sshd_config` file that controls X11 forwarding and ensure that it says `yes` (with no # sign before it), as follows:

```
X11Forwarding yes
```

5. Save if required by pressing *Ctrl + X, Y,* and *Enter* and reboot (if you need to change it) as follows:

```
sudo reboot
```

There's more...

SSH and X11 forwarding is a convenient way to control Raspberry Pi remotely; we will explore some additional tips on how to use it effectively in the following sections.

Running multiple programs with X11 forwarding

If you want to run an **X program**, but still be able to use the same Terminal console for other stuff, you can run the command in the background with `&` as follows:

```
leafpad &
```

Just remember that the more programs you run, the slower everything will get. You can switch to the background program by typing `fg` and check for background tasks with `bg`.

Running as a desktop with X11 forwarding

You can even run a complete desktop session through X11, although it isn't particularly user friendly and VNC will produce better results. To achieve this, you have to use `lxsession` instead of `startx` (in the way you would normally start the desktop from the Terminal).

An alternative is to use `lxpanel`, which provides the program menu bar from which you can start and run programs from the menu as you would on the desktop.

Running Pygame and Tkinter with X11 forwarding

You can get the following error (or similar) when running the **Pygame** or **Tkinter** scripts:

```
_tkinter.TclError: couldn't connect to display "localhost:10.0"
```

In this case, use the following command to fix the error:

```
sudo cp ~/.Xauthority ~root/
```

Sharing the home folder of Raspberry Pi with SMB

When you have Raspberry Pi connected to your network, you can access the home folder by setting up file sharing; this makes it much easier to transfer files and provides a quick and easy way to back up your data. **Server Message Block** (**SMB**) is a protocol that is compatible with Windows file sharing, OS X, and Linux.

Getting ready

Ensure that you have Raspberry Pi powered and running with a working connection to the internet.

You will also need another computer on the same local network to test the new share.

How to do it...

First, we need to install `samba`, a piece of software that handles folder sharing in a format that is compatible with Windows sharing methods:

1. Ensure that you use `update` as follows to obtain the latest list of available packages:

   ```
   sudo apt-get update
   sudo apt-get install samba
   ```

The install will require around 20 MB of space and take a few minutes.

2. Once the installation has completed, we can make a copy of the configuration file as follows to allow us to restore defaults if needed:

```
sudo cp /etc/samba/smb.conf /etc/samba/smb.conf.backup
sudo nano /etc/samba/smb.conf
```

Scroll down and find the section named Authentication; change the # security = user line to security = user.

As described in the file, this setting ensures that you have to enter your username and password for Raspberry Pi in order to access the files (this is important for shared networks).

Find the section called Share Definitions and [homes], and change the read only = yes line to read only = no.

This will allow us to view and also write files to the shared home folder. Once done, save and exit by pressing *Ctrl + X, Y,* and *Enter.*

> If you have changed the default user from pi to something else, substitute it in the following instructions.

3. Now, we can add pi (the default user) to use samba:

```
sudo pdbedit -a -u pi
```

4. Now, enter a password (you can use the same password as your login or select a different one, but avoid using the default Raspberry password, which would be very easy for someone to guess). Restart samba to use the new configuration file, as follows:

```
sudo /etc/init.d/samba restart
[ ok ] Stopping Samba daemons: nmbd smbd.
[ ok ] Starting Samba daemons: nmbd smbd.
```

5. To test, you will need to know either Raspberry Pi's hostname (the default hostname is raspberrypi) or its IP address. You can find both of these with the following command:

```
hostname
```

6. For the IP address, add `-I`:

    ```
    hostname -I
    ```

    On another computer on the network, enter the `\raspberrypipi` address in the explorer path.

    Depending on your network, the computer should locate Raspberry Pi on the network and prompt for a username and password. If it can't find the share using the `hostname`, you can use the IP address directly, where `192.168.1.69` should be changed to match the IP address `\192.168.1.69pi`.

Keeping Raspberry Pi up to date

The Linux image used by Raspberry Pi is often updated to include enhancements, fixes, and improvements to the system, as well as adding support for new hardware or changes made to the latest board. Many of the packages that you install can be updated too.

This is particularly important if you plan on using the same system image on another Raspberry Pi board (particularly a newer one), as older images will lack support for any wiring changes or alternative RAM chips. New firmware should work on older Raspberry Pi boards, but older firmware may not be compatible with the latest hardware.

Fortunately, you need not reflash your SD card every time there is a new release, since you can update it instead.

Getting ready

You will need to be connected to the internet to update your system. It is always advisable to make a backup of your image first (and at a minimum, make a copy of your important files).

You can check your current version of firmware with the `uname -a` command, as follows:

```
Linux raspberrypi 4.4.9-v7+ #884 SMP Fri May 6 17:28:59 BST 2016
armv7l GNU/Linux
```

The GPU firmware can be checked using the `/opt/vc/bin/vcgencmd version` command, as follows:

```
May   6 2016 13:53:23
Copyright (c) 2012 Broadcom
version 0cc642d53eab041e67c8c373d989fef5847448f8 (clean) (release)
```

This is important if you are using an older version of firmware (pre-November 2012) on a newer board, since the original Model B board was only 254 MB RAM. Upgrading allows the firmware to make use of the extra memory if available.

The `free -h` command will detail the RAM available to the main processor (the total RAM is split between the GPU and ARM cores) and will give the following output:

```
                    total      used       free      shared    buffers
cached
    Mem:            925M       224M       701M       7.1M        14M
123M
    -/+ buffers/cache:         86M        839M
    Swap:           99M        0B         99M
```

You can then recheck the preceding output following a reboot to confirm that they have been updated (although they may have already been the latest).

How to do it...

1. Before running any upgrades or installing any packages, it is worth ensuring you have the latest list of packages in the repository. The `update` command gets the latest list of available software and versions:

   ```
   sudo apt-get update
   ```

2. If you just want to obtain an upgrade of your current packages, `upgrade` will bring them all up to date:

   ```
   sudo apt-get upgrade
   ```

3. To ensure that you are running the latest release of Raspbian, you can run `dist-upgrade` (be warned: this can take an hour or so depending on the amount that needs to be upgraded). This will perform all the updates that `upgrade` will perform but will also remove redundant packages and clean up:

   ```
   sudo apt-get dist-upgrade
   ```

   Both methods will upgrade the software, including the firmware used at boot and startup (`bootcode.bin` and `start.elf`).

4. To update the firmware, the following command can be used:

   ```
   sudo rpi-update
   ```

There's more...

You will often find that you will want to perform a clean installation of your setup, however, this will mean you will have to install everything from scratch. To avoid this, I developed the Pi-Kitchen project (`https://github.com/PiHw/Pi-Kitchen`), based on the groundwork of *Kevin Hill*. This aims to provide a flexible platform for creating customized setups that can be automatically deployed to an SD card:

Pi Kitchen allows Raspberry Pi to be configured before powering up

The Pi-Kitchen allows a range of flavors to be configured, which can be selected from the NOOBS menu. Each flavor consists of a list of recipes, each providing a specific function or feature to the final operating system. Recipes can range from setting up custom drivers for Wi-Fi devices, to mapping shared drives on your network, to providing a fully functional web server out of the box, all combining to make your required setup.

This project is in beta, developed as a proof of concept, but once you have everything configured, it can be incredibly useful to deploy fully working setups directly onto an SD card. Ultimately, the project could be combined with Kevin Hill's advanced version of NOOBS, called **PINN Is Not NOOBS (PINN)**, which aims to allow extra features for advanced users, such as allowing operating systems and configurations to be stored on your network or on an external USB memory stick.

Dividing Text Data and Building Text Classifiers

This chapter presents the following topics:

- Building a text classifier
- Preprocessing data using tokenization
- Stemming text data
- Dividing text using chunking
- Building a bag-of-words model
- Applications of text classifiers

Introduction

This chapter presents recipes to build text classifiers. This includes extracting vital features from the database, training, testing, and validating the text classifier. Initially, a text classifier is trained using commonly used words. Later, the trained text classifier is used for prediction. Building a text classifier includes preprocessing the data using tokenization, stemming text data, dividing text using chunking, and building a bag-of-words model.

Building a text classifier

Classifier units are normally considered to separate a database into various classes. The Naive Bayes classifier scheme is widely considered in literature to segregate the texts based on the trained model. This section of the chapter initially considers a text database with keywords; feature extraction extracts the key phrases from the text and trains the classifier system. Then, **term frequency-inverse document frequency (tf-idf)** transformation is implemented to specify the importance of the word. Finally, the output is predicted and printed using the classifier system.

How to do it...

1. Include the following lines in a new Python file to add datasets:

```
from sklearn.datasets import fetch_20newsgroups
category_mapping = {'misc.forsale': 'Sellings',
'rec.motorcycles': 'Motorbikes',
        'rec.sport.baseball': 'Baseball', 'sci.crypt':
'Cryptography',
        'sci.space': 'OuterSpace'}

training_content = fetch_20newsgroups(subset='train',
categories=category_mapping.keys(), shuffle=True,
random_state=7)
```

2. Perform feature extraction to extract the main words from the text:

```
from sklearn.feature_extraction.text import CountVectorizer

vectorizing = CountVectorizer()
train_counts =
vectorizing.fit_transform(training_content.data)
print "nDimensions of training data:", train_counts.shape
```

3. Train the classifier:

```
from sklearn.naive_bayes import MultinomialNB
from sklearn.feature_extraction.text import TfidfTransformer

input_content = [
    "The curveballs of right handed pitchers tend to curve to
the left",
    "Caesar cipher is an ancient form of encryption",
    "This two-wheeler is really good on slippery roads"
]
```

```
tfidf_transformer = TfidfTransformer()
train_tfidf = tfidf_transformer.fit_transform(train_counts)
```

4. Implement the Multinomial Naive Bayes classifier:

```
classifier = MultinomialNB().fit(train_tfidf,
training_content.target)
input_counts = vectorizing.transform(input_content)
input_tfidf = tfidf_transformer.transform(input_counts)
```

5. Predict the output categories:

```
categories_prediction = classifier.predict(input_tfidf)
```

6. Print the output:

```
for sentence, category in zip(input_content,
categories_prediction):
    print 'nInput:', sentence, 'nPredicted category:',
category_mapping[training_content.target_names[category]]
```

The following screenshot provides examples of predicting the object based on the input from the database:

```
manju@manju-HP-Notebook:~/Documents$ python Building_text_classifier.py

Dimensions of training data: (2968, 40605)

Input: The curveballs of right handed pitchers tend to curve to the left
Predicted category: Baseball

Input: Caesar cipher is an ancient form of encryption
Predicted category: Cryptography

Input: This two-wheeler is really good on slippery roads
Predicted category: Motorbikes
manju@manju-HP-Notebook:~/Documents$ █
```

How it works...

The previous section of this chapter provided insight regarding the implemented classifier section and some sample results. The classifier section works based on a comparison between the previous text in the trained Naive Bayes with the key test in the test sequence.

See also

Please refer to the following articles:

- *Sentiment analysis algorithms and applications: A survey* at `https://www.sciencedirect.com/science/article/pii/S2090447914000550`.

- *Sentiment classification of online reviews: using sentence-based language model* to learn how sentiment prediction works at `https://www.tandfonline.com/doi/abs/10.1080/0952813X.2013.782352?src=recsysjournalCode=teta20`.

- *Sentiment analysis using product review data* and *Sentence-level sentiment analysis in the presence of modalities* to learn more about various metrics used in recommendation systems at `https://journalofbigdata.springeropen.com/articles/10.1186/s40537-015-0015-2` and ;`https://link.springer.com/chapter/10.1007/978-3-642-54903-8_1`.

Pre-processing data using tokenization

The pre-processing of data involves converting the existing text into acceptable information for the learning algorithm.

Tokenization is the process of dividing text into a set of meaningful pieces. These pieces are called tokens.

How to do it...

1. Introduce sentence tokenization:

```
from nltk.tokenize import sent_tokenize
```

2. Form a new text tokenizer:

```
tokenize_list_sent = sent_tokenize(text)
print "nSentence tokenizer:"
print tokenize_list_sent
```

3. Form a new word tokenizer:

```
from nltk.tokenize import word_tokenize
print "nWord tokenizer:"
print word_tokenize(text)
```

4. Introduce a new WordPunct tokenizer:

```
from nltk.tokenize import WordPunctTokenizer
word_punct_tokenizer = WordPunctTokenizer()
print "nWord punct tokenizer:"
print word_punct_tokenizer.tokenize(text)
```

The result obtained by the tokenizer is shown here. It divides a sentence into word groups:

```
manju@manju-HP-Notebook:~/Documents$ python tokenization.py

Sentence tokenizer:
['Tokenization is the process of dividing text into a set of meaningful pieces.'
, 'These pieces are called tokens.']

Word tokenizer:
['Tokenization', 'is', 'the', 'process', 'of', 'dividing', 'text', 'into', 'a',
'set', 'of', 'meaningful', 'pieces', '.', 'These', 'pieces', 'are', 'called', 't
okens', '.']

Word punct tokenizer:
['Tokenization', 'is', 'the', 'process', 'of', 'dividing', 'text', 'into', 'a',
'set', 'of', 'meaningful', 'pieces', '.', 'These', 'pieces', 'are', 'called', 't
okens', '.']
manju@manju-HP-Notebook:~/Documents$ 
```

Stemming text data

The stemming procedure involves creating a suitable word with reduced letters for the words of the tokenizer.

How to do it...

1. Initialize the stemming process with a new Python file:

```
from nltk.stem.porter import PorterStemmer
from nltk.stem.lancaster import LancasterStemmer
from nltk.stem.snowball import SnowballStemmer
```

2. Let's describe some words to consider, as follows:

```
words = ['ability', 'baby', 'college', 'playing', 'is',
'dream', 'election', 'beaches', 'image', 'group', 'happy']
```

3. Identify a group of `stemmers` to be used:

```
stemmers = ['PORTER', 'LANCASTER', 'SNOWBALL']
```

4. Initialize the necessary tasks for the chosen `stemmers`:

```
stem_porter = PorterStemmer()
stem_lancaster = LancasterStemmer()
stem_snowball = SnowballStemmer('english')
```

5. Format a table to print the results:

```
formatted_row = '{:>16}' * (len(stemmers) + 1)
print 'n', formatted_row.format('WORD', *stemmers), 'n'
```

6. Repeatedly check the list of words and arrange them using chosen `stemmers`:

```
for word in words:
    stem_words = [stem_porter.stem(word),
    stem_lancaster.stem(word),
    stem_snowball.stem(word)]
    print formatted_row.format(word, *stem_words)
```

The result obtained from the stemming process is shown in the following screenshot:

```
manju@manju-HP-Notebook:~$ cd Documents
manju@manju-HP-Notebook:~/Documents$ python stemming.py

        WORD        PORTER       LANCASTER       SNOWBALL

     ability        abil             abl           abil
        baby        babi            baby           babi
     college       colleg          colleg         colleg
     playing        play            play           play
          is          is              is             is
       dream       dream           dream          dream
    election       elect           elect          elect
     beaches       beach           beach          beach
       image        imag              im           imag
       group       group           group          group
       happy       happi           happy          happi
manju@manju-HP-Notebook:~/Documents$ █
```

Dividing text using chunking

The chunking procedure can be used to divide the large text into small, meaningful words.

How to do it...

1. Develop and import the following packages using Python:

```python
import numpy as np
from nltk.corpus import brown
```

2. Describe a function that divides text into chunks:

```python
# Split a text into chunks
def splitter(content, num_of_words):
    words = content.split(' ')
    result = []
```

3. Initialize the following programming lines to get the assigned variables:

```python
current_count = 0
current_words = []
```

4. Start the iteration using words:

```
for word in words:
    current_words.append(word)
    current_count += 1
```

5. After getting the essential amount of words, reorganize the variables:

```
if current_count == num_of_words:
    result.append(' '.join(current_words))
    current_words = []
    current_count = 0
```

6. Attach the chunks to the output variable:

```
result.append(' '.join(current_words))
return result
```

7. Import the data of `Brown corpus` and consider the first `10000` words:

```
if __name__=='__main__':
    # Read the data from the Brown corpus
    content = ' '.join(brown.words()[:10000])
```

8. Describe the word size in every chunk:

```
# Number of words in each chunk
num_of_words = 1600
```

9. Initiate a pair of significant variables:

```
chunks = []
counter = 0
```

10. Print the result by calling the `splitter` function:

```
num_text_chunks = splitter(content, num_of_words)
print "Number of text chunks =", len(num_text_chunks)
```

11. The result obtained after chunking is shown in the following screenshot:

```
manju@manju-HP-Notebook:~/Documents$ python chunking.py
Number of text chunks = 7
manju@manju-HP-Notebook:~/Documents$
```

Building a bag-of-words model

When working with text documents that include large words, we need to switch them to several types of arithmetic depictions. We need to formulate them to be suitable for machine learning algorithms. These algorithms require arithmetical information so that they can examine the data and provide significant details. The bag-of-words procedure helps us to achieve this. Bag-of-words creates a text model that discovers vocabulary using all the words in the document. Later, it creates the models for every text by constructing a histogram of all the words in the text.

How to do it...

1. Initialize a new Python file by importing the following file:

```
import numpy as np
from nltk.corpus import brown
from chunking import splitter
```

2. Define the `main` function and read the input data from `Brown corpus`:

```
if __name__=='__main__':
        content = ' '.join(brown.words()[:10000])
```

3. Split the text content into chunks:

```
num_of_words = 2000
num_chunks = []
count = 0
texts_chunk = splitter(content, num_of_words)
```

4. Build a vocabulary based on these `text` chunks:

```
for text in texts_chunk:
    num_chunk = {'index': count, 'text': text}
    num_chunks.append(num_chunk)
    count += 1
```

5. Extract a document word matrix, which effectively counts the amount of incidences of each word in the document:

```
from sklearn.feature_extraction.text
import CountVectorizer
```

6. Extract the document term `matrix`:

```
from sklearn.feature_extraction.text import CountVectorizer
vectorizer = CountVectorizer(min_df=5, max_df=.95)
matrix = vectorizer.fit_transform([num_chunk['text'] for
num_chunk in num_chunks])
```

7. Extract the vocabulary and print it:

```
vocabulary = np.array(vectorizer.get_feature_names())
print "nVocabulary:"
print vocabulary
```

8. Print the document term `matrix`:

```
print "nDocument term matrix:"
chunks_name = ['Chunk-0', 'Chunk-1', 'Chunk-2', 'Chunk-3',
'Chunk-4']
formatted_row = '{:>12}' * (len(chunks_name) + 1)
print 'n', formatted_row.format('Word', *chunks_name), 'n'
```

9. Iterate throughout the words, and print the reappearance of every word in various chunks:

```
for word, item in zip(vocabulary, matrix.T):
# 'item' is a 'csr_matrix' data structure
 result = [str(x) for x in item.data]
 print formatted_row.format(word, *result)
```

10. The result obtained after executing the bag-of-words model is shown as follows:

```
manju@manju-HP-Notebook:~$ cd Documents
manju@manju-HP-Notebook:~/Documents$ python bag_of_word.py

Vocabulary:
[u'about' u'after' u'against' u'aid' u'all' u'also' u'an' u'and' u'are'
 u'as' u'at' u'be' u'been' u'before' u'but' u'by' u'committee' u'congress'
 u'did' u'each' u'education' u'first' u'for' u'from' u'general' u'had'
 u'has' u'have' u'he' u'health' u'his' u'house' u'in' u'increase' u'is'
 u'it' u'last' u'made' u'make' u'may' u'more' u'no' u'not' u'of' u'on'
 u'one' u'only' u'or' u'other' u'out' u'over' u'pay' u'program'
 u'proposed' u'said' u'similar' u'state' u'such' u'take' u'than' u'that'
 u'the' u'them' u'there' u'they' u'this' u'time' u'to' u'two' u'under'
 u'up' u'was' u'were' u'what' u'which' u'who' u'will' u'with' u'would'
 u'year' u'years']
```

```
Document term matrix:
      Word   Chunk-0   Chunk-1   Chunk-2   Chunk-3   Chunk-4
     about      1         1         1         1         3
     after      2         3         2         1         3
   against      1         2         2         1         1
       aid      1         1         1         3         5
       all      2         2         5         2         1
      also      3         3         3         4         3
        an      5         7         5         7        10
       and     34        27        36        36        41
       are      5         3         6         3         2
        as     13         4        14        18         4
        at      5         7         9         3         6
        be     20        14         7        10        18
      been      7         1         6        15         5
    before      2         2         1         1         2
       but      3         3         2         9         5
        by      8        22        15        14        12
 committee      2        10         3         1         7
  congress      1         1         3         3         1
       did      2         1         1         2         2
      each      1         1         4         3         1
 education      3         2         3         1         1
     first      4         1         4         6         3
       for     22        19        24        27        20
      from      4         5         6         5         5
   general      2         2         2         3         6
       had      3         2         7         2         6
       has     10         2         5        20        11
      have      4         4         4         7         5
        he      4        13        12        13        29
    health      1         1         2         6         1
       his     10         6         9         3         7
     house      5         7         4         4         2
        in     38        27        37        49        45
  increase      3         1         1         4         1
        is     12         9        12        14         8
        it     18        16         5         6         9
      last      1         1         5         4         2
      made      1         1         7         4         3
      make      3         2         1         1         1
       may      1         1         2         2         1
      more      3         5         4         6         7
        no      4         1         1         7         3
       not      5         6         3        14         7
        of     61        69        76        56        53
        on     10        18        14        13        13
       one      4         5         3         4         9
      only      1         1         1         3         2
        or      4         4         5         5         4
     other      2         6         7         1         3
       out      3         3         3         4         1
      over      1         1         5         1         2
```

In order to understand how it works on a given sentence, refer to the following:

- *Introduction to Sentiment Analysis*, explained here: `https://blog.algorithmia.com/introduction-sentiment-analysis/`

Applications of text classifiers

Text classifiers are used to analyze customer sentiments, in product reviews, when searching queries on the internet, in social tags, to predict the novelty of research articles, and so on.

3
Using Python for Automation and Productivity

In this chapter, we will cover the following topics:

- Using Tkinter to create graphical user interfaces
- Creating a graphical Start menu application
- Displaying photo information in an application
- Organizing your photos automatically

Introduction

Until now, we have focused purely on command-line applications; however, there is much more to Raspberry Pi than just the command line. By using **graphical user interfaces (GUIs)**, it is often easier to obtain input from a user and provide feedback in a simpler way. After all, we continuously process multiple inputs and outputs all the time, so why limit ourselves to the procedural format of the command line when we don't have to?

Fortunately, Python can support this. Much like other programming languages, such as Visual Basic and C/C++/C#, this can be achieved using prebuilt objects that provide standard controls. We will use a module called **Tkinter** which provides a good range of controls (also referred to as **widgets**) and tools for creating graphical applications.

First, we will take an example, `encryptdecrypt.py`, and demonstrate how useful modules can be written and reused in a variety of ways. This is an example of good coding practice. We should aim to write code that can be tested thoroughly and then reused in many places.

Next, we will extend our previous examples by creating a small graphical Start menu application to run our favorite applications from.

Then, we will explore using **classes** within our applications to display and then to organize photos.

Using Tkinter to create graphical user interfaces

We will create a basic GUI to allow the user to enter information, and the program can then be used to encrypt and decrypt it.

Getting ready

You must ensure that this file is placed in the same directory.

Since we are using Tkinter (one of many available add-ons for Python), we need to ensure that it is installed. It should be installed by default on the standard Raspbian image. We can confirm it is installed by importing it from the Python prompt, as follows:

```
Python3
>>> import tkinter
```

If it is not installed, an `ImportError` exception will be raised, in which case you can install it using the following command (use *Ctrl + Z* to exit the Python prompt):

```
sudo apt-get install python3-tk
```

If the module did load, you can use the following command to read more about the module (use *Q* to quit when you are done reading):

```
>>>help(tkinter)
```

You can also get information about all the classes, functions, and methods within the module using the following command:

```
>>>help(tkinter.Button)
```

The following `dir` command will list any valid commands or variables that are in the scope of the `module`:

```
>>>dir(tkinter.Button)
```

You will see that our own modules will have the information about the functions marked by triple quotes; this will show up if we use the `help` command.

The command line will not be able to display the graphical displays created in this chapter, so you will have to start Raspberry Pi desktop (using the command `startx`), or if you are using it remotely.

Make sure you have **X11 forwarding** enabled and an **X server** running (see `Chapter 1`, *Getting Started with a Raspberry Pi 3 Computer*).

How to do it...

We will use the `tkinter` module to produce a GUI for the `encryptdecrypt.py` script.

To generate the GUI we will create the following `tkencryptdecrypt.py` script:

```python
#!/usr/bin/python3
#tkencryptdecrypt.py
import encryptdecrypt as ENC
import tkinter as TK

def encryptButton():
    encryptvalue.set(ENC.encryptText(encryptvalue.get(),
                                      keyvalue.get()))

def decryptButton():
    encryptvalue.set(ENC.encryptText(encryptvalue.get(),
                                      -keyvalue.get()))
#Define Tkinter application
root=TK.Tk()
root.title("Encrypt/Decrypt GUI")
#Set control & test value
encryptvalue = TK.StringVar()
encryptvalue.set("My Message")
keyvalue = TK.IntVar()
keyvalue.set(20)
prompt="Enter message to encrypt:"
key="Key:"

label1=TK.Label(root,text=prompt,width=len(prompt),bg='green')
textEnter=TK.Entry(root,textvariable=encryptvalue,
                   width=len(prompt))
encryptButton=TK.Button(root,text="Encrypt",command=encryptButton)
decryptButton=TK.Button(root,text="Decrypt",command=decryptButton)
label2=TK.Label(root,text=key,width=len(key))
keyEnter=TK.Entry(root,textvariable=keyvalue,width=8)
#Set layout
label1.grid(row=0,columnspan=2,sticky=TK.E+TK.W)
textEnter.grid(row=1,columnspan=2,sticky=TK.E+TK.W)
encryptButton.grid(row=2,column=0,sticky=TK.E)
decryptButton.grid(row=2,column=1,sticky=TK.W)
label2.grid(row=3,column=0,sticky=TK.E)
keyEnter.grid(row=3,column=1,sticky=TK.W)

TK.mainloop()
#End
```

Run the script using the following command:

```
python3 tkencryptdecrypt
```

How it works...

We start by importing two modules; the first is our own `encryptdecrypt` module and the second is the `tkinter` module. To make it easier to see which items have come from where, we use ENC/TK. If you want to avoid the extra reference, you can use `from <module_name> import *` to refer to the module items directly.

The `encryptButton()` and `decryptButton()` functions will be called when we click on the **Encrypt** and **Decrypt** buttons; they are explained in the following sections.

The main Tkinter window is created using the `Tk()` command, which returns the main window where all the widgets/controls can be placed.

We will define six controls as follows:

- `Label`: This displays the prompt **Enter message to encrypt:**
- `Entry`: This provides a textbox to receive the user's message to be encrypted
- `Button`: This is an **Encrypt** button to trigger the message to be encrypted
- `Button`: This is a **Decrypt** button to reverse the encryption
- `Label`: This displays the **Key:** field to prompt the user for an encryption key value
- `Entry`: This provides a second textbox to receive values for the encryption keys

These controls will produce a GUI similar to the one shown in the following screenshot:

The GUI to encrypt/decrypt messages

Let's take a look at the first `label1` definition:

```
label1=TK.Label(root,text=prompt,width=len(prompt),bg='green')
```

All controls must be linked to the application window; hence, we have to specify our Tkinter window `root`. The text used for the label is set by `text`; in this case, we have set it to a string named `prompt`, which has been defined previously with the text we require. We also set the `width` to match the number of characters of the message (while not essential, it provides a neater result if we add more text to our labels later), and finally, we set the background color using `bg='green'`.

Next, we define the text `Entry` box for our message:

```
textEnter=TK.Entry(root,textvariable=encryptvalue,
                   width=len(prompt))
```

We will define `textvariable`—a useful way to link a variable to the contents of the box which is a special string variable. We could access the `text` directly using `textEnter.get()`, but we shall use a `Tkinter StringVar()` object instead to access it indirectly. If required, this will allow us to separate the data we are processing from the code that handles the GUI layout. The `enycrptvalue` variable automatically updates the `Entry` widget it is linked to whenever the `.set()` command is used (and the `.get()` command obtains the latest value from the `Entry` widget).

Next, we have our two `Button` widgets, **Encrypt** and **Decrypt**, as follows:

```
encryptButton=TK.Button(root,text="Encrypt",command=encryptButton)
decryptButton=TK.Button(root,text="Decrypt",command=decryptButton)
```

In this case, we can set a function to be called when the `Button` widget is clicked by setting the `command` attribute. We can define the two functions that will be called when each button is clicked. In the following code snippet, we have the `encryptButton()` function, which will set the `encryptvalue StringVar` that controls the contents of the first `Entry` box. This string is set to the result we get by calling `ENC.encryptText()` with the message we want to encrypt (the current value of `encryptvalue`) and the `keyvalue` variable. The `decrypt()` function is exactly the same, except we make the `keyvalue` variable negative to decrypt the message:

```
def encryptButton():
    encryptvalue.set(ENC.encryptText(encryptvalue.get(),
                                      keyvalue.get())))
```

We then set the final `Label` and `Entry` widgets in a similar way. Note that `textvariable` can also be an integer (numerical value) if required, but there is no built-in check to ensure that only numbers can be entered. You will encounter a `ValueError` exception when the `.get()` command is used.

After we have defined all the widgets to be used in the Tkinter window, we have to set the layout. There are three ways to define the layout in Tkinter: *place, pack,* and *grid.*

The place layout allows us to specify the positions and sizes using exact pixel positions. The pack layout places the items in the window in the order that they have been added in. The grid layout allows us to place the items in a specific layout. It is recommended that you avoid the place layout wherever possible since any small change to one item can have a knock-on effect on the positions and sizes of all the other items; the other layouts account for this by determining their positions relative to the other items in the window.

We will place the items as laid out in the following screenshot:

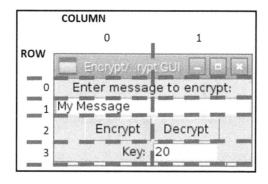

Grid layout for the Encrypt/Decrypt GUI

The positions of first two items in the GUI are set using the following code:

```
label1.grid(row=0,columnspan=2,sticky= TK.E+TK.W)
textEnter.grid(row=1,columnspan=2,sticky= TK.E+TK.W)
```

We can specify that the first Label and Entry box will span both columns (columnspan=2), and we can set the sticky values to ensure they span right to the edges. This is achieved by setting both the TK.E for the east and TK.W for the west sides. We'd use TK.N for the north and TK.S for the south sides if we needed to do the same vertically. If the column value is not specified, the grid function defaults to column=0. The other items are similarly defined.

The last step is to call TK.mainloop(), which allows Tkinter to run; this allows the buttons to be monitored for clicks and Tkinter to call the functions linked to them.

Creating a graphical application – Start menu

The example in this recipe shows how we can define our own variations of Tkinter objects to generate custom controls and dynamically construct a menu with them. We will also take a quick look at using threads to allow other tasks to continue to function while a particular task is being executed.

Getting ready

To view the GUI display, you will need a monitor displaying the Raspberry Pi desktop, or you need to be connected to another computer running the X server.

How to do it...

1. To create a graphical Start menu application, create the following graphicmenu.py script:

```
#!/usr/bin/python3
# graphicmenu.py
import tkinter as tk
from subprocess import call
import threading

#Define applications ["Display name","command"]
leafpad = ["Leafpad","leafpad"]
scratch = ["Scratch","scratch"]
pistore = ["Pi Store","pistore"]
```

```python
app_list = [leafpad,scratch,pistore]
APP_NAME = 0
APP_CMD  = 1

class runApplictionThread(threading.Thread):
    def __init__(self,app_cmd):
        threading.Thread.__init__(self)
        self.cmd = app_cmd
    def run(self):
        #Run the command, if valid
        try:
            call(self.cmd)
        except:
            print ("Unable to run: %s" % self.cmd)

class appButtons:
    def __init__(self,gui,app_index):
        #Add the buttons to window
        btn = tk.Button(gui,
text=app_list[app_index][APP_NAME],
                        width=30, command=self.startApp)
        btn.pack()
        self.app_cmd=app_list[app_index][APP_CMD]
    def startApp(self):
        print ("APP_CMD: %s" % self.app_cmd)
        runApplictionThread(self.app_cmd).start()

root = tk.Tk()
root.title("App Menu")
prompt = '     Select an application     '
label1 = tk.Label(root, text=prompt, width=len(prompt),
bg='green')
label1.pack()
#Create menu buttons from app_list
for index, app in enumerate(app_list):
    appButtons(root,index)
#Run the tk window
root.mainloop()
#End
```

2. The previous code produces the following application:

The App Menu GUI

How it works...

We create the Tkinter window as we did before; however, instead of defining all the items separately, we create a special class for the application buttons.

The class we create acts as a blueprint or specification of what we want the appButtons items to include. Each item will consist of a string value for app_cmd, a function called startApp(), and an __init__() function. The __init__() function is a special function (called a **constructor**) that is called when we create an appButtons item; it will allow us to create any setup that is required.

In this case, the __init__() function allows us to create a new **Tkinter** button with the text to be set to an item in app_list and the command to be called in the startApp() function when the button is clicked. The self keyword is used so that the command called will be the one that is part of the item; this means that each button will call a locally defined function that has access to the local data of the item.

We set the value of self.app_cmd to the command from app_list and make it ready for use via the startApp() function. We now create the startApp() function. If we run the application command here directly, the Tkinter window will freeze until the application we have opened is closed again. To avoid this, we can use the Python threading module, which allows us to perform multiple actions at the same time.

The `runApplicationThread()` class is created using the `threading.Thread` class as a template—this inherits all the features of the `threading.Thread` class in a new class. Just like our previous class, we provide an `__init__()` function for this as well. We first call the `__init__()` function of the inherited class to ensure it is set up correctly, and then we store the `app_cmd` value in `self.cmd`. After the `runApplicationThread()` function has been created and initialized, the `start()` function is called. This function is part of `threading.Thread`, which our class can use. When the `start()` function is called, it will create a separate application thread (that is, simulate running two things at the same time), allowing Tkinter to continue monitoring button clicks while executing the `run()` function within the class.

Therefore, we can place the code in the `run()` function to run the required application (using `call(self.cmd)`).

There's more...

One aspect that makes Python particularly powerful is that it supports the programming techniques used in **Object-Orientated Design** (**OOD**). This is commonly used by modern programming languages to help translate the tasks we want our program to perform into meaningful constructs and structures in code. The principle of OOD lies in the fact that we think of most problems as consisting of several objects (a GUI window, a button, and so on) that interact with each other to produce a desired result.

In the previous section, we found that we could use classes to create unique objects that could be reused multiple times. We created an `appButton` class, which generated an object with all the features of the class, including its own personal version of `app_cmd` that will be used by the `startApp()` function. Another object of the `appButton` type will have its own unrelated `[app_cmd]` data that its `startApp()` function will use.

You can see that classes are useful to keep together a collection of related variables and functions in a single object, and the class will hold its own data in one place. Having multiple objects of the same type (class), each with their own functions and data inside them, results in better program structure. The traditional approach would be to keep all the information in one place and send each item back and forth for various functions to process; however, this may become cumbersome in large systems.

The following diagram shows the organization of related functions and data:

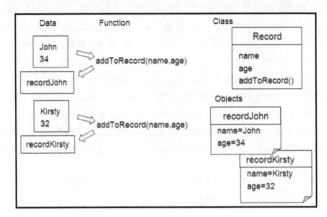

Data and functions

So far, we have used Python modules to separate parts of our programs into different files; this allows us to conceptually separate different parts of the program (an interface, encoder/decoder, or library of classes, such as Tkinter). Modules can provide code to control a particular bit of hardware, define an interface for the internet, or provide a library of common functionality; however, its most important function is to control the interface (the collection of functions, variables, and classes that are available when the item is imported). A well-implemented module should have a clear interface that is centered around how it is used, rather than how it is implemented. This allows you to create multiple modules that can be swapped and changed easily since they share the same interface. In our previous example, imagine how easy it would be to change the `encryptdecrypt` module for another one just by supporting `encryptText(input_text,key)`. Complex functionality can be split into smaller, manageable blocks that can be reused in multiple applications.

Python makes use of classes and modules all the time. Each time you import a library, such as `sys` or Tkinter or convert a value using `value.str()` and iterate through a list using `for...in`, you can use them without worrying about the details. You don't have to use classes or modules in every bit of code you write, but they are useful tools to keep in your programmer's toolbox for times when they fit what you are doing.

We will understand how classes and modules allow us to produce well-structured code that is easier to test and maintain by using them in the examples of this book.

Displaying photo information in an application

In this example, we shall create a utility class to handle photos that can be used by other applications (as modules) to access photo metadata and display preview images easily.

Getting ready

The following script makes use of **Python Image Library** (**PIL**); a compatible version for Python 3 is **Pillow**.

Pillow has not been included in the Raspbian repository (used by apt-get); therefore, we will need to install Pillow using a **Python Package Manager** called **PIP**.

To install packages for Python 3, we will use the Python 3 version of PIP (this requires 50 MB of available space).

The following commands can be used to install PIP:

```
sudo apt-get update
sudo apt-get install python3-pip
```

Before you use PIP, ensure that you have installed libjpeg-dev to allow Pillow to handle JPEG files. You can do this using the following command:

```
sudo apt-get install libjpeg-dev
```

Now you can install Pillow using the following PIP command:

```
sudo pip-3.2 install pillow
```

PIP also makes it easy to uninstall packages using uninstall instead of install.

Finally, you can confirm that it has installed successfully by running python3:

```
>>>import PIL
>>>help(PIL)
```

You should not get any errors and see lots of information about PIL and its uses (press *Q* to finish). Check the version installed as follows:

```
>>PIL.PILLOW_VERSION
```

You should see 2.7.0 (or similar).

PIP can also be used with Python 2 by installing pip-2.x using the following command:

```
sudo apt-get install python-pip
```

Any packages installed using sudo pip install will be installed just for Python 2.

How to do it...

To display photo information in an application, create the following photohandler.py script:

```
##!/usr/bin/python3
#photohandler.py
from PIL import Image
from PIL import ExifTags
import datetime
import os

#set module values
previewsize=240,240
defaultimagepreview="./preview.ppm"
filedate_to_use="Exif DateTime"
#Define expected inputs
ARG_IMAGEFILE=1
ARG_LENGTH=2
class Photo:
    def __init__(self,filename):
        """Class constructor"""
        self.filename=filename
        self.filevalid=False
        self.exifvalid=False
        img=self.initImage()
        if self.filevalid==True:
            self.initExif(img)
            self.initDates()
    def initImage(self):
        """opens the image and confirms if valid, returns Image"""
        try:
            img=Image.open(self.filename)
            self.filevalid=True
        except IOError:
```

```
            print ("Target image not found/valid %s" %
                    (self.filename))
            img=None
            self.filevalid=False
        return img
    def initExif(self,image):
        """gets any Exif data from the photo"""
        try:
            self.exif_info={
                ExifTags.TAGS[x]:y
                for x,y in image._getexif().items()
                if x in ExifTags.TAGS
            }
            self.exifvalid=True
        except AttributeError:
            print ("Image has no Exif Tags")
            self.exifvalid=False

    def initDates(self):
        """determines the date the photo was taken"""
        #Gather all the times available into YYYY-MM-DD format
        self.filedates={}
        if self.exifvalid:
            #Get the date info from Exif info
            exif_ids=["DateTime","DateTimeOriginal",
                    "DateTimeDigitized"]
            for id in exif_ids:
                dateraw=self.exif_info[id]
                self.filedates["Exif "+id]=
                            dateraw[:10].replace(":","-")
        modtimeraw = os.path.getmtime(self.filename)
        self.filedates["File ModTime"]="%s" %
            datetime.datetime.fromtimestamp(modtimeraw).date()
        createtimeraw = os.path.getctime(self.filename)
        self.filedates["File CreateTime"]="%s" %
            datetime.datetime.fromtimestamp(createtimeraw).date()

    def getDate(self):
        """returns the date the image was taken"""
        try:
            date = self.filedates[filedate_to_use]
        except KeyError:
            print ("Exif Date not found")
            date = self.filedates["File ModTime"]
        return date
    def previewPhoto(self):
        """creates a thumbnail image suitable for tk to display"""
        imageview=self.initImage()
```

```
imageview=imageview.convert('RGB')
imageview.thumbnail(previewsize,Image.ANTIALIAS)
imageview.save(defaultimagepreview,format='ppm')
return defaultimagepreview
```

The previous code defines our Photo class; it is of no use to us until we run it in the *There's more...* section and in the next example.

How it works...

We define a general class called Photo; it contains details about itself and provides functions to access **Exchangeable Image File Format (EXIF)** information and generate a preview image.

In the __init__() function, we set values for our class variables and call self.initImage(), which will open the image using the Image() function from the PIL. We then call self.initExif() and self.initDates() and set a flag to indicate whether the file was valid or not. If not valid, the Image() function would raise an IOError exception.

The initExif() function uses PIL to read the EXIF data from the img object, as shown in the following code snippet:

```
self.exif_info={
            ExifTags.TAGS[id]:y
            for id,y in image._getexif().items()
            if id in ExifTags.TAGS
            }
```

The previous code is a series of compound statements that results in self.exif_info being populated with a dictionary of tag names and their related values.

ExifTag.TAGS is a dictionary that contains a list of possible tag names linked with their IDs, as shown in the following code snippet:

```
ExifTag.TAGS={
4096: 'RelatedImageFileFormat',
513: 'JpegIFOffset',
514: 'JpegIFByteCount',
40963: 'ExifImageHeight',
...etc...}
```

The `image._getexif()` function returns a dictionary that contains all the values set by the camera of the image, each linked to their relevant IDs, as shown in the following code snippet:

```
Image._getexif()={
256: 3264,
257: 2448,
37378: (281, 100),
36867: '2016:09:28 22:38:08',
...etc...}
```

The `for` loop will go through each item in the image's EXIF value dictionary and check for its occurrence in the `ExifTags.TAGS` dictionary; the result will get stored in `self.exif_info`. The code for this is as follows:

```
self.exif_info={
'YResolution': (72, 1),
 'ResolutionUnit': 2,
 'ExposureMode': 0,
'Flash': 24,
...etc...}
```

Again, if there are no exceptions, we set a flag to indicate that the EXIF data is valid, or if there is no EXIF data, we raise an `AttributeError` exception.

The `initDates()` function allows us to gather all the possible file dates and dates from the EXIF data so that we can select one of them as the date we wish to use for the file. For example, it allows us to rename all the images to a filename in the standard date format. We create a `self.filedates` dictionary that we populate with three dates extracted from the EXIF information. We then add the filesystem dates (created and modified) just in case no EXIF data is available. The `os` module allows us to use `os.path.getctime()` and `os.path.getmtime()` to obtain an epoch value of the file creation. It can also be the date and time when the file was moved – and the file modification – when it was last written to (for example, it often refers to the date when the picture was taken). The epoch value is the number of seconds since January 1, 1970, but we can use `datetime.datetime.fromtimestamp()` to convert it into years, months, days, hours, and seconds. Adding `date()` simply limits it to years, months, and days.

Now, if the `Photo` class was to be used by another module, and we wished to know the date of the image that was taken, we could look at the `self.dates` dictionary and pick out a suitable date. However, this would require the programmer to know how the `self.dates` values are arranged, and if we later changed how they are stored, it would break their program. For this reason, it is recommended that we access data in a class through access functions so the implementation is independent of the interfaces (this process is known as **encapsulation**). We provide a function that returns a date when called; the programmer does not need to know that it could be one of the five available dates or even that they are stored as epoch values. Using a function, we can ensure that the interface will remain the same no matter how the data is stored or collected.

Finally, the last function we want the `Photo` class to provide is `previewPhoto()`. This function provides a method to generate a small thumbnail image and saves it as a **Portable Pixmap Format** (PPM) file. As we will discover in a moment, Tkinter allows us to place images on its `Canvas` widget, but unfortunately, it does not support JPEGs directly and only supports GIF or PPM. Therefore, we simply save a small copy of the image we want to display in the PPM format – with the added warning that the image pallet must be converted to RGB too – and then get Tkinter to load it onto the `Canvas` when required.

To summarize, the `Photo` class we have created is as follows:

Operations	Description
`__init__(self, filename)`	This is the object initializer.
`initImage(self)`	This returns `img`, a PIL-type image object.
`initExif(self, image)`	This extracts all the EXIF information, if any is present.
`initDates(self)`	This creates a dictionary of all the dates available from the file and photo information.
`getDate(self)`	This returns a string of the date when the photo was taken/created.
`previewPhoto(self)`	This returns a string of the filename of the previewed thumbnail.

The properties and their respective descriptions are as follows:

Properties	Description
self.filename	The filename of the photo.
self.filevalid	This is set to True if the file is opened successfully.
self.exifvalid	This is set to True if the photo contains EXIF information.
self.exif_info	This contains the EXIF information from the photo.
self.filedates	This contains a dictionary of the available dates from the file and photo information.

To test the new class, we will create some test code to confirm that everything is working as we expect; see the following section.

There's more...

We previously created the Photo class. Now we can add some test code to our module to ensure that it functions as we expect. We can use the __name__ ="__main__" attribute
as before to detect whether the module has been run directly or not.

We can add the subsequent section of code at the end of the photohandler.py script to produce the following test application, which looks as follows:

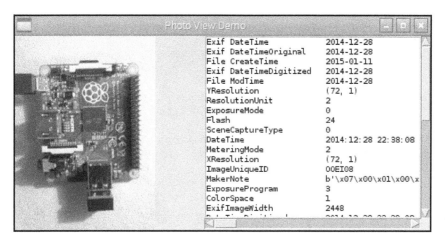

The Photo View Demo application

Add the following code at the end of `photohandler.py`:

```python
#Module test code
def dispPreview(aPhoto):
    """Create a test GUI"""
    import tkinter as TK

    #Define the app window
    app = TK.Tk()
    app.title("Photo View Demo")
    #Define TK objects
    # create an empty canvas object the same size as the image
    canvas = TK.Canvas(app, width=previewsize[0],
                        height=previewsize[1])
    canvas.grid(row=0,rowspan=2)
    # Add list box to display the photo data
    #(including xyscroll bars)
    photoInfo=TK.Variable()
    lbPhotoInfo=TK.Listbox(app,listvariable=photoInfo,
                            height=18,width=45,
                            font=("monospace",10))
    yscroll=TK.Scrollbar(command=lbPhotoInfo.yview,
                        orient=TK.VERTICAL)
    xscroll=TK.Scrollbar(command=lbPhotoInfo.xview,
                        orient=TK.HORIZONTAL)
    lbPhotoInfo.configure(xscrollcommand=xscroll.set,
                            yscrollcommand=yscroll.set)
    lbPhotoInfo.grid(row=0,column=1,sticky=TK.N+TK.S)
    yscroll.grid(row=0,column=2,sticky=TK.N+TK.S)
    xscroll.grid(row=1,column=1,sticky=TK.N+TK.E+TK.W)
    # Generate the preview image
    preview_filename = aPhoto.previewPhoto()
    photoImg = TK.PhotoImage(file=preview_filename)
    # anchor image to NW corner
    canvas.create_image(0,0, anchor=TK.NW, image=photoImg)
    # Populate infoList with dates and exif data
    infoList=[]
    for key,value in aPhoto.filedates.items():
        infoList.append(key.ljust(25) + value)
    if aPhoto.exifvalid:
        for key,value in aPhoto.exif_info.items():
            infoList.append(key.ljust(25) + str(value))
    # Set listvariable with the infoList
    photoInfo.set(tuple(infoList))

    app.mainloop()

def main():
```

```
    """called only when run directly, allowing module testing"""
    import sys
    #Check the arguments
    if len(sys.argv) == ARG_LENGTH:
        print ("Command: %s" % (sys.argv))
        #Create an instance of the Photo class
        viewPhoto = Photo(sys.argv[ARG_IMAGEFILE])
        #Test the module by running a GUI
        if viewPhoto.filevalid==True:
            dispPreview(viewPhoto)
    else:
        print ("Usage: photohandler.py imagefile")

if __name__=='__main__':
  main()
#End
```

The previous test code will run the main() function, which takes the filename of a photo to use and creates a new Photo object called viewPhoto. If viewPhoto is opened successfully, we will call dispPreview() to display the image and its details.

The dispPreview() function creates four Tkinter widgets to be displayed: a Canvas to load the thumbnail image, a Listbox widget to display the photo information, and two scroll bars to control the Listbox. First, we create a Canvas widget the size of the thumbnail image (previewsize).

Next, we create photoInfo, which will be our listvariable parameter linked to the Listbox widget. Since Tkinter doesn't provide a ListVar() function to create a suitable item, we use the generic type TK.Variable() and then ensure we convert it to a tuple type before setting the value. The Listbox widget gets added; we need to make sure that the listvariable parameter is set to photoInfo and also set the font to monospace. This will allow us to line up our data values using spaces, as monospace is a fixed width font, so each character takes up the same width as any other.

We define the two scroll bars, linking them to the `Listbox` widget, by setting the `Scrollbar` command parameters for vertical and horizontal scroll bars to `lbPhotoInfo.yview` and `lbPhotoInfo.xview`. Then, we adjust the parameters of the `Listbox` using the following command:

```
lbPhotoInfo.configure(xscrollcommand=xscroll.set,
                      yscrollcommand=yscroll.set)
```

The `configure` command allows us to add or change the widget's parameters after it has been created, in this case linking the two scroll bars so the `Listbox` widget can also control them if the user scrolls within the list.

As before, we make use of the grid layout to ensure that the `Listbox` widget has the two scroll bars placed correctly next to it and the `Canvas` widget is to the left of the `Listbox` widget.

We now use the `Photo` object to create the `preview.ppm` thumbnail file (using the `aPhoto.previewPhoto()` function) and create a `TK.PhotoImage` object that can then be added to the `Canvas` widget with the following command:

```
canvas.create_image(0,0, anchor=TK.NW, image=photoImg)
```

Finally, we use the date information that the `Photo` class gathers and the EXIF information (ensuring it is valid first) to populate the `Listbox` widget. We do this by converting each item into a list of strings that are spaced out using `.ljust(25)`—it adds left justification to the name and pads it out to make the string 25 characters wide. Once we have the list, we convert it to a tuple type and set the `listvariable` (`photoInfo`) parameter.

As always, we call `app.mainloop()` to start monitoring for events to respond to.

Organizing your photos automatically

Now that we have a class that allows us to gather information about photos, we can apply this information to perform useful tasks. In this case, we will use the file information to automatically organize a folder full of photos into a subset of folders based on the dates the photos were taken on.

The following screenshot shows the output of the script:

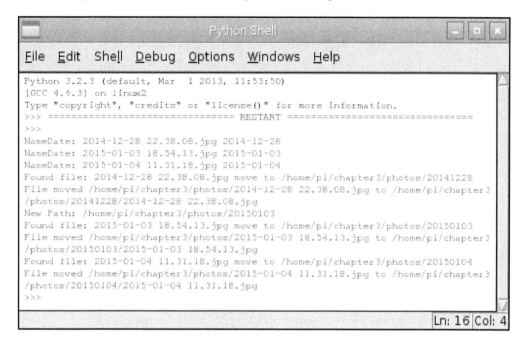

Script output to organize photos in folder

Getting ready

You will need a selection of photos placed in a folder on Raspberry Pi. Alternatively, you can insert a USB memory stick or a card reader with photos on it—they will be located in /mnt/. However, please make sure you test the scripts with a copy of your photos first, just in case there are any problems.

How to do it...

Create the following script in filehandler.py to automatically organize your photos:

```
#!/usr/bin/python3
#filehandler.py
import os
import shutil
import photohandler as PH
```

```
from operator import itemgetter

FOLDERSONLY=True
DEBUG=True
defaultpath=""
NAME=0
DATE=1

class FileList:
    def __init__(self,folder):
        """Class constructor"""
        self.folder=folder
        self.listFileDates()

    def getPhotoNamedates(self):
        """returns the list of filenames and dates"""
        return self.photo_namedates

    def listFileDates(self):
        """Generate list of filenames and dates"""
        self.photo_namedates = list()
        if os.path.isdir(self.folder):
            for filename in os.listdir(self.folder):
                if filename.lower().endswith(".jpg"):
                    aPhoto = PH.Photo(os.path.join(self.folder,filename))
                    if aPhoto.filevalid:
                        if (DEBUG):print("NameDate: %s %s"%
                                        (filename,aPhoto.getDate()))
                        self.photo_namedates.append((filename,
                                                    aPhoto.getDate()))
                        self.photo_namedates = sorted(self.photo_namedates,
                                        key=lambda date: date[DATE])

    def genFolders(self):
        """function to generate folders"""
        for i,namedate in enumerate(self.getPhotoNamedates()):
            #Remove the - from the date format
            new_folder=namedate[DATE].replace("-","")
            newpath = os.path.join(self.folder,new_folder)
            #If path does not exist create folder
            if not os.path.exists(newpath):
                if (DEBUG):print ("New Path: %s" % newpath)
                os.makedirs(newpath)
            if (DEBUG):print ("Found file: %s move to %s" %
                            (namedate[NAME],newpath))
            src_file = os.path.join(self.folder,namedate[NAME])
            dst_file = os.path.join(newpath,namedate[NAME])
            try:
```

```
        if (DEBUG):print ("File moved %s to %s" %
                        (src_file, dst_file))
        if (FOLDERSONLY==False):shutil.move(src_file, dst_file)
    except IOError:
        print ("Skipped: File not found")

def main():
    """called only when run directly, allowing module testing"""
    import tkinter as TK
    from tkinter import filedialog
    app = TK.Tk()
    app.withdraw()
    dirname = TK.filedialog.askdirectory(parent=app,
        initialdir=defaultpath,
        title='Select your pictures folder')
    if dirname != "":
        ourFileList=FileList(dirname)
        ourFileList.genFolders()

if __name__=="__main__":
    main()
#End
```

How it works...

We shall make a class called `FileList`; it will make use of the `Photo` class to manage the photos within a specific folder. There are two main steps for this: we first need to find all the images within the folder, and then generate a list containing both the filename and the photo date. We will use this information to generate new subfolders and move the photos into these folders.

When we create the `FileList` object, we will create the list using `listFileDates()`. We will then confirm that the folder provided is valid and use `os.listdir` to obtain the full list of files within the directory. We will check that each file is a JPEG file and obtain each photo's date (using the function defined in the `Photo` class). Next, we will add the filename and date as a tuple to the `self.photo_namedates` list.

Finally, we will use the built-in `sorted` function to place all the files in order of their date. While we don't need to do this here, this function would make it easier to remove duplicate dates if we were to use this module elsewhere.

The `sorted` function requires the list to be sorted, and, in this case, we want to sort it by the `date values`:

```
sorted(self.photo_namedates,key=lambda date:
date[DATE])
```

We will substitute `date[DATE]` with `lambda date:` as the value to sort by.

Once the `FileList` object has been initialized, we can use it by calling `genFolders()`. First, we convert the date text into a suitable format for our folders (YYYYMMDD), allowing our folders to be easily sorted in order of their date. Next, it will create the folders within the current directory if they don't already exist. Finally, it will move each of the files into the required subfolder.

We end up with our `FileList` class that is ready to be tested:

Operations	Description
`__init__(self,folder)`	This is the object initializer.
`getPhotoNamedates(self)`	This returns a list of the filenames of the dates of the photos.
`listFileDates(self)`	This creates a list of the filenames and dates of the photos in the folder.
`genFolders(self)`	This creates new folders based on a photo's date and moves the files into them.

The properties are listed as follows:

Properties	Description
`self.folder`	The folder we are working with.
`self.photo_namedates`	This contains a list of the filenames and dates.

The `FileList` class encapsulates all the functions and the relevant data together, keeping everything in one logical place:

Tkinter filediaglog.askdirectory() is used to select the photo directory

To test this, we use the Tkinter `filedialog.askdirectory()` widget to allow us to select a target directory of pictures. We use `app.withdrawn()` to hide the main Tkinter window since it isn't required this time. We just need to create a new `FileList` object and then call `genFolders()` to move all our photos to new locations!

Two additional flags have been defined in this script that provide extra control for testing. `DEBUG` allows us to enable or disable extra debugging messages by setting them to either `True` or `False`. Furthermore, `FOLDERSONLY`, when set to `True`, only generates the folders and doesn't move the files (this is helpful for testing whether the new subfolders are correct).

Once you have run the script, you can check if all the folders have been created correctly. Finally, change `FOLDERSONLY` to `True`, and your program will automatically move and organize your photos according to their dates the next time. It is recommended that you only run this on a copy of your photos, just in case you get an error.

4
Predicting Sentiments in Words

This chapter presents the following topics:

- Building a Naive Bayes classifier
- Logistic regression classifier
- Splitting the dataset for training and testing
- Evaluating the accuracy using cross-validation
- Analyzing the sentiment of a sentence
- Identifying patterns in text using topic modeling
- Application of sentiment analyses

Building a Naive Bayes classifier

A Naive Bayes classifier employs Bayes' theorem to construct a supervised model.

How to do it...

1. Import the following packages:

```
from sklearn.naive_bayes import GaussianNB
import numpy as np
import matplotlib.pyplot as plt
```

2. Use the following data file, which includes comma-separated arithmetical data:

```
in_file = 'data_multivar.txt'
a = []
b = []
with open(in_file, 'r') as f:
  for line in f.readlines():
      data = [float(x) for x in line.split(',')]
      a.append(data[:-1])
      b.append(data[-1])
a = np.array(a)
b = np.array(b)
```

3. Construct a Naive Bayes classifier:

```
classification_gaussiannb = GaussianNB()
classification_gaussiannb.fit(a, b)
b_pred = classification_gaussiannb.predict(a)
```

4. Calculate the accuracy of Naive Bayes:

```
correctness = 100.0 * (b == b_pred).sum() / a.shape[0]
print "correctness of the classification =",
round(correctness, 2), "%"
```

5. Plot the classifier result:

```
def plot_classification(classification_gaussiannb, a , b):
  a_min, a_max = min(a[:, 0]) - 1.0, max(a[:, 0]) + 1.0
  b_min, b_max = min(a[:, 1]) - 1.0, max(a[:, 1]) + 1.0
  step_size = 0.01
  a_values, b_values = np.meshgrid(np.arange(a_min, a_max,
step_size), np.arange(b_min, b_max, step_size))
  mesh_output1 =
classification_gaussiannb.predict(np.c_[a_values.ravel(),
b_values.ravel()])
  mesh_output2 = mesh_output1.reshape(a_values.shape)
  plt.figure()
  plt.pcolormesh(a_values, b_values, mesh_output2,
cmap=plt.cm.gray)
  plt.scatter(a[:, 0], a[:, 1], c=b , s=80,
edgecolors='black', linewidth=1,cmap=plt.cm.Paired)
```

6. Specify the boundaries of the figure:

```
plt.xlim(a_values.min(), a_values.max())
plt.ylim(b_values.min(), b_values.max())
```

```
# specify the ticks on the X and Y axes
plt.xticks((np.arange(int(min(a[:, 0])-1), int(max(a[:,
0])+1), 1.0)))
plt.yticks((np.arange(int(min(a[:, 1])-1), int(max(a[:,
1])+1), 1.0)))
plt.show()
plot_classification(classification_gaussiannb, a, b)
```

The accuracy obtained after executing a Naive Bayes classifier is shown in the
following screenshot:

```
manju@manju-HP-Notebook:~/Documents$ python Building_Naive_Bayes_classifier.py
correctness of the classification = 93.67 %
manju@manju-HP-Notebook:~/Documents$
```

See also

Please refer to the following articles:

- To get to know how the classifier works with an example refer to the
  following link:

  https://en.wikipedia.org/wiki/Naive_Bayes_classifier

- To learn more about text classification with the proposed classifier, refer to
  the following link:

  http://sebastianraschka.com/Articles/2014_naive_bayes_1.html

- To learn more about the Naive Bayes Classification Algorithm, refer to the
  following link:

  http://software.ucv.ro/~cmihaescu/ro/teaching/AIR/docs/Lab4-
  NaiveBayes.pdf

Logistic regression classifier

This approach can be chosen where the output can take only two values, 0 or 1,
pass/fail, win/lose, alive/dead, or healthy/sick, and so on. In cases where the
dependent variable has more than two outcome categories, it may be analyzed using
multinomial logistic regression.

How to do it...

1. After installing the essential packages, let's construct some training labels:

```
import numpy as np
from sklearn import linear_model
import matplotlib.pyplot as plt
a = np.array([[-1, -1], [-2, -1], [-3, -2], [1, 1], [2, 1],
[3, 2]])
b = np.array([1, 1, 1, 2, 2, 2])
```

2. Initiate the classifier:

```
classification =
linear_model.LogisticRegression(solver='liblinear', C=100)
classification.fit(a, b)
```

3. Sketch datapoints and margins:

```
def plot_classification(classification, a , b):
  a_min, a_max = min(a[:, 0]) - 1.0, max(a[:, 0]) + 1.0
  b_min, b_max = min(a[:, 1]) - 1.0, max(a[:, 1]) + 1.0
step_size = 0.01
  a_values, b_values = np.meshgrid(np.arange(a_min, a_max,
step_size), np.arange(b_min, b_max, step_size))
  mesh_output1 =
classification.predict(np.c_[a_values.ravel(),
b_values.ravel()])
  mesh_output2 = mesh_output1.reshape(a_values.shape)
  plt.figure()
  plt.pcolormesh(a_values, b_values, mesh_output2,
cmap=plt.cm.gray)
  plt.scatter(a[:, 0], a[:, 1], c=b , s=80,
edgecolors='black',linewidth=1,cmap=plt.cm.Paired)

  # specify the boundaries of the figure
  plt.xlim(a_values.min(), a_values.max())
  plt.ylim(b_values.min(), b_values.max())

  # specify the ticks on the X and Y axes
  plt.xticks((np.arange(int(min(a[:, 0])-1), int(max(a[:,
0])+1), 1.0)))
  plt.yticks((np.arange(int(min(a[:, 1])-1), int(max(a[:,
1])+1), 1.0)))
  plt.show()
  plot_classification(classification, a, b)
```

The command to execute logistic regression is shown in the following screenshot:

```
manju@manju-HP-Notebook:~/Documents$ python logistic_regression.py
```

Splitting the dataset for training and testing

Splitting helps to partition the dataset into training and testing sequences.

How to do it...

1. Add the following code fragment into the same Python file:

```
from sklearn import cross_validation
from sklearn.naive_bayes import GaussianNB
import numpy as np
import matplotlib.pyplot as plt
in_file = 'data_multivar.txt'
a = []
b = []
with open(in_file, 'r') as f:
  for line in f.readlines():
    data = [float(x) for x in line.split(',')]
    a.append(data[:-1])
    b.append(data[-1])
a = np.array(a)
b = np.array(b)
```

2. Allocate 75% of data for training and 25% of data for testing:

```
a_training, a_testing, b_training, b_testing =
cross_validation.train_test_split(a, b, test_size=0.25,
random_state=5)
classification_gaussiannb_new = GaussianNB()
classification_gaussiannb_new.fit(a_training, b_training)
```

3. Evaluate the classifier performance on test data:

```
b_test_pred = classification_gaussiannb_new.predict(a_testing)
```

4. Compute the accuracy of the classifier system:

```
correctness = 100.0 * (b_testing == b_test_pred).sum() /
a_testing.shape[0]
print "correctness of the classification =",
round(correctness, 2), "%"
```

5. Plot the datapoints and the boundaries for test data:

```
def plot_classification(classification_gaussiannb_new,
a_testing , b_testing):
  a_min, a_max = min(a_testing[:, 0]) - 1.0, max(a_testing[:,
0]) + 1.0
  b_min, b_max = min(a_testing[:, 1]) - 1.0, max(a_testing[:,
1]) + 1.0
  step_size = 0.01
  a_values, b_values = np.meshgrid(np.arange(a_min, a_max,
step_size), np.arange(b_min, b_max, step_size))
  mesh_output =
classification_gaussiannb_new.predict(np.c_[a_values.ravel(),
b_values.ravel()])
  mesh_output = mesh_output.reshape(a_values.shape)
  plt.figure()
  plt.pcolormesh(a_values, b_values, mesh_output,
cmap=plt.cm.gray)
  plt.scatter(a_testing[:, 0], a_testing[:, 1], c=b_testing ,
s=80, edgecolors='black', linewidth=1,cmap=plt.cm.Paired)
  # specify the boundaries of the figure
  plt.xlim(a_values.min(), a_values.max())
  plt.ylim(b_values.min(), b_values.max())
  # specify the ticks on the X and Y axes
  plt.xticks((np.arange(int(min(a_testing[:, 0])-1),
int(max(a_testing[:, 0])+1), 1.0)))
  plt.yticks((np.arange(int(min(a_testing[:, 1])-1),
int(max(a_testing[:, 1])+1), 1.0)))
  plt.show()
plot_classification(classification_gaussiannb_new, a_testing,
b_testing)
```

The accuracy obtained while splitting the dataset is shown in the following screenshot:

```
manju@manju-HP-Notebook:~/Documents$ python Splitting_dataset.py
/usr/local/lib/python2.7/dist-packages/sklearn/cross_validation.py:41: Deprecati
onWarning: This module was deprecated in version 0.18 in favor of the model_sele
ction module into which all the refactored classes and functions are moved. Also
 note that the interface of the new CV iterators are different from that of this
 module. This module will be removed in 0.20.
  "This module will be removed in 0.20.", DeprecationWarning)
correctness of the classification = 92.0 %
manju@manju-HP-Notebook:~/Documents$
```

Evaluating the accuracy using cross-validation

Cross-validation is essential in machine learning. Initially, we split the datasets into a train set and a test set. Next, in order to construct a robust classifier, we repeat this procedure, but we need to avoid overfitting the model. Overfitting indicates that we get excellent prediction results for the train set, but very poor results for the test set. Overfitting causes poor generalization of the model.

How to do it...

1. Import the packages:

```
from sklearn import cross_validation
from sklearn.naive_bayes import GaussianNB
import numpy as np
in_file = 'cross_validation_multivar.txt'
a = []
b = []
with open(in_file, 'r') as f:
  for line in f.readlines():
    data = [float(x) for x in line.split(',')]
    a.append(data[:-1])
    b.append(data[-1])
a = np.array(a)
b = np.array(b)
classification_gaussiannb = GaussianNB()
```

2. Compute the accuracy of the classifier:

```
num_of_validations = 5
accuracy =
cross_validation.cross_val_score(classification_gaussiannb, a,
b, scoring='accuracy', cv=num_of_validations)
print "Accuracy: " + str(round(100* accuracy.mean(), 2)) + "%"
f1 =
cross_validation.cross_val_score(classification_gaussiannb, a,
b, scoring='f1_weighted', cv=num_of_validations)
print "f1: " + str(round(100*f1.mean(), 2)) + "%"
precision =
cross_validation.cross_val_score(classification_gaussiannb,a,
b, scoring='precision_weighted', cv=num_of_validations)
print "Precision: " + str(round(100*precision.mean(), 2)) +
"%"
recall =
cross_validation.cross_val_score(classification_gaussiannb, a,
b, scoring='recall_weighted', cv=num_of_validations)
print "Recall: " + str(round(100*recall.mean(), 2)) + "%"
```

3. The result obtained after executing cross-validation is shown as follows:

```
manju@manju-HP-Notebook:~/Documents$ python cross_validation.py
/usr/local/lib/python2.7/dist-packages/sklearn/cross_validation.py:41: DeprecationWarning: This module was deprecated in version 0.18 in favor
of the model_selection module into which all the refactored classes and functions are moved. Also note that the interface of the new CV iterato
rs are different from that of this module. This module will be removed in 0.20.
  "This module will be removed in 0.20.", DeprecationWarning)
Accuracy: 75.13%
f1: 74.73%
Precision: 74.61%
Recall: 75.13%
manju@manju-HP-Notebook:~/Documents$ 
```

In order to know how it works on a given sentence dataset, refer to the following:

- Introduction to logistic regression:

  https://machinelearningmastery.com/logistic-regression-for-machine-learning/

Analyzing the sentiment of a sentence

Sentiment analysis refers to procedures of finding whether a specified part of text is positive, negative, or neutral. This technique is frequently considered to find out how people think about a particular situation. It evaluates the sentiments of consumers in different forms, such as advertising campaigns, social media, and e-commerce customers.

How to do it...

1. Create a new file and import the chosen packages:

```
import nltk.classify.util
from nltk.classify import NaiveBayesClassifier
from nltk.corpus import movie_reviews
```

2. Describe a function to extract features:

```
def collect_features(word_list):
    word = []
    return dict([(word, True) for word in word_list])
```

3. Adopt movie reviews in NLTK as training data:

```
if __name__=='__main__':
    plus_filenum = movie_reviews.fileids('pos')
    minus_filenum = movie_reviews.fileids('neg')
```

4. Divide the data into positive and negative reviews:

```
    feature_pluspts =
[(collect_features(movie_reviews.words(fileids=[f])),
'Positive') for f in plus_filenum]
    feature_minuspts =
[(collect_features(movie_reviews.words(fileids=[f])),
'Negative') for f in minus_filenum]
```

5. Segregate the data into training and testing datasets:

```
    threshold_fact = 0.8
    threshold_pluspts = int(threshold_fact *
len(feature_pluspts))
    threshold_minuspts = int(threshold_fact *
len(feature_minuspts))
```

6. Extract the features:

```
    feature_training = feature_pluspts[:threshold_pluspts] +
feature_minuspts[:threshold_minuspts]
    feature_testing = feature_pluspts[threshold_pluspts:] +
feature_minuspts[threshold_minuspts:]
    print "nNumber of training datapoints:",
len(feature_training)
    print "Number of test datapoints:", len(feature_testing)
```

7. Consider the Naive Bayes classifier and train it with an assigned objective:

```
    # Train a Naive Bayes classifiers
    classifiers = NaiveBayesClassifier.train(feature_training)
    print "nAccuracy of the
classifiers:",nltk.classify.util.accuracy(classifiers,feature_
testing)
    print "nTop 10 most informative words:"
    for item in
classifiers.most_informative_features()[:10]:print item[0]
    # Sample input reviews
    in_reviews = [
    "The Movie was amazing",
    "the movie was dull. I would never recommend it to anyone.",
    "The cinematography is pretty great in the movie",
    "The direction was horrible and the story was all over the
place"
    ]
    print "nPredictions:"
    for review in in_reviews:
      print "nReview:", review
    probdist =
classifiers.prob_classify(collect_features(review.split()))
    predict_sentiment = probdist.max()
    print "Predicted sentiment:", predict_sentiment
    print "Probability:",
round(probdist.prob(predict_sentiment), 2)
```

8. The result obtained for sentiment analysis is shown as follows:

```
manju@manju-HP-Notebook:~/Documents$ python sentiment_analysis.py

Number of training datapoints: 1600
Number of test datapoints: 400

Accuracy of the classifiers: 0.735

Top 10 most informative words:
outstanding
insulting
vulnerable
ludicrous
uninvolving
astounding
avoids
fascination
animators
darker

Predictions:

Review: The Movie was amazing

Review: the movie was dull. I would never recommend it to anyone.

Review: The cinematography is pretty great in the movie

Review: The direction was horrible and the story was all over the place
Predicted sentiment: Negative
Probability: 0.51
manju@manju-HP-Notebook:~/Documents$
```

Identifying patterns in text using topic modeling

The theme modeling refers to the procedure of recognizing hidden patterns in manuscript information. The objective is to expose some hidden thematic configuration in a collection of documents.

How to do it...

1. Import the following packages:

```
from nltk.tokenize import RegexpTokenizer
from nltk.stem.snowball import SnowballStemmer
from gensim import models, corpora
from nltk.corpus import stopwords
```

2. Load the input data:

```
def load_words(in_file):
  element = []
  with open(in_file, 'r') as f:
    for line in f.readlines():
      element.append(line[:-1])
  return element
```

3. Class to pre-process text:

```
classPreprocedure(object):
  def __init__(self):
    # Create a regular expression tokenizer
    self.tokenizer = RegexpTokenizer(r'w+')
```

4. Obtain a list of stop words to terminate the program execution:

```
self.english_stop_words= stopwords.words('english')
```

5. Create a Snowball stemmer:

```
self.snowball_stemmer = SnowballStemmer('english')
```

6. Define a function to perform tokenizing, stop word removal, and stemming:

```
def procedure(self, in_data):
# Tokenize the string
    token = self.tokenizer.tokenize(in_data.lower())
```

7. Eliminate stop words from the text:

```
    tokenized_stopwords = [x for x in token if not x in
self.english_stop_words]
```

8. Implement stemming on the tokens:

```
    token_stemming = [self.snowball_stemmer.stem(x) for x in
tokenized_stopwords]
```

9. Return the processed tokens:

```
    return token_stemming
```

10. Load the input data from the main function:

```
if __name__=='__main__':
# File containing input data
    in_file = 'data_topic_modeling.txt'
# Load words
    element = load_words(in_file)
```

11. Create an object:

```
    preprocedure = Preprocedure()
```

12. Process the file and extract the tokens:

```
    processed_tokens = [preprocedure.procedure(x) for x in
element]
```

13. Create a dictionary based on the tokenized documents:

```
    dict_tokens = corpora.Dictionary(processed_tokens)
    corpus = [dict_tokens.doc2bow(text) for text in
processed_tokens]
```

14. Develop an LDA model, define required parameters, and initialize the LDA objective:

```
num_of_topics = 2
num_of_words = 4
ldamodel =
models.ldamodel.LdaModel(corpus,num_topics=num_of_topics,
id2word=dict_tokens, passes=25)
    print "Most contributing words to the topics:"
    for item in ldamodel.print_topics(num_topics=num_of_topics,
num_words=num_of_words):
        print "nTopic", item[0], "==>", item[1]
```

15. The result obtained when `topic_modelling.py` is executed is shown in the following screenshot:

```
manju@manju-HP-Notebook:~/Documents$ python topic_modeling.py
Most contributing words to the topics:

Topic 0 ==> 0.067*"drive" + 0.066*"pressur" + 0.039*"caus" + 0.039*"doctor"

Topic 1 ==> 0.090*"sugar" + 0.064*"father" + 0.064*"sister" + 0.038*"practic"
manju@manju-HP-Notebook:~/Documents$
```

Applications of sentiment analysis

Sentiment analysis is used in social media such as Facebook and Twitter, to find the sentiments (positive/negative) of the general public over an issue. They are also used to establish the sentiments of people regarding advertisements and how people feel about your product, brand, or service.

5

Detecting Edges and Contours in Images

This chapter presents the following topics:

- Loading, displaying, and saving images
- Image flipping and scaling
- Erosion and dilation
- Image segmentation
- Blurring and sharpening images
- Detecting edges in images
- Histogram equalization
- Detecting corners in images

Introduction

Image processing plays a vital role in almost all engineering and medical applications to extract and evaluate the region of interest from gray/color images. Image processing methods include pre-processing, feature extraction, and classification. Pre-processing is used to enhance the quality of the image; this includes adaptive thresholding, contrast enhancement, histogram equalization, and edge detection. Feature extraction techniques are used to extract prominent features from images that can later be used for classification.

The procedures to build an image pre-processing scheme are presented in the chapter.

Loading, displaying, and saving images

This section presents how to work on images by means of OpenCV-Python. Furthermore, we discuss how to load, display, and save images.

How to do it...

1. Import the Computer Vision package - cv2:

   ```
   import cv2
   ```

2. Read the image using the built-in imread function:

   ```
   image = cv2.imread('image_1.jpg')
   ```

3. Display the original image using the built-in imshow function:

   ```
   cv2.imshow("Original", image)
   ```

4. Wait until any key is pressed:

   ```
   cv2.waitKey(0)
   ```

5. Save the image using the built-in imwrite function:

   ```
   cv2.imwrite("Saved Image.jpg", image)
   ```

6. The command used to execute the Python program Load_Display_Save.py is shown here:

   ```
   manju@manju-HP-Notebook:~/Documents$ python Load_Display_Save.py
   ```

7. The result obtained after executing Load_Display_Save.py is shown here:

Image flipping

In the image flipping operation, we can flip the input images horizontally, vertically, horizontal, and vertically.

How to do it...

1. Import the Computer Vision package - cv2:

   ```
   import cv2
   ```

2. Read the image using the built-in imread function:

   ```
   image = cv2.imread('image_2.jpg')
   ```

3. Display the original image using the built-in imshow function:

```
cv2.imshow("Original", image)
```

4. Wait until any key is pressed:

```
cv2.waitKey(0)
```

5. Perform the required operation on the test image:

```
# cv2.flip is used to flip images
# Horizontal flipping of images using value '1'
flipping = cv2.flip(image, 1)
```

6. Display the horizontally flipped image:

```
# Display horizontally flipped image
cv2.imshow("Horizontal Flipping", flipping)
```

7. Wait until any key is pressed:

```
cv2.waitKey(0)
```

8. Perform vertical flipping of input image:

```
# Vertical flipping of images using value '0'
flipping = cv2.flip(image, 0)
```

9. Display the vertically flipped image:

```
cv2.imshow("Vertical Flipping", flipping)
```

10. Wait until any key is pressed:

```
cv2.waitKey(0)
```

11. Display the processed image:

```
# Horizontal & Vertical flipping of images using value '-1'
flipping = cv2.flip(image, -1)
# Display horizontally & vertically flipped image
cv2.imshow("Horizontal & Vertical Flipping", flipping)
# Wait until any key is pressed
cv2.waitKey(0)
```

12. Stop the execution and display the result:

```
# Close all windows
cv2.destroyAllWindows()
```

13. The command used to execute the `Flipping.py` Python program is shown here:

```
manju@manju-HP-Notebook:~/Documents$ python Flipping.py
```

14. The original and horizontally flipped images obtained after executing `Flipping.py` are shown here:

Following is the horizontally flipped picture:

15. Vertically, and horizontally and vertically, flipped images obtained after executing `Flipping.py` are shown here:

Following horizontally and vertically flipped picture:

Image scaling

Image scaling is used to modify the dimensions of the input image based on requirements. Three types of scaling operators are commonly used in OpenCV, and they are cubic, area, and linear interpolations.

How to do it...

1. Create a new Python file and import the following packages:

   ```
   # Scaling (Resizing) Images - Cubic, Area, Linear
   Interpolations
   # Interpolation is a method of estimating values between known
   data points
   # Import Computer Vision package - cv2
   import cv2
   # Import Numerical Python package - numpy as np
   import numpy as np
   ```

2. Read the image using the built-in imread function:

   ```
   image = cv2.imread('image_3.jpg')
   ```

3. Display the original image using the built-in imshow function:

   ```
   cv2.imshow("Original", image)
   ```

4. Wait until any key is pressed:

   ```
   cv2.waitKey()
   ```

5. Adjust the image size based on the operator's command:

   ```
   # cv2.resize(image, output image size, x scale, y scale,
   interpolation)
   ```

6. Adjust the image size using cubic interpolation:

   ```
   # Scaling using cubic interpolation
   scaling_cubic = cv2.resize(image, None, fx=.75, fy=.75,
   interpolation = cv2.INTER_CUBIC)
   ```

7. Show the output image:

   ```
   # Display cubic interpolated image
   cv2.imshow('Cubic Interpolated', scaling_cubic)
   ```

8. Wait until any key is pressed:

   ```
   cv2.waitKey()
   ```

9. Adjust the image size using area interpolation:

    ```
    # Scaling using area interpolation
    scaling_skewed = cv2.resize(image, (600, 300), interpolation =
    cv2.INTER_AREA)
    ```

10. Show the output image:

    ```
    # Display area interpolated image
    cv2.imshow('Area Interpolated', scaling_skewed)
    ```

11. Wait for the instruction from the operator:

    ```
    # Wait until any key is pressed
    cv2.waitKey()
    ```

12. Adjust the image size using linear interpolation:

    ```
    # Scaling using linear interpolation
    scaling_linear  = cv2.resize(image, None, fx=0.5, fy=0.5,
    interpolation = cv2.INTER_LINEAR)
    ```

13. Show the output image:

    ```
    # Display linear interpolated image
    cv2.imshow('Linear Interpolated', scaling_linear)
    ```

14. Wait until any key is pressed:

    ```
    cv2.waitKey()
    ```

15. After completing the image scaling task, terminate the program execution:

    ```
    # Close all windows
    cv2.destroyAllWindows()
    ```

16. The command used to execute the `Scaling.py` Python program is shown here:

    ```
    manju@manju-HP-Notebook:~/Documents$ python Scaling.py
    ```

17. The original image used for scaling is shown here:

18. Linear interpolated output obtained after executing the `Scaling.py` file is shown here:

19. The area-interpolated output obtained after executing the `Scaling.py` file is shown here:

20. The cubic-interpolated output obtained after executing the `Scaling.py` file is shown here:

Erosion and dilation

Erosion and dilation are morphological operations. Erosion removes pixels at the boundaries of objects in an image and dilation adds pixels to the boundaries of objects in an image.

How to do it...

1. Import the Computer Vision package – cv2:

```
import cv2
```

2. Import the numerical Python package – numpy as np:

```
import numpy as np
```

3. Read the image using the built-in imread function:

```
image = cv2.imread('image_4.jpg')
```

4. Display the original image using the built-in `imshow` function:

```
cv2.imshow("Original", image)
```

5. Wait until any key is pressed:

```
cv2.waitKey(0)
```

6. Given shape and type, fill it with ones:

```
# np.ones(shape, dtype)
# 5 x 5 is the dimension of the kernel, uint8: is an unsigned
integer (0 to 255)
kernel = np.ones((5,5), dtype = "uint8")
```

7. `cv2.erode` is the built-in function used for erosion:

```
# cv2.erode(image, kernel, iterations)
erosion = cv2.erode(image, kernel, iterations = 1)
```

8. Display the image after erosion using the built-in `imshow` function:

```
cv2.imshow("Erosion", erosion)
```

9. Wait until any key is pressed:

```
cv2.waitKey(0)
```

10. `cv2.dilate` is the built-in function used for dilation:

```
# cv2.dilate(image, kernel, iterations)
dilation = cv2.dilate(image, kernel, iterations = 1)
```

11. Display the image after dilation using the built-in `imshow` function:

```
cv2.imshow("Dilation", dilation)
```

12. Wait until any key is pressed:

```
cv2.waitKey(0)
```

13. Close all windows:

```
cv2.destroyAllWindows()
```

14. The command used to execute the `Erosion_Dilation.py` file is shown here:

```
manju@manju-HP-Notebook:~/Documents$ python Erosion_Dilation.py
```

15. The input image used to execute the `Erosion_Dilation.py` file is shown here:

16. The eroded image obtained after executing the `Erosion_Dilation.py` file is shown here:

17. The dilated image obtained after executing the `Erosion_Dilation.py` file is shown here:

Image segmentation

Segmentation is a process of partitioning images into different regions. Contours are lines or curves around the boundary of an object. Image segmentation using contours is discussed in this section.

How to do it...

1. Import the Computer Vision package - cv2:

```
import cv2
# Import Numerical Python package - numpy as np
import numpy as np
```

2. Read the image using the built-in imread function:

```
image = cv2.imread('image_5.jpg')
```

3. Display the original image using the built-in imshow function:

```
cv2.imshow("Original", image)
```

4. Wait until any key is pressed:

```
cv2.waitKey(0)
```

5. Execute the Canny edge detection system:

```
# cv2.Canny is the built-in function used to detect edges
# cv2.Canny(image, threshold_1, threshold_2)
canny = cv2.Canny(image, 50, 200)
```

6. Display the edge detected output image using the built-in imshow function:

```
cv2.imshow("Canny Edge Detection", canny)
```

7. Wait until any key is pressed:

```
cv2.waitKey(0)
```

8. Execute the contour detection system:

```
# cv2.findContours is the built-in function to find contours
# cv2.findContours(canny, contour retrieval mode, contour
approximation mode)
# contour retrieval mode: cv2.RETR_LIST (retrieves all
contours)
# contour approximation mode: cv2.CHAIN_APPROX_NONE (stores
all boundary points)
contours, hierarchy = cv2.findContours(canny, cv2.RETR_LIST,
cv2.CHAIN_APPROX_NONE)
```

9. Sketch the contour on the image:

```
# cv2.drawContours is the built-in function to draw contours
# cv2.drawContours(image, contours, index of contours, color,
thickness)
cv2.drawContours(image, contours, -1, (255,0,0), 10)
# index of contours = -1 will draw all the contours
```

10. Show the sketched contour of the image:

```
# Display contours using imshow built-in function
cv2.imshow("Contours", image)
```

11. Wait until any key is pressed:

```
cv2.waitKey()
```

12. Terminate the program and display the result:

```
# Close all windows
cv2.destroyAllWindows()
```

13. The result obtained after executing the `Image_Segmentation.py` file is shown here:

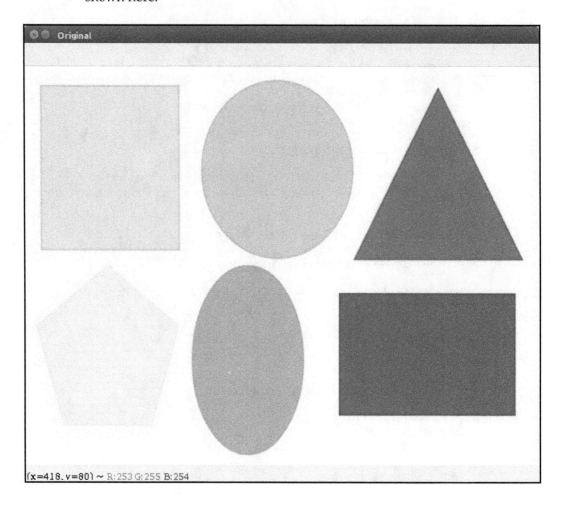

Following is the edge detection output:

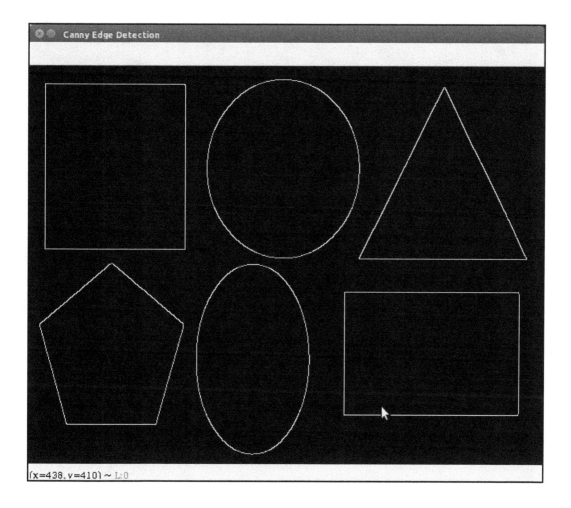

Blurring and sharpening images

Blurring and sharpening are image processing operations used to enhance the input images.

How to do it...

1. Import the Computer Vision package - `cv2`:

```
import cv2
# Import Numerical Python package - numpy as np
import numpy as np
```

2. Read the image using the built-in `imread` function:

```
image = cv2.imread('image_6.jpg')
```

3. Display the original image using the built-in `imshow` function:

```
cv2.imshow("Original", image)
```

4. Wait until any key is pressed:

```
cv2.waitKey(0)
```

5. Execute the pixel level action with the blurring operation:

```
# Blurring images: Averaging, cv2.blur built-in function
# Averaging: Convolving image with normalized box filter
# Convolution: Mathematical operation on 2 functions which
produces third function.
# Normalized box filter having size 3 x 3 would be:
# (1/9)   [[1, 1, 1],
#          [1, 1, 1],
#          [1, 1, 1]]
blur = cv2.blur(image,(9,9)) # (9 x 9) filter is used
```

6. Display the blurred image:

```
cv2.imshow('Blurred', blur)
```

7. Wait until any key is pressed:

```
cv2.waitKey(0)
```

8. Execute the pixel level action with the sharpening operation:

```
# Sharpening images: Emphasizes edges in an image
kernel = np.array([[-1,-1,-1],
                   [-1,9,-1],
                   [-1,-1,-1]])
# If we don't normalize to 1, image would be brighter or
darker respectively
# cv2.filter2D is the built-in function used for sharpening
images
# cv2.filter2D(image, ddepth, kernel)
# ddepth = -1, sharpened images will have same depth as
original image
sharpened = cv2.filter2D(image, -1, kernel)
```

9. Display the sharpened image:

```
cv2.imshow('Sharpened', sharpened)
```

10. Wait until any key is pressed:

```
cv2.waitKey(0)
```

11. Terminate the program execution:

```
# Close all windows
cv2.destroyAllWindows()
```

12. The command used to execute the `Blurring_Sharpening.py` Python program file is shown here:

```
manju@manju-HP-Notebook:~/Documents$ python Blurring_Sharpening.py
```

13. The input image used to execute the `Blurring_Sharpening.py` file is shown here:

14. The blurred image obtained after executing
    the `Blurring_Sharpening.py` file is shown here:

15. The sharpened image obtained after executing
    the `Blurring_Sharpening.py` file is shown here:

Detecting edges in images

Edge detection is used to detect the borders in images. It provides the details
regarding the shape and the region properties. This includes perimeter, major axis
size, and minor axis size.

How to do it...

1. Import the necessary packages:

```
import sys
import cv2
import numpy as np
```

2. Read the input image:

```
in_file = sys.argv[1]
image = cv2.imread(in_file, cv2.IMREAD_GRAYSCALE)
```

3. Implement the Sobel edge detection scheme:

```
horizontal_sobel = cv2.Sobel(image, cv2.CV_64F, 1, 0, ksize=5)
vertical_sobel = cv2.Sobel(image, cv2.CV_64F, 0, 1, ksize=5)
laplacian_img = cv2.Laplacian(image, cv2.CV_64F)
canny_img = cv2.Canny(image, 30, 200)
```

4. Display the input image and its corresponding output:

```
cv2.imshow('Original', image)
cv2.imshow('horizontal Sobel', horizontal_sobel)
cv2.imshow('vertical Sobel', vertical_sobel)
cv2.imshow('Laplacian image', laplacian_img)
cv2.imshow('Canny image', canny_img)
```

5. Wait for the instruction from the operator:

```
cv2.waitKey()
```

6. Display the input image and the corresponding results:

```
cv2.imshow('Original', image)
cv2.imshow('horizontal Sobel', horizontal_sobel)
cv2.imshow('vertical Sobel', vertical_sobel)
cv2.imshow('Laplacian image', laplacian_img)
cv2.imshow('Canny image', canny_img)
```

7. Wait for the instruction from the operator:

```
cv2.waitKey()
```

8. The command used to execute the `Detecting_edges.py` Python program file, along with the input image (`baby.jpg`), is shown here:

```
manju@manju-HP-Notebook:~/Documents$ python Detecting_edges.py baby.jpg
```

9. The input image and the horizontal Sobel filter output obtained after executing the `Detecting_edges.py` file is shown here:

10. The vertical Sobel filter output and the Laplacian image output obtained after executing the `Detecting_edges.py` file is shown here:

Following is the Laplacian image output:

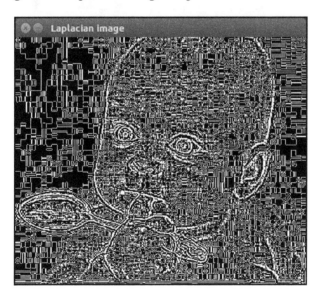

11. The `Canny` edge detection output obtained after executing the `Detecting_edges.py` file is shown here:

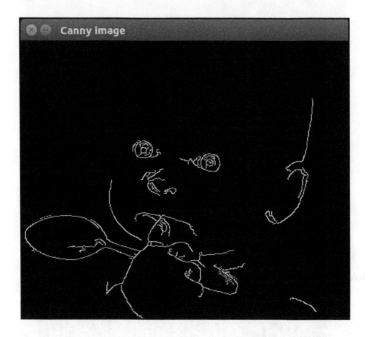

How it works...

Readers can refer to the following document to learn what edge detection is and its impact on test pictures:

`http://citeseerx.ist.psu.edu/viewdoc/summary?doi=10.1.1.301.927`

See also

Please refer to the following document:

- `https://www.tutorialspoint.com/dip/concept_of_edge_detection.htm`

Histogram equalization

Histogram equalization is used to enhance the visibility and the contrast of images. It is performed by varying the image intensities. These procedures are clearly described here.

How to do it...

1. Import the necessary packages:

```
import sys
import cv2
import numpy as np
```

2. Load the input image:

```
in_file = sys.argv[1]
image = cv2.imread(in_file)
```

3. Convert the RGB image into grayscale:

```
image_gray = cv2.cvtColor(image, cv2.COLOR_BGR2GRAY)
cv2.imshow('Input grayscale image', image_gray)
```

4. Regulate the histogram of the grayscale image:

```
image_gray_histoeq = cv2.equalizeHist(image_gray)
cv2.imshow('Histogram equalized - grayscale image',
image_gray_histoeq)
```

5. Regulate the histogram of the RGB image:

```
image_yuv = cv2.cvtColor(image, cv2.COLOR_BGR2YUV)
image_yuv[:,:,0] = cv2.equalizeHist(image_yuv[:,:,0])
image_histoeq = cv2.cvtColor(image_yuv, cv2.COLOR_YUV2BGR)
```

6. Display the output image:

```
cv2.imshow('Input image', image)
cv2.imshow('Histogram equalized - color image', image_histoeq)
cv2.waitKey()
```

7. The command used to execute the `histogram.py` Python program file, along with the input image (`finger.jpg`), is shown here:

```
manju@manju-HP-Notebook:~/Documents$ python histogram.py finger.jpg
```

8. The input image used to execute the `histogram.py` file is shown here:

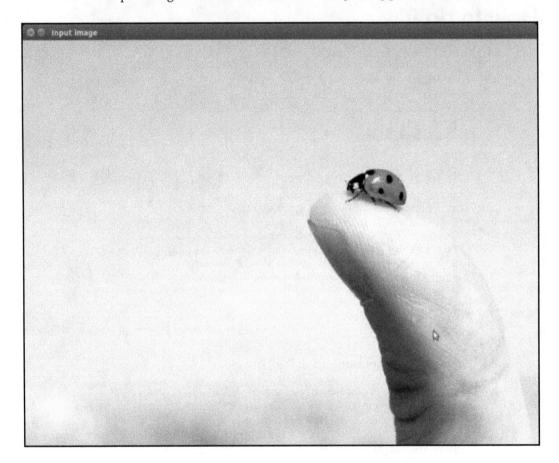

9. The histogram equalized grayscale image obtained after executing the `histogram.py` file is shown here:

10. The histogram equalized color image obtained after executing the `histogram.py` file is shown here:

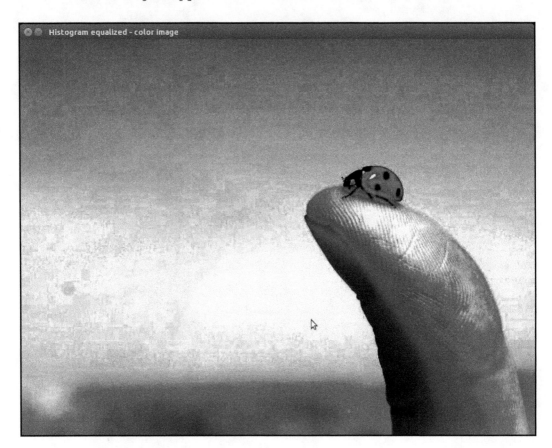

Detecting corners in images

Corners are borders in images used to extract special features that infer the content of an image. Corner detection is frequently used in image registration, video tracking, image mosaics, motion detection, 3D modelling, panorama stitching, and object recognition.

How to do it...

1. Import the necessary packages:

   ```
   import sys
   import cv2
   import numpy as np
   ```

2. Load the input image:

   ```
   in_file = sys.argv[1]
   image = cv2.imread(in_file)
   cv2.imshow('Input image', image)
   image_gray1 = cv2.cvtColor(image, cv2.COLOR_BGR2GRAY)
   image_gray2 = np.float32(image_gray1)
   ```

3. Implement the Harris corner detection scheme:

   ```
   image_harris1 = cv2.cornerHarris(image_gray2, 7, 5, 0.04)
   ```

4. Dilate the input image and construct the corners:

   ```
   image_harris2 = cv2.dilate(image_harris1, None)
   ```

5. Implement image thresholding:

   ```
   image[image_harris2 > 0.01 * image_harris2.max()] = [0, 0, 0]
   ```

6. Display the input image:

   ```
   cv2.imshow('Harris Corners', image)
   ```

7. Wait for the instruction from the operator:

   ```
   cv2.waitKey()
   ```

8. The command used to execute the `Detecting_corner.py` Python program file, along with the input image (`box.jpg`), is shown here:

```
manju@manju-HP-Notebook:~/Documents$ python Detecting_corner.py box.jpg
```

9. The input image used to execute the `Detecting_corner.py` file is shown here:

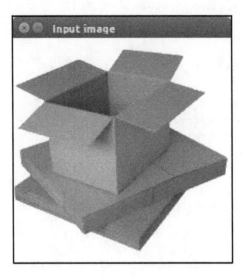

10. **Harris Corners** obtained after executing the `Detecting_corner.py` file are shown here:

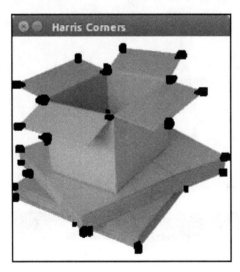

In order to learn how it works for an input image, refer to the following:

- Image corner detection involves finding the edges/corners in the given picture. It can be used to extract the vital shape features from grayscale and RGB pictures. Refer to this survey paper on edge and corner detection:

  ```
  https://pdfs.semanticscholar.org/24dd/
  6c2c08f5601e140aad5b9170e0c7485f6648.pdf.
  ```

6

Building Face Detector and Face Recognition Applications

This chapter presents the following topics:

- Introduction to the face recognition system
- Building a face detector application
- Building a face recognition application
- Applications of a face recognition system

Introduction

In recent years, face recognition has emerged as one of the hottest research areas. A face recognition system is a computer program with the ability to detect and recognize faces. In order to recognize a person, it considers their unique facial features. Recently, it has been adopted in several security and surveillance installations to ensure safety in high-risk areas, residential zones, private and public buildings, and so on.

Building a face detector application

In this section, we discuss how human faces can be detected from webcam images. A USB webcam needs to be connected to Raspberry Pi 3 to implement real-time human face detection.

How to do it...

1. Import the necessary packages:

```
import cv2
import numpy as np
```

2. Load the face cascade file:

```
frontalface_cascade=
cv2.CascadeClassifier('haarcascade_frontalface_alt.xml')
```

3. Check whether the face cascade file has been loaded:

```
if frontalface_cascade.empty():
    raiseIOError('Unable to load the face cascade classifier xml
file')
```

4. Initialize the video capture object:

```
capture = cv2.VideoCapture(0)
```

5. Define the scaling factor:

```
scale_factor = 0.5
```

6. Perform the operation until the *Esc* key is pressed:

```
# Loop until you hit the Esc key
while True:
```

7. Capture the current frame and resize it:

```
ret, frame = capture.read()
frame = cv2.resize(frame, None, fx=scale_factor,
fy=scale_factor,
            interpolation=cv2.INTER_AREA)
```

8. Convert the image frame into grayscale:

```
gray_image = cv2.cvtColor(frame, cv2.COLOR_BGR2GRAY)
```

9. Run the face detector on the grayscale image:

```
face_rectangle =
frontalface_cascade.detectMultiScale(gray_image, 1.3, 5)
```

10. Draw the rectangles box:

```
for (x,y,w,h) in face_rectangle:
    cv2.rectangle(frame, (x,y), (x+w,y+h), (0,255,0), 3)
```

11. Display the output image:

```
cv2.imshow('Face Detector', frame)
```

12. Check whether the *Esc* key has been pressed for operation termination:

```
a = cv2.waitKey(1)
if a == 10:
    break
```

13. Stop the video capturing and terminate the operation:

```
capture.release()
cv2.destroyAllWindows()
```

The result obtained in the human face detection system is shown here:

Building a face recognition application

Face recognition is a technique that is performed after face detection. The detected human face is compared with the images stored in the database. It extracts features from the input image and matches them with human features stored in the database.

How to do it...

1. Import the necessary packages:

```
import cv2
import numpy as np
from sklearn import preprocessing
```

2. Load the encoding and decoding task operators:

```
class LabelEncoding(object):
    # Method to encode labels from words to numbers
    def encoding_labels(self, label_wordings):
        self.le = preprocessing.LabelEncoder()
        self.le.fit(label_wordings)
```

3. Implement word-to-number conversion for the input label:

```
def word_to_number(self, label_wordings):
    return int(self.le.transform([label_wordings])[0])
```

4. Convert the input label from a number to word:

```
def number_to_word(self, label_number):
    return self.le.inverse_transform([label_number])[0]
```

5. Extract images and labels from the input path:

```
def getting_images_and_labels(path_input):
    label_wordings = []
```

6. Iterate the procedure for the input path and append the files:

```
for roots, dirs, files in os.walk(path_input):
    for fname in (x for x in files if x.endswith('.jpg')):
        fpath = os.path.join(roots, fname)
        label_wordings.append(fpath.split('/')[-2])
```

7. Initialize the variables and parse the input register:

```
images = []
le = LabelEncoding()
le.encoding_labels(label_wordings)
labels = []
# Parse the input directory
for roots, dirs, files in os.walk(path_input):
    for fname in (x for x in files if x.endswith('.jpg')):
        fpath = os.path.join(roots, fname)
```

8. Read the grayscale image:

```
img = cv2.imread(fpath, 0)
```

9. Extract the label:

```
names = fpath.split('/')[-2]
```

10. Perform face detection:

```
face = faceCascade.detectMultiScale(img, 1.1, 2,
minSize=(100,100))
```

11. Iterate the procedure with face rectangles:

```
for (x, y, w, h) in face:
    images.append(img[y:y+h, x:x+w])
    labels.append(le.word_to_number(names))
return images, labels, le
if __name__=='__main__':
    path_cascade = "haarcascade_frontalface_alt.xml"
    train_img_path = 'faces_dataset/train'
    path_img_test = 'faces_dataset/test'
```

12. Load the face cascade file:

```
faceCascade = cv2.CascadeClassifier(path_cascade)
```

13. Initialize face detection with local binary patterns:

```
face_recognizer = cv2.createLBPHFaceRecognizer()
```

14. Extract the face features from the training face dataset:

```
imgs, labels, le = getting_images_and_labels(train_img_path)
```

15. Train the face detection system:

```
print "nTraining..."
face_recognizer.train(imgs, np.array(labels))
```

16. Test the face detection system:

```
print 'nPerforming prediction on test images...'
flag_stop = False
for roots, dirs, files in os.walk(path_img_test):
  for fname in (x for x in files if x.endswith('.jpg')):
    fpath = os.path.join(roots, fname)
```

17. Validate the face recognition system:

```
predicting_img = cv2.imread(fpath, 0)
      # Detect faces
face = faceCascade.detectMultiScale(predicting_img, 1.1,
        2, minSize=(100,100))
      # Iterate through face rectangles
for (x, y, w, h) in face:
  # Predict the output
  index_predicted, config = face_recognizer.predict(
predicting_img[y:y+h, x:x+w])
  # Convert to word label
  person_predicted = le.number_to_word(index_predicted)
  # Overlay text on the output image and display it
  cv2.putText(predicting_img, 'Prediction: ' +
person_predicted,
            (10,60), cv2.FONT_HERSHEY_SIMPLEX, 2,
(255,255,255), 6)
  cv2.imshow("Recognizing face", predicting_img)
  a = cv2.waitKey(0)
  if a == 27:
    flag = True
    break
  if flag_stop:
  break
```

The face recognition output obtained is shown here:

How it works...

Face recognition systems are widely used to implement personal security systems. Readers can refer to the article *The system of face detection based on OpenCV* at `http://ieeexplore.ieee.org/document/6242980/`.

See also *Study of Face Detection Algorithm for Real-time Face Detection System* at `http://ieeexplore.ieee.org/document/5209668`.

See also

Please refer to the following articles:

- http://www.ex-sight.com/technology.htm
- https://www.eurotech.com/en/products/devices/face+recognition+systems
- https://arxiv.org/ftp/arxiv/papers/1403/1403.0485.pdf

Applications of a face recognition system

Face recognition is widely used in security, healthcare, and marketing. Industries are developing novel face recognition systems using deep learning to recognize fraud, identify the difference between human faces and photographs, and so on. In healthcare, face recognition, combined with other computer vision algorithms, is used to detect facial skin diseases.

Using Python to Drive Hardware

7

In this chapter, we will cover the following topics:

- Controlling an LED
- Responding to a button
- The controlled shutdown button
- The GPIO keypad input
- Multiplexed color LEDs
- Writing messages using persistence of vision

Introduction

One of the key features of a Raspberry Pi computer that sets it apart from most other home/office computers is that it has the ability to directly interface with other hardware. The **general-purpose input/output** (**GPIO**) pins on the Raspberry Pi can control a wide range of low-level electronics, from **light-emitting diodes** (**LEDs**) to switches, sensors, motors, servos, and even extra displays.

This chapter will focus on connecting the Raspberry Pi with some simple circuits and getting to grips with using Python to control and respond to the connected components.

The Raspberry Pi hardware interface consists of 40 pins located along one side of the board.

The GPIO pins and their layout will vary slightly according to the particular model you have.

The Raspberry Pi 3, Raspberry Pi 2, and Raspberry Pi B+ all have the same 40-pin layout.

The older Raspberry Pi 1 models (nonplus types) have a 26-pin header, which is the same as the 1-26 pins of the newer models.

Function	GPIO.BOARD		Function
3V3	1	2	5V
SDA1 ARM	3	4	5V
SCL1 ARM	5	6	GND
	7	8	TX
GND	9	10	RX
SPI1 CE1	11	12	PWM0/SPI1 CE0
	13	14	GND
	15	16	
3v3	17	18	
SPI0 MOSI	19	20	GND
SPI0 MISO	21	22	
SPI0 SCLK	23	24	SPI0 CE0
GND	25	26	SPI0 CE1
SDA0 VC	27	28	SCL0 VC
	29	30	GND
	31	32	PWM0
PWM1	33	34	GND
SPI1 MISO/PWM1	35	36	SPI1 CE2
	37	38	SPI1 MOSI
GND	39	40	SPI1 SCLK

Raspberry Pi 2, Raspberry Pi B+, and Raspberry Pi Model Plus GPIO header pins (pin functions)

The layout of the connector is shown in the preceding diagram; the pin numbers are shown as seen from pin 1 of the GPIO header.

Pin 1 is at the end that is nearest to the SD card, as shown in the following photo:

The Raspberry Pi GPIO header location

Care should be taken when using the GPIO header, since it also includes power pins (3V3 and 5 V), as well as **ground (GND)** pins. All of the GPIO pins can be used as standard GPIO, but several also have special functions; these are labeled and highlighted with different colors.

It is common for engineers to use a 3V3 notation to specify values in schematics in order to avoid using decimal places that could easily be missed (using 33V rather than 3.3V would cause severe damage to the circuitry). The same can be applied to the values of other components, such as resistors, for example, 1.2K ohms can be written as 1K2 ohms.

The **TX** and **RX** pins are used for serial communications, and with the aid of a voltage-level converter, information can be transferred via a serial cable to another computer or device.

We also have the **SDA** and **SCL** pins, which are able to support a two-wire bus communication protocol called I^2C (there are two I^2C channels on Raspberry Pi 3 and Model Plus boards: **channel 1 ARM**, which is for general use, and **channel 0 VC**, which is typically used for identifying **hardware attached on top** (HAT) modules). There are also the **SPI MOSI**, **SPI MISO**, **SPI SCLK**, **SPI CE0**, and **SPI CE1** pins, which support another type of bus protocol called **SPI** for high-speed data. Finally, we have the **PWM0/1** pin, which allows a **pulse-width modulation** signal to be generated, which is useful for servos and generating analog signals.

However, we will focus on using just the standard GPIO functions in this chapter. The GPIO pin layout is shown in the following diagram:

GPIO.BCM	Function	GPIO.BOARD		Function	GPIO.BCM
<50mA	3V3	1	2	5V	
BCM GPIO02	SDA1 ARM	3	4	5V	
BCM GPIO03	SCL1 ARM	5	6	GND	
BCM GPIO04		7	8	TX	BCM GPIO14
	GND	9	10	RX	BCM GPIO15
BCM GPIO17	SPI1 CE1	11	12	PWM0/SPI1 CE0	BCM GPIO18
BCM GPIO27		13	14	GND	
BCM GPIO22		15	16		BCM GPIO23
<50mA	3v3	17	18		BCM GPIO24
BCM GPIO10	SPI0 MOSI	19	20	GND	
BCM GPIO9	SPI0 MISO	21	22		BCM GPIO25
BCM GPIO11	SPI0 SCLK	23	24	SPI0 CE0	BCM GPIO08
	GND	25	26	SPI0 CE1	BCM GPIO07
BCM GPIO00	SDA0 VC	27	28	SCL0 VC	BCM GPIO01
BCM GPIO05		29	30	GND	
BCM GPIO06		31	32	PWM0	BCM GPIO 12
BCM GPIO13	PWM1	33	34	GND	
BCM GPIO19	SPI1 MISO/PWM1	35	36	SPI1 CE2	BCM GPIO16
BCM GPIO26		37	38	SPI1 MOSI	BCM GPIO20
	GND	39	40	SPI1 SCLK	BCM GPIO21

Raspberry Pi GPIO header pins (GPIO.BOARD and GPIO.BCM)

The Raspberry Pi Rev 2 (pre-July 2014) has the following differences compared to the Raspberry Pi 2 GPIO layout:

- 26-GPIO-pin header (matching the first 26 pins).
- An additional secondary set of eight holes (P5) located next to the pin header. The details are as follows:

GPIO.BCM	Function	GPIO.BOARD		Function	GPIO.BCM
<50mA	3V3	2	1	5V	
BCM GPIO29	SCL0 VC	4	3	SDA0	BCM GPIO28
BCM GPIO31		6	5		BCM GPIO23
	GND	8	7	GND	

Raspberry Pi Rev 2 P5 GPIO header pins

- The original Raspberry Pi Rev 1 (pre-October 2012) has only 26 GPIO pins in total, (matching the first 26 pins of the current Raspberry Pi, except for the following details:

GPIO.BCM	Function	GPIO.BOARD
BCM GPIO00	SDA0	3
BCM GPIO01	SCL0	5
BCM GPIO21		13

Raspberry Pi Rev 1 GPIO header differences

The RPi.GPIO library can reference the pins on the Raspberry Pi using one of two systems. The numbers shown in the center refer to the physical position of the pins, and are also the numbers referenced by the RPi.GPIO library when in **GPIO.BOARD** mode. The numbers on the outside (**GPIO.BCM**) are the actual reference numbers of the physical ports of the processor that indicate which of the pins are wired (which is why they are not in any specific order). They are used when the mode is set to **GPIO.BCM**, and they allow control of the GPIO header pins as well as any peripherals connected to other GPIO lines. This includes the LED on the add-on camera on BCM GPIO 4 and the status LED on the board. However, this can also include the GPIO lines used for reading/writing to the SD card, which would cause serious errors if interfered with.

If you use other programming languages to access the GPIO pins, the numbering scheme may be different, so it will be helpful if you are aware of the BCM GPIO references, which refer to the physical GPIO ports of the processor.

Be sure to check out the Appendix, *Hardware and Software List*, which lists all the items used in this chapter and the places that you can obtain them from.

Controlling an LED

The hardware equivalent of `hello world` is an LED flash, which is a great test to ensure that everything is working and that you have wired it correctly. To make it a little more interesting, I've suggested using a **red, blue, and green (RGB)** LED, but feel free to use separate LEDs if that is all you have available.

Getting ready

You will need the following equipment:

- 4 x DuPont female-to-male patch wires
- Mini breadboard (170 tie points) or a larger one
- RGB LED (common cathode)/3 standard LEDs (ideally red, green, and blue)
- Breadboard wire (solid core)
- 3 x 470 ohm resistors

Each of the preceding components shouldn't cost many dollars and can be reused for other projects afterwards. The breadboard is a particularly useful item that allows you to try out your own circuits without needing to solder them:

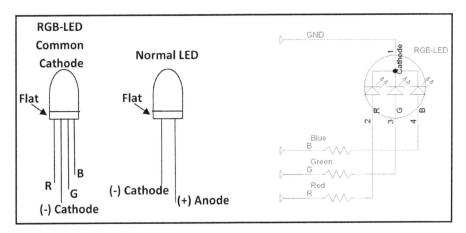

Diagrams of an RGB LED, a standard LED, and an RGB circuit

The following diagram shows the breadboard circuitry:

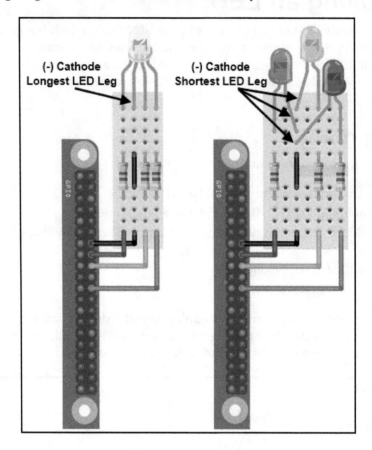

The wiring of an RGB LED/standard LEDs connected to the GPIO header

There are several different kinds of RGB LEDs available, so check the datasheet of your component to confirm the pin order and type you have. Some are RGB, so ensure that you wire accordingly or adjust the RGB_ pin settings in the code. You can also get common anode variants, which will require the anode to be connected to 3V3 (GPIO-pin 1) for it to light up (and they will also require RGB_ENABLE and RGB_DISABLE to be set to 0 and 1 respectively).

The breadboard and component diagrams of this book have been created using a free tool called **Fritzing** (www.fritzing.org); it is great for planning your own Raspberry Pi projects.

How to do it...

1. Create the `ledtest.py` script as follows:

```python
#!/usr/bin/python3
#ledtest.py
import time
import RPi.GPIO as GPIO
# RGB LED module
#HARDWARE SETUP
# GPIO
# 2[======XRG=B==]26[=======]40
# 1[=============]25[=======]39
# X=GND R=Red G=Green B=Blue
#Setup Active States
#Common Cathode RGB-LED (Cathode=Active Low)
RGB_ENABLE = 1; RGB_DISABLE = 0

#LED CONFIG - Set GPIO Ports
RGB_RED = 16; RGB_GREEN = 18; RGB_BLUE = 22
RGB = [RGB_RED,RGB_GREEN,RGB_BLUE]

def led_setup():
  #Setup the wiring
  GPIO.setmode(GPIO.BOARD)
  #Setup Ports
  for val in RGB:
    GPIO.setup(val,GPIO.OUT)

def main():
  led_setup()
  for val in RGB:
    GPIO.output(val,RGB_ENABLE)
    print("LED ON")
    time.sleep(5)
    GPIO.output(val,RGB_DISABLE)
    print("LED OFF")

try:
  main()
finally:
  GPIO.cleanup()
  print("Closed Everything. END")
#End
```

2. The `RPi.GPIO` library will require `sudo` permissions to access the GPIO pin hardware, so you will need to run the script using the following command:

```
sudo python3 ledtest.py
```

When you run the script, you should see the red, green, and blue parts of the LED (or each LED, if you're using separate ones) light up in turn. If not, double-check your wiring or confirm that the LED is working by temporarily connecting the red, green, or blue wire to the 3V3 pin (pin 1 of the GPIO header).

The `sudo` command is required for most hardware-related scripts because it isn't normal for users to directly control hardware at such a low level. For example, setting or clearing a control pin that is part of the SD card controller could corrupt data being written to it. Therefore, for security purposes, superuser permissions are required to stop programs from using hardware by accident (or with malicious intent).

How it works...

To access the GPIO pins using Python, we import the `RPi.GPIO` library, which allows direct control of the pins through the module functions. We also require the `time` module to pause the program for a set number of seconds.

We then define values for the LED wiring and active states (see *Controlling the GPIO current* segment in the *There's more...* section of this recipe).

Before the GPIO pins are used by the program, we need to set them up by specifying the numbering method—`GPIO.BOARD`—and the direction—`GPIO.OUT` or `GPIO.IN` (in this case, we set all the RGB pins to outputs). If a pin is configured as an output, we will be able to set the pin state; similarly, if it is configured as an input, we will be able to read the pin state.

Next, we control the pins using `GPIO.ouput()` by stating the number of the GPIO pin and the state we want it to be in (1 = high/on and 0 = low/off). We switch each LED on, wait five seconds, and then switch it back off.

Finally, we use `GPIO.cleanup()` to return the GPIO pins back to their original default state and release control of the pins for use by other programs.

There's more...

Using the GPIO pins on the Raspberry Pi must be done with care since these pins are directly connected to the main processor of the Raspberry Pi without any additional protection. Caution must be used as any incorrect wiring will probably damage the Raspberry Pi processor and cause it to stop functioning altogether.

Alternatively, you could use one of the many modules available that plug directly into the GPIO header pins (reducing the chance of wiring mistakes):

For example, the Pi-Stop is a simple pre-built LED board that simulates a set of traffic lights, designed to be a stepping stone for those who are interested in controlling hardware but want to avoid the risk of damaging their Raspberry Pi. After the basics have been mastered, it also makes an excellent indicator to aid debugging.

Just ensure that you update the LED CONFIG pin references in the ledtest.py script to reference the pin layout and location used for the hardware you are using.

See the Appendix, *Hardware and Software List*, for a list of Raspberry Pi hardware retailers.

Controlling the GPIO current

Each GPIO pin is only able to handle a certain current before it burns out (a maximum of 16 mA from a single pin or 30 mA in total), and similarly, the RGB LED should be limited to no more than 100 mA. By adding a resistor before or after an LED, we will be able to limit the current that will be passed through it and control how bright it is (more current will equal a brighter LED).

Since we may wish to power more than one LED at a time, we typically aim to set the current as low as we can get away with while still providing enough power to light up the LED.

We can use Ohm's law to tell us how much resistance to use to provide a particular current. The law is as shown in the following diagram:

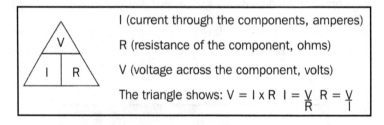

Ohm's law: The relationship between the current, resistance, and voltage in electrical circuits

We will aim for a minimum current (3 mA) and maximum current (16 mA), while still producing a reasonably bright light from each of the LEDs. To get a balanced output for the RGB LEDs, I tested different resistors until they provided a near white light (when viewed through a card). A 470 ohm resistor was selected for each one (your LEDs may differ slightly):

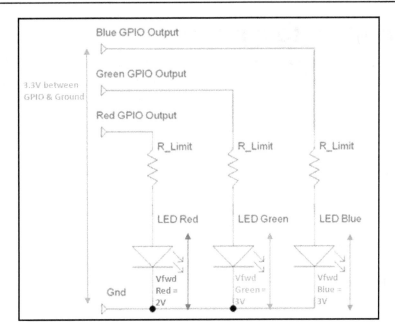

Resistors are needed to limit the current that passes through the LEDs

The voltage across the resistor is equal to the GPIO voltage (**Vgpio** = 3.3V) minus the voltage drop on the particular LED (**Vfwd**); we can then use this resistance to calculate the current used by each of the LEDs, as shown in the following formulas:

$$V_{R\_Limit} = (Vgpio\text{-}Vfwd)$$

$$I = \frac{V_{R\_Limit}}{R} = \frac{(3.3\text{-}2)}{470} = \frac{1.3}{470} = 2.8mA \text{ for the Red LED}$$

$$I = \frac{V_{R\_Limit}}{R} = \frac{(3.3\text{-}3)}{470} = \frac{0.3}{470} = 0.64mA \text{ each for the Green and Blue LEDs}$$

We can calculate the current drawn by each of the LEDs

Responding to a button

Many applications using the Raspberry Pi require that actions are activated without requiring a keyboard and screen to be attached to it. The GPIO pins provide an excellent way for the Raspberry Pi to be controlled by your own buttons and switches without a mouse/keyboard and screen.

Getting ready

You will need the following equipment:

- 2 x DuPont female-to-male patch wires
- Mini breadboard (170 tie points) or a larger one
- Push-button switch (momentary close) or a wire connection to make/break the circuit
- Breadboard wire (solid core)
- 1K ohm resistor

The switches are as shown in the following diagram:

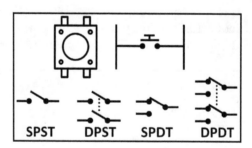

The push-button switch and other types of switch

The switches used in the following examples are **single-pole, single-throw** (**SPST**), momentary close, push-button switches. **Single pole** (**SP**) means that there is one set of contacts that makes a connection. In the case of the push switch used here, the legs on each side are connected together with a single-pole switch in the middle. A **double-pole** (**DP**) switch acts just like a SP switch, except that the two sides are separated electrically, allowing you to switch two separate components on/off at the same time.

Single throw (**ST**) means the switch will make a connection with just one position; the other side will be left open. **Double throw** (**DT**) means both positions of the switch will connect to different parts.

Momentary close means that the button will close the switch when pressed and automatically open it when released. A **latched** push-button switch will remain closed until it is pressed again.

Trying a speaker or headphone with Raspberry Pi

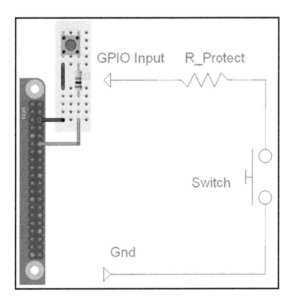

The layout of the button circuit

We will use sound in this example, so you will also need speakers or headphones attached to the audio socket of the Raspberry Pi.

You will need to install a program called `flite` using the following command, which will let us make the Raspberry Pi talk:

```
sudo apt-get install flite
```

After it has been installed, you can test it with the following command:

```
sudo flite -t "hello I can talk"
```

If it is a little too quiet (or too loud), you can adjust the volume (0-100 percent) using the following command:

```
amixer set PCM 100%
```

How to do it...

Create the `btntest.py` script as follows:

```python
#!/usr/bin/python3
#btntest.py
import time
import os
import RPi.GPIO as GPIO
#HARDWARE SETUP
# GPIO
# 2[==X==1=======]26[=======]40
# 1[=============]25[=======]39
#Button Config
BTN = 12

def gpio_setup():
  #Setup the wiring
  GPIO.setmode(GPIO.BOARD)
  #Setup Ports
  GPIO.setup(BTN,GPIO.IN,pull_up_down=GPIO.PUD_UP)

def main():
  gpio_setup()
  count=0
  btn_closed = True
  while True:
    btn_val = GPIO.input(BTN)
    if btn_val and btn_closed:
```

```
        print("OPEN")
        btn_closed=False
    elif btn_val==False and btn_closed==False:
        count+=1
        print("CLOSE %s" % count)
        os.system("flite -t '%s'" % count)
        btn_closed=True
    time.sleep(0.1)


try:
  main()
finally:
  GPIO.cleanup()
  print("Closed Everything. END")
#End
```

How it works...

As in the previous recipe, we set up the GPIO pin as required, but this time as an input, and we also enable the internal pull-up resistor (see *Pull-up and pull-down resistor circuits* in the *There's more...* section of this recipe for more information) using the following code:

```
GPIO.setup(BTN, GPIO.IN, pull_up_down=GPIO.PUD_UP)
```

After the GPIO pin is set up, we create a loop that will continuously check the state of BTN using GPIO.input(). If the value returned is false, the pin has been connected to 0V (ground) through the switch, and we will use flite to count out loud for us each time the button is pressed.

Since we have called the main function from within a try/finally condition, it will still call GPIO.cleanup() even if we close the program using *Ctrl* + *Z*.

We use a short delay in the loop; this ensures that any noise from the contacts on the switch is ignored. This is because when we press the button, there isn't always perfect contact as we press or release it, and it may produce several triggers if we press it again too quickly. This is known as **software debouncing**; we ignore the bounce in the signal here.

There's more...

The Raspberry Pi GPIO pins must be used with care; voltages used for inputs should be
within specific ranges, and any current drawn from them should be minimized using protective resistors.

Safe voltages

We must ensure that we only connect inputs that are between 0 (ground) and 3V3. Some processors use voltages between 0V and 5V, so extra components are required to interface safely with them. Never connect an input or component that uses 5V unless you are certain it is safe, or you will damage the GPIO ports of the Raspberry Pi.

Pull-up and pull-down resistor circuits

The previous code sets the GPIO pins to use an internal pull-up resistor. Without a pull-up resistor (or pull-down resistor) on the GPIO pin, the voltage is free to float somewhere between 3V3 and 0V, and the actual logical state remains undetermined (sometimes 1 and sometimes 0).

Raspberry Pi's internal pull-up resistors are 50K ohm-65K ohm, and the pull-down resistors are 50K ohm-65K ohm. External pull-up/pull-down resistors are often used in GPIO circuits (as shown in the following diagram), typically using 10K ohm or larger for similar reasons (giving a very small current draw when they are not active).

A pull-up resistor allows a small amount of current to flow through the GPIO pin and will provide a high voltage when the switch isn't pressed. When the switch is pressed, the small current is replaced by the larger one flowing to 0V, so we get a low voltage on the GPIO pin instead. The switch is active low and logic 0 when pressed. It works as shown in the following diagram:

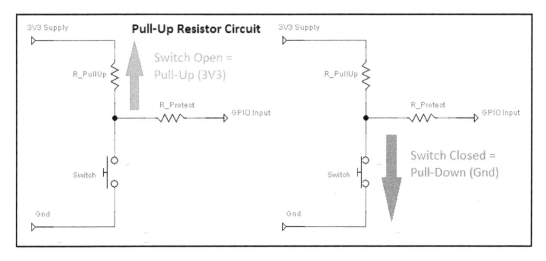

A pull-up resistor circuit

Pull-down resistors work in the same way, except the switch is active high (the GPIO pin is logic 1 when pressed). It works as shown in the following diagram:

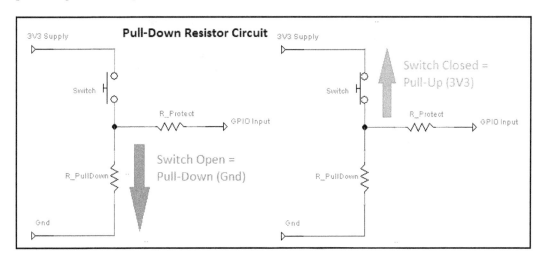

A pull-down resistor circuit

Protection resistors

In addition to the switch, the circuit includes a resistor in series with the switch to protect the GPIO pin, as shown in the following diagram:

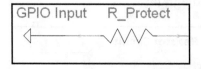

A GPIO protective current-limiting resistor

The purpose of the protection resistor is to protect the GPIO pin if it is accidentally set as an output rather than an input. Imagine, for instance, that we have our switch connected between the GPIO and ground. Now the GPIO pin is set as an output and switched on (driving it to 3V3) as soon as we press the switch, without a resistor present, the GPIO pin will be directly connected to 0V. The GPIO will still try to drive it to 3V3; this will cause the GPIO pin to burn out (since it will use too much current to drive the pin to the high state). If we use a 1K ohm resistor here, the pin is able to be driven high using an acceptable amount of current ($I = V/R = 3.3/1K = 3.3$ mA).

A controlled shutdown button

The Raspberry Pi should always be shut down correctly to avoid the SD card being corrupted (by losing power while performing a write operation to the card). This can pose a problem if you don't have a keyboard or screen connected (you might be running an automated program or controlling it remotely over a network and forget to turn it off) as you can't type the command or see what you are doing. By adding our own buttons and LED indicator, we can easily command a shutdown and reset, and then start up again to indicate when the system is active.

Getting ready

You will need the following equipment:

- 3 x DuPont female-to-male patch wires
- Mini breadboard (170 tie points) or a larger one
- Push-button switch (momentary close)

- General-purpose LED
- 2 x 470 ohm resistors
- Breadboard wire (solid core)

The entire layout of the shutdown circuit will look as shown in the following figure:

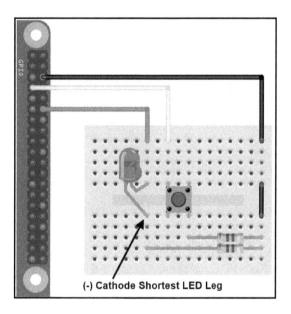

(-) Cathode Shortest LED Leg

The controlled shutdown circuit layout

How to do it...

1. Create the `shtdwn.py` script as follows:

```
#!/usr/bin/python3
#shtdwn.py
import time
import RPi.GPIO as GPIO
import os

# Shutdown Script
DEBUG=True #Simulate Only
SNDON=True
#HARDWARE SETUP
# GPIO
# 2[==X==L=======]26[=======]40
```

```
#  1[===1=========]25[=======]39

#BTN CONFIG - Set GPIO Ports
GPIO_MODE=GPIO.BOARD
SHTDWN_BTN = 7 #1
LED = 12        #L

def gpio_setup():
  #Setup the wiring
  GPIO.setmode(GPIO_MODE)
  #Setup Ports
  GPIO.setup(SHTDWN_BTN,GPIO.IN,pull_up_down=GPIO.PUD_UP)
  GPIO.setup(LED,GPIO.OUT)

def doShutdown():
  if(DEBUG):print("Press detected")
  time.sleep(3)
  if GPIO.input(SHTDWN_BTN):
    if(DEBUG):print("Ignore the shutdown (<3sec)")
  else:
    if(DEBUG):print ("Would shutdown the RPi Now")
    GPIO.output(LED,0)
    time.sleep(0.5)
    GPIO.output(LED,1)
    if(SNDON):os.system("flite -t 'Warning commencing power
down 3 2 1'")
    if(DEBUG==False):os.system("sudo shutdown -h now")
    if(DEBUG):GPIO.cleanup()
    if(DEBUG):exit()

def main():
  gpio_setup()
  GPIO.output(LED,1)
  while True:
    if(DEBUG):print("Waiting for >3sec button press")
    if GPIO.input(SHTDWN_BTN)==False:
       doShutdown()
    time.sleep(1)

try:
  main()
finally:
  GPIO.cleanup()
  print("Closed Everything. END")
#End
```

2. To get this script to run automatically (once we have tested it), we can place the script in the `~/bin` (we can use `cp` instead of `mv` if we just want to copy it) and add it to `crontab` with the following code:

```
mkdir ~/bin
mv shtdwn.py ~/bin/shtdwn.py
crontab -e
```

3. At the end of the file, we add the following code:

```
@reboot sudo python3 ~/bin/shtdwn.py
```

How it works...

This time, when we set up the GPIO pin, we define the pin connected to the shutdown button as an input and the pin connected to the LED as an output. We turn the LED on to indicate that the system is running.

By setting the DEBUG flag to True, we can test the functionality of our script without causing an actual shutdown (by reading the terminal messages); we just need to ensure that we set DEBUG to False when using the script for real.

We enter a while loop and check the pin every second to see whether the GPIO pin is set to LOW (that is, to check whether the switch has been pressed); if so, we enter the doShutdown() function.

The program will wait for three seconds and then test again to see whether the button is still being pressed. If the button is no longer being pressed, we return to the previous while loop. However, if it is still being pressed after three seconds, the program will flash the LED and trigger the shutdown (and also provide an audio warning using flite).

When we are happy with how the script is operating, we can disable the DEBUG flag (by setting it to False) and add the script to crontab. crontab is a special program that runs in the background and allows us to schedule (at specific times, dates, or periodically) programs and actions when the system is started (@reboot). This allows the script to be started automatically every time the Raspberry Pi is powered up. When we press and hold the shutdown button for more than three seconds, it safely shuts down the system and enters a low power state (the LED switches off just before this, indicating that it is safe to remove the power shortly after). To restart the Raspberry Pi, we briefly remove the power; this will restart the system, and the LED will light up when the Raspberry Pi has loaded.

There's more...

We can extend this example further using the reset header by adding extra functionality and making use of additional GPIO connections (if available).

Resetting and rebooting Raspberry Pi

The Raspberry Pi has holes for mounting a reset header (marked **RUN** on the Raspberry Pi 3/2 and **P6** on the Raspberry Pi 1 Model A and Model B Rev 2). The reset pin allows the device to be reset using a button rather than removing the micro USB connector each time to cycle the power:

Raspberry Pi reset headers - on the left, Raspberry Pi Model A/B (Rev2), and on the right, Raspberry Pi 3

To make use of it, you will need to solder a wire or pin header to the Raspberry Pi and connect a button to it (or briefly touch a wire between the two holes each time). Alternatively, we can extend our previous circuit, as shown in the following diagram:

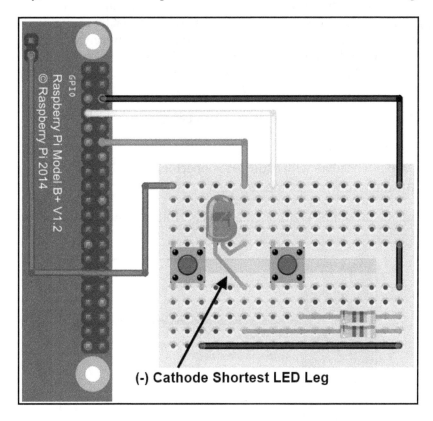

(-) Cathode Shortest LED Leg

The controlled shutdown circuit layout and reset button

We can add this extra button to our circuit, which can be connected to the reset header (this is the hole nearest the middle on the Raspberry Pi 3 or closest to the edge on other models). This pin, when temporarily pulled low by connecting to ground (such as the hole next to it or by another ground point, such as pin 6 of the GPIO header), will reset the Raspberry Pi and allow it to boot up again following a shutdown.

Adding extra functions

Since we now have the script monitoring the shutdown button all the time, we can add extra buttons/switches/jumpers to be monitored at the same time. This will allow us to trigger specific programs or set up particular states just by changing the inputs. The following example allows us to easily switch between automatic DHCP networking (the default networking setup) and using a direct IP address, as used in the *Networking directly to a laptop or computer* recipe of `Chapter 1`, *Getting Started with a Raspberry Pi 3 Computer*, for direct LAN connections.

Add the following components to the previous circuit:

- A 470 ohm resistor
- Two pin headers with a jumper connector (or, optionally, a switch)
- Breadboard wire (solid core)

After adding the preceding components, our controlled shutdown circuit now looks as follows:

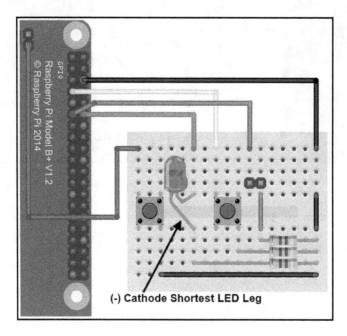

The controlled shutdown circuit layout, reset button, and jumper pins

In the previous script, we add an additional input to detect the status of the LAN_SWA pin (the jumper pins we added to the circuit) using the following code:

```
LAN_SWA = 11      #2
```

Ensure that it is set up as an input (with a pull-up resistor) in the gpio_setup() function using the following code:

```
GPIO.setup(LAN_SWA, GPIO.IN, pull_up_down=GPIO.PUD_UP)
```

Add a new function to switch between the LAN modes and read out the new IP address. The doChangeLAN() function checks whether the status of the LAN_SWA pin has changed since the last call, and if so, it sets the network adapter to DHCP or sets the direct LAN settings accordingly (and uses flite to speak the new IP setting, if available). Finally, the LAN being set for direct connection causes the LED to flash slowly while that mode is active. Use the following code to do this:

```
def doChangeLAN(direct):
  if(DEBUG):print("Direct LAN: %s" % direct)
  if GPIO.input(LAN_SWA) and direct==True:
    if(DEBUG):print("LAN Switch OFF")
    cmd="sudo dhclient eth0"
    direct=False
    GPIO.output(LED,1)
  elif GPIO.input(LAN_SWA)==False and direct==False:
    if(DEBUG):print("LAN Switch ON")
    cmd="sudo ifconfig eth0 169.254.69.69"
    direct=True
  else:
    return direct
  if(DEBUG==False):os.system(cmd)
  if(SNDON):os.system("hostname -I | flite")
  return direct
```

Add another function, flashled(), which will just toggle the state of the LED each time it is called. The code for this function is as follows:

```
def flashled(ledon):
  if ledon:
    ledon=False
  else:
    ledon=True
  GPIO.output(LED,ledon)
  return ledon
```

Finally, we adjust the main loop to also call `doChangeLAN()` and use the result to decide whether we call `flashled()` using `ledon` to keep track of the LED's previous state each time. The `main()` function should now be updated as follows:

```
def main():
    gpio_setup()
    GPIO.output(LED,1)
    directlan=False
    ledon=True
    while True:
        if(DEBUG):print("Waiting for >3sec button press")
        if GPIO.input(SHTDWN_BTN)==False:
            doShutdown()
        directlan= doChangeLAN(directlan)
        if directlan:
            flashled(ledon)
        time.sleep(1)
```

The GPIO keypad input

We have seen how we can monitor inputs on the GPIO to launch applications and control the Raspberry Pi; however, sometimes we need to control third-party programs. Using the `uInput` library, we can emulate key presses from a keyboard (or even mouse movement) to control any program using our own custom hardware.

For more information about using uInput, visit `http://tjjr.fi/sw/python-uinput/`.

Getting ready

Perform the following steps to install `uInput`:

1. First, we need to download `uInput`.

   You will need to download the `uInput` Python library from GitHub (~50 KB) using the following commands:

   ```
   wget
   https://github.com/tuomasjjrasanen/python-uinput/archive/master.zip
   unzip master.zip
   ```

The library will unzip to a directory called `python-uinput-master`.

2. Once completed, you can remove the ZIP file using the following command:

```
rm master.zip
```

3. Install the required packages using the following commands (if you have installed them already, the `apt-get` command will ignore them):

```
sudo apt-get install python3-setuptools python3-dev
sudo apt-get install libudev-dev
```

4. Compile and install `uInput` using the following commands:

```
cd python-uinput-master
sudo python3 setup.py install
```

5. Finally, we load the new `uinput` kernel module using the following command:

```
sudo modprobe uinput
```

To ensure it is loaded upon startup, we can add `uinput` to the `modules` file using the following command:

```
sudo nano /etc/modules
```

Put `uinput` on a new line in the file and save it (*Ctrl* + *X*, *Y*).

6. Create the following circuit using the following equipment:
   - Breadboard (half-sized or larger)
   - 7 x DuPont female-to-male patch wires
   - Six push buttons
   - 6 x 470 ohm resistors

- Breadboarding wire (solid core)

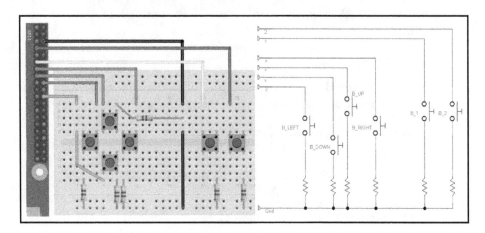

GPIO keypad circuit layout

The keypad circuit can also be built into a permanent circuit by soldering the components into a Vero prototype board (also known as a stripboard), as shown in the following photo:

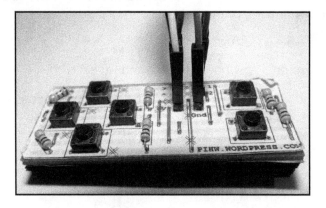

GPIO keypad Pi hardware module

 This circuit is available as a solder-yourself kit from PiHardware.com.

7. Connect the circuit to the Raspberry Pi GPIO pins by matching the appropriate buttons with the appropriate pins, as shown in the following table:

	Button	GPIO pin
GND		6
v	B_DOWN	22
<	B_LEFT	18
^	B_UP	15
>	B_RIGHT	13
1	B_1	11
2	B_2	7

How to do it...

Create a gpiokeys.py script as follows:

```
#!/usr/bin/python3
#gpiokeys.py
import time
import RPi.GPIO as GPIO
import uinput

#HARDWARE SETUP
# GPIO
# 2[==G=====<=V==]26[=======]40
# 1[===2=1>^=====]25[=======]39
B_DOWN  = 22      #V
B_LEFT  = 18    #<
B_UP    = 15    #^
B_RIGHT = 13    #>
B_1   = 11    #1
B_2   = 7    #2

DEBUG=True
BTN = [B_UP,B_DOWN,B_LEFT,B_RIGHT,B_1,B_2]
MSG = ["UP","DOWN","LEFT","RIGHT","1","2"]

#Setup the DPad module pins and pull-ups
def dpad_setup():
  #Set up the wiring
  GPIO.setmode(GPIO.BOARD)
  # Setup BTN Ports as INPUTS
  for val in BTN:
```

```
        # set up GPIO input with pull-up control
        #(pull_up_down can be:
        #    PUD_OFF, PUD_UP or PUD_DOWN, default PUD_OFF)
        GPIO.setup(val, GPIO.IN, pull_up_down=GPIO.PUD_UP)

def main():
    #Setup uinput
    events = (uinput.KEY_UP,uinput.KEY_DOWN,uinput.KEY_LEFT,
            uinput.KEY_RIGHT,uinput.KEY_ENTER,uinput.KEY_ENTER)
    device = uinput.Device(events)
    time.sleep(2)  # seconds
    dpad_setup()
    print("DPad Ready!")

    btn_state=[False,False,False,False,False,False]
    key_state=[False,False,False,False,False,False]
    while True:
        #Catch all the buttons pressed before pressing the related keys
        for idx, val in enumerate(BTN):
            if GPIO.input(val) == False:
                btn_state[idx]=True
            else:
                btn_state[idx]=False

        #Perform the button presses/releases (but only change state once)
        for idx, val in enumerate(btn_state):
            if val == True and key_state[idx] == False:
                if DEBUG:print (str(val) + ":" + MSG[idx])
                device.emit(events[idx], 1) # Press.
                key_state[idx]=True
            elif val == False and key_state[idx] == True:
                if DEBUG:print (str(val) + ":!" + MSG[idx])
                device.emit(events[idx], 0) # Release.
                key_state[idx]=False

        time.sleep(.1)
try:
    main()
finally:
    GPIO.cleanup()
#End
```

How it works...

First, we import `uinput` and define the wiring of the keypad buttons. For each of the buttons in BTN, we enable them as inputs, with internal pull-ups enabled.

Next, we set up `uinput`, defining the keys we want to emulate and adding them to the `uinput.Device()` function. We wait a few seconds to allow `uinput` to initialize, set the initial button and key states, and start our `main` loop.

The `main` loop is split into two sections: the first section checks through the buttons and records the states in `btn_state`, and the second section compares the `btn_state` with the current `key_state` array. This way, we can detect a change in `btn_state` and call `device.emit()` to toggle the state of the key.

To allow us to run this script in the background, we can run it with &, as shown in the following command:

```
sudo python3 gpiokeys.py &
```

The & character allows the command to run in the background, so we can continue with the command line to run other programs. You can use `fg` to bring it back to the foreground, or `%1`, `%2`, and so on if you have several commands running. Use `jobs` to get a list.

You can even put a process/program on hold to get to Command Prompt by pressing *Ctrl + Z* and then resume it with `bg` (which will let it run in the background).

There's more...

We can do more using `uinput` to provide hardware control for other programs, including those that require mouse input.

Generating other key combinations

You can create several different key mappings in your file to support different programs. For instance, the `events_z80` key mapping would be useful for a spectrum emulator, such as **Fuse** (browse to http://raspi.tv/2012/how-to-install-fuse-zx-spectrum-emulator-on-raspberry -pi for more details). The `events_omx` key mappings are suitable for controlling video played through the OMXPlayer using the following command:

```
omxplayer filename.mp4
```

You can get a list of keys supported by `omxplayer` by using the `-k` parameter.

Replace the line that defines the `events` list with a new key mapping, and select different ones by assigning them to events using the following code:

```
events_dpad = (uinput.KEY_UP,uinput.KEY_DOWN,uinput.KEY_LEFT,
                uinput.KEY_RIGHT,uinput.KEY_ENTER,uinput.KEY_ENTER)
events_z80 = (uinput.KEY_Q,uinput.KEY_A,uinput.KEY_O,
                uinput.KEY_P,uinput.KEY_M,uinput.KEY_ENTER)
events_omx = (uinput.KEY_EQUAL,uinput.KEY_MINUS,uinput.KEY_LEFT,
                uinput.KEY_RIGHT,uinput.KEY_P,uinput.KEY_Q)
```

You can find all the KEY definitions in the `input.h` file; you can view it using the `less` command (press *Q* to exit), as shown in the following command:

```
less /usr/include/linux/input.h
```

Emulating mouse events

The `uinput` library can emulate mouse and joystick events, as well as keyboard presses. To use the buttons to simulate a mouse, we can adjust the script to use mouse events (as well as defining `mousemove` to set the step size of the movement) using the following code:

```
MSG = ["M_UP","M_DOWN","M_LEFT","M_RIGHT","1","Enter"]
events_mouse=(uinput.REL_Y,uinput.REL_Y, uinput.REL_X,
            uinput.REL_X,uinput.BTN_LEFT,uinput.BTN_RIGHT)
mousemove=1
```

We also need to modify the button handling to provide continuous movement, as we don't need to keep track of the state of the keys for the mouse. To do so, use the following code:

```
#Perform the button presses/releases
```

```
#(but only change state once)
for idx, val in enumerate(btn_state):
  if MSG[idx] == "M_UP" or MSG[idx] == "M_LEFT":
    state = -mousemove
  else:
    state = mousemove
  if val == True:
    device.emit(events[idx], state) # Press.
  elif val == False:
    device.emit(events[idx], 0) # Release.
time.sleep(0.01)
```

Multiplexed color LEDs

The next example in this chapter demonstrates that some seemingly simple hardware can produce some impressive results if controlled with software. For this, we will go back to using RGB LEDs. We will use five RGB LEDs that are wired so that we only need to use eight GPIO pins to control their red, green, and blue elements using a method called **hardware multiplexing** (see the *Hardware multiplexing* subsection in the *There's more...* section of this recipe).

Getting ready

You will need the RGB LED module shown in the following picture:

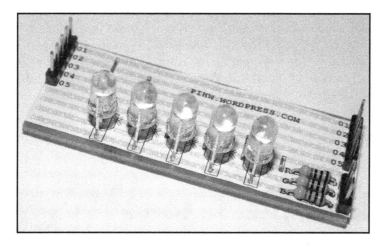

The RGB LED module from PiHardware.com

As you can see in the preceding photo, the RGB LED module from `http://pihardware.com/` comes with GPIO pins and a DuPont female-to-female cable for connecting it. Although there are two sets of pins labelled from 1 to 5, only one side needs to be connected.

Alternatively, you can recreate your own with the following circuit using five common cathode RGB LEDs, 3 x 470 ohm resistors, and a Vero prototype board (or large breadboard). The circuit will look as shown in the following diagram:

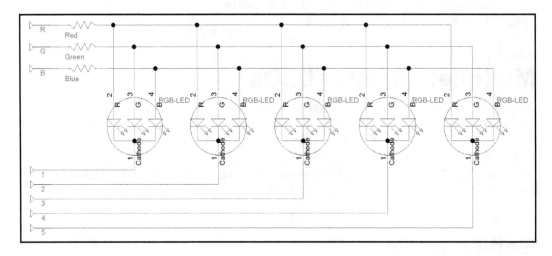

Circuit diagram for the RGB LED module

 Strictly speaking, we should use 15 resistors in this circuit (one for each RGB LED element), which will avoid interference from LEDs sharing the same resistor, and will also prolong the life of the LEDs themselves if switched on together. However, there is only a slight advantage in using this, particularly since we intend to drive each RGB LED independently of the other four to achieve multi-color effects.

You will need to connect the circuit to the Raspberry Pi GPIO header as follows:

RGB LED		1		2	3		4			
Rpi GPIO pin	2 4 6 8	10	12	14	16	18	20	22 24 26 28 30 32 34 36 38 40		
Rpi GPIO pin	1 3 5 7 9	11	13	15	17	19	21	23 25 27 29 31 33 35 37 39		
RGB LED			5		R	G	B			

How to do it...

Create the `rgbled.py` script and perform the following steps:

1. Import all the required modules and define the values to be used with the help of the following code:

```python
#!/usr/bin/python3
#rgbled.py
import time
import RPi.GPIO as GPIO

#Setup Active states
#Common Cathode RGB-LEDs (Cathode=Active Low)
LED_ENABLE = 0; LED_DISABLE = 1
RGB_ENABLE = 1; RGB_DISABLE = 0
#HARDWARE SETUP
# GPIO
# 2[=====1=23=4==]26[=======]40
# 1[===5=RGB=====]25[=======]39
#LED CONFIG - Set GPIO Ports
LED1 = 12; LED2 = 16; LED3 = 18; LED4 = 22; LED5 = 7
LED = [LED1,LED2,LED3,LED4,LED5]
RGB_RED = 11; RGB_GREEN = 13; RGB_BLUE = 15
RGB = [RGB_RED,RGB_GREEN,RGB_BLUE]
#Mixed Colors
RGB_CYAN = [RGB_GREEN,RGB_BLUE]
RGB_MAGENTA = [RGB_RED,RGB_BLUE]
RGB_YELLOW = [RGB_RED,RGB_GREEN]
RGB_WHITE = [RGB_RED,RGB_GREEN,RGB_BLUE]
RGB_LIST = [RGB_RED,RGB_GREEN,RGB_BLUE,RGB_CYAN,
            RGB_MAGENTA,RGB_YELLOW,RGB_WHITE]
```

2. Define functions to set up the GPIO pins using the following code:

```python
def led_setup():
  '''Setup the RGB-LED module pins and state.'''
  #Set up the wiring
  GPIO.setmode(GPIO.BOARD)
  # Setup Ports
  for val in LED:
    GPIO.setup(val, GPIO.OUT)
  for val in RGB:
    GPIO.setup(val, GPIO.OUT)
  led_clear()
```

3. Define our utility functions to help control the LEDs using the following code:

```python
def led_gpiocontrol(pins,state):
    '''This function will control the state of
    a single or multiple pins in a list.'''
    #determine if "pins" is a single integer or not
    if isinstance(pins,int):
        #Single integer - reference directly
        GPIO.output(pins,state)
    else:
        #if not, then cycle through the "pins" list
        for i in pins:
            GPIO.output(i,state)

def led_activate(led,color):
    '''Enable the selected led(s) and set the required color(s)
    Will accept single or multiple values'''
    #Enable led
    led_gpiocontrol(led,LED_ENABLE)
    #Enable color
    led_gpiocontrol(color,RGB_ENABLE)

def led_deactivate(led,color):
    '''Deactivate the selected led(s) and set the required
    color(s) will accept single or multiple values'''
    #Disable led
    led_gpiocontrol(led,LED_DISABLE)
    #Disable color
    led_gpiocontrol(color,RGB_DISABLE)
def led_time(led, color, timeon):
    '''Switch on the led and color for the timeon period'''
    led_activate(led,color)
    time.sleep(timeon)
    led_deactivate(led,color)

def led_clear():
    '''Set the pins to default state.'''
    for val in LED:
        GPIO.output(val, LED_DISABLE)
    for val in RGB:
        GPIO.output(val, RGB_DISABLE)

def led_cleanup():
    '''Reset pins to default state and release GPIO'''
    led_clear()
    GPIO.cleanup()
```

4. Create a test function to demonstrate the functionality of the module:

```
def main():
    '''Directly run test function.
    This function will run if the file is executed directly'''
    led_setup()
    led_time(LED1,RGB_RED,5)
    led_time(LED2,RGB_GREEN,5)
    led_time(LED3,RGB_BLUE,5)
    led_time(LED,RGB_MAGENTA,2)
    led_time(LED,RGB_YELLOW,2)
    led_time(LED,RGB_CYAN,2)

if __name__=='__main__':
    try:
        main()
    finally:
        led_cleanup()
#End
```

How it works...

To start with, we define the hardware setup by defining the states required to **Enable** and **Disable** the LED depending on the type of RGB LED (common cathode) used. If you are using a common anode device, just reverse the **Enable** and **Disable** states.

Next, we define the GPIO mapping to the pins to match the wiring we did previously.

We also define some basic color combinations by combining red, green, and/or blue together, as shown in the following diagram:

Red Green Blue	000	001	010	011	100	101	110	111
LED State	OFF	Blue	Green	Cyan	Red	Magenta	Yellow	White

LED color combinations

We define a series of useful functions, the first being `led_setup()`, which will set the GPIO numbering to `GPIO.BOARD` and define all the pins that are to be used as outputs. We also call a function named `led_clear()`, which will set the pins to the default state with all the pins disabled.

This means that the LED pins, 1-5 (the common cathode on each LED), are set to HIGH, while the RGB pins (the separate anodes for each color) are set to LOW.

We create a function called led_gpiocontrol() that will allow us to set the state of one or more pins. The isinstance() function allows us to test a value to see whether it matches a particular type (in this case, a single integer); then we can either set the state of that single pin or iterate through the list of pins and set each one.

Next, we define two functions, led_activate() and led_deactivate(), which will enable and disable the specified LED and color. Finally, we define led_time(), which will allow us to specify an LED, color, and time to switch it on for.

We also create led_cleanup() to reset the pins (and LEDs) to the default values and call GPIO.cleanup() to release the GPIO pins in use.

This script is intended to become a library file, so we will use the if __name__=='__main__' check to only run our test code when running the file directly:

By checking the value of __name__, we can determine whether the file was run directly (it will equal __main__) or whether it was imported by another Python script.

This allows us to define a special test code that is only executed when we directly load and run the file. If we include this file as a module in another script, then this code will not be executed.

As before, we will use try/finally to allow us to always perform cleanup actions, even if we exit early.

To test the script, we will set the LEDs to light up in various colors, one after another.

There's more...

We can create a few different colors by switching on one or more parts of the RGB LED at a time. However, with some clever programming, we can create a whole spectrum of colors. Also, we can display different colors on each LED, seemingly at the same time.

Hardware multiplexing

An LED requires a high voltage on the anode side and a lower voltage on the cathode side in order to light up. The RGB LEDs used in the circuit are common cathodes, so we must apply a high voltage (3V3) on the RGB pins and a low voltage (0V) on the cathode pin (wired to pins 1 to 5 for each of the LEDs).

The cathode and RGB pin states are as follows:

RGB-LED	Cathode (1-5)	RGB Pins	Result	Status
	HIGH	HIGH	LED OFF	LED "Disabled"
	HIGH	LOW	LED OFF	
	LOW	HIGH	LED ON	LED "Enabled"
	LOW	LOW	LED OFF	

Cathode and RGB pin states

Therefore, we can enable one or more of the RGB pins, but still control which of the LEDs are lit. We enable the pins of the LEDs we want to light up and disable the ones we don't. This allows us to use far fewer pins than we would need to control each of the 15 RGB lines separately.

Displaying random patterns

We can add new functions to our library to produce different effects, such as generating random colors. The following function uses randint() to get a value between 1 and the number of colors. We ignore any values that are over the number of the available colors so that we can control how often the LEDs are switched off. Perform the following steps to add the required functions:

1. Add the randint() function from the random module to the rgbled.py script using the following code:

   ```
   from random import randint
   ```

2. Now add led_rgbrandom() using the following code:

   ```
   def led_rgbrandom(led, period, colors):
       ''' Light up the selected led, for period in seconds,
       in one of the possible colors. The colors can be
   ```

```
      1 to 3 for RGB, or 1-6 for RGB plus combinations,
      1-7 includes white. Anything over 7 will be set as
      OFF (larger the number more chance of OFF).'''
value = randint(1,colors)
if value < len(RGB_LIST):
    led_time(led,RGB_LIST[value-1],period)
```

3. Use the following commands in the `main()` function to create a series of flashing LEDs:

```
for i in range(20):
  for j in LED:
    #Select from all, plus OFF
    led_rgbrandom(j,0.1,20)
```

Mixing multiple colors

Until now, we have only displayed a single color at a time on one or more of the LEDs. If you consider how the circuit is wired up, you might wonder how we can get one LED to display one color and another a different one at the same time. The simple answer is that we don't need to-we just do it quickly!

All we need to do is display one color at a time, but change it back and forth, so quickly that the color looks like a mix of the two (or even a combination of the three red/green/blue LEDs). Fortunately, this is something that computers such as the Raspberry Pi can do very easily, even allowing us to combine the RGB elements to make multiple shades of colors across all five LEDs. Perform the following steps to mix the colors:

1. Add combo color definitions to the top of the `rgbled.py` script, after the definition of the mixed colors, using the following code:

```
#Combo Colors
RGB_AQUA = [RGB_CYAN,RGB_GREEN]
RGB_LBLUE = [RGB_CYAN,RGB_BLUE]
RGB_PINK = [RGB_MAGENTA,RGB_RED]
RGB_PURPLE = [RGB_MAGENTA,RGB_BLUE]
RGB_ORANGE = [RGB_YELLOW,RGB_RED]
RGB_LIME = [RGB_YELLOW,RGB_GREEN]
RGB_COLORS = [RGB_LIME,RGB_YELLOW,RGB_ORANGE,RGB_RED,
              RGB_PINK,RGB_MAGENTA,RGB_PURPLE,RGB_BLUE,
              RGB_LBLUE,RGB_CYAN,RGB_AQUA,RGB_GREEN]
```

The preceding code will provide the combination of colors needed to create our shades, with RGB_COLORS providing a smooth progression through the shades.

2. Next, we need to create a function called led_combo() to handle single or multiple colors. The code for the function will be as follows:

```
def led_combo(pins,colors,period):
  #determine if "colors" is a single integer or not
  if isinstance(colors,int):
    #Single integer - reference directly
    led_time(pins,colors,period)
  else:
    #if not, then cycle through the "colors" list
    for i in colors:
      led_time(pins,i,period)
```

3. Now we can create a new script, rgbledrainbow.py, to make use of the new functions in our rgbled.py module. The rgbledrainbow.py script will be as follows:

```
#!/usr/bin/python3
#rgbledrainbow.py
import time
import rgbled as RGBLED

def next_value(number,max):
  number = number % max
  return number

def main():
  print ("Setup the RGB module")
  RGBLED.led_setup()

  # Multiple LEDs with different Colors
  print ("Switch on Rainbow")
  led_num = 0
  col_num = 0
  for l in range(5):
    print ("Cycle LEDs")
    for k in range(100):
      #Set the starting point for the next set of colors
      col_num = next_value(col_num+1,len(RGBLED.RGB_COLORS))
      for i in range(20):  #cycle time
        for j in range(5): #led cycle
          led_num = next_value(j,len(RGBLED.LED))
          led_color = next_value(col_num+led_num,
```

```
                                        len(RGBLED.RGB_COLORS))
                RGBLED.led_combo(RGBLED.LED[led_num],
                                RGBLED.RGB_COLORS[led_color],0.001)

        print ("Cycle COLORs")
        for k in range(100):
            #Set the next color
            col_num = next_value(col_num+1,len(RGBLED.RGB_COLORS))
            for i in range(20): #cycle time
                for j in range(5): #led cycle
                    led_num = next_value(j,len(RGBLED.LED))
                    RGBLED.led_combo(RGBLED.LED[led_num],
                                    RGBLED.RGB_COLORS[col_num],0.001)
        print ("Finished")

if __name__=='__main__':
    try:
        main()
    finally:
        RGBLED.led_cleanup()
#End
```

The `main()` function will first cycle through the LEDs, setting each color from the `RGB_COLORS` array on all the LEDs. Then, it will cycle through the colors, creating a rainbow effect across the LEDs:

Cycling through multiple colors on the five RGB LEDs

Writing messages using persistence of vision

Persistence of vision (POV) displays can produce an almost magical effect, displaying images in the air by moving a line of LEDs back and forth very quickly or around in circles. The effect works because your eyes are unable to adjust fast enough to separate out the individual flashes of light, and so you observe a merged image (the message or picture being displayed):

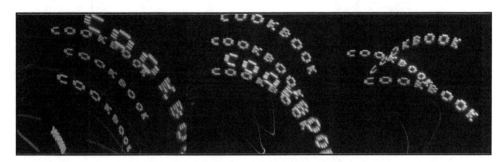

Persistence of vision using RGB LEDs

Getting ready

This recipe uses the RGB LED kit used in the previous recipe; you will also need the following additional items:

- Breadboard (half-sized or larger)
- 2 x DuPont female-to-male patch wires
- Tilt switch (the ball-bearing type is suitable)
- 1 x 470 ohm resistor (R_Protect)
- Breadboard wire (solid core)

The tilt switch should be added to the RGB LED (as described in the *Getting ready* section of the *Multiplexed color LEDs* recipe). The tilt switch is wired as follows:

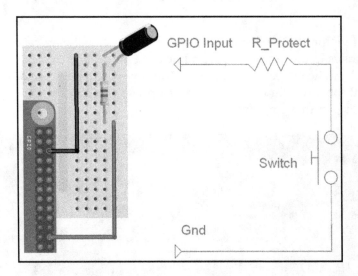

The tilt switch is connected to GPIO Input (GPIO pin 24) and Gnd (GPIO pin 6)

To reproduce the POV image, you will need to be able to quickly move the LEDs and tilt the switch back and forth. Note how the tilt switch is mounted angled to the side, so the switch will open when moved to the left. It is recommended that the hardware is mounted onto a length of wood or similar piece of equipment. You can even use a portable USB battery pack along with a Wi-Fi dongle to power and control the Raspberry Pi through a remote connection (see the *Connecting Remotely to the Raspberry Pi over the Network using SSH (and X11 forwarding)* recipe in Chapter 1, *Getting Started with a Raspberry Pi 3 Computer*, for details):

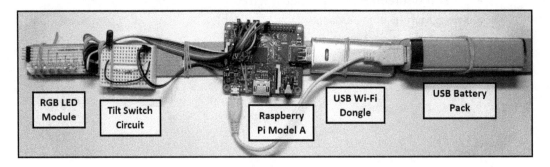

Persistence of vision hardware setup

You will also need the completed `rgbled.py` file, which we will extend further in the *How to do it...* section.

How to do it...

1. Create a script called `tilt.py` to report the state of the tilt switch:

```python
#!/usr/bin/python3
#tilt.py
import RPi.GPIO as GPIO
#HARDWARE SETUP
# GPIO
# 2[===========T=]26[=======]40
# 1[=============]25[=======]39
#Tilt Config
TILT_SW = 24

def tilt_setup():
    #Setup the wiring
    GPIO.setmode(GPIO.BOARD)
    #Setup Ports
    GPIO.setup(TILT_SW,GPIO.IN,pull_up_down=GPIO.PUD_UP)

def tilt_moving():
    #Report the state of the Tilt Switch
    return GPIO.input(TILT_SW)

def main():
    import time
    tilt_setup()
    while True:
        print("TILT %s"% (GPIO.input(TILT_SW)))
        time.sleep(0.1)

if __name__=='__main__':
    try:
        main()
    finally:
        GPIO.cleanup()
        print("Closed Everything. END")
#End
```

2. You can test the script by running it directly with the following command:

```
sudo python3 tilt.py
```

3. Add the following `rgbled_pov()` function to the `rgbled.py` script we created previously; this will allow us to display a single line of our image:

```
def rgbled_pov(led_pattern,color,ontime):
    '''Disable all the LEDs and re-enable the LED pattern in the
required color'''
    led_deactivate(LED,RGB)
    for led_num,col_num in enumerate(led_pattern):
        if col_num >= 1:
            led_activate(LED[led_num],color)
    time.sleep(ontime)
```

4. We will now create the following file, called `rgbledmessage.py`, to perform the required actions to display our message. First, we will import the modules used: the updated `rgbled` module, the new `tilt` module, and the Python `os` module. Initially, we set `DEBUG` to `True`, so the Python terminal will display additional information while the script is running:

```
#!/usr/bin/python3
# rgbledmessage.py
import rgbled as RGBLED
import tilt as TILT
import os

DEBUG = True
```

5. Add a `readMessageFile()` function to read the content of the `letters.txt` file and then add `processFileContent()` to generate a **Python dictionary** of the LED patterns for each letter:

```
def readMessageFile(filename):
    assert os.path.exists(filename), 'Cannot find the message
file: %s' % (filename)
    try:
        with open(filename, 'r') as theFile:
        fileContent = theFile.readlines()
    except IOError:
        print("Unable to open %s" % (filename))
    if DEBUG:print ("File Content START:")
    if DEBUG:print (fileContent)
    if DEBUG:print ("File Content END")
    dictionary = processFileContent(fileContent)
    return dictionary

def processFileContent(content):
    letterIndex = [] #Will contain a list of letters stored in
the file
```

```
letterList = []   #Will contain a list of letter formats
letterFormat = [] #Will contain the format of each letter
firstLetter = True
nextLetter = False
LETTERDIC={}
#Process each line that was in the file
for line in content:
  # Ignore the # as comments
  if '#' in line:
    if DEBUG:print ("Comment: %s"%line)
  #Check for " in the line = index name
  elif '"' in line:
    nextLetter = True
    line = line.replace('"','') #Remove " characters
    LETTER=line.rstrip()
    if DEBUG:print ("Index: %s"%line)
  #Remaining lines are formatting codes
  else:
    #Skip firstLetter until complete
    if firstLetter:
      firstLetter = False
      nextLetter = False
      lastLetter = LETTER
    #Move to next letter if needed
    if nextLetter:
      nextLetter = False
      LETTERDIC[lastLetter]=letterFormat[:]
      letterFormat[:] = []
      lastLetter = LETTER
    #Save the format data
    values = line.rstrip().split(' ')
    row = []
    for val in values:
      row.append(int(val))
    letterFormat.append(row)
LETTERDIC[lastLetter]=letterFormat[:]
#Show letter patterns for debugging
if DEBUG:print ("LETTERDIC: %s" %LETTERDIC)
if DEBUG:print ("C: %s"%LETTERDIC['C'])
if DEBUG:print ("O: %s"%LETTERDIC['O'])
return LETTERDIC
```

6. Add a `createBuffer()` function, which will convert a message into a series of LED patterns for each letter (assuming the letter is defined by the `letters.txt` file):

```
def createBuffer(message,dictionary):
  buffer=[]
  for letter in message:
    try:
      letterPattern=dictionary[letter]
    except KeyError:
      if DEBUG:print("Unknown letter %s: use _"%letter)
      letterPattern=dictionary['_']
    buffer=addLetter(letterPattern,buffer)
  if DEBUG:print("Buffer: %s"%buffer)
  return buffer

def addLetter(letter,buffer):
  for row in letter:
    buffer.append(row)
  buffer.append([0,0,0,0,0])
  buffer.append([0,0,0,0,0])
  return buffer
```

7. Next, we define a `displayBuffer()` function to display the LED patterns using the `rgbled_pov()` function in the `rgbled` module:

```
def displayBuffer(buffer):
  position=0
  while(1):
    if(TILT.tilt_moving()==False):
      position=0
    elif (position+1)<len(buffer):
      position+=1
      if DEBUG:print("Pos:%s
ROW:%s"%(position,buffer[position]))
      RGBLED.rgbled_pov(buffer[position],RGBLED.RGB_GREEN,0.001)
      RGBLED.rgbled_pov(buffer[position],RGBLED.RGB_BLUE,0.001)
```

8. Finally, we create a `main()` function to perform each of the required steps:
   1. Set up the hardware components (RGB LEDs and the tilt switch).
   2. Read the `letters.txt` file.
   3. Define the dictionary of LED letter patterns.
   4. Generate a buffer to represent the required message.
   5. Display the buffer using the `rgbled` module and control it with the `tilt` module:

```
def main():
    RGBLED.led_setup()
    TILT.tilt_setup()
    dict=readMessageFile('letters.txt')
    buffer=createBuffer('_COOKBOOK_',dict)
    displayBuffer(buffer)
if __name__=='__main__':
    try:
        main()
    finally:
        RGBLED.led_cleanup()
        print("Closed Everything.  END")
#End
```

9. Create the following file, called `letters.txt`, to define the LED patterns needed to display the example '_COOKBOOK_' message. Note that this file only needs to define a pattern for each unique letter or symbol in the message:

```
#COOKBOOK
"C"
0 1 1 1 0
1 0 0 0 1
1 0 0 0 1
"O"
0 1 1 1 0
1 0 0 0 1
1 0 0 0 1
0 1 1 1 0
"K"
1 1 1 1 1
0 1 0 1 0
1 0 0 0 1
"B"
1 1 1 1 1
1 0 1 0 1
0 1 0 1 0
"_"
0 0 0 0 0
0 0 0 0 0
0 0 0 0 0
0 0 0 0 0
0 0 0 0 0
```

How it works...

The first function, `readMessageFile()`, will open and read the contents of a given file. This will then use `processFileContent()` to return a Python dictionary containing the corresponding patterns for the letters defined in the file provided. Each line in the file is processed, ignoring any line containing a # character and checking for " characters to indicate the name of the LED pattern that follows after. After the file has been processed, we end up with a Python dictionary that contains LED patterns for the `'_'`, `'C'`, `'B'`, `'K'`, and `'O'` characters:

```
'_': [[0, 0, 0, 0, 0], [0, 0, 0, 0, 0], [0, 0, 0, 0, 0], [0, 0, 0, 0,
0], [0, 0, 0, 0, 0]]
'C': [[0, 1, 1, 1, 0], [1, 0, 0, 0, 1], [1, 0, 0, 0, 1]]
'B': [[1, 1, 1, 1, 1], [1, 0, 1, 0, 1], [0, 1, 0, 1, 0]]
'K': [[1, 1, 1, 1, 1], [0, 1, 0, 1, 0], [1, 0, 0, 0, 1]]
'O': [[0, 1, 1, 1, 0], [1, 0, 0, 0, 1], [1, 0, 0, 0, 1], [0, 1, 1, 1,
0]]
```

Now that we have a selection of letters to choose from, we can create a sequence of LED patterns using the `createBuffer()` function. As the name suggests, the function will build up a buffer of LED patterns by looking up each letter in the message and adding the related pattern row by row. If a letter isn't found in the dictionary, then a space will be used instead.

Finally, we now have a list of LED patterns ready to display. To control when we start the sequence, we will use the TILT module and check the status of the tilt switch:

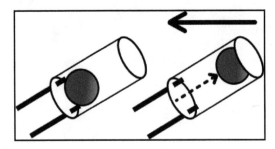

The tilt switch position when not moving (left) and moving (right)

The tilt switch consists of a small ball bearing enclosed in a hollow, insulated cylinder; the connection between the two pins is closed when the ball is resting at the bottom of the cylinder. The tilt switch is open when the ball is moved to the other end of the cylinder, out of contact of the pins:

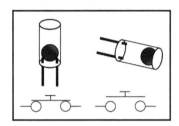

The tilt switch circuit with the switch closed and with the switch open

The tilt switch circuit shown previously will allow GPIO pin 24 to be connected to the ground when the switch is closed. Then, if we read the pin, it will return `False` when it is at rest. By setting the GPIO pin as an input and enabling the internal pull-up resistor, when the tilt switch is open, it will report `True`.

If the tilt switch is open (reporting `True`), then we will assume the unit is being moved and begin displaying the LED sequences, incrementing the current position each time we display a row of the LED pattern. Just to make the pattern a little more colorful (just because we can!) we repeat each row in another color. As soon as the `TILT.tilt_moving()` function reports that we have stopped moving or that we are moving in the opposite direction, we will reset the current position, ready to start the whole pattern all over again:

The message is displayed by the RGB LEDs - here, we are using green and blue together

When the RGB LED module and tilt switch are moved back and forth, we should see the message displayed in the air!

Try experimenting with different color combinations, speeds, and arm waviness to see what effects you can produce. You could even create a similar setup mounted on a wheel to produce a continuous POV effect.

8
Sensing and Displaying Real-World Data

In this chapter, we will cover the following topics:

- Using devices with the I²C bus
- Reading analog data using an analog-to-digital converter
- Logging and plotting data
- Extending the Raspberry Pi GPIO with an I/O expander
- Capturing data in an SQLite database
- Viewing data from your own web server
- Sensing and sending data to online services

Introduction

In this chapter, we will learn how to collect analog data from the real world and process it so we can display, log, graph, and share the data and make use of it in our programs.

We will extend the capabilities of the Raspberry Pi by interfacing with **analog-to-digital converters** (**ADCs**), LCD alphanumeric displays, and digital port expanders using Raspberry Pi's GPIO connections.

Using devices with the I²C bus

Raspberry Pi can support several higher-level protocols that a wide range of devices can easily be connected to. In this chapter, we shall focus on the most common bus, called **I-squared-C** (**I²C**). It provides a medium-speed bus for communicating with devices over two wires. In this section, we shall use I²C to interface with an 8-bit ADC. This device will measure an analog signal, convert it to a relative value between 0 and 255, and send the value as a digital signal (represented by 8-bits) over the I²C bus to the Raspberry Pi.

The advantages of I²C can be summarized as follows:

- Maintains a low pin/signal count, even with numerous devices on the bus
- Adapts to the needs of different slave devices
- Readily supports multiple masters
- Incorporates ACK/NACK functionality for improved error handling

Getting ready

The I²C bus is not enabled in all Raspberry Pi images; therefore, we need to enable the module and install some supporting tools. Newer versions of Raspbian use **device trees** to handle hardware peripherals and drivers.

In order to make use of the I²C bus, we need to enable the ARM I²C in the `bootconfig.txt` file.

You can do this automatically using the following command:

```
sudo raspi-config
```

Select **Advanced Options** from the menu and then select **I²C**, as shown in the following screenshot. When asked, select **Yes** to enable the interface and then click **Yes** to load the module by default:

```
┌─────────┤ Raspberry Pi Software Configuration Tool (raspi-config) ├─────────┐
│                                                                              │
│   A1 Overscan              You may need to configure oversca                 │
│   A2 Hostname              Set the visible name for this Pi                   │
│   A3 Memory Split          Change the amount of memory made                  │
│   A4 SSH                   Enable/Disable remote command lin                 │
│   A5 Device Tree           Enable/Disable the use of Device                  │
│   A6 SPI                   Enable/Disable automatic loading                   │
│   A7 I2C                   Enable/Disable automatic loading                   │
│   A8 Serial                Enable/Disable shell and kernel m                  │
│   A9 Audio                 Force audio out through HDMI or 3                  │
│   A0 Update                Update this tool to the latest ve                  │
│                                                                              │
│                                                                              │
│              <Select>                        <Back>                          │
│                                                                              │
└──────────────────────────────────────────────────────────────────────────┘
```

The raspi-config menu

From the menu, select **I2C** and select **Yes** to enable the interface and to load the module by default.

The `raspi-config` program enables the `I2C_ARM` interface by altering `/boot/config.txt` to include `dtparam=i2c_arm=on`. The other bus (I2C_VC) is typically reserved for interfacing with Raspberry Pi HAT add-on boards (to read the configuration information from the on-board memory devices); however, you can enable this using `dtparam=i2c_vc=on`.

If you wish, you can also enable the SPI using the `raspi-config` list, which is another type of bus.

Next, we should include the I²C module to be loaded upon turning the Raspberry Pi on, as follows:

```
sudo nano /etc/modules
```

Add the following on separate lines and save (*Ctrl + X, Y, Enter*):

```
i2c-dev
i2c-bcm2708
```

Similarly, we can also enable the SPI module by adding `spi-bcm2708`.

Next, we will install some tools to use I²C devices directly from the command line, as follows:

```
sudo apt-get update
sudo apt-get install i2c-tools
```

Finally, shut down the Raspberry Pi before attaching the hardware in order to allow the changes to be applied, as follows:

```
sudo halt
```

You will need a PCF8591 module (retailers of these are listed in the Appendix, *Hardware and Software List*) or you can obtain the PCF8591 chip separately and build your own circuit (see the *There's more...* section for details on the circuit):

The PCF8591 ADC and sensor module from dx.com

Connect the **GND**, **VCC**, **SDA**, and **SCL** pins to the Raspberry Pi GPIO header as follows:

I²C Device	Raspberry Pi GPIO		I²C Device
VCC	1	2	
SDA	3	4	
SCL	5	6	GND

I2C connections on the Raspberry Pi GPIO header

 You can use the same I²C tools/code with other I²C devices by studying the datasheet of the device to find out what messages to send/read and which registers are used to control your device.

How to do it...

1. The `i2cdetect` command is used to detect the I²C devices (the `--y` option skips any warnings about possible interference with other hardware that could be connected to the I²C bus). The following commands are used to scan both the buses:

   ```
   sudo i2cdetect -y 0
   sudo i2cdetect -y 1
   ```

2. Depending on your Raspberry Pi board revision, the address of the device should be listed on bus 0 (for Model B Rev1 boards) or bus 1 (for Raspberry Pi 2 and 3, and Raspberry Pi 1 Model A and Model B Revision 2). By default, the PCF8591 address is `0x48`:

I²C bus number to use	Bus 00	Bus 11
Raspberry Pi 2 and 3	HAT ID (I2C_VC)	GPIO (I2C_ARM)
Model A and Model B Revision 2	P5	GPIO
Model B Revision 1	GPIO	N/A

3. The following screenshot shows the output of `i2cdetect`:

The PCF8591 address (48) is displayed here on bus 1

If nothing is listed, shut down and double-check your connections (the ADC module from `www.dx.com` will switch on a red LED when powered).

If you receive an error stating that the `/dev/i2c1` bus doesn't exist, you can perform the following checks:

- Ensure that the `/etc/modprobe.d/raspi-blacklist.conf` file is empty (that is, that the modules haven't been blacklisted), using the following command to view the file:

```
sudo nano /etc/modprobe.d/raspi-blacklist.conf
```

- If there is anything in the file (such as `blacklist i2c-bcm2708`), remove it and save

- Check `/boot/config` and ensure there isn't a line that contains `device_tree_param=` (this will disable support for the new device tree configurations and disable support for some Raspberry Pi HAT add-on boards)

- Check whether the modules have been loaded by using `lsmod` and look for `i2c-bcm2708` and `i2c_dev`

4. Using the detected bus number (0 or 1) and the device address (0x48), use `i2cget` to read from the device (after a power up or channel change, you will need to read the device twice to see the latest value), as follows:

```
sudo i2cget -y 1 0x48
sudo i2cget -y 1 0x48
```

5. To read from channel 1 (this is the temperature sensor on the module), we can use `i2cset` to write 0x01 to the PCF8591 control register. Again, use two reads to get a new sample from channel 1, as follows:

```
sudo i2cset -y 1 0x48 0x01
sudo i2cget -y 1 0x48
sudo i2cget -y 1 0x48
```

6. To cycle through each of the input channels, use `i2cset` to set the control register to `0x04`, as follows:

```
sudo i2cset -y 1 0x48 0x04
```

7. We can also control the AOUT pin using the following command to set it fully on (lighting up the LED D1):

```
sudo i2cset -y 1 0x48 0x40 0xff
```

8. Finally, we can use the following command to set it fully off (switching off the LED D1):

```
sudo i2cset -y 1 0x48 0x40 0x00
```

How it works...

The first read from the device after it has been switched on will return `0x80` and will also trigger the new sample from channel 0. If you read it a second time, it will return the sample previously read and generate a fresh sample. Each reading will be an 8-bit value (ranging from `0` to `255`), representing the voltage to VCC (in this case, 0 V to 3.3 V). On the www.dx.com module, channel 0 is connected to a light sensor, so if you cover up the module with your hand and resend the command, you will observe a change in the values (darker means a higher value and lighter means a lower one). You will find that the readings are always one behind; this is because, as it returns the previous sample, it captures the next sample.

We use the following command to specify a particular channel to read:

```
sudo i2cset -y 1 0x48 0x01
```

This changes the channel that is read to channel 1 (this is marked as **AIN1** on the module). Remember, you will need to perform two reads before you see data from the newly selected channel. The following table shows the channels and pin names, as well as which jumper connectors enable/disable each of the sensors:

Channel	0	1	2	3
Pin Name	AIN0	AIN1	AIN2	AIN3
Sensor	Light-Dependent Resistor	Thermistor	External Pin	Potentiometer
Jumper	P5	P4		P6

Next, we control the AOUT pin by setting the analog output enable flag (bit 6) of the control register and using the next value to set the analog voltage (0V-3.3V, 0x00-0xFF), as follows:

```
sudo i2cset -y 1 0x48 0x40 0xff
```

Finally, you can set bit 2 (0x04) to auto increment and cycle through the input channels as follows:

```
sudo i2cset -y 1 0x48 0x04
```

Each time you run i2cget -y 1 0x48, the next channel will be selected, starting with channel AIN0, then running from AIN1 through to AIN3 and back to AIN0 again.

To understand how to set a particular bit in a value, it helps to look at the binary representation of the number. The 8-bit value 0x04 can be written as b0000 0100 in binary (0x indicates the value is written in hexadecimal, or hex, and b indicates a binary number).

Bits within binary numbers are counted from right to left, starting with 0 - that is, MSB 7 6 5 4 3 2 1 0 LSB.

Bit 7 is known as the **most significant bit** (**MSB**) and bit 0 is known as the **least significant bit** (**LSB**). Therefore, by setting bit 2, we end up with b0000 0100 (which is 0x04).

There's more...

The I²C bus allows us to easily connect multiple devices using only a few wires. The PCF8591 chip can be used to connect your own sensors to the module or just the chip.

Using multiple I²C devices

All commands on the I²C bus are addressed to a specific I²C device (many have the option to set some pins high or low to select additional addresses and allow multiple devices to exist on the same bus). Each device must have a unique address so that only one device will respond at any one time. The PCF8591 starting address is 0x48, with additional addresses selectable by the three address pins to 0x4F. This allows up to eight PCF8591 devices to be used on the same bus.

If you decide to use the I2C_VC bus that is located on GPIO pins 27 and 2828 (or on the P5 header on Model A and Revision 2 Model B devices), you may need to add a 1k8 ohm pull-up resistor between the I²C lines and 3.3 V. These resistors are already present on the I²C bus on the GPIO connector. However, some I²C modules, including the PCF8591 module, have their own resistors fitted, so it will work without the extra resistors.

I²C bus and level shifting

The I²C bus consists of two wires, one data (SDA), and one clock (SCL). Both are passively pulled to VCC (on the Raspberry Pi, this is 3.3 V) with pull-up resistors. The Raspberry Pi will control the clock by pulling it low every cycle and the data line can be pulled low by Raspberry Pi to send commands or by the connected device to respond with data:

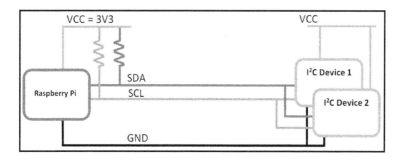

The Raspberry Pi I²C pins include pull-up resistors on SDA and SCL

Since the slave devices can only pull the data line to **GND**, the device may be powered by 3.3 V or even 5 V without the risk of driving the GPIO pins too high (remember that the Raspberry Pi GPIO is not able to handle voltages over 3.3 V). This should work as long as the I²C bus of the device can recognize the logic maximum a 3.3 V rather than 5 V. The I²C device must not have its own pull-up resistors fitted, as this will cause the GPIO pins to be pulled to the supply voltage of the I²C device.

Note that the PCF8591 module used in this chapter has resistors fitted; therefore, we must only use **VCC = 3V3**. A bidirectional logic level converter can be used to overcome any issues with logic levels. One such device is the **Adafruit** I²C bidirectional logic level translator module, which is shown in the following image:

Adafruit I²C Bidirectional logic level translator module

In addition to ensuring that any logic voltages are at suitable levels for the device you are using, it will allow the bus to be extended over longer wires (the level shifter will also act as a bus repeater).

Using just the PCF8591 chip or adding alternative sensors

A circuit diagram of the PCF8591 module without the sensors attached is shown in the following diagram:

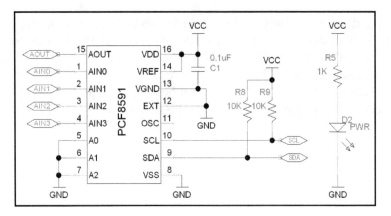

Circuit diagram of the PCF8591 module without sensor attachment

As you can see, excluding the sensors, there are only five additional components. We have a power-filtering capacitor (C1) and a power-indicating LED (D2) with a current-limiting resistor (R5), all of which are optional.

Note that the module includes two 10K pull-up resistors (R8 and R9) for SCL and SDA signals. However, since the GPIO I^{2}C connections on the Raspberry Pi also include pull-up resistors, these are not needed on the module (and could be removed). It also means we should only connect this module to VCC = 3.3 V (if we use 5 V, then voltages on SCL and SDA will be around 3.56 V, which is too high for the Raspberry Pi GPIO pins).

The sensors on the PCF891 module are all resistive, so the voltage level that is present on the analog input will change between **GND** and **VCC** as the resistance of the sensor changes:

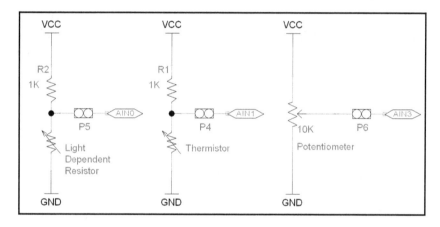

A potential divider circuit. This provides voltage proportional to the sensor's resistance.

The module uses a circuit known as a potential divider. The resistor at the top balances the resistance provided by the sensor at the bottom to provide a voltage that is somewhere between **VCC** and **GND.**

The output voltage (V_{out}) of the potential divider can be calculated as follows:

$$V_{out} = \frac{R_t}{(R_t + R_b)} \times VCC$$

R_t and R_b are the resistance values at the top and bottom, respectively, and VCC is the supply voltage.

The potentiometer in the module has the 10K ohm resistance split between the top and bottom, depending on the position of the adjuster. So, halfway, we have 5K ohm on each side and an output voltage of 1.65 V; a quarter of the way (clockwise), we have 2.5K ohm and 7.5K ohm, producing 0.825 V.

 I haven't shown the AOUT circuit, which is a resistor and LED. However, as you will find, an LED isn't suited to indicate an analog output (except to show the on/off states).

For more sensitive circuits, you can use more complex circuits, such as a **Wheatstone bridge** (which allows the detection of very small changes in resistance), or you can use dedicated sensors that output an analog voltage based on their readings (such as a **TMP36** temperature sensor). The PCF891 also supports the differential input mode, where the input of one channel can be compared to the input of another (the resultant reading will be the difference between the two).

For more information on the PCF8591 chip, refer to the datasheet at
`http://www.nxp.com/documents/data_sheet/PCF8591.pdf`.

Reading analog data using an analog-to-digital converter

The I^{2}C tools (used in the previous section) are very useful for debugging I^{2}C devices in the command line, but they are not practical for use within Python, as they would be slow and require significant overhead to use. Fortunately, there are several Python libraries that provide I^{2}C support, allowing the efficient use of I^{2}C to communicate with connected devices and providing easy operation.

We will use such a library to create our own Python module that will allow us to quickly and easily obtain data from the ADC device and use it in our programs. The module is designed in such a way that other hardware or data sources may be put in its place without impacting the remaining examples.

Getting ready

To use the I²C bus using Python 3, we will use *Gordon Henderson's* WiringPi2 (see `http://wiringpi.com/` for more details).

The easiest way to install `wiringpi2` is by using `pip` for Python 3. The `pip` is a package manager for Python that works in a similar way to `apt-get`. Any packages you wish to install will be automatically downloaded and installed from an online repository.

To install `pip`, use the following command:

```
sudo apt-get install python3-dev python3-pip
```

Then, install `wiringpi2` with the following command:

```
sudo pip-3.2 install wiringpi2
```

Once the installation has completed, you should see the following, indicating success:

```
ngPi/wiringPi/wiringSerial.o build/temp.linux-armv6l-3.2/WiringPi/wiringPi/wirin
gShift.o build/temp.linux-armv6l-3.2/wiringpi_wrap.o -o build/lib.linux-armv6l-3
.2/_wiringpi2.cpython-32mu.so

Successfully installed wiringpi2
Cleaning up...
pi@raspberrypi:~$
```

Successfully installed WiringPi2

You will need the PCF8591 module wired as it was previously used in the I²C connections of the Raspberry Pi:

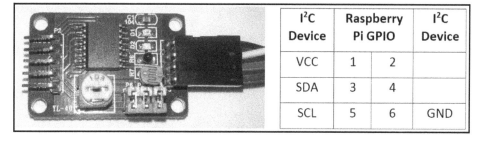

I²C Device	Raspberry Pi GPIO		I²C Device
VCC	1	2	
SDA	3	4	
SCL	5	6	GND

The PCF8591 module and pin connections to the Raspberry Pi GPIO connector

How to do it...

In the next section, we shall write a script to allow us to gather data that we will then use later on in this chapter.

Create the following script, `data_adc.py`, as follows:

1. First, import the modules and create the variables we will use, as follows:

```
#!/usr/bin/env python3
#data_adc.py
import wiringpi2
import time

DEBUG=False
LIGHT=0;TEMP=1;EXT=2;POT=3
ADC_CH=[LIGHT,TEMP,EXT,POT]
ADC_ADR=0x48
ADC_CYCLE=0x04
BUS_GAP=0.25
DATANAME=["0:Light","1:Temperature",
          "2:External","3:Potentiometer"]
```

2. Create the `device` class with a constructor to initialize it, as follows:

```
class device:
  # Constructor:
  def __init__(self,addr=ADC_ADR):
    self.NAME = DATANAME
    self.i2c = wiringpi2.I2C()
    self.devADC=self.i2c.setup(addr)
    pwrup = self.i2c.read(self.devADC) #flush powerup value
    if DEBUG==True and pwrup!=-1:
      print("ADC Ready")
    self.i2c.read(self.devADC) #flush first value
    time.sleep(BUS_GAP)
    self.i2c.write(self.devADC,ADC_CYCLE)
    time.sleep(BUS_GAP)
    self.i2c.read(self.devADC) #flush first value
```

3. Within the class, define a function to provide a list of channel names, as follows:

```
def getName(self):
  return self.NAME
```

4. Define another function (still as part of the class) to return a new set of samples from the ADC channels, as follows:

```
def getNew(self):
  data=[]
  for ch in ADC_CH:
    time.sleep(BUS_GAP)
    data.append(self.i2c.read(self.devADC))
  return data
```

5. Finally, after the device class, create a test function to exercise our new `device` class, as follows. This is only to be run when the script is executed directly:

```
def main():
  ADC = device(ADC_ADR)
  print (str(ADC.getName()))
  for i in range(10):
    dataValues = ADC.getNew()
    print (str(dataValues))
    time.sleep(1)

if __name__=='__main__':
  main()
#End
```

You can run the test function of this module using the following command:

```
sudo python3 data_adc.py
```

How it works...

We start by importing wiringpi2 so we can communicate with our I²C device later on. We will create a class to contain the required functionality to control the ADC. When we create the class, we can initialize wiringpi2 in such a way that it is ready to use the I²C bus (using wiringpi2.I2C()), and we will set up a generic I²C device with the chip's bus address (using self.i2c.setup(0x48)).

wiringpi2 also has a dedicated class to use with the PCF8591 chip; however, in this case, it is more useful to use the standard I²C functionality to illustrate how any I²C device can be controlled using wiringpi2. By referring to the device datasheet, you can use similar commands to communicate to any connected I²C device (whether it is directly supported or not).

As before, we perform a device read and configure the ADC to cycle through the channels, but instead of i2cget and i2cset, we use the `wiringpi2` read and write functions of the I2C object. Once initialized, the device will be ready to read the analog signals on each of the channels.

The class will also have two member functions. The first function, getName(), returns a list of channel names (which we can use to correlate our data to its source) and the second function, getNew(), returns a new set of data from all the channels. The data is read from the ADC using the i2c.read() function, and since we have already put it into cycle mode, each read will be from the next channel.

As we plan to reuse this class later on, we will use the if __name__ test to allow us to define a code to run when we execute the file directly. Within our main() function, we create the ADC, which is an instance of our new device class. We can choose to select a non-default address if we need to; otherwise, the default address for the chip will be used. We use the getName() function to print out the names of the channels and then we can collect data from the ADC (using getNew()) and display them.

There's more...

The following allows us to define an alternative version of the device class in data_adc.py so it can be used in place of the ADC module. This will allow the remaining sections of the chapter to be tried without needing any specific hardware.

Gathering analog data without hardware

If you don't have an ADC module available, there is a wealth of data available from within Raspberry Pi that you can use instead.

Create the data_local.py script as follows:

```
#!/usr/bin/env python3
#data_local.py
import subprocess
from random import randint
import time

MEM_TOTAL=0
MEM_USED=1
MEM_FREE=2
MEM_OFFSET=7
DRIVE_USED=0
```

```
DRIVE_FREE=1
DRIVE_OFFSET=9
DEBUG=False
DATANAME=["CPU_Load","System_Temp","CPU_Frequency",
          "Random","RAM_Total","RAM_Used","RAM_Free",
          "Drive_Used","Drive_Free"]

def read_loadavg():
  # function to read 1 minute load average from system uptime
  value = subprocess.check_output(
          ["awk '{print $1}' /proc/loadavg"], shell=True)
  return float(value)

def read_systemp():
  # function to read current system temperature
  value = subprocess.check_output(
          ["cat /sys/class/thermal/thermal_zone0/temp"],
          shell=True)
  return int(value)

def read_cpu():
  # function to read current clock frequency
  value = subprocess.check_output(
          ["cat /sys/devices/system/cpu/cpu0/cpufreq/"+
           "scaling_cur_freq"], shell=True)
  return int(value)
def read_rnd():
  return randint(0,255)

def read_mem():
  # function to read RAM info
  value = subprocess.check_output(["free"], shell=True)
  memory=[]
  for val in value.split()[MEM_TOTAL+
                           MEM_OFFSET:MEM_FREE+
                           MEM_OFFSET+1]:
    memory.append(int(val))
  return(memory)
def read_drive():
  # function to read drive info
  value = subprocess.check_output(["df"], shell=True)
  memory=[]
  for val in value.split()[DRIVE_USED+
                           DRIVE_OFFSET:DRIVE_FREE+
                           DRIVE_OFFSET+1]:
    memory.append(int(val))
  return(memory)
```

```
class device:
  # Constructor:
  def __init__(self,addr=0):
    self.NAME=DATANAME
  def getName(self):
    return self.NAME

  def getNew(self):
    data=[]
    data.append(read_loadavg())
    data.append(read_systemp())
    data.append(read_cpu())
    data.append(read_rnd())
    memory_ram = read_mem()
    data.append(memory_ram[MEM_TOTAL])
    data.append(memory_ram[MEM_USED])
    data.append(memory_ram[MEM_FREE])
    memory_drive = read_drive()
    data.append(memory_drive[DRIVE_USED])
    data.append(memory_drive[DRIVE_FREE])
    return data

def main():
  LOCAL = device()
  print (str(LOCAL.getName()))
  for i in range(10):
    dataValues = LOCAL.getNew()
    print (str(dataValues))
    time.sleep(1)

if __name__=='__main__':
  main()
#End
```

The preceding script allows us to gather system information from the Raspberry Pi using the following commands (the `subprocess` module allows us to capture the results and process them):

- CPU speed:

    ```
    cat /sys/devices/system/cpu/cpu0/cpufreq/scaling_cur_freq
    ```

- CPU load:

    ```
    awk '{print $1}' /proc/loadavg
    ```

- Core temperature (scaled by 1,000):

    ```
    cat /sys/class/thermal/thermal_zone0/temp
    ```

- Drive info:

    ```
    df
    ```

- RAM info:

    ```
    free
    ```

Each data item is sampled using one of the functions. In the case of the drive and RAM information, we split the response into a list (separated by spaces) and select the items that we want to monitor (such as available memory and used drive space).

This is all packaged up to function in the same way as the data_adc.py file and the device class (so you can choose to use either in the following examples just by swapping the data_adc include with data_local).

Logging and plotting data

Now that we are able to sample and collect a lot of data, it is important that we can capture and analyze it. For this, we will make use of a Python library called matplotlib, which includes lots of useful tools for manipulating, graphing, and analyzing data. We will use pyplot (which is a part of matplotlib) to produce graphs of our captured data. For more information on pyplot, go to http://matplotlib.org/users/pyplot_tutorial.html.

It is a MATLAB-style data visualization framework for Python.

Getting ready

To use pyplot, we will need to install matplotlib.

Because of a problem with the `matplotlib` installer, performing the installation using `pip-3.2` doesn't always work correctly. The method that follows will overcome this problem by performing all the steps `pip` does manually; however, this can take over 30 minutes to complete.

To save time, you can try the `pip` installation, which is much quicker. If it doesn't work, you can install it using the aforementioned manual method.

Use the following commands to try to install `matplotlib` using `pip`:

```
sudo apt-get install tk-dev python3-tk libpng-dev
sudo pip-3.2 install numpy
sudo pip-3.2 install matplotlib
```

You can confirm that `matplotlib` has been installed by running `python3` and trying to import it from the Python Terminal, as follows:

`import matplotlib`

If the installation fails, it will respond with the following:

```
ImportError: No module named matplotlib
```

Otherwise, there will be no errors.

Use the following steps to install `matplotlib` manually:

1. Install the support packages as follows:

    ```
    sudo apt-get install tk-dev python3-tk python3-dev libpng-dev
    sudo pip-3.2 install numpy
    sudo pip-3.2 install matplotlib
    ```

2. Download the source files from the Git repository (the command should be a single line) as follows:

    ```
    wget
    https://github.com/matplotlib/matplotlib/archive/master.zip
    ```

3. Unzip and open the `matplotlib-master` folder that is created, as follows:

```
unzip master.zip
rm master.zip
cd matplotlib-master
```

4. Run the setup file to build (this will take a while) and install it as follows:

```
sudo python3 setup.py build
sudo python3 setup.py install
```

5. Test the installation in the same way as the automated install.

We will either need the PCF8591 ADC module (and `wiringpi2`, installed as before), or we can use the `data_local.py` module from the previous section (just replace `data_adc` with `data_local` in the import section of the script). We also need to have `data_adc.py` and `data_local.py` in the same directory as the new script, depending on which you use.

How to do it...

1. Create a script called `log_adc.py`:

```python
#!/usr/bin/python3
#log_adc.c
import time
import datetime
import data_adc as dataDevice

DEBUG=True
FILE=True
VAL0=0;VAL1=1;VAL2=2;VAL3=3 #Set data order
FORMATHEADER = "t%st%st%st%st%s"
FORMATBODY = "%dt%st%ft%ft%ft%f"

if(FILE):f = open("data.log",'w')

def timestamp():
  ts = time.time()
  return datetime.datetime.fromtimestamp(ts).strftime(
                                    '%Y-%m-%d %H:%M:%S')

def main():
    counter=0
    myData = dataDevice.device()
```

```
        myDataNames = myData.getName()
        header = (FORMATHEADER%("Time",
                            myDataNames[VAL0],myDataNames[VAL1],
                            myDataNames[VAL2],myDataNames[VAL3]))
        if(DEBUG):print (header)
        if(FILE):f.write(header+"n")
        while(1):
          data = myData.getNew()
          counter+=1
          body = (FORMATBODY%(counter,timestamp(),
                          data[0],data[1],data[2],data[3]))
          if(DEBUG):print (body)
          if(FILE):f.write(body+"n")
          time.sleep(0.1)

try:
  main()
finally:
  f.close()
#End
```

2. Create a second script called `log_graph.py`, as follows:

```
#!/usr/bin/python3
#log_graph.py
import numpy as np
import matplotlib.pyplot as plt

filename = "data.log"
OFFSET=2
with open(filename) as f:
    header = f.readline().split('t')
data = np.genfromtxt(filename, delimiter='t', skip_header=1,
                    names=['sample', 'date', 'DATA0',
                            'DATA1', 'DATA2', 'DATA3'])
fig = plt.figure(1)
ax1 = fig.add_subplot(211)#numrows, numcols, fignum
ax2 = fig.add_subplot(212)
ax1.plot(data['sample'],data['DATA0'],'r',
        label=header[OFFSET+0])
ax2.plot(data['sample'],data['DATA1'],'b',
        label=header[OFFSET+1])
ax1.set_title("ADC Samples")
ax1.set_xlabel('Samples')
ax1.set_ylabel('Reading')
ax2.set_xlabel('Samples')
ax2.set_ylabel('Reading')
```

```
leg1 = ax1.legend()
leg2 = ax2.legend()

plt.show()
#End
```

How it works...

The first script, `log_adc.py`, allows us to collect data and write it to a log file.

We can use the ADC device by importing `data_adc` as the `dataDevice`, or we can import `data_local` to use the system data. The numbers given to `VAL0` through `VAL3` allow us to change the order of the channels (and, if using the `data_local` device, select the other channels). We can also define the format string for the header and each line in the log file (to create a file with data separated by tabs) using `%s`, `%d`, and `%f` to allow us to substitute strings, integers, and float values, as shown in the following table:

	Time	0:Light	1:Temperature	2:External	3:Potentiometer
1	2014-02-20 21:24:15	207.00000	216.00000	130.00000	255.00000
2	2014-02-20 21:24:16	207.00000	216.00000	152.00000	255.00000
3	2014-02-20 21:24:17	207.00000	216.00000	145.00000	255.00000
4	2014-02-20 21:24:18	207.00000	216.00000	123.00000	255.00000
5	2014-02-20 21:24:19	207.00000	216.00000	128.00000	255.00000

The table of data captured from the ADC sensor module

When logging in to the file (when `FILE=True`), we open `data.log` in write mode using the `'w'` option (this will overwrite any existing files; to append to a file, use `'a'`).

As part of our data log, we generate `timestamp` using `time` and `datetime` to get the current **epoch time** (this is the number of milliseconds since January 1, 1970) using the `time.time()` command. We convert the value into a more friendly `year-month-day hour:min:sec` format using `strftime()`.

The `main()` function starts by creating an instance of our `device` class (we made this in the previous example), which will supply the data. We fetch the channel names from the `data` device and construct the `header` string. If `DEBUG` is set to `True`, the data is printed to the screen; if `FILE` is set to `True`, it will be written to the file.

In the main loop, we use the `getNew()` function of the device to collect data and format it to display on the screen or be logged to the file. The `main()` function is called using the `try: finally:` command, which will ensure that when the script is aborted, the file will be closed correctly.

The second script, `log_graph.py`, allows us to read the log file and produce a graph of the recorded data, as shown in the following diagram:

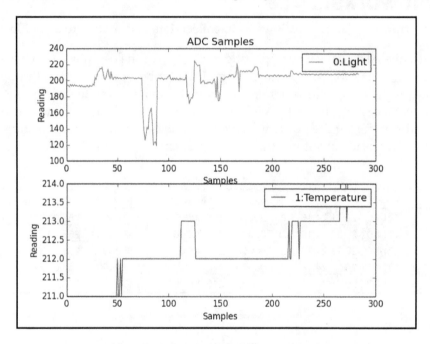

Graphs produced by log_graph.py from the light and temperature sensors

We start by opening up the log file and reading the first line; this contains the header information (which we can then use to identify the data later on). Next, we use `numpy`, a specialist Python library that extends how we can manipulate data and numbers. In this case, we use it to read in the data from the file, split it up based on the tab delimiter, and provide identifiers for each of the data channels.

We define a figure to hold our graphs, adding two subplots (located in a 2 x 1 grid at positions 1 and 2 in the grid - set by the values `211` and `212`). Next, we define the values we want to plot, providing the x values (`data['sample']`), the y values (`data['DATA0']`), the `color` value (`'r'` for Red or `'b'` for Blue), and `label` (set to the heading text we read previously from the top of the file).

Finally, we set a title and the x and y labels for each subplot, enable legends (to show the labels), and display the plot (using `plt.show()`).

There's more...

Now that we have the ability to see the data we have been capturing, we can take things even further by displaying it as we sample it. This will allow us to instantly see how the data reacts to changes in the environment or stimuli. We can also calibrate our data so that we can assign the appropriate scaling to produce measurements in real units.

Plotting live data

Besides plotting data from files, we can use `matplotlib` to plot sensor data as it is sampled. To achieve this, we can use the `plot-animation` feature, which automatically calls a function to collect new data and update our plot.

Create the following script, called `live_graph.py`:

```python
#!/usr/bin/python3
#live_graph.py
import numpy as np
import matplotlib.pyplot as plt
import matplotlib.animation as animation
import data_local as dataDevice

PADDING=5
myData = dataDevice.device()
dispdata = []
timeplot=0
fig, ax = plt.subplots()
line, = ax.plot(dispdata)

def update(data):
  global dispdata,timeplot
  timeplot+=1
  dispdata.append(data)
```

```
    ax.set_xlim(0, timeplot)
    ymin = min(dispdata)-PADDING
    ymax = max(dispdata)+PADDING
    ax.set_ylim(ymin, ymax)
    line.set_data(range(timeplot),dispdata)
    return line

def data_gen():
    while True:
        yield myData.getNew()[1]/1000

ani = animation.FuncAnimation(fig, update,
                              data_gen, interval=1000)
plt.show()
#End
```

We start by defining our dataDevice object and creating an empty array, dispdata[], which will hold all the data which has been collected. Next, we define our subplot and the line we are going to plot.

The FuncAnimation() function allows us to update a figure (fig) by defining an update function and a generator function. The generator function (data_gen()) will be called every interval (1,000 ms) and will produce a data value.

This example uses the core temperature reading that, when divided by 1,000, gives the actual temperature in degC:

To use the ADC data instead, change the import for dataDevice to data_adc and adjust the following line to use a channel other than [1] and apply a scaling that is different from 1,000:

```
yield myData.getNew()[1]/1000
```

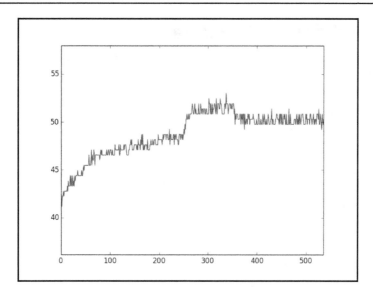

Raspberry Pi plotting in real time

The data value is passed to the update() function, which allows us to add it to our dispdata[] array that will contain all the data values to be displayed in the plot. We adjust the *x* axis range to be near the min and max values of the data. We also adjust the *y* axis to grow as we continue to sample more data.

The FuncAnimation() function requires the data_gen() object to be a special type of function called a generator. A generator function produces a continuous series of values each time it is called, and can even use its previous state to calculate the next value if required. This is used to perform continuous calculations for plotting; this is why it is used here. In our case, we just want to run the same sampling function (new_data()) continuously so that each time it is called, it will yield a new sample.

Finally, we update the *x* and *y* axes data with our dispdata[] array (using the set_data() function), which will plot our samples against the number of seconds we are sampling. To use other data, or to plot data from the ADC, adjust the import for dataDevice and select the required channel (and scaling) in the data_gen() function.

Scaling and calibrating data

You may have noticed that it can sometimes be difficult to interpret data read from an ADC, since the value is just a number. A number isn't much help on its own; all it can tell you is that the environment is slightly hotter or slightly darker than the previous sample. However, if you can use another device to provide comparable values (such as the current room temperature), you can then calibrate your sensor data to provide more useful real-world information.

To obtain a rough calibration, we shall use two samples to create a linear fit model that can then be used to estimate real-world values for other ADC readings (this assumes the sensor itself is mostly linear in its response). The following diagram shows a linear fit graph using two readings at 25 and 30 degrees Celsius, providing estimated ADC values for other temperatures:

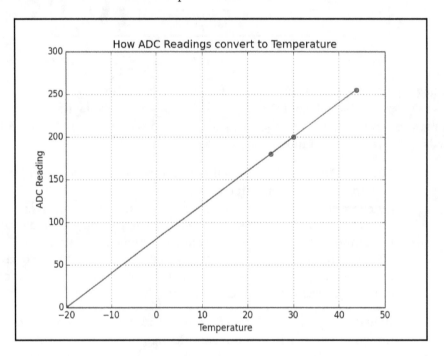

Samples are used to linearly calibrate temperature sensor readings

We can calculate our model using the following function:

```
def linearCal(realVal1,readVal1,realVal2,readVal2):
    #y=Ax+C
    A = (realVal1-realVal2)/(readVal1-readVal2)
    C = realVal1-(readVal1*A)
    cal = (A,C)
    return cal
```

This will return `cal`, which will contain the model slope (`A`) and offset (`C`).

We can then use the following function to calculate the value of any reading by using the calculated `cal` values for that channel:

```
def calValue(readVal,cal = [1,0]):
    realVal = (readVal*cal[0])+cal[1]
    return realVal
```

For more accuracy, you can take several samples and use linear interpolation between the values (or fit the data to other, more complex mathematical models), if required.

Extending the Raspberry Pi GPIO with an I/O expander

As we have seen, making use of the higher-level bus protocols allows us to connect to more complex hardware quickly and easily. The I²C can be put to great use by using it to expand the available I/O on the Raspberry Pi, as well as providing additional circuit protection (and, in some cases, additional power to drive more hardware).

There are lots of devices available that provide I/O expansion over the I²C bus (and also SPI), but the most commonly used is a 28-pin device, MCP23017, which provides 16 additional digital input/output pins. Being an I²C device, it only requires the two signals (SCL and SDA connections, plus ground, and power) and will happily function with other I²C devices on the same bus.

We shall see how the Adafruit I²C 16x2 RGB LCD Pi Plate makes use of one of these chips to control an LCD alphanumeric display and keypad over the I²C bus (without the I/O expander, this would normally require up to 15 GPIO pins).

Boards from other manufacturers will also work. A 16x2 LCD module and I²C-to-serial interface module can be combined to have our own low cost I²C LCD module.

Getting ready

You will need the Adafruit I²C 16x2 RGB LCD Pi Plate (which also includes five keypad buttons), shown in the following photo:

Adafruit I²C 16x2 RGB LCD Pi Plate with keypad buttons

The Adafruit I²C 16x2 RGB LCD Pi Plate directly connects to the GPIO connector of Raspberry Pi.

As before, we can use the PCF8591 ADC module or use the `data_local.py` module from the previous section (use `data_adc` or `data_local` in the import section of the script). The `data_adc.py` and `data_local.py` files should be in the same directory as the new script.

The LCD Pi Plate only requires four pins (SDA, SCL, GND, and 5V); it connects over the whole GPIO header. If we want to use it with other devices, such as the PCF8591 ADC module, then something similar to a TriBorg from PiBorg (which splits the GPIO port into three) can be used to add ports.

How to do it...

1. Create the following script, called `lcd_i2c.py`:

```
#!/usr/bin/python3
```

```
#lcd_i2c.py
import wiringpi2
import time
import datetime
import data_local as dataDevice

AF_BASE=100
AF_E=AF_BASE+13;      AF_RW=AF_BASE+14;    AF_RS=AF_BASE+15
AF_DB4=AF_BASE+12;    AF_DB5=AF_BASE+11;   AF_DB6=AF_BASE+10
AF_DB7=AF_BASE+9

AF_SELECT=AF_BASE+0; AF_RIGHT=AF_BASE+1; AF_DOWN=AF_BASE+2
AF_UP=AF_BASE+3;     AF_LEFT=AF_BASE+4;  AF_BACK=AF_BASE+5

AF_GREEN=AF_BASE+6; AF_BLUE=AF_BASE+7;  AF_RED=AF_BASE+8
BNK=" "*16 #16 spaces

def gpiosetup():
  global lcd
  wiringpi2.wiringPiSetup()
  wiringpi2.mcp23017Setup(AF_BASE,0x20)
  wiringpi2.pinMode(AF_RIGHT,0)
  wiringpi2.pinMode(AF_LEFT,0)
  wiringpi2.pinMode(AF_SELECT,0)
  wiringpi2.pinMode(AF_RW,1)
  wiringpi2.digitalWrite(AF_RW,0)
  lcd=wiringpi2.lcdInit(2,16,4,AF_RS,AF_E,
                        AF_DB4,AF_DB5,AF_DB6,AF_DB7,0,0,0,0)

def printLCD(line0="",line1=""):
  wiringpi2.lcdPosition(lcd,0,0)
  wiringpi2.lcdPrintf(lcd,line0+BNK)
  wiringpi2.lcdPosition(lcd,0,1)
  wiringpi2.lcdPrintf(lcd,line1+BNK)

def checkBtn(idx,size):
  global run
  if wiringpi2.digitalRead(AF_LEFT):
    idx-=1
    printLCD()
  elif wiringpi2.digitalRead(AF_RIGHT):
    idx+=1
    printLCD()
  if wiringpi2.digitalRead(AF_SELECT):
    printLCD("Exit Display")
    run=False
  return idx%size
```

```
def main():
  global run
  gpiosetup()
  myData = dataDevice.device()
  myDataNames = myData.getName()
  run=True
  index=0
  while(run):
    data = myData.getNew()
    printLCD(myDataNames[index],str(data[index]))
    time.sleep(0.2)
    index = checkBtn(index,len(myDataNames))

main()
#End
```

2. With the LCD module connected, run the script as follows:

sudo python3 lcd_i2c.py

Select the data channel you want to display using the left and right buttons and press the **SELECT** button to exit.

How it works...

The `wiringpi2` library has excellent support for I/O expander chips, like the one used for the Adafruit LCD character module. To use the Adafruit module, we need to set up the pin mapping for all the pins of MCP23017 Port A, as shown in the following table (then, we set up the I/O expander pins with an offset of `100`):

Name	SELECT	RIGHT	DOWN	UP	LEFT	GREEN	BLUE	RED
MCP23017 Port A	A0	A1	A2	A3	A4	A6	A7	A8
WiringPi pin	100	101	102	103	104	106	107	108

The pin mapping for all of MCP23017 Port B's pins is as follows:

Name	DB7	DB6	DB5	DB4	E	RW	RS
MCP23017 Port B	B1	B2	B3	B4	B5	B6	B7
WiringPi pin	109	110	111	112	113	114	115

To set up the LCD screen, we initialize `wiringPiSetup()` and the I/O expander, `mcp23017Setup()`. We then specify the pin offset and bus address of the I/O expander. Next, we set all the hardware buttons as inputs (using `pinMode(pin number,0)`), and the RW pin of the LCD to an output. The `wiringpi2` LCD library expects the RW pin to be set to `LOW` (forcing it into read-only mode), so we set the pin to `LOW` (using `digitalWrite(AF_RW,0)`).

We create an `lcd` object by defining the number of rows and columns of the screen and stating whether we are using a 4- or 8-bit data mode (we are using four of the eight data lines, so we will be using 4-bit mode). We also provide the pin mapping of the pins we are using (the last four are set to `0` since we are only using four data lines).

Now, we will create a function called `PrintLCD()`, which will allow us to send strings to show on each line of the display. We use `lcdPosition()` to set the cursor position on the `lcd` object for each line and then print the text for each line. We also add some blank spaces at the end of each line to ensure the full line is overwritten.

The next function, `checkBtn()`, briefly checks the left/right and select buttons to see if they have been pressed (using the `digitalRead()` function). If the left/right button has been pressed, then the index is set to the previous/next item in the array. If the **SELECT** button is pressed, then the `run` flag is set to `False` (this will exit the main loop, allowing the script to finish).

The `main()` function calls `gpiosetup()` to create our `lcd` object; then, we create our `dataDevice` object and fetch the data names. Within the main loop, we get new data; then, we use our `printLCD()` function to display the data name on the top line and the data value on the second line. Finally, we check to see whether the buttons have been pressed and set the index to our data as required.

There's more...

Using an expander chip such as the MCP23017 provides an excellent way to increase the amount of hardware connectivity to the Raspberry Pi while also providing an additional layer of protection (it is cheaper to replace the expander chip Raspberry Pi).

I/O expander voltages and limits

The port expander only uses a small amount of power when in use, but if you are powering it using the 3.3 V supply, then you will still only be able to draw a maximum of 50 mA in total from all the pins. If you draw too much power, then you may experience system freezes or corrupted read/writes on the SD card.

If you power the expander using the 5V supply, then you can draw up to the maximum power the expander can support (around a maximum of 25 mA per pin and 125 mA in total), as long as your USB power supply is powerful enough.

We must remember that if the expander is powered with a 5 V supply, the inputs/outputs and interrupt lines will also be 5 V and should never be connected back to the Raspberry Pi (without using level shifters to translate the voltage down to 3.3 V).

By changing the wiring of the address pins (A0, A1, and A2) on the expander chip, up to eight modules can be used on the same I^{2}C bus simultaneously. To ensure there is enough current available for each, we would need to use a separate 3.3 V supply. A linear regulator such as LM1117-3.3 would be suitable (this would provide up to 800 mA at 3.3 V, 100 mA for each), and only needs the following simple circuit:

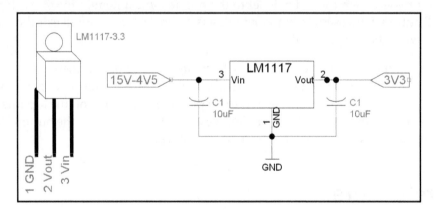

The LM1117 linear voltage regulator circuit

The following diagram shows how a voltage regulator can be connected to the I/O expander (or other device) to provide more current for driving extra hardware:

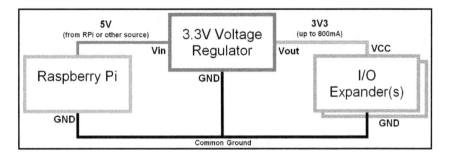

Using a voltage regulator with the Raspberry Pi

The input voltage (Vin) is provided by the Raspberry Pi (for example, from the GPIO pin header, such as 5 V pin 2). However, Vin could be provided by any other power supply (or battery pack) as long as it is between 4.5 V and 15 V and is able to provide enough current. The important part is to ensure that the ground connections (GND) of the Raspberry Pi, the power supply (if a separate one is used), the regulator, and the I/O expander are all connected together (as a common ground).

Using your own I/O expander module

You can use one of the I/O expander modules that are available (or just the MCP23017 chip in the following circuit) to control most HD44780-compatible LCD displays:

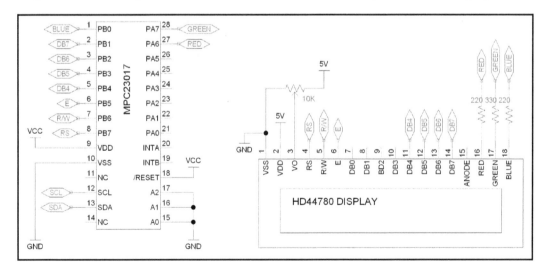

The I/O expander and a HD44780-compatible display

The D-Pad circuit, u*sing Python-to-drive hardware,* can also be connected to the remaining port A pins of the expander (PA0 to button 1, PA1 to right, PA2 to down, PA3 to up, PA4 to left, and PA5 to button 2). As in the previous example, the buttons will be PA0 to PA4 (WiringPi pin number 100 to 104); apart from these, we have the second button added to PA5 (WiringPi pin number 105).

Directly controlling an LCD alphanumeric display

Alternatively, you can also drive the screen directly from the Raspberry Pi with the following connections:

 We are not using the I²C bus here.

LCD	VSS	VDD	V0	RS	RW	E	DB4	DB5	DB6	DB7
LCD Pin	1	2	3	4	5	6	11	12	13	14
Raspberry Pi GPIO	6 (GND)	2 (5V)	Contrast	11	13 (GND)	15	12	16	18	22

The preceding table lists the connections required between the Raspberry Pi and the HD44780-compatible, alphanumeric display module.

The contrast pin (V0) can be connected to a variable resistor as before (with one side connected to the 5 V supply and the other to GND); although, depending on the screen, you may find you can connect directly to GND/5 V to obtain the maximum contrast.

The wiringpi2 LCD library assumes that the RW pin is connected to GND (read only); this avoids the risk that the LCD will send data back if it is connected directly to the Raspberry Pi (this would be a problem since the screen is powered by 5 V and will send data using 5 V logic).

Ensure that you update the code with the new AF_XX references and refer to the physical pin number by changing the setup within the gpiosetup() function. We can also skip the setup of the MCP23017 device.

Have a look at the following commands:

```
wiringpi2.wiringPiSetup()
wiringpi2.mcp23017Setup(AF_BASE,0x20)
```

Replace the preceding commands with the following command:

```
wiringpi.wiringPiSetupPhys()
```

You can see that we only need to change the pin references to switch between using the I/O expander and not using it, which shows how convenient the `wiringpi2` implementation is.

Capturing data in an SQLite database

Databases are a perfect way to store lots of structured data while maintaining the ability to access and search for specific data. **Structured Query Language (SQL)** is a standardized set of commands to update and query databases. For this example, we will use SQLite (a lightweight, self-contained implementation of an SQL database system).

In this chapter, we will gather raw data from our ADC (or local data source) and build our own database. We can then use a Python library called `sqlite3` to add data to a database and then query it:

##	Timestamp	0:Light	1:Temperature	2:External	3:Potentiometer
0	2015-06-16 21:30:51	225	212	122	216
1	2015-06-16 21:30:52	225	212	148	216
2	2015-06-16 21:30:53	225	212	113	216
3	2015-06-16 21:30:54	225	212	137	216
4	2015-06-16 21:30:55	225	212	142	216
5	2015-06-16 21:30:56	225	212	115	216
6	2015-06-16 21:30:57	225	212	149	216
7	2015-06-16 21:30:58	225	212	128	216
8	2015-06-16 21:30:59	225	212	123	216
9	2015-06-16 21:31:02	225	212	147	216

Getting ready

To capture data in our database, we will install SQLite so that it is ready to be used with Python's `sqlite3` built-in module. Use the following command to install SQLite:

```
sudo apt-get install sqlite3
```

Next, we will perform some basic operations with SQLite to see how to use SQL queries.

Run SQLite directly, creating a new `test.db` database file with the following command:

```
sqlite3 test.db
SQLite version 3.7.13 2012-06-11 02:05:22
Enter ".help" for instructions
Enter SQL statements terminated with a ";"
sqlite>
```

This will open an SQLite console, within which we enter SQL commands directly. For example, the following commands will create a new table, add some data, display the content, and then remove the table:

```
CREATE TABLE mytable (info TEXT, info2 TEXT,);
INSERT INTO mytable VALUES ("John","Smith");
INSERT INTO mytable VALUES ("Mary","Jane");
John|Smith
Mary|Jane
DROP TABLE mytable;
.exit
```

You will need the same hardware setup as the previous recipe, as detailed in the *Getting ready* section of the *Using devices with the I²C bus* recipe.

How to do it...

Create the following script, called `mysqlite_adc.py`:

```python
#!/usr/bin/python3
#mysql_adc.py
import sqlite3
import datetime
import data_adc as dataDevice
import time
```

```
import os


DEBUG=True
SHOWSQL=True
CLEARDATA=False
VAL0=0;VAL1=1;VAL2=2;VAL3=3 #Set data order
FORMATBODY="%5s %8s %14s %12s %16s"
FORMATLIST="%5s %12s %10s %16s %7s"
DATEBASE_DIR="/var/databases/datasite/"
DATEBASE=DATEBASE_DIR+"mydatabase.db"
TABLE="recordeddata"
DELAY=1 #approximate seconds between samples

def captureSamples(cursor):
    if(CLEARDATA):cursor.execute("DELETE FROM %s" %(TABLE))
    myData = dataDevice.device()
    myDataNames=myData.getName()

    if(DEBUG):print(FORMATBODY%("##",myDataNames[VAL0],
                                myDataNames[VAL1],myDataNames[VAL2],
                                myDataNames[VAL3]))
    for x in range(10):
        data=myData.getNew()
        for i,dataName in enumerate(myDataNames):
            sqlquery = "INSERT INTO %s (itm_name, itm_value) "
%(TABLE) +
                        "VALUES('%s', %s)"
                        %(str(dataName),str(data[i]))
            if (SHOWSQL):print(sqlquery)
            cursor.execute(sqlquery)

        if(DEBUG):print(FORMATBODY%(x,
                                    data[VAL0],data[VAL1],
                                    data[VAL2],data[VAL3]))
        time.sleep(DELAY)
    cursor.commit()

def displayAll(connect):
    sqlquery="SELECT * FROM %s" %(TABLE)
    if (SHOWSQL):print(sqlquery)
    cursor = connect.execute (sqlquery)
    print(FORMATLIST%("","Date","Time","Name","Value"))

    for x,column in enumerate(cursor.fetchall()):
       print(FORMATLIST%(x,str(column[0]),str(column[1]),
                         str(column[2]),str(column[3])))
```

```
def createTable(cursor):
    print("Create a new table: %s" %(TABLE))
    sqlquery="CREATE TABLE %s (" %(TABLE) +
            "itm_date DEFAULT (date('now','localtime')), " +
            "itm_time DEFAULT (time('now','localtime')), " +
            "itm_name, itm_value)"
    if (SHOWSQL):print(sqlquery)
    cursor.execute(sqlquery)
    cursor.commit()

def openTable(cursor):
    try:
        displayAll(cursor)
    except sqlite3.OperationalError:
        print("Table does not exist in database")
        createTable(cursor)
    finally:
        captureSamples(cursor)
        displayAll(cursor)

try:
    if not os.path.exists(DATEBASE_DIR):
        os.makedirs(DATEBASE_DIR)
    connection = sqlite3.connect(DATEBASE)
    try:
        openTable(connection)
    finally:
        connection.close()
except sqlite3.OperationalError:
    print("Unable to open Database")
finally:
    print("Done")

#End
```

If you do not have the ADC module hardware, you can capture local data by setting the `dataDevice` module as `data_local`. Ensure you have `data_local.py` (from the *There's more...* section in the *Reading analog data using an analog-to-digital converter* recipe) in the same directory as the following script:

```
import data_local as dataDevice
```

This will capture the local data (RAM, CPU activity, temperature, and so on) to the SQLite database instead of ADC samples.

How it works...

When the script is first run, it will create a new SQLite database file called
mydatabase.db, which will add a table named recordeddata. The table is
generated by createTable(), which runs the following SQLite command:

```
CREATE TABLE recordeddata
(
    itm_date DEFAULT (date('now','localtime')),
    itm_time DEFAULT (time('now','localtime')),
    itm_name,
    itm_value
)
```

The new table will contain the following data items:

Name	Description
itm_date	Used to store the date of the data sample. When the data record is created, the current date (using date('now','localtime')) is applied as the default value.
itm_time	Used to store the time of the data sample. When the data record is created, the current time (using time('now','localtime')) is applied as the default value.
itm_name	Used to record the name of the sample.
itm_value	Used to keep the sampled value.

We then use the same method to capture 10 data samples from the ADC as we did in
the *Logging and plotting data* recipe previously (as shown in the captureSamples()
function). However, this time, we will then add the captured data into our new
SQLite database table, using the following SQL command (applied using
cursor.execute(sqlquery)):

```
INSERT INTO recordeddata
    (itm_name, itm_value) VALUES ('0:Light', 210)
```

The current date and time will be added by default to each record as it is created. We end up with a set of 40 records (4 records for every cycle of ADC samples captured), which are now stored in the SQLite database:

```
        Date        Time              Name     Value
0   2015-07-03   21:02:54          0:Light       210
1   2015-07-03   21:02:54   1:Temperature       210
2   2015-07-03   21:02:54       2:External       107
3   2015-07-03   21:02:54   3:Potentiometer      40
4   2015-07-03   21:02:55          0:Light       211
5   2015-07-03   21:02:55   1:Temperature       210
6   2015-07-03   21:02:55       2:External       156
7   2015-07-03   21:02:55   3:Potentiometer      39
```

Eight ADC samples have been captured and stored in the SQLite database

After the records have been created, we must remember to call `cursor.commit()`, which will save all the new records to the database.

The last part of the script calls `displayAll()`, which will use the following SQL command:

SELECT * FROM recordeddata

This will select all of the data records in the `recordeddata` table, and we use `cursor.fetch()` to provide the selected data as a list we can iterate through:

```
for x,column in enumerate(cursor.fetchall()):
    print(FORMATLIST%(x,str(column[0]),str(column[1]),
                      str(column[2]),str(column[3])))
```

This allows us to print out the full contents of the database, displaying the captured data.

Note that here we use the `try`, `except`, and `finally` constructs in this script to attempt to handle the mostly likely scenario that users will face when running the script.

First, we ensure that if the database directory doesn't exist, we create it. Next, we try opening the database file; this process will automatically create a new database file if one doesn't already exist. If either of these initial steps fail (because they don't have read/write permissions, for example) we cannot continue, so we report that we cannot open the database and simply exit the script.

Next, we try to open the required table within the database and display it. If the database file is brand new, this operation will always fail, as it will be empty. However, if this occurs, we just catch the exception and create the table before continuing with the script to add our sampled data to the table and display it.

This allows the script to gracefully handle potential problems, take corrective action, and then continue smoothly. The next time the script is run, the database and table will already exist, so we won't need to create them a second time, and we can append the sample data to the table within the same database file.

There's more...

There are many variants of SQL servers available (such as MySQL, Microsoft SQL Server, and PostgreSQL), however they should at least have the following primary commands (or equivalent):

CREATE, INSERT, SELECT, WHERE, UPDATE, SET, DELETE, and **DROP**

You should find that even if you choose to use a different SQL server to the SQLite one used here, the SQL commands will be relatively similar.

The CREATE TABLE command

The CREATE TABLE command is used to define a new table by specifying the column names (and also to set default values, if desired):

```
CREATE TABLE table_name (
    column_name1 TEXT,
    column_name2 INTEGER DEFAULT 0,
    column_name3 REAL )
```

The previous SQL command will create a new table called table_name, containing three data items. One column will contain text, other integers (for example, 1, 3, -9), and finally, one column will contain real numbers (for example, 5.6, 3.1749, 1.0).

The INSERT command

The INSERT command will add a particular entry to a table in the database:

```
INSERT INTO table_name (column_name1name1, column_name2name2,
column_name3)name3)
    VALUES ('Terry'Terry Pratchett', 6666, 27.082015)082015)
```

This will enter the values provided into the corresponding columns in the table.

The SELECT command

The SELECT command allows us to specify a particular column or columns from the database table, returning a list of records with the data:

```
SELECT column_name1, column_name2 FROM table_name
```

It can also allow us to select all of the items, using this command:

```
SELECT * FROM table_name
```

The WHERE command

The WHERE command is used to specify specific entries to be selected, updated, or deleted:

```
SELECT * FROM table_name
    WHERE column_name1= 'Terry Pratchett'
```

This will SELECT any records where the column_name1 matches 'Terry Pratchett'.

The UPDATE command

The UPDATE command will allow us to change (SET) the values of data in each of the specified columns. We can also combine this with the WHERE command to limit the records the change is applied to:

```
UPDATE table_name
    SET column_name2=49name2=49,column_name3=30name3=30.111997
    WHERE column_name1name1= 'Douglas Adams'Adams';
```

The DELETE command

The DELETE command allows any records selected using WHERE to be removed from the specified table. However, if the whole table is selected, using DELETE * FROM table_name will delete the entire contents of the table:

```
DELETE FROM table_name
    WHERE columncolumn_name2=9999
```

The DROP command

The DROP command allows a table to be removed completely from the database:

```
DROP table_name
```

Be warned that this will permanently remove all the data that was stored in the specified table and the structure.

Viewing data from your own webserver

Gathering and collecting information into databases is very helpful, but if it is locked inside a database or a file, it isn't of much use. However, if we allow the stored data to be viewed via a web page, it will be far more accessible; not only can we view the data from other devices, but we can also share it with others on the same network.

We shall create a local web server to query and display the captured SQLite data and allow it to be viewed through a PHP web interface. This will allow the data to be viewed, not only via the web browser on the Raspberry Pi, but also on other devices, such as cell phones or tablets, on the local network:

Press button to remove the table data
Delete

Recorded Data
2015-08-06 21:45:49 System_Temp 43850
2015-08-06 21:45:50 System_Temp 43850
2015-08-06 21:45:51 System_Temp 43312
2015-08-06 21:45:52 System_Temp 43850
2015-08-06 21:45:53 System_Temp 43312
2015-08-06 21:45:54 System_Temp 43850
2015-08-06 21:45:55 System_Temp 43312
2015-08-06 21:45:56 System_Temp 43312
2015-08-06 21:45:57 System_Temp 43850
2015-08-06 21:45:59 System_Temp 43312
2015-08-06 21:46:10 1:Temperature 211
2015-08-06 21:46:12 1:Temperature 212
2015-08-06 21:46:14 1:Temperature 212
2015-08-06 21:46:16 1:Temperature 212
2015-08-06 21:46:18 1:Temperature 211
2015-08-06 21:46:20 1:Temperature 212
2015-08-06 21:46:22 1:Temperature 212
2015-08-06 21:46:24 1:Temperature 211
2015-08-06 21:46:26 1:Temperature 211
2015-08-06 21:46:28 1:Temperature 212
Done

Data captured in the SQLite database displayed via a web page

Using a web server to enter and display information is a powerful way to allow a wide range of users to interact with your projects. The following example demonstrates a web server setup that can be customized for a variety of uses.

Getting ready

Ensure you have completed the previous recipe so that the sensor data has been collected and stored in the SQLite database. We need to install a web server (**Apache2**) and enable PHP support to allow SQLite access.

Use these commands to install a web server and PHP:

```
sudo apt-get update
sudo aptitude install apache2 php5 php5-sqlite
```

The /var/www/ directory is used by the web server; by default, it will load index.html (or index.php) – otherwise, it will just display a list of the links to the files within the directory.

To test whether the web server is running, create a default index.html page. To do this, you will need to create the file using sudo permissions (the /var/www/ directory is protected from changes made by normal users). Use the following command:

```
sudo nano /var/www/index.html
```

Create index.html with the following content:

```
<h1>It works!</h1>
```

Close and save the file (using *Ctrl + X*, *Y* and *Enter*).

If you are using the Raspberry Pi with a screen, you can check whether it is working by loading the desktop:

```
startx
```

Then, open the web browser (**epiphany-browser**) and enter http://localhost as the address. You should see the following test page, indicating that the web server is active:

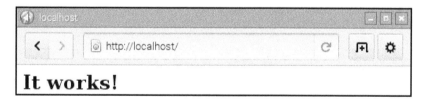

Raspberry Pi browser displaying the test page, located at http://localhost

If you are using the Raspberry Pi remotely or it is connected to your network, you should also be able to view the page on another computer on your network. First, identify the IP address of the Raspberry Pi (using sudo hostname -I) and then use this as the address in your web browser. You may even find you can use the actual hostname of the Raspberry Pi (by default, this is http://raspberrypi/).

If you are unable to see the web page from another computer, ensure that you do not have a firewall enabled (on the computer itself, or on your router) that could be blocking it.

Next, we can test that PHP is operating correctly. We can create a web page called test.php, and ensure that it is located in the /var/www/ directory:

```php
<?php
  phpinfo();
?>;
```

The PHP web page to view the data in the SQLite database has the following details:

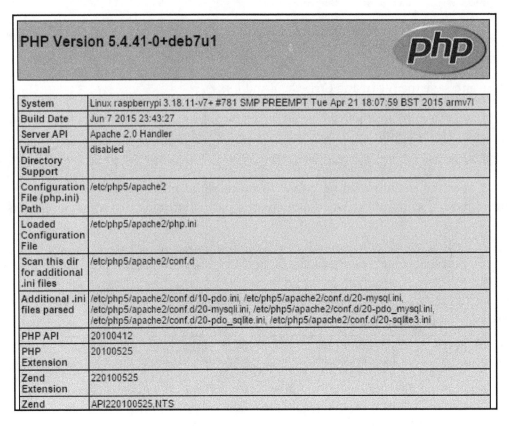

PHP Version 5.4.41-0+deb7u1	

System	Linux raspberrypi 3.18.11-v7+ #781 SMP PREEMPT Tue Apr 21 18:07:59 BST 2015 armv7l
Build Date	Jun 7 2015 23:43:27
Server API	Apache 2.0 Handler
Virtual Directory Support	disabled
Configuration File (php.ini) Path	/etc/php5/apache2
Loaded Configuration File	/etc/php5/apache2/php.ini
Scan this dir for additional .ini files	/etc/php5/apache2/conf.d
Additional .ini files parsed	/etc/php5/apache2/conf.d/10-pdo.ini, /etc/php5/apache2/conf.d/20-mysql.ini, /etc/php5/apache2/conf.d/20-mysqli.ini, /etc/php5/apache2/conf.d/20-pdo_mysql.ini, /etc/php5/apache2/conf.d/20-pdo_sqlite.ini, /etc/php5/apache2/conf.d/20-sqlite3.ini
PHP API	20100412
PHP Extension	20100525
Zend Extension	220100525
Zend	API220100525,NTS

Viewing the test.php page at http://localhost/test.php

We are now ready to write our own PHP web page to view the data in the SQLite database.

How to do it...

1. Create the following PHP files and save them in the web server directory named /var/www/./.

2. Use the following command to create the PHP file:

   sudo nano /var/www/show_data_lite.php

3. The show_data_lite.php file should contain the following:

```
<head>
<title>DatabaseDatabase Data</title>
<meta http-equiv="refresh" content="10" >
</head>
<body>

Press button to remove the table data
<br>
<input type="button" onclick="location.href =
'del_data_lite.php';" value="Delete">
<br><br>
<b>Recorded Data</b><br>
<?php
$db = new
PDO("sqlite:/var/databases/datasitedatasite/mydatabase.db");
//SQL query
$strSQL = "SELECT * FROM recordeddatarecordeddata WHERE
itmitm_name LIKE '%'%temp%'";
//Execute the query
$response = $db->query($strSQL);
//Loop through the response
while($column = $response->fetch())
{
    //Display the content of the response
    echo $column[0] . " ";
    echo $column[1] . " ";
    echo $column[2] . " ";
    echo $column[3] . "<br />";
}
?>
Done
</body>
</html>
```

4. Use the following command to create the PHP file:

```
sudo nano /var/www/del_data_lite.php
<html>
<body>
Remove all the data in the table.
<br>
<?php
$db = new
PDO("sqlite:/var/databases/datasitedatasite/mydatabase.db");
//SQL query
$strSQL = "DROPDROP TABLErecordeddata recordeddata";
//ExecuteExecute the query
$response = $db->query($strSQL);

if ($response == 1)
    {
        echo "Result: DELETED DATA";
    }
else
    {
        echo "Error: Ensure table exists and database directory
is owned
by www-data";
    }
?>
<br><br>
Press button to return to data display.
<br>
<input type="button" onclick="location.href =
'show'show_data_lite.php';" value="Return">
</body>
</html>
```

In order for the PHP code to delete the table within the database, it needs to be writable by the web server. Use the following command to allow it to be writable:

```
sudo chown www-data /var/databases/datasite -R
```

5. The `show_data_lite.php` file will appear as a web page if you open it in a web browser by using the following address:

```
http://localhost/showshow_data_lite.php
```

6. Alternatively, you can open the web page (on another computer within your network, if you wish) by referencing the IP address of the Raspberry Pi (use `hostname -I` to confirm the IP address):

```
http://192.168.1.101/showshow_data_lite.php
```

You may be able to use the hostname instead (by default, this would make the address `http://raspberrypi/show_data_lite.php`). However, this may depend upon your network setup.

If there is no data present, ensure that you run the `mysqlite_adc.py` script to capture additional data.

7. To make the `show_data_lite.php` page display automatically when you visit the web address of your Raspberry Pi (instead of the *It works!* page), we can change the `index.html` to the following:

```
<meta http-equiv="refresh" content="0;
URL='show_data_lite.php' " />
```

This will automatically redirect the browser to load our `show_data_lite.php` **page**.

How it works...

The `show_data_lite.php` file shall display the temperature data that has been stored within the SQLite database (either from the ADC samples or local data sources).

The `show_data_lite.php` file consists of standard HTML code, as well as a special PHP code section. The HTML code sets ACD Data as the title on the head section of the page and uses the following command to make the page automatically reload every 10 seconds:

```
<meta http-equiv="refresh" content="10" >
```

Next, we define a Delete button, which will load the `del_data_lite.php` **page** when clicked:

```
<input type="button" onclick="location.href = 'del_data_lite.php';"
value="Delete">
```

Finally, we use the PHP code section to load the SQLite database and display the Channel 0 data.

We use the following PHP command to open the SQLite database we have previously stored data in (located at `/var/databases/testsites/mydatabase.db`):

```
$db = new PDO("sqlite:/var/databases/testsite/mydatabase.db");
```

Next, we use the following SQLite query to select all the entries where the zone includes `0:` in the text (for example, `0:Light`):

```
SELECT * FROM recordeddatarecordeddata WHERE itm_namename LIKE
'%temp%''
```

 Note that even though we are now using PHP, the queries we use with the SQLite database are the same as we would use when using the `sqlite3` Python module.

We now collect the query result in the `$response` variable:

```
$response = $db->query($strSQL);
Allowing us to use fetch() (like we used cursor.fetchall() previously)
to list all the data columns in each of the data entries within the
response.
while($column = $response->fetch())
{
    //Display the content of the response
    echo $column[0] . " ";
    echo $column[1] . " ";
    echo $column[2] . " ";
    echo $column[3] . "<br />";
}
?>
```

The `del_data_lite.php` file is fairly similar; it starts by reopening the `mydatabase.db` file as before. It then executes the following SQLite query:

```
DROP TABLE recordeddata
```

As described in the *There's more...* section, this will remove the `recordeddata` table from the database. If the `response` isn't equal to 1, the action was not completed. The most likely reason for this is that the directory that contains the `mydatabase.db` file isn't writable by the web server (see the note in the *How to do it...* section about changing the file owner to `www-data`).

Finally, we provide another button that will take the user back to the `show_data_lite.php` page (which will show that the recorded data has now been cleared):

Remove all the data in the table.
Result: DELETED DATA

Press button to return to data display.
Return

Show_data_lite.php

There's more...

You may have noticed that this recipe has focused more on HTML and PHP than Python (yes, check the cover – this is still a book for Python programmers!). However, it is important to remember that a key part of engineering is integrating and combining different technologies to produce the desired results.

By design, Python lends itself well to this kind of task since it allows easy customization and integration with a huge range of other languages and modules. We could just do it all in Python but why not make use of the existing solutions, instead? After all, they are usually well documented, have undergone extensive testing, and often meet industry standards.

Security

SQL databases are used in many places to store a wide range of information, from product information to customer details. In such circumstances, users may be required to enter information that is then formed into SQL queries. In a poorly implemented system, a malicious user may be able to include additional SQL syntax in their response, allowing them to compromise the SQL database (perhaps by accessing sensitive information, altering it, or simply deleting it).

For example, when asking for a username within a web page, the user could enter the following text:

```
John; DELETE FROM Orders
```

If this was used directly to construct the SQL query, we would end up with the following:

```
SELECT * FROM Users WHERE UserName = John; DELETE FROM CurrentOrders
```

We have just allowed the attacker to delete everything in the CurrentOrders table!

Using user input to form part of SQL queries means we have to be careful what commands we allow to be executed. In this example, the user may be able to wipe out potentially important information, which could be very costly for a company and its reputation.

This technique is called SQL injection, and is easily protected against by using the parameters option of the SQLite execute() function. We can replace our Python SQLite query with a safer version, as follows:

```
sqlquery = "INSERT INTO %s (itm_name, itm_value) VALUES(?, ?)"
% (TABLE)
cursor.execute(sqlquery, (str(dataName), str(data[i])))
```

Instead of blindly building the SQL query, the SQLite module will first check that the provided parameters are valid values to enter into the database. Then, it will ensure that no additional SQL actions will result from inserting them into the command. Finally, the value of the dataName and data[i] parameters will be used to replace the ? characters to generate the final safe SQLite query.

Using MySQL instead

SQLite, which is used in this recipe, is just one of many SQL databases available. It is helpful for small projects that only require relatively small databases and minimal resources. However, for larger projects that require additional features (such as user accounts to control access and additional security), you can use alternatives, such as MySQL.

To use a different SQL database, you will need to adjust the Python code that we used to capture the entries using a suitable Python module.

For MySQL (`mysql-server`), we can use a Python-3-compatible library called
PyMySQL to interface with it. See the PyMySQL website
(`https://github.com/PyMySQL/PyMySQL`) for additional information about how to use
this library.

To use PHP with MySQL, you will also need PHP MySQL (`php5-mysql`); for more
information, see the excellent resource at W3 Schools
(`http://www.w3schools.com/php/php_mysql_connect.asp`).

You will notice that although there are small differences between SQL
implementations, the general concepts and commands should now be familiar to you,
whichever one you select.

Sensing and sending data to online services

In this section, we shall make use of an online service called Xively. The service
allows us to connect, transmit, and view data online. Xively makes use of a common
protocol that is used for transferring information over HTTP called **REpresentational
State Transfer (REST)**. REST is used by many services, such as Facebook and Twitter,
using various keys and access tokens to ensure data is transferred securely between
authorized applications and verified sites.

You can perform most REST operations (methods such as `POST`, `GET`, `SET`, and so on)
manually using a Python library called `requests`
(`http://docs.python-requests.org`).

However, it is often easier to make use of specific libraries available for the service
you intend to use. They will handle the authorization process and provide access
functions, and if the service changes, the library can be updated rather than your
code.

We will use the `xively-python` library, which provides Python functions to allow
us to easily interact with the site.

For details about the `xively-python` library, refer to
`http://xively.github.io/xively-python/`.

The data collected by Xively is shown in the following screenshot:

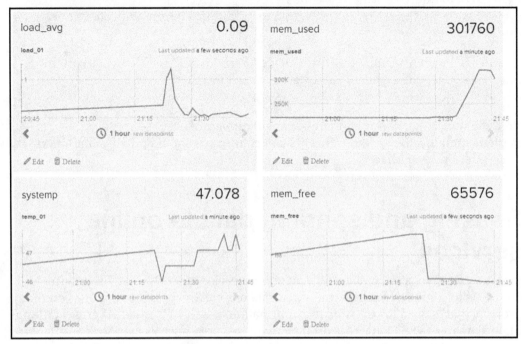

Xively collects and graphs data transferred using REST

Getting ready

You will need to create an account at www.xively.com, which we will use to receive our data. Go to the site and sign up for a free developer account:

Signing up and creating a Xively account

Once you have registered and verified your account, you can follow the instructions that will take you through a test drive example. This will demonstrate how you can link to data from your smartphone (gyroscopic data, location, and so on), which will give you a taste of what we can do with the Raspberry Pi.

When you log in, you will be taken to the **Development Devices** dashboard (located in the **WebTools** drop-down menu):

Adding a new device

Select **+Add Device** and fill in the details, giving your device a name and setting **Device** as **Private**.

You will now see the control page for your remote device, which contains all the information you need to connect it and also where your data will be displayed:

```
API Keys

Auto-generated MyDevice device key for
feed 399948883

CcRxJbP5TuHp1PiOGVrN2kTGeXVsb6QZRJU236v6PjO
dtzze
permissions  READ,UPDATE,CREATE,DELETE
private accesss
```

Example API key and feed number (this will be unique for your device)

Although there is a lot of information on this page, you only need two key pieces of information:

- The API key (which is the long code in the `API Keys` section), as follows:

      `API_KEY = CcRxJbP5TuHp1PiOGVrN2kTGeXVsb6QZRJU236v6PjOdtzze`

- The feed number (referred to in the `API Keys` section and also listed at the top of the page), as follows:

      `FEED_ID = 399948883`

Now that we have the details we need to connect with Xively, we can focus on the Raspberry Pi side of things.

We will use `pip-3.2` to install Xively, as follows:

```
sudo pip-3.2 install xively-python
```

Ensure that the following is reported:

```
Successfully installed xively-python requests
```

You are now ready to send some data from your Raspberry Pi.

How to do it...

Create the following script, called `xivelyLog.py`. Ensure that you set FEED_ID and API_KEY within the code to match the device you created:

```python
#!/usr/bin/env python3
#xivelylog.py
import xively
import time
import datetime
import requests
from random import randint
import data_local as dataDevice

# Set the FEED_ID and API_KEY from your account
FEED_ID = 399948883
API_KEY = "CcRxJbP5TuHp1PiOGVrN2kTGeXVsb6QZRJU236v6PjOdtzze"
api = xively.XivelyAPIClient(API_KEY) # initialize api client
DEBUG=True

myData = dataDevice.device()
myDataNames=myData.getName()

def get_datastream(feed,name,tags):
  try:
    datastream = feed.datastreams.get(name)
    if DEBUG:print ("Found existing datastream")
    return datastream
  except:
    if DEBUG:print ("Creating new datastream")
    datastream = feed.datastreams.create(name, tags=tags)
    return datastream

def run():
  print ("Connecting to Xively")
  feed = api.feeds.get(FEED_ID)
  if DEBUG:print ("Got feed" + str(feed))
  datastreams=[]
  for dataName in myDataNames:
    dstream = get_datastream(feed,dataName,dataName)
    if DEBUG:print ("Got %s datastream:%s"%(dataName,dstream))
    datastreams.append(dstream)

  while True:
    data=myData.getNew()
    for idx,dataValue in enumerate(data):
      if DEBUG:
```

```
        print ("Updating %s: %s" % (dataName,dataValue))
      datastreams[idx].current_value = dataValue
      datastreams[idx].at = datetime.datetime.utcnow()
    try:
      for ds in datastreams:
        ds.update()
    except requests.HTTPError as e:
      print ("HTTPError({0}): {1}".format(e.errno, e.strerror))
    time.sleep(60)

run()
#End
```

How it works...

First, we initialize the Xively API client, to which we supply the API_KEY (this authorizes us to send data to the Xively device we created previously). Next, we use FEED_ID to link us to the specific feed we want to send the data to. Finally, we request the data stream to connect to (if it doesn't already exist in the feed, the get_datastream() function will create one for us).

For each data stream in the feed, we supply a name function and tags (these are keywords that help us identify the data; we can use our data names for this).

Once we have defined our data streams, we enter the main loop. Here, we gather our data values from dataDevice. We then set the current_value function and also the timestamp of the data for each data item and apply them to our data stream objects.

Finally, when all the data is ready, we update each of the data streams and the data is sent to Xively, appearing within a few moments on the dashboard of the device.

We can log in to our Xively account and view data as it comes in, using a standard web browser. This provides the means to send data and remotely monitor it anywhere in the world (perhaps from several Raspberry Pis at once, if required). The service even supports the creation of triggers that can send additional messages back if certain items go out of expected ranges, reach specific values, or match set criteria. The triggers can, in turn, be used to control other devices or raise alerts, and so on. They can also be used in other platforms, such as ThingSpeak or plot.ly.

See also

The AirPi Air Quality and Weather project (http://airpi.es) shows you how to add your own sensors or use their AirPi kit to create your own air quality and weather station (with data logging to your own Xively account). The site also allows you to share your Xively data feeds with others around the world.

9
Building Neural Network Modules for Optical Character Recognition

This chapter presents the following topics:

- Using the **Optical Character Recognition (OCR)** system
- Visualizing optical characters using the software
- Building an optical character recognizer using neural networks
- Application of the OCR system

Introduction

The OCR system is used to convert images of text into letters, words, and sentences. It is widely used in various fields to convert/extract the information from the image. It is also used in signature recognition, automated data evaluation, and security systems. It is commercially used to validate data records, passport documents, invoices, bank statements, computerized receipts, business cards, printouts of static data, and so on. OCR is a field of research in pattern recognition, artificial intelligence, and computer vision.

Visualizing optical characters

Optical character visualization is a common method of digitizing printed texts so that such texts can be electronically edited, searched, stored compactly, and displayed online. Currently, they are widely used in cognitive computing, machine translation, text-to-speech conversion, text mining, and so on.

How to do it...

1. Import the following packages:

```
import os
import sys
import cv2
import numpy as np
```

2. Load the input data:

```
in_file = 'words.data'
```

3. Define the visualization parameters:

```
scale_factor = 10
s_index = 6
e_index = -1
h, w = 16, 8
```

4. Loop until you encounter the *Esc* key:

```
with open(in_file, 'r') as f:
  for line in f.readlines():
    information = np.array([255*float(x) for x in
line.split('t')[s_index:e_index]])
    image = np.reshape(information, (h,w))
    image_scaled = cv2.resize(image, None, fx=scale_factor,
fy=scale_factor)
    cv2.imshow('Image', image_scaled)
    a = cv2.waitKey()
    if a == 10:
      break
```

5. Type `python visualize_character.py` to execute the code:

```
manju@manju-HP-Notebook:~/Documents$ python visualize_characters.py
```

6. The result obtained when `visualize_character.py` is executed is shown here:

Building an optical character recognizer using neural networks

This section describes the neural network based optical character identification scheme.

How to do it...

1. Import the following packages:

```
import numpy as np
import neurolab as nl
```

2. Read the input file:

```
in_file = 'words.data'
```

3. Consider 20 data points to build the neural network based system:

```
# Number of datapoints to load from the input file
num_of_datapoints = 20
```

4. Represent the distinct characters:

```
original_labels = 'omandig'
# Number of distinct characters
num_of_charect = len(original_labels)
```

5. Use 90% of data for training the neural network and the remaining 10% for testing:

```
train_param = int(0.9 * num_of_datapoints)
test_param = num_of_datapoints - train_param
```

6. Define the dataset extraction parameters:

```
s_index = 6
e_index = -1
```

7. Build the dataset:

```
information = []
labels = []
with open(in_file, 'r') as f:
  for line in f.readlines():
    # Split the line tabwise
    list_of_values = line.split('t')
```

8. Implement an error check to confirm the characters:

```
if list_of_values[1] not in original_labels:
  continue
```

9. Extract the label and attach it to the main list:

```
label = np.zeros((num_of_charect , 1))
label[original_labels.index(list_of_values[1])] = 1
labels.append(label)
```

10. Extract the character and add it to the main list:

```
extract_char = np.array([float(x) for x in
list_of_values[s_index:e_index]])
    information.append(extract_char)
```

11. Exit the loop once the required dataset has been loaded:

```
if len(information) >= num_of_datapoints:
    break
```

12. Convert information and labels to NumPy arrays:

```
information = np.array(information)
labels = np.array(labels).reshape(num_of_datapoints,
num_of_charect)
```

13. Extract the number of dimensions:

```
num_dimension = len(information[0])
```

14. Create and train the neural network:

```
neural_net = nl.net.newff([[0, 1] for _ in
range(len(information[0]))], [128, 16, num_of_charect])
neural_net.trainf = nl.train.train_gd
error = neural_net.train(information[:train_param,:],
labels[:train_param,:], epochs=10000, show=100, goal=0.01)
```

15. Predict the output for the test input:

```
p_output = neural_net.sim(information[train_param:, :])
print "nTesting on unknown data:"
  for i in range(test_param):
    print "nOriginal:", original_labels[np.argmax(labels[i])]
    print "Predicted:",
original_labels[np.argmax(p_output[i])]
```

16. The result obtained when `optical_character_recognition.py` is executed is shown in the following screenshot:

```
manju@manju-HP-Notebook:~/Documents$ python optical_charecter_recognition.py
Epoch: 100; Error: 7.872634174;
Epoch: 200; Error: 6.9598487099;
Epoch: 300; Error: 3.69162674976;
Epoch: 400; Error: 1.28277091966;
Epoch: 500; Error: 1.46603655023;
Epoch: 600; Error: 1.14465834785;
Epoch: 700; Error: 1.54577830363;
Epoch: 800; Error: 0.739356427701;
Epoch: 900; Error: 0.997718413015;
Epoch: 1000; Error: 0.496692038186;
Epoch: 1100; Error: 0.445750401977;
Epoch: 1200; Error: 0.433701255714;
Epoch: 1300; Error: 0.139799043752;
Epoch: 1400; Error: 0.162959312047;
Epoch: 1500; Error: 0.0415268342145;
Epoch: 1600; Error: 0.0218423266053;
Epoch: 1700; Error: 0.0242494495199;
Epoch: 1800; Error: 0.0335171101107;
Epoch: 1900; Error: 0.0211101742172;
Epoch: 2000; Error: 0.013270542884;
Epoch: 2100; Error: 0.0107846817182;
Epoch: 2200; Error: 0.0114038385711;
Epoch: 2300; Error: 0.0136432946878;
Epoch: 2400; Error: 0.0142994078988;
Epoch: 2500; Error: 0.0125231282293;
Epoch: 2600; Error: 0.0112677556235;
Epoch: 2700; Error: 0.0182870005799;
Epoch: 2800; Error: 0.0223704819025;
Epoch: 2900; Error: 0.0109798464676;
The goal of learning is reached

Testing on unknown data:

Original: o
Predicted: o

Original: m
Predicted: n
```

How it works...

A neural network-supported optical character recognition system is constructed to extract the text from the images. This procedure involves training the neural network system, testing, and validation using the character dataset.

Readers can refer to the article *Neural network based optical character recognition system* to learn the basic principles behind OCR: `http://ieeexplore.ieee.org/document/6419976/`.

See also

Please refer to the following:

- `https://searchcontentmanagement.techtarget.com/definition/OCR-optical-character-recognition`
- `https://thecodpast.org/2015/09/top-5-ocr-apps/`
- `https://convertio.co/ocr/`

Applications of an OCR system

An OCR system is widely used to convert/extract the text (the alphabet and numbers) from an image. The OCR system is widely used to validate business documents, in automatic number plate recognition, and in key character extraction from documents. It is also used to make electronic images of printed documents searchable and to build assistive technology for blind and visually impaired users.

10
Arithmetic Operations, Loops, and Blinky Lights

Now let's take a look at this chapter, where we will review arithmetic operations and variables in Python. We will also discuss strings and accepting user inputs in Python. You will learn about the Raspberry Pi's GPIO and its features and write code in Python that makes an LED blink using the Raspberry Pi Zero's GPIO. We will also discuss a practical application of controlling the Raspberry Pi's GPIO.

In this chapter, we will cover the following topics:

- Arithmetic operations in Python
- Bitwise operators in Python
- Logical operators in Python
- Data types and variables in Python
- Loops in Python
- Raspberry Pi Zero's GPIO interface.

Hardware required for this chapter

In this chapter, we will be discussing examples where we will be controlling the Raspberry Pi's GPIO. We will need a breadboard, jumper wires, LEDs, and some resistors (330 or 470 Ohms) to discuss these examples.

We will also need some optional hardware that we will discuss in the last section of this chapter.

Arithmetic operations

Python enables performing all the standard arithmetic operations. Let's launch the Python interpreter and learn more:

- **Addition**: Two numbers can be added using the + operand. The result is printed on the screen. Try the following example using the python interpreter:

  ```
  >>>123+456
  579
  ```

- **Subtraction**: Two numbers can be added using the – operand:

  ```
  >>>456-123
  333
  >>>123-456
  -333
  ```

- **Multiplication**: Two numbers can be multiplied as follows:

  ```
  >>>123*456
  56088
  ```

- **Division**: Two numbers can be divided as follows:

  ```
  >>>456/22
  20.727272727272727
  >>>456/2.0
  228.0
  >>>int(456/228)
  2
  ```

- **Modulus operator**: In Python, the modulus operator (%) returns the remainder of a division operation:

  ```
  >>>4%2
  0
  >>>3%2
  1
  ```

- The **floor operator** (//) is the opposite of the modulus operator. This operator returns the floor of the quotient, that is, the integer result, and discards the fractions:

```
>>>9//7
1
>>>7//3
2
>>>79//25
3
```

Bitwise operators in Python

In Python, it is possible to perform bit-level operations on numbers. This is especially helpful while parsing information from certain sensors. For example, Some sensors share their output at a certain frequency. When a new data point is available, a certain bit is set indicating that the data is available. Bitwise operators can be used to check whether a particular bit is set before retrieving the datapoint from the sensor.

If you are interested in a deep dive on bitwise operators, we recommend getting started at https://en.wikipedia.org/wiki/Bitwise_operation.

Consider the numbers 3 and 2 whose binary equivalents are 011 and 010, respectively. Let's take a look at different operators that perform the operation on every bit of the number:

- **The AND operator**: The AND operator is used to perform the AND operation on two numbers. Try this using the Python interpreter:

```
>>>3&2
2
```

This is equivalent to the following AND operation:

```
0 1 1 &
0 1 0
--------
0 1 0 (the binary representation of the number 2)
```

- **The OR operator**: The OR operator is used to perform the OR operation on two numbers as follows:

```
>>>3|2
3
```

This is equivalent to the following OR operation:

```
0 1 1 OR
0 1 0
--------
0 1 1 (the binary representation of the number 3)
```

- **The NOT operator**: The NOT operator flips the bits of a number. see the following example:

```
>>>~1
-2
```

In the preceding example, the bits are flipped, that is, 1 as 0 and 0 as 1. So, the binary representation of 1 is 0001 and when the bitwise NOT operation is performed, the result is 1110. The interpreter returns the result as -2 because negative numbers are stored as their *two's complement*. The two's complement of 1 is -2.

 For a better understanding of two's complement and so on, we recommend reading the following articles, https://wiki.python.org/moin/BitwiseOperators and https://en.wikipedia.org/wiki/Two's_complement.

- **The XOR operator**: An exclusive OR operation can be performed as follows:

```
>>>3^2
1
```

- **Left shift operator**: The left shift operator enables shifting the bits of a given value to the left by the desired number of places. For example, bit shifting the number 3 to the left gives us the number 6. The binary representation of the number 3 is 0011. Left shifting the bits by one position will give us 0110, that is, the number 6:

```
>>>3<<1
6
```

- **Right shift operator**: The right shift operator enables shifting the bits of a given value to the right by the desired number of places. Launch the command-line interpreter and try this yourself. What happens when you bit shift the number 6 to the right by one position?

Logical operators

Logical operators are used to check different conditions and execute the code accordingly. For example, detecting a button interfaced to the Raspberry Pi's GPIO being pressed and executing a specific task as a consequence. Let's discuss the basic logical operators:

- **EQUAL**: The EQUAL (==) operator is used to compare if two values are equal:

```
>>>3==3
True
>>>3==2
False
```

- **NOT EQUAL**: The NOT EQUAL (!=) operator compares two values and returns True if they are not equal:

```
>>>3!=2
True
>>>2!=2
False
```

- **GREATER THAN**: This operator (>) returns True if one value is greater than the other value:

```
>>>3>2
True
>>>2>3
False
```

- **LESS THAN**: This operator compares two values and returns `True` if one value is smaller than the other:

```
>>>2<3
True
>>>3<2
False
```

- **GREATER THAN OR EQUAL TO (>=)**: This operator compares two values and returns `True` if one value is greater/bigger than or equal to the other value:

```
>>>4>=3
True
>>>3>=3
True
>>>2>=3
False
```

- **LESS THAN OR EQUAL TO (<=)**: This operator compares two values and returns `True` if one value is smaller than or equal to the other value:

```
>>>2<=2
True
>>>2<=3
True
>>>3<=2
False
```

Data types and variables in Python

In Python, **variables** are used to store a result or a value in the computer's memory during the execution of a program. Variables enable easy access to a specific location on the computer's memory and enables writing user-readable code.

For example, let's consider a scenario where a person wants a new ID card from an office or a university. The person would be asked to fill out an application form with relevant information, including their name, department, and emergency contact information. The form would have the requisite fields. This would enable the office manager to refer to the form while creating a new ID card.

Similarly, variables simplify code development by providing means to store information in the computer's memory. It would be very difficult to write code if one had to write code keeping the storage memory map in mind. For example, it is easier to use the variable called name rather than a specific memory address like `0x3745092`.

There are different kinds of data types in Python. Let's review the different data types:

- In general, names, street addresses, and so on are a combination of alphanumeric characters. In Python, they are stored as *strings*. Strings in Python are represented and stored in variables as follows:

```
>>>name = 'John Smith'
>>>address = '123 Main Street'
```

- *Numbers* in Python could be stored as follows:

```
>>>age = 29
>>>employee_id = 123456
>>>height = 179.5
>>>zip_code = 94560
```

- Python also enables storing *boolean* variables. For example, a person's organ donor status can be either as `True` or `False`:

```
>>>organ_donor = True
```

- It is possible to *assign* values to multiple variables at the same time:

```
>>>a = c= 1
>>>b = a
```

- A variable may be *deleted* as follows:

```
>>>del(a)
```

There are other data types in Python, including lists, tuples, and dictionaries. We will discuss this in detail in the next chapter.

Reading inputs from the user

Now, we will discuss a simple program where we ask the user to enter two numbers and the program returns the sum of two numbers. For now, we are going to pretend that the user always provides a valid input.

In Python, user input to a Python program can be provided using the `input()` function (https://docs.python.org/3/library/functions.html#input):

```
var = input("Enter the first number: ")
```

In the preceding example, we are making use of the `input()` function to seek the user's input of the number. The `input()` function takes the prompt (`"Enter the first number: "`) as an argument and returns the user input. In this example, the user input is stored in the variable, `var`. In order to add two numbers, we make use of the `input()` function to request user to provide two numbers as input:

```
var1 = input("Enter the first number: ")
var2 = input("Enter the second number: ")
total = int(var1) + int(var2)
print("The sum is %d" % total)
```

We are making use of the `input()` function to seek user input on two numbers. In this case, the user number is stored in `var1` and `var2`, respectively.
The user input is a string. We need to convert them into integers before adding them. We can convert a string to an integer using the `int()` function (https://docs.python.org/3/library/functions.html#int).

The `int()` function takes the string as an argument and returns the converted integer. The converted integers are added and stored in the variable, `total`. The preceding example is available for download along with this chapter as `input_function.py`.

 If the user input is invalid, the `int()` function will throw an exception indicating that an error has occurred. Hence, we assumed that user inputs are valid in this example. In a later chapter, we will discuss catching exceptions that are caused by invalid inputs.

The following snapshot shows the program output:

```
pi@raspberrypi: ~/Documents/pywpi/chapter_2
File  Edit  Tabs  Help
pi@raspberrypi:~/Documents/pywpi/chapter_2 $ python3 input_function.py
Enter the first number: 3
Enter the second number: 2
The sum is 5
```

The input_function.py output

The formatted string output

Let's revisit the example discussed in the previous section. We printed the result as follows:

```
print("The sum is %d" % total)
```

In Python, it is possible to format a string to display the result. In the earlier example, we make use of %d to indicate that it is a placeholder for an integer variable. This enables printing the string with the integer. Along with the string that is passed an argument to the print() function, the variable that needs to be printed is also passed an argument. In the earlier example, the variables are passed using the % operator. It is also possible to pass multiple variables:

```
print("The sum of %d and %d is %d" % (var1, var2, total))
```

It is also possible to format a string as follows:

```
print("The sum of 3 and 2 is {total}".format(total=5))
```

The str.format() method

The `format()` method enables formatting the string using braces (`{ }`) as placeholders. In the preceding example, we use `total` as a placeholder and use the format method of the string class to fill each place holder.

An exercise for the reader

Make use of the `format()` method to format a string with more than one variable.

Let's build a console/command-line application that takes inputs from the user and print it on the screen. Let's create a new file named `input_test.py`, (available along with this chapter's downloads) take some user inputs and print them on the screen:

```
name = input("What is your name? ")
address = input("What is your address? ")
age = input("How old are you? ")

print("My name is " + name)
print("I am " + age + " years old")
print("My address is " + address)
```

Execute the program and see what happens:

```
pi@raspberrypi:~/Documents/pywpi/chapter_2 $ python3 input_test.py
What is your name? Sai
What is your address? 123 Main Street, Newark, CA
How old are you? 29
My name is Sai
I am 29 years old
My address is 123 Main Street, Newark, CA
```

The input_test.py output

The preceding example is available for download along with this chapter as `input_test.py`.

Another exercise for the reader

Repeat the earlier example using the string formatting techniques.

Concatenating strings

In the preceding example, we printed the user inputs in combination with another string. For example, we took the user input name and printed the sentence as My name is Sai. The process of appending one string to another is called **concatenation**.

In Python, strings can be concatenated by adding + between two strings:

```
name = input("What is your name? ")
print("My name is " + name)
```

It is possible to concatenate two strings, but it is not possible to concatenate an integer. Let's consider the following example:

```
id = 5
print("My id is " + id)
```

It would throw an error implying that integers and strings cannot be combined:

```
Traceback (most recent call last):
  File "<stdin>", line 1, in <module>
TypeError: Can't convert 'int' object to str implicitly
```

An exception

It is possible to convert an integer to string and concatenate it to another string:

```
print("My id is " + str(id))
```

This would give the following result:

```
>>> print("My id is " + str(id))
My id is 5
```

Loops in Python

Sometimes, a specific task has to be repeated several times. In such cases, we could use **loops**. In Python, there are two types of loops, namely the `for` loop and `while` loop. Let's review them with specific examples.

A for loop

In Python, a `for` loop is used to execute a task for *n* times. A for loop iterates through each element of a sequence. This sequence could be a dictionary, list, or any other iterator. For example, let's discuss an example where we execute a loop:

```python
for i in range(0, 10):
    print("Loop execution no: ", i)
```

In the preceding example, the `print` statement is executed 10 times:

```
Loop execution no: 0
Loop execution no: 1
Loop execution no: 2
Loop execution no: 3
Loop execution no: 4
Loop execution no: 5
Loop execution no: 6
Loop execution no: 7
Loop execution no: 8
Loop execution no: 9
```

In order to execute the `print` task 10 times, the `range()` function (https://docs.python.org/2/library/functions.html#range) was used. The `range` function generates a list of numbers for a start and stop values that are passed as an arguments to the function. In this case, 0 and 10 are passed as arguments to the `range()` function. This returns a list containing numbers from 0 to 9. The `for` loop iterates through the code block for each element in steps of 1. The `range` function can also generate a list of numbers in steps of 2. This is done by passing the start value, stop value, and the step value as arguments to the `range()` function:

```python
for i in range(0, 20, 2):
    print("Loop execution no: ", i)
```

In this example, 0 is the start value, 20 is the stop value, and 2 is the step value. This generates a list of 10 numbers in steps of two:

```
Loop execution no: 0
Loop execution no: 2
Loop execution no: 4
Loop execution no: 6
Loop execution no: 8
Loop execution no: 10
Loop execution no: 12
Loop execution no: 14
Loop execution no: 16
Loop execution no: 18
```

The range function can be used to count down from a given number. Let's say we would like to count down from 10 to 1:

```
for i in range(10, 0, -1):
    print("Count down no: ", i)
```

The output would be something like:

```
Count down no:  10
Count down no:  9
Count down no:  8
Count down no:  7
Count down no:  6
Count down no:  5
Count down no:  4
Count down no:  3
Count down no:  2
Count down no:  1
```

The general syntax of the range function is range(start, stop, step_count). It generates a sequence of numbers from start to n-1 where n is the stop value.

Indentation

Note the *indentation* in the for loop block:

```
for i in range(10, 1, -1):
    print("Count down no: ", i)
```

Python executes the block of code under the for loop statement. It is one of the features of the Python programming language. It executes any piece of code under the for loop as long as it has same level of indentation:

```
for i in range(0,10):
    #start of block
    print("Hello")
    #end of block
```

The indentation has the following two uses:

- It makes the code readable
- It helps us identify the block of code to be executed in a loop

It is important to pay attention to indentation in Python as it directly affects how a piece of code is executed.

Nested loops

In Python, it is possible to implement *a loop within a loop*. For example, let's say we have to print x and y coordinates of a map. We can use nested loops to implement this:

```
for x in range(0,3):
    for y in range(0,3):
        print(x,y)
```

The expected output is:

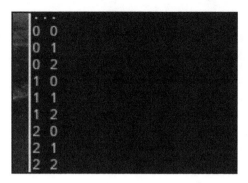

Be careful about code indentation in nested loops as it may throw errors. Consider the following example:

```
for x in range(0,10):
    for y in range(0,10):
    print(x,y)
```

The Python interpreter would throw the following error:

```
SyntaxError: expected an indented block
```

This is visible in the following screenshot:

```
>>> for x in range(0, 10):
...       for y in range(0, 10):
...       print(x,y)
  File "<stdin>", line 3
    print(x,y)
        ^
IndentationError: expected an indented block
```

Hence, it is important to pay attention to indentation in Python (especially nested loops) to successfully execute the code. IDLE's text editor automatically indents code as you write them. This should aid with understanding indentation in Python.

A while loop

while loops are used when a specific task is supposed to be executed until a specific condition is met. while loops are commonly used to execute code in an infinite loop. Let's look at a specific example where we would like to print the value of i from 0 to 9:

```
i=0
while i<10:
   print("The value of i is ",i)
   i+=1
```

Inside the while loop, we increment i by 1 for every iteration. The value of i is incremented as follows:

```
i += 1
```

This is equivalent to i = i+1.

This example would execute the code until the value of i is less than 10. It is also possible to execute something in an infinite loop:

```
i=0
while True:
   print("The value of i is ",i)
   i+=1
```

The execution of this infinite loop can be stopped by pressing *Ctrl + C* on your keyboard.

It is also possible to have nested while loops:

```
i=0
j=0
while i<10:
   while j<10:
     print("The value of i,j is ",i,",",j)
     i+=1
     j+=1
```

Similar to `for` loops, `while` loops also rely on the indented code block to execute a piece of code.

Python enables printing a combination of strings and integers as long as they are presented as arguments to the `print` function separated by commas. In the earlier-mentioned example, `The value of i,j is, i` are arguments to the `print` function. You will learn more about functions and arguments in the next chapter. This feature enables formatting the output string to suit our needs.

Raspberry Pi's GPIO

The Raspberry Pi Zero comes with a 40-pin GPIO header. Out of these 40 pins, we can use 26 pins either to read inputs (from sensors) or control outputs. The other pins are power supply pins (**5V**, **3.3V**, and **Ground** pins):

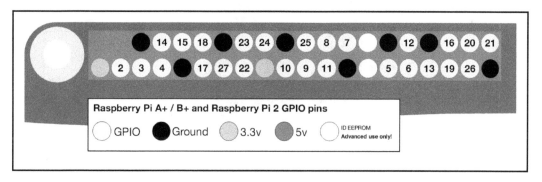

Raspberry Pi Zero GPIO mapping (source: https://www.raspberrypi.org/documentation/usage/gpio-plus-and-raspi2/README.md)

We can use up to 26 pins of the Raspberry Pi's GPIO to interface appliances and control them. But, there are certain pins that have an alternative function.

The earlier image shows the mapping of the Raspberry Pi's GPIO pins. The numbers in the circle correspond to the pin numbers on the Raspberry Pi's processor. For example, GPIO pin **2** (second pin from the left on the bottom row) corresponds to the GPIO pin **2** on the Raspberry Pi's processor and not the physical pin location on the GPIO header.

In the beginning, it might be confusing to try and understand the pin mapping. Keep a GPIO pin handout (available for download along with this chapter) for your reference. It takes some time to get used to the GPIO pin mapping of the Raspberry Pi Zero.

 The Raspberry Pi Zero's GPIO pins are 3.3V tolerant, that is, if a voltage greater than 3.3V is applied to the pin, it may permanently damage the pin. When set to *high*, the pins are set to 3.3V and 0V when the pins are set to low.

Blinky lights

Let's discuss an example where we make use of the Raspberry Pi Zero's GPIO. We will interface an LED to the Raspberry Pi Zero and make it blink *on* and *off* with a 1-second interval.

Let's wire up the Raspberry Pi zero to get started:

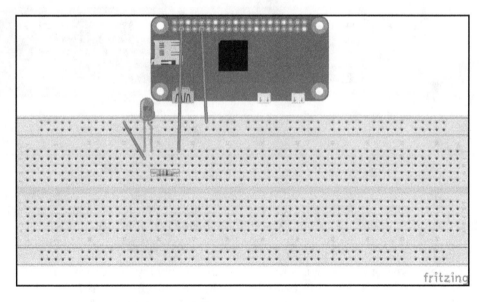

Blinky schematic generated using Fritzing

In the preceding schematic, the GPIO pin 2 is connected to the anode (the longest leg) of the LED. The cathode of the LED is connected to the ground pin of the Raspberry Pi Zero. A 330 Ohm current limiting resistor is also used to limit the flow of the current.

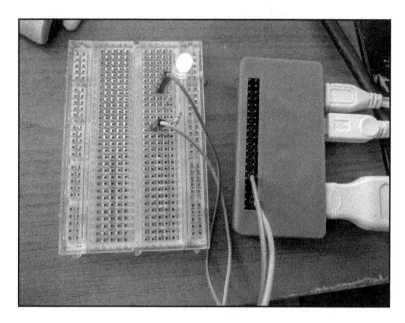

Breadboard connections to the Raspberry Pi Zero

Code

We will make use of the `python3-gpiozero` library (`https://gpiozero.readthedocs.io/en/v1.3.1/`). The **Raspbian Jessie** OS image comes with the pre-installed library. It is very simple to use, and it is the best option to get started as a beginner. It supports a standard set of devices that helps us get started easily.

For example, in order to interface an LED, we need to import the `LED` class from the `gpiozero` library:

```
from gpiozero import LED
```

We will be turning the LED *on* and *off* at a 1-second interval. In order to do so, we will be *importing* the `time` library. In Python, we need to import a library to make use of it. Since we interfaced the LED to the GPIO pin 2, let's make a mention of that in our code:

```
import time

led = LED(2)
```

We just created a variable named `led` and defined that we will be making use of GPIO pin 2 in the `LED` class. Let's make use of a `while` loop to turn the LED on and off with a 1-second interval.

The `gpiozero` library's LED class comes with functions named `on()` and `off()` to set the GPIO pin 2 to high and low, respectively:

```
while True:
    led.on()
    time.sleep(1)
    led.off()
    time.sleep(1)
```

In Python's time library, there is a `sleep` function that enables introducing a 1-second delay between turning on/off the LED. This is executed in an infinite loop! We just built a practical example using the Raspberry Pi Zero.

Putting all the code together in a file named `blinky.py` (available for download along with this book), run the code from the command-line terminal (alternatively, you may use IDLE3):

```
python3 blinky.py
```

The applications of GPIO control

Now that we have implemented our first example, let's discuss some possible applications of being able to control the GPIO. We could use the Raspberry Pi's GPIO to control the lights in our homes. We will make use of the same example to control a table lamp!

There is a product called the **PowerSwitch Tail**
II (`http://www.powerswitchtail.com/Pages/default.aspx`) that enables interfacing
AC appliances like a table lamp to a Raspberry Pi. The PowerSwitch Tail comes with
control pins (that can take a 3.3V high signal) that could be used to turn on/off a lamp.
The switch comes with the requisite circuitry/protection to interface it directly to a
Raspberry Pi Zero:

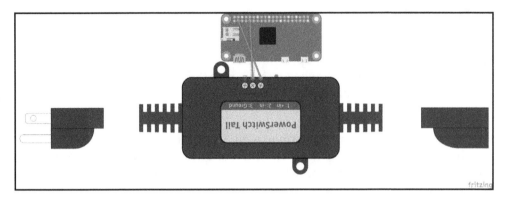

The Pi Zero interfaced to the PowerSwitch Tail II

Let's take the same example from the previous section and connect the GPIO pin 2 to
the **+in** pin of the PowerSwitch Tail. Let's connect the ground pin of the Raspberry Pi
Zero's GPIO header to the PowerSwitch Tail's **-in** pain. The PowerSwitch Tail should
be connected to the AC mains. The lamp should be connected to the AC output of the
switch. If we use the same piece of code and connect a lamp to the PowerSwitch Tail,
we should be able to turn on/off with a 1-second interval.

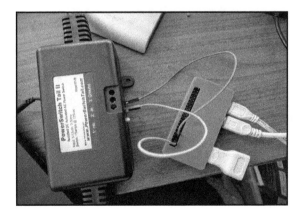

PowerSwitch Tail II connected to a Raspberry Pi Zero

This appliance control using the LED blinking code is just an example. It is not recommended to turn on/off a table lamp at such short intervals.

Summary

In this chapter, we reviewed the integers, boolean, and string data types as well as arithmetic operations and logical operators in Python. We also discussed accepting user inputs and loops. We introduced ourselves to the Raspberry Pi Zero's GPIO and discussed an LED blinking example. We took the same example to control a table lamp!

Have you heard of the chat application named *Slack*? How about controlling a table lamp at home from your laptop at work? If that piques your interest, work with us toward that over the next few chapters.

11
Conditional Statements, Functions, and Lists

In this chapter, we will build upon what you learned in the previous chapter. You will learn about conditional statements and how to make use of logical operators to check conditions using conditional statements. Next, you will learn to write simple functions in Python and discuss interfacing inputs to the Raspberry Pi's GPIO header using a tactile switch (momentary push button). We will also discuss motor control (this is a run-up to the final project) using the Raspberry Pi Zero and control the motors using the switch inputs. Let's get to it!

In this chapter, we will discuss the following topics:

- Conditional statements in Python
    - Using conditional inputs to take actions based on GPIO pin states
  - Breaking out of loops using conditional statement
- Functions in Python
    - GPIO callback functions
- Motor control in Python

Conditional statements

In Python, conditional statements are used to determine if a specific condition is met by testing whether a condition is `true` or `false`. Conditional statements are used to determine how a program is executed. For example, conditional statements could be used to determine whether it is time to turn on the lights. The syntax is as follows:

```
if condition_is_true:

    do_something()
```

The condition is usually tested using a logical operator, and the set of tasks under the indented block is executed. Let's consider the example, `check_address_if_statement.py` (available for download with this chapter) where the user input to a program needs to be verified using a `yes` or `no` question:

```
check_address = input("Is your address correct(yes/no)? ")
if check_address == "yes":
  print("Thanks. Your address has been saved")
if check_address == "no":
  del(address)
  print("Your address has been deleted. Try again")
```

In this example, the program expects a `yes` or `no` input. If the user provides the input `yes`, the condition `if check_address == "yes"` is `true`, the message `Your address has been saved` is printed on the screen.

Likewise, if the user input is `no`, the program executes the indented code block under the logical test condition `if check_address == "no"` and deletes the variable `address`.

An if-else statement

In the preceding example, we used an `if` statement to test each condition. In Python, there is an alternative option named the `if-else` statement. The `if-else` statement enables testing an alternative condition if the main condition is not `true`:

```
check_address = input("Is your address correct(yes/no)? ")
if check_address == "yes":
  print("Thanks. Your address has been saved")
else:
  del(address)
  print("Your address has been deleted. Try again")
```

In this example, if the user input is yes, the indented code block under if is executed. Otherwise, the code block under else is executed.

if-elif-else statement

In the preceding example, the program executes any piece of code under the else block for any user input other than yes that is if the user pressed the return key without providing any input or provided random characters instead of no, the if-elif-else statement works as follows:

```
check_address = input("Is your address correct(yes/no)? ")
if check_address == "yes":
  print("Thanks. Your address has been saved")
elif check_address == "no":
  del(address)
  print("Your address has been deleted. Try again")
else:
  print("Invalid input. Try again")
```

If the user input is yes, the indented code block under the if statement is executed. If the user input is no, the indented code block under elif (*else-if*) is executed. If the user input is something else, the program prints the message: Invalid input. Try again.

It is important to note that the code block indentation determines the block of code that needs to be executed when a specific condition is met. We recommend modifying the indentation of the conditional statement block and find out what happens to the program execution. This will help understand the importance of indentation in Python.

In the three examples that we discussed so far, it could be noted that an if statement does not need to be complemented by an else statement. The else and elif statements need to have a preceding if statement or the program execution would result in an error.

Breaking out of loops

Conditional statements can be used to break out of a loop execution (`for` loop and `while` loop). When a specific condition is met, an `if` statement can be used to break out of a loop:

```
i = 0
while True:
  print("The value of i is ", i)
  i += 1
  if i > 100:
    break
```

In the preceding example, the `while` loop is executed in an infinite loop. The value of `i` is incremented and printed on the screen. The program breaks out of the `while` loop when the value of `i` is greater than `100` and the value of `i` is printed from 1 to 100.

The applications of conditional statements: executing tasks using GPIO

In the previous chapter, we discussed interfacing outputs to the Raspberry Pi's GPIO. Let's discuss an example where a simple push button is pressed. A button press is detected by reading the GPIO pin state. We are going to make use of conditional statements to execute a task based on the GPIO pin state.

Let us connect a button to the Raspberry Pi's GPIO. All you need to get started are a button, pull-up resistor, and a few jumper wires. The figure given later shows an illustration on connecting the push button to the Raspberry Pi Zero. One of the push button's terminals is connected to the ground pin of the Raspberry Pi Zero's GPIO pin.

The schematic of the button's interface is shown here:

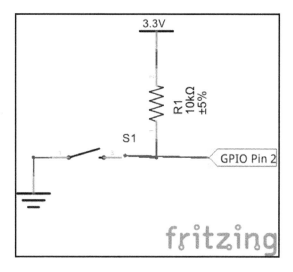

Raspberry Pi GPIO schematic

The other terminal of the push button is pulled up to 3.3V using a 10 K resistor. The junction of the push button terminal and the 10 K resistor is connected to the GPIO pin 2 (refer to the BCM GPIO pin map shared in the earlier chapter).

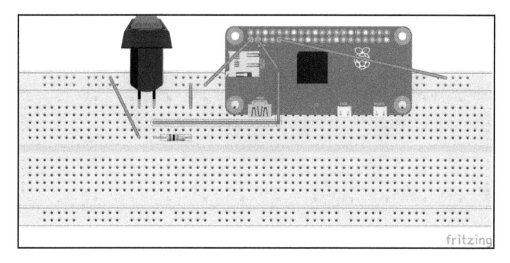

Interfacing the push button to the Raspberry Pi Zero's GPIO - an image generated using Fritzing

Let's review the code required to review the button state. We make use of loops and conditional statements to read the button inputs using the Raspberry Pi Zero.

We will be making use of the `gpiozero` library introduced in the previous chapter. The code sample for this section is `GPIO_button_test.py` and available for download along with this chapter.

In a later chapter, we will discuss **object-oriented programming (OOP)**. For now, let's briefly discuss the concept of classes for this example. A **class** in Python is a blueprint that contains all the attributes that define an object. For example, the `Button` class of the `gpiozero` library contains all attributes required to interface a button to the Raspberry Pi Zero's GPIO interface. These attributes include button states and functions required to check the button states and so on. In order to interface a button and read its states, we need to make use of this blueprint. The process of creating a copy of this blueprint is called instantiation.

Let's get started with importing the `gpiozero` library and instantiate the `Button` class of the `gpiozero` library (we will discuss Python's classes, objects, and their attributes in a later chapter). The button is interfaced to GPIO pin 2. We need to pass the pin number as an argument during instantiation:

```
from gpiozero import Button

#button is interfaced to GPIO 2
button = Button(2)
```

The `gpiozero` library's documentation is available at http://gpiozero. readthedocs.io/en/v1.2.0/api_input.html. According to the documentation, there is a variable named `is_pressed` in the `Button` class that could be tested using a conditional statement to determine if the button is pressed:

```
if button.is_pressed:
    print("Button pressed")
```

Whenever the button is pressed, the message `Button pressed` is printed on the screen. Let's stick this code snippet inside an infinite loop:

```
from gpiozero import Button

#button is interfaced to GPIO 2
button = Button(2)

while True:
  if button.is_pressed:
    print("Button pressed")
```

In an infinite `while` loop, the program constantly checks for a button press and prints the message as long as the button is being pressed. Once the button is released, it goes back to checking whether the button is pressed.

Breaking out a loop by counting button presses

Let's review another example where we would like to count the number of button presses and break out of the infinite loop when the button has received a predetermined number of presses:

```
i = 0
while True:
  if button.is_pressed:
    button.wait_for_release()
    i += 1
    print("Button pressed")

  if i >= 10:
    break
```

The preceding example is available for downloading along with this chapter as `GPIO_button_loop_break.py`.

In this example, the program checks for the state of the `is_pressed` variable. On receiving a button press, the program can be paused until the button is released using the `wait_for_release` method. When the button is released, the variable used to store the number of presses is incremented by one.

The program breaks out of the infinite loop, when the button has received 10 presses.

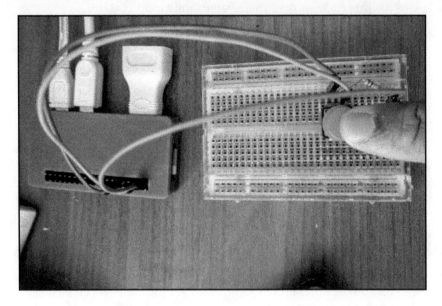

A red momentary push button interfaced to Raspberry Pi Zero GPIO pin 2

Functions in Python

We briefly discussed functions in Python. Functions execute a predefined set of task. `print` is one example of a function in Python. It enables printing something to the screen. Let's discuss writing our own functions in Python.

A function can be declared in Python using the `def` keyword. A function could be defined as follows:

```
def my_func():
    print("This is a simple function")
```

In this function `my_func`, the `print` statement is written under an indented code block. Any block of code that is indented under the function definition is executed when the function is called during the code execution. The function could be executed as `my_func()`.

Passing arguments to a function:

A function is always defined with parentheses. The parentheses are used to pass any requisite arguments to a function. Arguments are parameters required to execute a function. In the earlier example, there are no arguments passed to the function.

Let's review an example where we pass an argument to a function:

```
def add_function(a, b):
  c = a + b
  print("The sum of a and b is ", c)
```

In this example, a and b are arguments to the function. The function adds a and b and prints the sum on the screen. When the function `add_function` is called by passing the arguments 3 and 2 as `add_function(3,2)` where a is 3 and b is 2, respectively.

Hence, the arguments a and b are required to execute function, or calling the function without the arguments would result in an error. Errors related to missing arguments could be avoided by setting default values to the arguments:

```
def add_function(a=0, b=0):
  c = a + b
  print("The sum of a and b is ", c)
```

The preceding function expects two arguments. If we pass only one argument to this function, the other defaults to zero. For example, `add_function(a=3)`, b defaults to 0, or `add_function(b=2)`, a defaults to 0. When an argument is not furnished while calling a function, it defaults to zero (declared in the function).

Similarly, the `print` function prints any variable passed as an argument. If the `print` function is called without any arguments, a blank line is printed.

Returning values from a function

Functions can perform a set of defined operations and finally return a value at the end. Let's consider the following example:

```
def square(a):
    return a**2
```

In this example, the function returns a square of the argument. In Python, the `return` keyword is used to return a value requested upon completion of execution.

The scope of variables in a function

There are two types of variables in a Python program: local and global variables. **Local variables** are local to a function, that is, it is a variable declared within a function is accessible within that function. The example is as follows:

```
def add_function():
    a = 3
    b = 2
    c = a + b
    print("The sum of a and b is ", c)
```

In this example, the variables a and b are local to the function `add_function`. Let's consider an example of a **global variable**:

```
a = 3
b = 2
def add_function():
    c = a + b
    print("The sum of a and b is ", c)

add_function()
```

In this case, the variables a and b are declared in the main body of the Python script. They are accessible across the entire program. Now, let's consider this example:

```
a = 3
def my_function():
    a = 5
    print("The value of a is ", a)

my_function()
print("The value of a is ", a)
```

The program output is:

```
The value of a is

5

The value of a is

3
```

In this case, when `my_function` is called, the value of a is 5 and the value of a is 3 in the `print` statement of the main body of the script. In Python, it is not possible to explicitly modify the value of global variables inside functions. In order to modify the value of a global variable, we need to make use of the `global` keyword:

```
a = 3
def my_function():
   global a
   a = 5
   print("The value of a is ", a)

my_function()
print("The value of a is ", a)
```

In general, it is not recommended to modify variables inside functions as it is not a very safe practice of modifying variables. The best practice would be passing variables as arguments and returning the modified value. Consider the following example:

```
a = 3
def my_function(a):
   a = 5
   print("The value of a is ", a)
   return a

a = my_function(a)
print("The value of a is ", a)
```

In the preceding program, the value of a is 3. It is passed as an argument to `my_function`. The function returns 5, which is saved to a. We were able to safely modify the value of a.

GPIO callback functions

Let's review some uses of functions with the GPIO example. Functions can be used in order to handle specific events related to the GPIO pins of the Raspberry Pi. For example, the gpiozero library provides the capability of calling a function either when a button is pressed or released:

```
from gpiozero import Button

def button_pressed():
   print("button pressed")
```

```
def button_released():
  print("button released")

#button is interfaced to GPIO 2
button = Button(2)
button.when_pressed = button_pressed
button.when_released = button_released

while True:
  pass
```

In this example, we make use of the attributes `when_pressed` and `when_released` of the library's GPIO class. When the button is pressed, the function `button_pressed` is executed. Likewise, when the button is released, the function `button_released` is executed. We make use of the `while` loop to avoid exiting the program and keep listening for button events. The `pass` keyword is used to avoid an error and nothing happens when a `pass` keyword is executed.

This capability of being able to execute different functions for different events is useful in applications like *home automation*. For example, it could be used to turn on lights when it is dark and vice versa.

DC motor control in Python

In this section, we will discuss motor control using the Raspberry Pi Zero. Why discuss motor control? As we progress through different topics in this book, we will culminate in building a mobile robot. Hence, we need to discuss writing code in Python to control a motor using a Raspberry Pi.

In order to control a motor, we need an **H-bridge motor driver** (Discussing H-bridge is beyond our scope. There are several resources for H-bridge motor drivers: `http://www.mcmanis.com/chuck/robotics/tutorial/h-bridge/`). There are several motor driver kits designed for the Raspberry Pi. In this section, we will make use of the following kit: `https://www.pololu.com/product/2753`.

The **Pololu** product page also provides instructions on how to connect the motor. Let's get to writing some Python code to operate the motor:

```
from gpiozero import Motor
from gpiozero import OutputDevice
import time

motor_1_direction = OutputDevice(13)
motor_2_direction = OutputDevice(12)
```

```
motor = Motor(5, 6)

motor_1_direction.on()
motor_2_direction.on()

motor.forward()

time.sleep(10)

motor.stop()

motor_1_direction.off()
motor_2_direction.off()
```

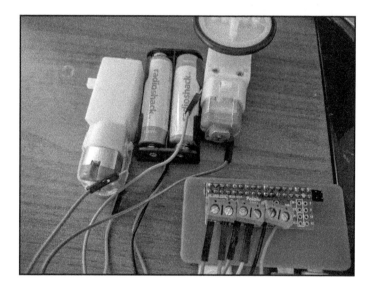

Raspberry Pi based motor control

In order to control the motor, let's declare the pins, the motor's speed pins and direction pins. As per the motor driver's documentation, the motors are controlled by GPIO pins 12, 13 and 5, 6, respectively.

```
from gpiozero import Motor
from gpiozero import OutputDevice
import time

motor_1_direction = OutputDevice(13)
motor_2_direction = OutputDevice(12)

motor = Motor(5, 6)
```

Controlling the motor is as simple as turning on the motor using the `on()` method and moving the motor in the forward direction using the `forward()` method:

```
motor.forward()
```

Similarly, reversing the motor direction could be done by calling the `reverse()` method. Stopping the motor could be done by:

```
motor.stop()
```

Some mini-project challenges for the reader

Here are some of mini-project challenged for our readers:

- In this chapter, we discussed interfacing inputs for the Raspberry Pi and controlling motors. Think about a project where we could drive a mobile robot that reads inputs from whisker switches and operate a mobile robot. Is it possible to build a wall following robot in combination with the limit switches and motors?
- We discussed controlling a DC motor in this chapter. How do we control a stepper motor using a Raspberry Pi?
- How can we interface a motion sensor to control the lights at home using a Raspberry Pi Zero?

Summary

In this chapter, we discussed conditional statements and the applications of conditional statements in Python. We also discussed functions in Python, passing arguments to a function, returning values from a function and scope of variables in a Python program. We discussed callback functions and motor control in Python.

12
Communication Interfaces

So far, we have discussed loops, conditional statements, and functions in Python. We also discussed interfacing output devices and simple digital input devices.

In this chapter, we will discuss the following communication interfaces:

- UART – serial port
- Serial Peripheral Interface
- I²C interface

 We will be making use of different sensors/electronic components to demonstrate writing code in Python for these interfaces. We leave it up to you to pick a component of your choice to explore these communication interfaces.

UART – serial port

Universal Asynchronous Receiver/Transmitter (UART), a serial port, is a communication interface where the data is transmitted serially in bits from a sensor to the host computer. Using a serial port is one of the oldest forms of communication protocol. It is used in data logging where microcontrollers collect data from sensors and transmit the data via a serial port. There are also sensors that transmit data via serial communication as responses to incoming commands.

We will not go into the theory behind serial port communications (there's plenty of theory available on the Web at
`https://en.wikipedia.org/wiki/Universal_asynchronous_receiver/transmitter`)
. We will be discussing the use of the serial port to interface different sensors with the Raspberry Pi.

Raspberry Pi Zero's UART port

Typically, UART ports consist of a receiver (*Rx*) and a transmitter (*Tx*) pin that receive and transmit data. The Raspberry Pi's GPIO header comes with an UART port. The GPIO pins 14 (the *Tx* pin) and 15 (is the *Rx* pin) serve as the UART port for the Raspberry Pi:

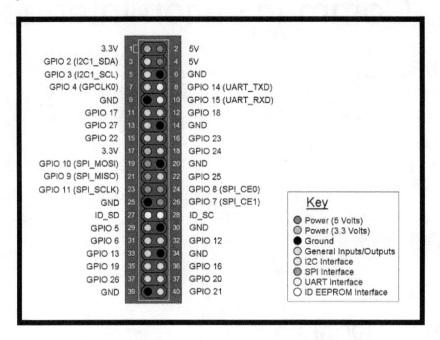

GPIO pins 14 and 15 are the UART pins (image source: https://www.rs-online.com/designspark/introducing-the-raspberry-pi-b-plus)

Setting up the Raspberry Pi Zero serial port

In order to use the serial port to talk to sensors, the serial port login/console needs to be disabled. In the **Raspbian** OS image, this is enabled by default as it enables easy debugging.

The serial port login can be disabled via `raspi-config`:

1. Launch the terminal and run this command:

```
sudo raspi-config
```

2. Select **Advanced Options** from the main menu of `raspi-config`:

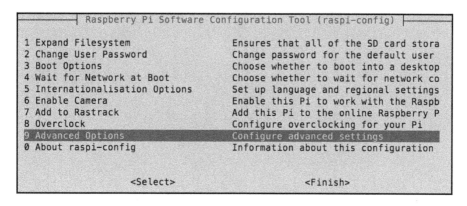

```
        ┤ Raspberry Pi Software Configuration Tool (raspi-config) ├
 1 Expand Filesystem              Ensures that all of the SD card stora
 2 Change User Password           Change password for the default user
 3 Boot Options                   Choose whether to boot into a desktop
 4 Wait for Network at Boot       Choose whether to wait for network co
 5 Internationalisation Options   Set up language and regional settings
 6 Enable Camera                  Enable this Pi to work with the Raspb
 7 Add to Rastrack                Add this Pi to the online Raspberry P
 8 Overclock                      Configure overclocking for your Pi
 9 Advanced Options               Configure advanced settings
 0 About raspi-config             Information about this configuration


                <Select>                        <Finish>
```

Select Advanced Options from the raspi-config menu

3. Select the **A8 Serial** option from the drop-down menu:

```
        ┤ Raspberry Pi Software Configuration Tool (raspi-config) ├
A1 Overscan                    You may need to configure overscan if  ↑
A2 Hostname                    Set the visible name for this Pi on a  ▓
A3 Memory Split                Change the amount of memory made avai   ▓
A4 SSH                         Enable/Disable remote command line ac   ▓
A5 Device Tree                 Enable/Disable the use of Device Tree   ▓
A6 SPI                         Enable/Disable automatic loading of S   ▓
A7 I2C                         Enable/Disable automatic loading of I   ■
A8 Serial                      Enable/Disable shell and kernel messa   ▓
A9 Audio                       Force audio out through HDMI or 3.5mm   ▓
AA GL Driver                   Enable/Disable experimental desktop G   ↓


                <Select>                        <Back>
```

Select A8 Serial from the dropdown

4. Disable serial login:

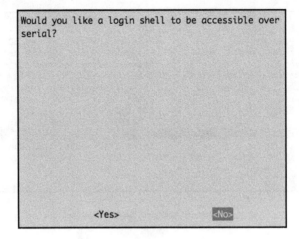

Disable serial login

5. Finish the configuration and reboot at the end:

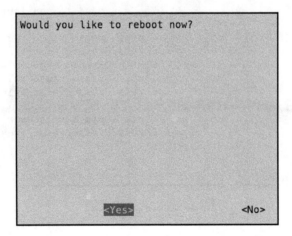

Save config and reboot

Example 1 – interfacing a carbon dioxide sensor to the Raspberry Pi

We will be making use of the K30 carbon dioxide sensor (its documentation is available here, `http://co2meters.com/Documentation/Datasheets/DS30-01%20-%20K30.pdf`). It has a range of 0-10,000 ppm, and the sensor provides it carbon dioxide concentration readings via serial port as a response to certain commands from the Raspberry Pi.

The following diagram shows the connections between the Raspberry Pi and the K30 carbon dioxide sensor:

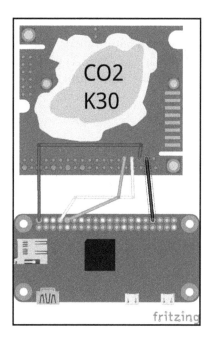

K30 carbon dioxide sensor interfaced with the Raspberry Pi

The receiver (*Rx*) pin of the sensor is connected to the transmitter (*Tx*-**GPIO 14 (UART_TXD)**) pin of the Raspberry Pi Zero (the yellow wire in the preceding figure). The transmitter (*Tx*) pin of the sensor is connected to the receiver (*Rx*-**GPIO 15 (UART_RXD)**) pin of the Raspberry Pi Zero (the green wire in the preceding figure).

In order to power the sensor, the G+ pin of the sensor (the red wire in the preceding figure) is connected to the **5V** pin of the Raspberry Pi Zero. The G0 pin of the sensor is connected to the **GND** pin of the Raspberry Pi Zero (black wire in the earlier figure).

Typically, serial port communication is initiated by specifying the baud rate, the number of bits in a frame, stop bit, and flow control.

Python code for serial port communication

We will make use of the **pySerial** library (https://pyserial.readthedocs.io/en/latest/shortintro.html#opening-serial-ports) for interfacing the carbon dioxide sensor:

1. As per the sensor's documentation, the sensor output can be read by initiating the serial port at a baud rate of 9600, no parity, 8 bits, and 1 stop bit. The GPIO serial port is `ttyAMA0`. The first step in interfacing with the sensor is initiating serial port communication:

   ```
   import serial
   ser = serial.Serial("/dev/ttyAMA0")
   ```

2. As per the sensor documentation (http://co2meters.com/Documentation/Other/SenseAirCommGuide.zip), the sensor responds to the following command for the carbon dioxide concentration:

Reading CO2							
Request:							
Description	Address 1byte	Command 1-byte	Address (see I2C guide) 2-bytes		N- Bytes to Read 1-byte	Checksum 2-bytes	
Example (reads CO2)	0xFE	0x44	0x00	0x08	0x02	0x9F	0x25
Command Bytes: 0x46- EEPROM Read, 0x44 – RAM Read							

Command to read carbon dioxide concentration from the sensor-borrowed from the sensor datasheet

3. The command can be transmitted to the sensor as follows:

   ```
   ser.write(bytearray([0xFE, 0x44, 0x00, 0x08, 0x02, 0x9F, 0x25]))
   ```

4. The sensor responds with a 7-byte response, which can be read as follows:

   ```
   resp = ser.read(7)
   ```

5. The sensor's response is in the following format:

Response							
Description	Address 1byte	Command 1-byte	Count 1-byte	N- Bytes Read n-bytes			Checksum 2-bytes
Example (cont.)	0xFE	0x44	0x02	0x01	0x90		

Carbon dioxide sensor response

6. According to the datasheet, the sensor data size is 2 bytes. Each byte can be used to store a value of 0 and 255. Two bytes can be used to store values up to 65,535 (255 * 255). The carbon dioxide concentration could be calculated from the message as follows:

```
high = resp[3]
low = resp[4]
co2 = (high*256) + low
```

7. Put it all together:

```
import serial
import time
import array
ser = serial.Serial("/dev/ttyAMA0")
print("Serial Connected!")
ser.flushInput()
time.sleep(1)

while True:
    ser.write(bytearray([0xFE, 0x44, 0x00, 0x08,
    0x02, 0x9F, 0x25]))
    # wait for sensor to respond
    time.sleep(.01)
    resp = ser.read(7)
    high = resp[3]
    low = resp[4]
    co2 = (high*256) + low
    print()
    print()
    print("Co2 = " + str(co2))
    time.sleep(1)
```

8. Save the code to a file and try executing it.

I²C communication

Inter-Integrated Circuit (I²C) communication is a type of serial communication that allows interfacing multiple sensors to the computer. I²C communication consists of two wires of a clock and a data line. The Raspberry Pi Zero's clock and data pins for I²C communication are **GPIO 3 (SCL)** and **GPIO 2 (SDA)**, respectively. In order to communicate with multiple sensors over the same bus, sensors/actuators that communicate via I²C protocol are usually addressed by their 7-bit address. It is possible to have two or more Raspberry Pi boards talking to the same sensor on the same I²C bus. This enables building a sensor network around the Raspberry Pi.

The I²C communication lines are open drain lines; hence, they are pulled up using resistors, as shown in the following figure:

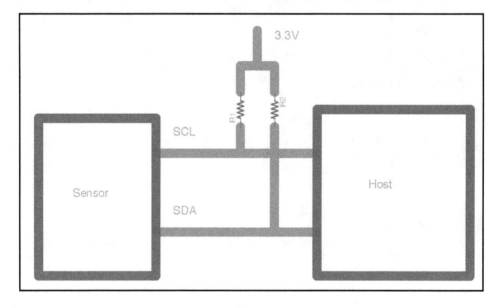

I²C setup

Let's review an example of I²C communication using an example.

Example 2 – PiGlow

The **PiGlow** is a piece of add-on hardware for the Raspberry Pi that consists of 18 LEDs interfaced with the **SN3218** chip. This chip permits controlling the LEDs via the I²C interface. The chip's 7-bit address is 0x54.

To interface the add-on hardware, the **SCL** pin is connected to **GPIO 3** and **SDA** pin to **GPIO 2**; the ground pins and the power supply pins are connected to the counterparts of the add-on hardware, respectively.

The PiGlow comes with a library that comes which abstracts the I²C communication: `https://github.com/pimoroni/piglow`.

Although the library is a wrapper around the I²C interface for the library, we recommend reading through the code to understand the internal mechanism to operate the LEDs:

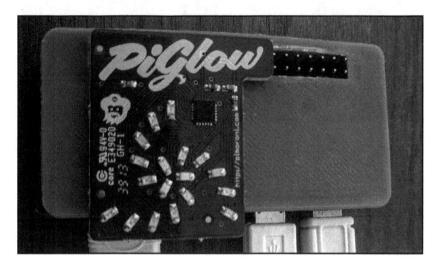

PiGlow stacked on top of the Raspberry Pi

Installing libraries

The PiGlow library may be installed by running the following from the command-line terminal:

```
curl get.pimoroni.com/piglow | bash
```

Example

On the completion of installation, switch to the example folder (`/home/pi/Pimoroni/piglow`) and run one of the examples:

```
python3 bar.py
```

It should run *blinky* light effects as shown in the following figure:

Blinky lights on the PiGlow

Similarly, there are libraries to talk to real-time clocks, LCD displays, and so on using I²C communication. If you are interested in writing your own interface that provides the nitty-gritty detail of I²C communication with sensors/output devices, check out this book's accompanying website for some examples.

Example 3 – Sensorian add-on hardware for the Raspberry Pi

The **Sensorian** is an add-on hardware designed for the Raspberry Pi. This add-on hardware comes with different types of sensors, including a light sensor, barometer, accelerometer, LCD display interface, flash memory, capacitive touch sensors, and a real-time clock.

The sensors on this add-on hardware is sufficient to learn using all the communication interfaces discussed in this chapter:

Sensorian hardware stacked on top of the Raspberry Pi Zero

In this section, we will discuss an example where we will measure the ambient light levels using a Raspberry Pi Zero via the I^{2}C interface. The sensor on the add-on hardware board is the **APDS-9300** sensor (`www.avagotech.com/docs/AV02-1077EN`).

I^{2}C drivers for the lux sensor

The drivers are available from the GitHub repository for the Sensorian hardware (`https://github.com/sensorian/sensorian-firmware.git`). Let's clone the repository from the command-line terminal:

```
git clone https://github.com/sensorian/sensorian-firmware.git
```

Let's make use of the drivers (which is available in the `~/sensorian-firmware/Drivers_Python/APDS-9300` folder) to read the values from the two ADC channels of the sensor:

```python
import time
import APDS9300 as LuxSens
import sys

AmbientLight = LuxSens.APDS9300()
while True:
    time.sleep(1)
    channel1 = AmbientLight.readChannel(1)
    channel2 = AmbientLight.readChannel(0)
    Lux = AmbientLight.getLuxLevel(channel1,channel2)
    print("Lux output: %d." % Lux)
```

With the ADC values available from both the channel, the ambient light value can be calculated by the driver using the following formula (retrieved from the sensor datasheet):

CH1/CH0	Sensor Lux Formula
$0 \leq CH1/CH0 \leq 0.52$	Sensor Lux = $(0.0315 \times CH0) - (0.0593 \times CH0 \times ((CH1/CH0)^{1.4}))$
$0.52 \leq CH1/CH0 \leq 0.65$	Sensor Lux = $(0.0229 \times CH0) - (0.0291 \times CH1)$
$0.65 \leq CH1/CH0 \leq 0.80$	Sensor Lux = $(0.0157 \times CH0) - (0.0180 \times CH1)$
$0.80 \leq CH1/CH0 \leq 1.30$	Sensor Lux = $(0.00338 \times CH0) - (0.00260 \times CH1)$
$CH1/CH0 \geq 1.30$	Sensor Lux = 0

Ambient light levels calculated using the ADC values

This calculation is performed by the attribute `getLuxLevel`. Under normal lighting conditions, the ambient light level (measured in lux) was around 2. The measured output was 0 when we covered the lux sensor with the palm. This sensor could be used to measure ambient light and adjust the room lighting accordingly.

Challenge

We discussed measuring ambient light levels using the lux sensor. How do we make use of the lux output (ambient light levels) to control the room lighting?

The SPI interface

There is another type of serial communication interface named the **Serial Peripheral Interface (SPI)**. This interface has to be enabled via `raspi-config` (this is similar to enabling serial port interface earlier in this chapter). Using the SPI interface is similar to that of I²C interface and the serial port.

Typically, an SPI interface consists of a clock line, data-in, data-out, and a **Slave Select (SS)** line. Unlike I²C communication (where we could connect multiple masters), there can be only one master (the Raspberry Pi Zero), but multiple slaves on the same bus. The **SS** pin enables selecting a specific sensor that the Raspberry Pi Zero is reading/writing data when there are multiple sensors connected to the same bus.

Example 4 – writing to external memory chip

Let's review an example where we write to a flash memory chip on the Sensorian add-on hardware via the SPI interface. The drivers for the SPI interface and the memory chip are available from the same GitHub repository.

Since we already have the drivers downloaded, let's review an example available with drivers:

```
import sys
import time
import S25FL204K as Memory
```

Let's initialize and write the message `hello` to the memory:

```
Flash_memory = Memory.S25FL204K()
Flash_memory.writeStatusRegister(0x00)
message = "hello"
flash_memory.writeArray(0x000000,list(message), message.len())
```

Now, let's try to read the data we just wrote to the external memory:

```
data = flash_memory.readArray(0x000000, message.len())
print("Data Read from memory: ")
print(''.join(data))
```

The code sample is available for download with this chapter (`memory_test.py`).

We were able to demonstrate using the SPI to read/write to an external memory chip.

Challenge to the reader

In the figure here, there is an LED strip (https://www.adafruit.com/product/306) interfaced to the SPI interface of the Raspberry Pi add on hardware using the Adafruit Cobbler (https://www.adafruit.com/product/914). We are providing a clue on how to interface the LED strip to the Raspberry Pi Zero. We would like to see if you are able to find a solution to interface the LED strip by yourself. Refer to this book's website for the answer.

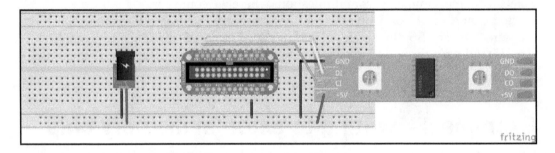

LED strip interfaced with the Adafruit Cobbler for the Raspberry Pi Zero

Summary

In this chapter, we have discussed different communication interfaces that are available on the Raspberry Pi Zero. These interfaces include I²C, SPI, and UART. We will be making use of these interfaces in our final projects. We discussed these interfaces using a carbon dioxide sensor, LED driver, and a sensor platform. In the next chapter, we will discuss object-oriented programming and its distinct advantages. We will discuss the need for object-oriented programming using an example. Object-oriented programming can be especially helpful in scenarios where you have to write your own drivers to control a component of your robot or write an interface library for a sensor.

13
Data Types and Object-Oriented Programming in Python

In this chapter, we will discuss data types and **object-oriented programming** (OOP) in Python. We will discuss data types including lists, dictionaries, tuples and sets in Python. We will also discuss OOP, it's necessity and how to write object-oriented code in Python for Raspberry Pi based projects (such as, using OOP to control appliances at home). We will discuss making use of OOP in a Raspberry Pi Zero project.

Lists

In Python, a list is a data type (its documentation is available here, `https://docs.python.org/3.4/tutorial/datastructures.html#`) that could be used to store elements in a sequence.

 The topics discussed in this chapter can be difficult to grasp unless used in practice. Any example that is represented using this notation: >>> indicates that it could be tested using the Python interpreter.

A list may consist of strings, objects (discussed in detail in this chapter) or numbers, and so on. For instance, the following are examples of lists:

```
>>> sequence = [1, 2, 3, 4, 5, 6]
>>> example_list = ['apple', 'orange', 1.0, 2.0, 3]
```

In the preceding set of examples, the `sequence` list consists of numbers between 1 and 6 while the `example_list` list consists of a combination of strings, integer, and floating-point numbers. A list is represented by square brackets (`[]`). Items can be added to a list separated by commas:

```
>>> type(sequence)
<class 'list'>
```

Since a list is an ordered sequence of elements, the elements of a list could be fetched by iterating through the list elements using a `for` loop as follows:

```
for item in sequence:
    print("The number is ", item)
```

The output is something as follows:

```
The number is  1
The number is  2
The number is  3
The number is  4
The number is  5
The number is  6
```

Since Python's loop can iterate through a sequence of elements, it fetches each element and assigns it to `item`. This item is printed on the console.

Operations that could be performed on a list

In Python, the attributes of a data type can be retrieved using the `dir()` method. For example, the attributes available for the `sequence` list can be retrieved as follows:

```
>>> dir(sequence)
['__add__', '__class__', '__contains__', '__delattr__',
'__delitem__', '__dir__', '__doc__', '__eq__',
'__format__', '__ge__', '__getattribute__', '__getitem__',
'__gt__', '__hash__', '__iadd__', '__imul__', '__init__',
'__iter__', '__le__', '__len__', '__lt__', '__mul__',
'__ne__', '__new__', '__reduce__', '__reduce_ex__',
'__repr__', '__reversed__', '__rmul__', '__setattr__',
'__setitem__', '__sizeof__', '__str__', '__subclasshook__',
'append', 'clear', 'copy', 'count', 'extend', 'index',
'insert', 'pop', 'remove', 'reverse', 'sort']
```

These attributes enable performing different operations on a list. Let's discuss each attribute in detail.

Append element to list:

It is possible to add an element using the `append()` method:

```
>>> sequence.append(7)
>>> sequence
[1, 2, 3, 4, 5, 6, 7]
```

Remove element from list:

The `remove()` method finds the first instance of the element (passed an argument) and removes it from the list. Let's consider the following examples:

- **Example 1:**

```
>>> sequence = [1, 1, 2, 3, 4, 7, 5, 6, 7]
>>> sequence.remove(7)
>>> sequence
[1, 1, 2, 3, 4, 5, 6, 7]
```

- **Example 2:**

```
>>> sequence.remove(1)
>>> sequence
[1, 2, 3, 4, 5, 6, 7]
```

- **Example 3:**

```
>>> sequence.remove(1)
>>> sequence
[2, 3, 4, 5, 6, 7]
```

Retrieving the index of an element

The `index()` method returns the position of an element in a list:

```
>>> index_list = [1, 2, 3, 4, 5, 6, 7]
>>> index_list.index(5)
4
```

In this example, the method returns the index of the element 5. Since Python uses zero-based indexing that is the index is counted from 0 and hence the index of the element 5 is 4:

```
random_list = [2, 2, 4, 5, 5, 5, 6, 7, 7, 8]
>>> random_list.index(5)
3
```

In this example, the method returns the position of the first instance of the element. The element 5 is located at the third position.

Popping an element from the list

The pop() method enables removing an element from a specified position and return it:

```
>>> index_list = [1, 2, 3, 4, 5, 6, 7]
>>> index_list.pop(3)
4
>>> index_list
[1, 2, 3, 5, 6, 7]
```

In this example, the index_list list consists of numbers between 1 and 7. When the third element is popped by passing the index position (3) as an argument, the number 4 is removed from the list and returned.

If no arguments are provided for the index position, the last element is popped and returned:

```
>>> index_list.pop()
7
>>> index_list
[1, 2, 3, 5, 6]
```

In this example, the last element (7) was popped and returned.

Counting the instances of an element:

The count() method returns the number of times an element appears in a list. For example, the element appears twice in the list: random_list.

```
>>> random_list = [2, 9, 8, 4, 3, 2, 1, 7]
>>> random_list.count(2)
2
```

Inserting element at a specific position:

The `insert()` method enables adding an element at a specific position in the list. For example, let's consider the following example:

```
>>> day_of_week = ['Monday', 'Tuesday', 'Thursday',
'Friday', 'Saturday']
```

In the list, `Wednesday` is missing. It needs to be positioned between `Tuesday` and `Thursday` at position 2 (Python uses **zero based indexing** that is the positions/indexes of elements are counted as 0, 1, 2, and so on.). It could be added using insert as follows:

```
>>> day_of_week.insert(2, 'Wednesday')
>>> day_of_week
['Monday', 'Tuesday', 'Wednesday', 'Thursday',
'Friday', 'Saturday']
```

Challenge to the reader

In the preceding list, `Sunday` is missing. Use the `insert` attribute of lists to insert it at the correct position.

Extending a list

Two lists can be combined together using the `extend()` method. The `day_of_week` and `sequence` lists can be combined as follows:

```
>>> day_of_week.extend(sequence)
>>> day_of_week
['Monday', 'Tuesday', 'Wednesday', 'Thursday', 'Friday',
'Saturday', 1, 2, 3, 4, 5, 6]
```

Lists can also be combined as follows:

```
>>> [1, 2, 3] + [4, 5, 6]
[1, 2, 3, 4, 5, 6]
```

It is also possible to add a list as an element to another list:

```
sequence.insert(6, [1, 2, 3])
>>> sequence
[1, 2, 3, 4, 5, 6, [1, 2, 3]]
```

Clearing the elements of a list

All the elements of a list could be deleted using the `clear()` method:

```
>>> sequence.clear()
>>> sequence
[]
```

Sorting the elements of a list

The elements of a list could be sorted using the `sort()` method:

```
random_list = [8, 7, 5, 2, 2, 5, 7, 5, 6, 4]
>>> random_list.sort()
>>> random_list
[2, 2, 4, 5, 5, 5, 6, 7, 7, 8]
```

When a list consists of a collection of strings, they are sorted in the alphabetical order:

```
>>> day_of_week = ['Monday', 'Tuesday', 'Thursday',
'Friday', 'Saturday']
>>> day_of_week.sort()
>>> day_of_week
['Friday', 'Monday', 'Saturday', 'Thursday', 'Tuesday']
```

Reverse the order of elements in list

The `reverse()` method enables the reversing the order of the list elements:

```
>>> random_list = [8, 7, 5, 2, 2, 5, 7, 5, 6, 4]
>>> random_list.reverse()
>>> random_list
[4, 6, 5, 7, 5, 2, 2, 5, 7, 8]
```

Create copies of a list

The `copy()` method enables creating copies of a list:

```
>>> copy_list = random_list.copy()
>>> copy_list
[4, 6, 5, 7, 5, 2, 2, 5, 7, 8]
```

Accessing list elements

The list elements could be accessed by specifying the index position of the `list_name[i]` element. For example, the zeroth list element of the `random_list` list could be accessed as follows:

```
>>> random_list = [4, 6, 5, 7, 5, 2, 2, 5, 7, 8]
>>> random_list[0] 4>>> random_list[3] 7
```

Accessing a set of elements within a list

It is possible to access elements between specified indices. For example, it is possible to retrieve all elements between indices 2 and 4:

```
>>> random_list[2:5]
[5, 7, 5]
```

The first six elements of a list could be accessed as follows:

```
>>> random_list[:6]
[4, 6, 5, 7, 5, 2]
```

The elements of a list could be printed in the reverse order as follows:

```
>>> random_list[::-1]
[8, 7, 5, 2, 2, 5, 7, 5, 6, 4]
```

Every second element in the list could be fetched as follows:

```
>>> random_list[::2]
[4, 5, 5, 2, 7]
```

It is also possible to fetch every second element after the second element after skipping the first two elements:

```
>>> random_list[2::2]
[5, 5, 2, 7]
```

List membership

It is possible to check if a value is a member of a list using the `in` keyword. For example:

```
>>> random_list = [2, 1, 0, 8, 3, 1, 10, 9, 5, 4]
```

In this list, we could check if the number 6 is a member:

```
>>> 6 in random_list
False
>>> 4 in random_list
True
```

Let's build a simple game!

This exercise consists of two parts. In the first part, we will review building a list containing ten random numbers between 0 and 10. The second part is a challenge to the reader. Perform the following steps:

1. The first step is creating an empty list. Let's create an empty list called `random_list`. An empty list can be created as follows:

   ```
   random_list = []
   ```

2. We will be making use of Python's `random` module (https://docs.python.org/3/library/random.html) to generate random numbers. In order to generate random numbers between 0 and 10, we will make use of the `randint()` method from the `random` module:

   ```
   random_number = random.randint(0,10)
   ```

3. Let's append the generated number to the list. This operation is repeated 10 times using a `for` loop:

   ```
   for index in range(0,10):
           random_number = random.randint(0, 10)
           random_list.append(random_number)
   print("The items in random_list are ")
   print(random_list)
   ```

4. The generated list looks something like this:

   ```
   The items in random_list are
   [2, 1, 0, 8, 3, 1, 10, 9, 5, 4]
   ```

We discussed generating a list of random numbers. The next step is taking user input where we ask the user to make a guess for a number between 0 and 10. If the number is a member of the list, the message `Your guess is correct` is printed to the screen, else, the message `Sorry! Your guess is incorrect` is printed. We leave the second part as a challenge to the reader. Get started with the `list_generator.py` code sample available for download with this chapter.

Dictionaries

A dictionary (`https://docs.python.org/3.4/tutorial/datastructures.html#dictionaries`) is a data type that is an unordered collection of key and value pairs. Each key in a dictionary has an associated value. An example of a dictionary is:

```
>>> my_dict = {1: "Hello", 2: "World"}
>>> my_dict
{1: 'Hello', 2: 'World'}
```

A dictionary is created by using the braces `{}`. At the time of creation, new members are added to the dictionary in the following format: `key: value` (shown in the preceding example). In the previous example 1 and 2 are keys while `'Hello'` and `'World'` are the associated values. Each value added to a dictionary needs to have an associated key.

The elements of a dictionary do not have an order i.e. the elements cannot be retrieved in the order they were added. It is possible to retrieving the values of a dictionary by iterating through the keys. Let's consider the following example:

```
>>> my_dict = {1: "Hello", 2: "World", 3: "I", 4: "am",
5: "excited", 6: "to", 7: "learn", 8: "Python" }
```

There are several ways to print the keys or values of a dictionary:

```
>>> for key in my_dict:

...

print(my_dict[value])

...

Hello
```

```
World

I

am

excited

to

learn

Python
```

In the preceding example, we iterate through the keys of the dictionary and retrieve the value using the key, `my_dict[key]`. It is also possible to retrieve the values using the `values()` method available with dictionaries:

```
>>> for value in my_dict.values():

...

print(value)

...

Hello

World

I

am

excited

to

learn

Python
```

The keys of a dictionary can be an integer, string, or a tuple. The keys of a dictionary need to be unique and it is immutable, that is a key cannot be modified after creation. Duplicates of a key cannot be created. If a new value is added to an existing key, the latest value is stored in the dictionary. Let's consider the following example:

- A new key/value pair could be added to a dictionary as follows:

```
>>> my_dict[9] = 'test'

>>> my_dict

{1: 'Hello', 2: 'World', 3: 'I', 4: 'am', 5: 'excited',
6: 'to', 7: 'learn', 8: 'Python', 9: 'test'}
```

- Let's try creating a duplicate of the key 9:

```
>>> my_dict[9] = 'programming'

>>> my_dict

{1: 'Hello', 2: 'World', 3: 'I', 4: 'am', 5: 'excited',
6: 'to', 7: 'learn', 8: 'Python', 9: 'programming'}
```

- As shown in the preceding example, when we try to create a duplicate, the value of the existing key is modified.
- It is possible to have multiple values associated with a key. For example, as a list or a dictionary:

```
>>> my_dict = {1: "Hello", 2: "World", 3: "I", 4: "am",
"values": [1, 2, 3,4, 5], "test": {"1": 1, "2": 2} }
```

Dictionaries are useful in scenarios like parsing CSV files and associating each row with a unique key. Dictionaries are also used to encode and decode JSON data

Tuples

A tuple (pronounced either like *two-ple* or *tuh-ple*) is an immutable data type that are ordered and separated by a comma. A tuple can be created as follows:

```
>>> my_tuple = 1, 2, 3, 4, 5

>>> my_tuple

(1, 2, 3, 4, 5)
```

Since tuples are immutable, the value at a given index cannot be modified:

```
>>> my_tuple[1] = 3
Traceback (most recent call last):
  File "<stdin>", line 1, in <module>
TypeError: 'tuple' object does not support item assignment
```

A tuple can consist of a number, string, or a list. Since lists are mutable, if a list is a member of a tuple, it can be modified. For example:

```
>>> my_tuple = 1, 2, 3, 4, [1, 2, 4, 5]
>>> my_tuple[4][2] = 3
>>> my_tuple
(1, 2, 3, 4, [1, 2, 3, 5])
```

Tuples are especially useful in scenarios where the value cannot be modified. Tuples are also used to return values from a function. Let's consider the following example:

```
>>> for value in my_dict.items():

...

print(value)

...

(1, 'Hello')

(2, 'World')

(3, 'I')

(4, 'am')

('test', {'1': 1, '2': 2})

('values', [1, 2, 3, 4, 5])
```

In the preceding example, the `items()` method returns a list of tuples.

Sets

A set (`https://docs.python.org/3/tutorial/datastructures.html#sets`) is an unordered collection of immutable elements without duplicate entries. A set could be created as follows:

```
>>> my_set = set([1, 2, 3, 4, 5])

>>> my_set

{1, 2, 3, 4, 5}
```

Now, let's add a duplicate list to this set:

```
>>> my_set.update([1, 2, 3, 4, 5])

>>> my_set

{1, 2, 3, 4, 5}
```

Sets enable avoid duplication of entries and saving the unique entries. A single element can be added to a set as follows:

```
>>> my_set = set([1, 2, 3, 4, 5])

>>> my_set.add(6)

>>> my_set

{1, 2, 3, 4, 5, 6}
```

Sets are used to test memberships of an element among different sets. There are different methods that are related to membership tests. We recommend learning about each method using the documentation on sets (run `help(my_set)` to find the different methods available for membership tests).

OOP in Python

OOP is a concept that helps simplifying your code and eases application development. It is especially useful in reusing your code. Object-oriented code enables reusing your code for sensors that use the communications interface. For example, all sensors that are equipped with a UART port could be grouped together using object-oriented code.

One example of OOP is the **GPIO Zero library** (`https://www.raspberrypi.org/blog/gpio-zero-a-friendly-python-api-for-phys ical-computing/`) used in previous chapters. In fact, everything is an object in Python.

Object-oriented code is especially helpful in collaboration with other people on a project. For example, you could implement a sensor driver using object-oriented code in Python and document its usage. This enables other developers to develop an application without paying attention to the nitty-gritty detail behind the sensor's interface. OOP provides modularity to an application that simplifies application development. We are going to review an example in this chapter that demonstrates the advantage of OOP. In this chapter, we will be making use of OOP to bring modularity to our project.

Let's get started!

Revisiting the student ID card example

Let's revisit the ID card example from Chapter 10, *Arithmetic Operations, Loops, and Blinky Lights* (input_test.py). We discussed writing a simple program that captures and prints the information belonging to a student. A student's contact information could be retrieved and stored as follows:

```
name = input("What is your name? ")
address = input("What is your address? ")
age = input("How old are you? ")
```

Now, consider a scenario where the information of 10 students has to be saved and retrieved at any point during program execution. We would need to come up with a nomenclature for the variables used to save the student information. It would be a clutter if we use 30 different variables to store information belonging to each student. This is where object oriented programming can be really helpful.

Let's rewrite this example using OOP to simplify the problem. The first step in OOP is declaring a structure for the object. This is done by defining a class. The class determines the functions of an object. Let's write a Python class that defines the structure for a student object.

Class

Since we are going to save student information, the class is going to be called Student. A class is defined using the class keyword as follows:

```
class Student(object):
```

Thus, a class called Student has been defined. Whenever a new object is created, the method __init__() (the underscore indicate that the init method is a magic method, that is it is a function that is called by Python when an object is created) is called internally by Python.

This method is defined within the class:

```
class Student(object):
    """A Python class to store student information"""

    def __init__(self, name, address, age):
        self.name = name
        self.address = address
        self.age = age
```

In this example, the arguments to the __init__ method include name, age and address. These arguments are called **attributes**. These attributes enable creating a unique object that belongs to the Student class. Hence, in this example, while creating an instance of the Student class, the attributes name, age, and address are required arguments.

Let's create an object (also called an instance) belonging to the Student class:

```
student1 = Student("John Doe", "123 Main Street, Newark, CA", "29")
```

In this example, we created an object belonging to the Student class called student1 where John Doe (name), 29 (age) and 123 Main Street, Newark, CA(address) are attributes required to create an object. When we create an object that belongs to the Student class by passing the requisite arguments (declared earlier in the __init__() method of the Student class), the __init__() method is automatically called to initialize the object. Upon initialization, the information related to student1 is stored under the object student1.

Now, the information belonging to student1 could be retrieved as follows:

```
print(student1.name)
print(student1.age)
print(student1.address)
```

Now, let's create another object called student2:

```
student2 = Student("Jane Doe", "123 Main Street, San Jose, CA", "27")
```

We created two objects called `student1` and `student2`. Each object's attributes are accessible as `student1.name`, `student2.name` and so on. In the absence of object oriented programming, we will have to create variables like `student1_name`, `student1_age`, `student1_address`, `student2_name`, `student2_age` and `student2_address` and so on. Thus, OOP enables modularizing the code.

Adding methods to a class

Let's add some methods to our `Student` class that would help retrieve a student's information:

```
class Student(object):
    """A Python class to store student information"""

    def __init__(self, name, age, address):
        self.name = name
        self.address = address
        self.age = age

    def return_name(self):
        """return student name"""
        return self.name

    def return_age(self):
        """return student age"""
        return self.age

    def return_address(self):
        """return student address"""
        return self.address
```

In this example, we have added three methods namely `return_name()`, `return_age()` and `return_address()` that returns the attributes `name`, `age` and `address` respectively. These methods of a class are called **callable attributes**. Let's review a quick example where we make use of these callable attributes to print an object's information.

```
student1 = Student("John Doe", "29", "123 Main Street, Newark, CA")
print(student1.return_name())
print(student1.return_age())
print(student1.return_address())
```

So far, we discussed methods that retrieves information about a student. Let's include a method in our class that enables updating information belonging to a student. Now, let's add another method to the class that enables updating address by a student:

```
def update_address(self, address):
    """update student address"""
    self.address = address
    return self.address
```

Let's compare the `student1` object's address before and after updating the address:

```
print(student1.address())
print(student1.update_address("234 Main Street, Newark, CA"))
```

This would print the following output to your screen:

```
123 Main Street, Newark, CA
234 Main Street, Newark, CA
```

Thus, we have written our first object-oriented code that demonstrates the ability to modularize the code. The preceding code sample is available for download along with this chapter as `student_info.py`.

Doc strings in Python

In the object oriented example, you might have noticed a sentence enclosed in triple double quotes:

```
"""A Python class to store student information"""
```

This is called a **doc string**. The doc string is used to document information about a class or a method. Doc strings are especially helpful while trying to store information related to the usage of a method or a class (this will be demonstrated later in this chapter). Doc strings are also used at the beginning of a file to store multi-line comments related to an application or a code sample. Doc strings are ignored by the Python interpreter and they are meant to provide documentation about a class to fellow programmers.

Similarly, the Python interpreter ignores any single line comment that starts with a # sign. Single line comments are generally used to make a specific note on a block of code. The practice of including well-structured comments makes your code readable.

For example, the following code snippet informs the reader that a random number between 0 and 9 is generated and stored in the variable rand_num:

```
# generate a random number between 0 and 9
rand_num = random.randrange(0,10)
```

On the contrary, a comment that provides no context is going to confuse someone who is reviewing your code:

```
# Todo: Fix this later
```

It is quite possible that you may not be able to recall what needs fixing when you revisit the code later.

self

In our object-oriented example, the first argument to every method had an argument called self. self refers to the instance of the class in use and the self keyword is used as the first argument in methods that interact with the instances of the class. In the preceding example, self refers to the object student1. It is equivalent to initializing an object and accessing it as follows:

```
Student(student1, "John Doe", "29", "123 Main Street, Newark, CA")
Student.return_address(student1)
```

The self keyword simplifies how we access an object's attributes in this case. Now, let's review some examples where we make use of OOP involving the Raspberry Pi.

Speaker controller

Let's write a Python class (tone_player.py in **downloads**) that plays a musical tone indicating that the boot-up of your Raspberry Pi is complete. For this section, you will need a USB sound card and a speaker interfaced to the USB hub of the Raspberry Pi.

Let's call our class TonePlayer. This class should be capable of controlling the speaker volume and playing any file passed as an argument while creating an object:

```
class TonePlayer(object):
    """A Python class to play boot-up complete tone"""

    def __init__(self, file_name):
        self.file_name = file_name
```

In this case, the file that has to be played by the `TonePlayer` class has to be passed an argument. For example:

```
tone_player = TonePlayer("/home/pi/tone.wav")
```

We also need to be able to set the volume level at which the tone has to be played. Let's add a method to do the same:

```
def set_volume(self, value):
    """set tone sound volume"""
    subprocess.Popen(["amixer", "set", "'PCM'", str(value)],
    shell=False)
```

In the `set_volume` method, we make use of Python's `subprocess` module to run the Linux system command that adjusts the sound drive volume.

The most essential method for this class is the `play` command. When the `play` method is called, we need to play the tone sound using Linux's a `play` command:

```
def play(self):
    """play the wav file"""
    subprocess.Popen(["aplay", self.file_name], shell=False)
```

Put it all together:

```
import subprocess

class TonePlayer(object):
    """A Python class to play boot-up complete tone"""

    def __init__(self, file_name):
        self.file_name = file_name

    def set_volume(self, value):
        """set tone sound volume"""
        subprocess.Popen(["amixer", "set", "'PCM'", str(value)],
        shell=False)

    def play(self):
        """play the wav file"""
        subprocess.Popen(["aplay", self.file_name], shell=False)


if __name__ == "__main__":
    tone_player = TonePlayer("/home/pi/tone.wav")
    tone_player.set_volume(75)
    tone_player.play()
```

Save the `TonePlayer` class to your Raspberry Pi (save it to a file called `tone_player.py`) and use a tone sound file from sources like *freesound* (`https://www.freesound.org/people/zippi1/sounds/18872/`). Save it to a location of your choice and try running the code. It should play the tone sound at the desired volume!

Now, edit `/etc/rc.local` and add the following line to the end of the file (right before the `exit 0` line):

```
python3 /home/pi/toneplayer.py
```

This should play a tone whenever the Pi boots up!

Light control daemon

Let's review another example where we implement a simple daemon using OOP that turns on/off lights at specified times of the day. In order to be able to perform tasks at scheduled times, we will make use of the `schedule` library (`https://github.com/dbader/schedule`). It could be installed as follows:

```
sudo pip3 install schedule
```

Let's call our class, `LightScheduler`. It should be capable of accepting start and top times to turn on/off lights at given times. It should also provide override capabilities to let the user turn on/off lights as necessary. Let's assume that the light is controlled using **PowerSwitch Tail II** (`http://www.powerswitchtail.com/Pages/default.aspx`). It is interfaced as follows:

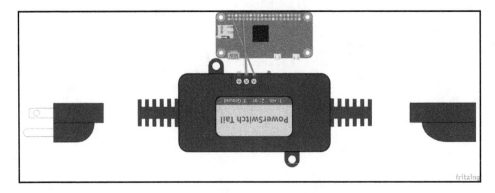

Raspberry Pi Zero interfaced to the PowerSwitch Tail II

The following is the `LightSchedular` class created:

```
class LightScheduler(object):
    """A Python class to turn on/off lights"""

    def __init__(self, start_time, stop_time):
        self.start_time = start_time
        self.stop_time = stop_time
        # lamp is connected to GPIO pin2.
        self.lights = OutputDevice(2)
```

Whenever an instance of `LightScheduler` is created, the GPIO pin is initialized to control the PowerSwitch Tail II. Now, let's add methods to turn on/off lights:

```
def init_schedule(self):
    # set the schedule
    schedule.every().day.at(self.start_time).do(self.on)
    schedule.every().day.at(self.stop_time).do(self.off)

def on(self):
    """turn on lights"""
    self.lights.on()

def off(self):
    """turn off lights"""
    self.lights.off()
```

In the `init_schedule()` method, the start and stop times that were passed as arguments are used to initialize `schedule` to turn on/off the lights at the specified times.

Put it together, we have:

```
import schedule
import time
from gpiozero import OutputDevice

class LightScheduler(object):
    """A Python class to turn on/off lights"""

    def __init__(self, start_time, stop_time):
        self.start_time = start_time
        self.stop_time = stop_time
        # lamp is connected to GPIO pin2.
        self.lights = OutputDevice(2)

    def init_schedule(self):
        # set the schedule
```

```
            schedule.every().day.at(self.start_time).do(self.on)
            schedule.every().day.at(self.stop_time).do(self.off)

    def on(self):
        """turn on lights"""
        self.lights.on()

    def off(self):
        """turn off lights"""
        self.lights.off()


if __name__ == "__main__":
    lamp = LightScheduler("18:30", "9:30")
    lamp.on()
    time.sleep(50)
    lamp.off()
    lamp.init_schedule()
    while True:
        schedule.run_pending()
        time.sleep(1)
```

In the preceding example, the lights are scheduled to be turned on at 6:30 p.m. and turned off at 9:30 a.m. Once the jobs are scheduled, the program enters an infinite loop where it awaits task execution. This example could be run as a daemon by executing the file at start-up (add a line called `light_scheduler.py` to `/etc/rc.local`). After scheduling the job, it will continue to run as a daemon in the background.

> This is just a basic introduction to OOP and its applications (keeping the beginner in mind). Refer to this book's website for more examples on OOP.

Summary

In this chapter, we discussed lists and the advantages of OOP. We discussed OOP examples using the Raspberry Pi as the center of the examples. Since the book is targeted mostly towards beginners, we decided to stick to the basics of OOP while discussing examples. There are advanced aspects that are beyond the scope of the book. We leave it up to the reader to learn advanced concepts using other examples available on this book's site.

File I/O and Python Utilities
14

In this chapter, we are going to discuss file I/O, that is reading, writing and appending to file in detail. We are also going to discuss Python utilities that enable manipulating files and interacting with the operating system. Each topic has a different level of complexity that we will discuss using an example. Let's get started!

File I/O

We are discussing file I/O for two reasons:

- In the world of Linux operating systems, everything is a file. Interaction with peripherals on the Raspberry Pi is similar to reading from/writing to a file. For example: In `Chapter 12`, *Communication Interfaces*, we discussed serial port communication. You should be able to observe that serial port communication is like a file read/write operation.
- We use file I/O in some form in every project. For example: Writing sensor data to a CSV file or reading pre-configured options for a web server, and so on.

Hence, we thought it would be useful to discuss file I/O in Python as its own chapter (detailed documentation available from here: `https://docs.python.org/3/tutorial/inputoutput.html#reading-and-writing-files`) and discuss examples where it could play a role while developing applications on the Raspberry Pi Zero.

Reading from a file

Let's create a simple text file, `read_file.txt` with the following text: `I am learning Python Programming using the Raspberry Pi Zero` and save it to the code samples directory (or any location of your choice).

To read from a file, we need to make use of the Python's in-built function: open to open the file. Let's take a quick look at a code snippet that demonstrates opening a text file to read its content and print it to the screen:

```
if __name__ == "__main__":
    # open text file to read
    file = open('read_line.txt', 'r')
    # read from file and store it to data
    data = file.read()
    print(data)
    file.close()
```

Let's discuss this code snippet in detail:

1. The first step in reading the contents of the text file is opening the file using the in-built function open. The file in question needs to be passed as an argument along with a flag r that indicates we are opening the file to read the contents (We will discuss other flag options as we discuss each reading/writing files.)

2. Upon opening the file, the open function returns a pointer (address to the file object) that is stored in the file variable.

   ```
   file = open('read_line.txt', 'r')
   ```

3. This file pointer is used to read the contents of the file and print it to the screen:

   ```
   data = file.read()
   print(data)
   ```

4. After reading the contents of the file, the file is closed by calling the close() function.

Run the preceding code snippet (available for download along with this chapter—read_from_file.py) using IDLE3 or the command-line terminal. The contents of the text file would be printed to the screen as follows:

```
I am learning Python Programming using the Raspberry Pi Zero
```

Reading lines

Sometimes, it is necessary to read the contents of a file by line-by-file. In Python, there are two options to do this: readline() and readlines():

- readline(): As the name suggests, this in-built function enables reading one line at a time. Let's review this using an example:

```python
if __name__ == "__main__":
    # open text file to read
    file = open('read_line.txt', 'r')

    # read a line from the file
    data = file.readline()
    print(data)

    # read another line from the file
    data = file.readline()
    print(data)

    file.close()
```

When the preceding code snippet is executed (available for download as read_line_from_file.py along with this chapter), the read_line.txt file is opened and a single line is returned by the readline() function. This line is stored in the variable data. Since the function is called twice in this program, the output is as follows:

I am learning Python Programming using the Raspberry Pi Zero.

This is the second line.

A new line is returned every time the readline function is called and it returns an empty string when the end-of-file has reached.

- readlines(): This function reads the entire content of a file in lines and stores each it to a list:

```python
if __name__ == "__main__":
    # open text file to read
    file = open('read_lines.txt', 'r')

    # read a line from the file
    data = file.readlines()
    for line in data:
        print(line)

    file.close()
```

Since the lines of the files is stored as a list, it could be retrieved by iterating through the list:

```
data = file.readlines()
    for line in data:
        print(line)
```

The preceding code snippet is available for download along with this chapter as `read_lines_from_file.py`.

Writing to a file

Perform the following steps in order to write to a file:

1. The first step in writing to a file is opening a file with the write flag: w. If the file name that was passed as an argument doesn't exist, a new file is created:

```
file = open('write_file.txt', 'w')
```

2. Once the file is open, the next step is passing the string to be written as argument to the write() function:

```
file.write('I am excited to learn Python using
Raspberry Pi Zero')
```

3. Let's put the code together where we write a string to a text file, close it, re-open the file and print the contents of the file to the screen:

```
if __name__ == "__main__":
    # open text file to write
    file = open('write_file.txt', 'w')
    # write a line from the file
    file.write('I am excited to learn Python using
    Raspberry Pi Zero \n')
    file.close()

    file = open('write_file.txt', 'r')
    data = file.read()
    print(data)
    file.close()
```

4. The preceding code snippet is available for download along with this chapter (`write_to_file.py`).

5. When the preceding code snippet is executed, the output is shown as follows:

```
I am excited to learn Python using Raspberry Pi Zero
```

Appending to a file

Whenever a file is opened using the write flag w, the contents of the file are deleted and opened afresh to write data. There is an alternative flag a that enables appending data to the end of the file. This flag also creates a new file if the file (that is passed as an argument to open) doesn't exist. Let's consider the code snippet below where we append a line to the text file write_file.txt from the previous section:

```
if __name__ == "__main__":
    # open text file to append
    file = open('write_file.txt', 'a')
    # append a line from the file
    file.write('This is a line appended to the file\n')
    file.close()

    file = open('write_file.txt', 'r')
    data = file.read()
    print(data)
    file.close()
```

When the preceding code snippet is executed (available for download along with this chapter—append_to_file.py), the string This is a line appended to the file is appended to the end of the text of the file. The contents of the file will include the following:

```
I am excited to learn Python using Raspberry Pi Zero
This is a line appended to the file
```

seek

Once a file is opened, the file pointer that is used in file I/O moves from the beginning to the end of the file. It is possible to move the pointer to a specific position and read the data from that position. This is especially useful when we are interested in a specific line of a file. Let's consider the text file write_file.txt from the previous example. The contents of the file include:

```
I am excited to learn Python using Raspberry Pi Zero
This is a line appended to the file
```

Let's try to skip the first line and read only the second line using seek:

```
if __name__ == "__main__":
    # open text file to read

    file = open('write_file.txt', 'r')

    # read the second line from the file
    file.seek(53)

    data = file.read()
    print(data)
    file.close()
```

In the preceding example (available for download along with this chapter as seek_in_file.py), the seek function is used to move the pointer to byte 53 that is the end of first line. Then the file's contents are read and stored into the variable. When this code snippet is executed, the output is as follows:

This is a line appended to the file

Thus, seek enables moving the file pointer to a specific position.

Read n bytes

The seek function enables moving the pointer to a specific position and reading a byte or n bytes from that position. Let's re-visit reading write_file.txt and try to read the word excited in the sentence I am excited to learn Python using Raspberry Pi Zero.

```
if __name__ == "__main__":
    # open text file to read and write
    file = open('write_file.txt', 'r')

    # set the pointer to the desired position
    file.seek(5)
    data = file.read(1)
    print(data)

    # rewind the pointer
    file.seek(5)
    data = file.read(7)
    print(data)
    file.close()
```

The preceding code can be explained in the following steps:

1. In the first step, the file is opened using the `read` flag and the file pointer is set to the fifth byte (using `seek`)—the position of the letter `e` in the contents of the text file.

2. Now, we read one byte from the file by passing it as an argument to the `read` function. When an integer is passed as an argument, the `read` function returns the corresponding number of bytes from the file. When no argument is passed, it reads the entire file. The `read` function returns an empty string if the file is empty:

```
file.seek(5)
data = file.read(1)
print(data)
```

3. In the second part, we try to read the word `excited` from the text file. We rewind the position of the pointer back to the fifth byte. Then we read seven bytes from the file (length of the word `excited`).

4. When the code snippet is executed (available for download along with this chapter as `seek_to_read.py`), the program should print the letter `e` and the word `excited`:

```
file.seek(5)
data = file.read(7)
print(data)
```

r+

We discussed reading and writing to files using the `r` and `w` flags. There is another called `r+`. This flag enables reading and writing to a file. Let's review an example that enables us to understand this flag.

Let's review the contents of `write_file.txt` once again:

```
I am excited to learn Python using Raspberry Pi Zero
This is a line appended to the file
```

Let's modify the second line to read: `This is a line that was modified`. The code sample is available for download along with this chapter as `seek_to_write.py`.

```
if __name__ == "__main__":
    # open text file to read and write
```

```
file = open('write_file.txt', 'r+')

# set the pointer to the desired position
file.seek(68)
file.write('that was modified \n')

# rewind the pointer to the beginning of the file
file.seek(0)
data = file.read()
print(data)
file.close()
```

Let's review how this example works:

1. The first step in this example is opening the file using the r+ flag. This enables reading and writing to the file.
2. The next step is moving to the 68th byte of the file
3. The that was modified string is written to the file at this position. The spaces at the end of the string are used to overwrite the original content of the second sentence.
4. Now, the file pointer is set to the beginning of the file and its contents are read.
5. When the preceding code snippet is executed, the modified file contents are printed to the screen as follows:

```
I am excited to learn Python using Raspberry Pi Zero
This is a line that was modified
```

There is another a+ flag that enables appending data to the end of the file and reading at the same time. We will leave this to the reader to figure out using the examples discussed so far.

 We have discussed different examples on reading and writing to files in Python. It can be overwhelming without sufficient experience in programming. We strongly recommend working through the different code samples provided in this chapter

Challenge to the reader

Use the a+ flag to open the write_file.txt file (discussed in different examples) and append a line to the file. Set the file pointer using seek and print its contents. You may open the file only once in the program.

The with keyword

So far, we discussed different flags that could be used to open files in different modes. The examples we discussed followed a common pattern—open the file, perform read/write operations and close the file. There is an elegant way of interacting with files using the `with` keyword.

If there are any errors during the execution of the code block that interacts with a file, the `with` keyword ensures that the file is closed and the associated resources are cleaned up on exiting the code block. As always, let's review the `with` keyword with an example:

```
if __name__ == "__main__":
    with open('write_file.txt', 'r+') as file:
        # read the contents of the file and print to the screen
        print(file.read())
        file.write("This is a line appended to the file")

        #rewind the file and read its contents
        file.seek(0)
        print(file.read())
    # the file is automatically closed at this point
    print("Exited the with keyword code block")
```

In the preceding example (`with_keyword_example`), we skipped closing the file as the `with` keyword takes care of closing the file once the execution of the indented code block is complete. The `with` keyword also takes care of closing the file while leaving the code block due to an error. This ensures that the resources are cleaned up properly in any scenario. Going forward, we will be using the `with` keyword for file I/O.

configparser

Let's discuss some aspects of Python programming that is especially helpful while developing applications using the Raspberry Pi. One such tool is the `configparser` available in Python. The `configparser` module (`https://docs.python.org/3.4/library/configparser.html`) is used to read/write config files for applications.

In software development, config files are generally used to store constants such as access credentials, device ID, and so on In the context of a Raspberry Pi, configparser could be used to store the list of all GPIO pins in use, addresses of sensors interfaced via the I^2C interface, and so on. Let's discuss three examples where we learn making use of the configparser module. In the first example we will create a config file using the configparser.

In the second example, we will make use of the configparser to read the config values and in the third example, we will discuss modifying config files in the final example.

Example 1:

In the first example, let's create a config file that stores information including device ID, GPIO pins in use, sensor interface address, debug switch, and access credentials:

```
import configparser

if __name__ == "__main__":
    # initialize ConfigParser
    config_parser = configparser.ConfigParser()

    # Let's create a config file
    with open('raspi.cfg', 'w') as config_file:
        #Let's add a section called ApplicationInfo
        config_parser.add_section('AppInfo')

        #let's add config information under this section
        config_parser.set('AppInfo', 'id', '123')
        config_parser.set('AppInfo', 'gpio', '2')
        config_parser.set('AppInfo', 'debug_switch', 'True')
        config_parser.set('AppInfo', 'sensor_address', '0x62')

        #Let's add another section for credentials
        config_parser.add_section('Credentials')
        config_parser.set('Credentials', 'token', 'abcxyz123')
        config_parser.write(config_file)
    print("Config File Creation Complete")
```

Let's discuss the preceding code example (available for download along with this chapter as `config_parser_write.py`) in detail:

1. The first step is importing the `configparser` module and creating an instance of the `ConfigParser` class. This instance is going to be called `config_parser`:

   ```
   config_parser = configparser.ConfigParser()
   ```

2. Now, we open a config file called `raspi.cfg` using the `with` keyword. Since the file doesn't exist, a new config file is created.

3. The config file is going to consist of two sections namely `AppInfo` and `Credentials`.

4. The two sections could be created using the `add_section` method as follows:

   ```
   config_parser.add_section('AppInfo')
   config_parser.add_section('Credentials')
   ```

5. Each section is going to consist of different set of constants. Each constant could be added to the relevant section using the `set` method. The required arguments to the `set` method include the section name (under which the parameter/constant is going to be located), the name of the parameter/constant and its corresponding value. For example: The `id` parameter can be added to the `AppInfo` section and assigned a value of `123` as follows:

   ```
   config_parser.set('AppInfo', 'id', '123')
   ```

6. The final step is saving these config values to the file. This is accomplished using the `config_parser` method, `write`. The file is closed once the program exits the indented block under the `with` keyword:

   ```
   config_parser.write(config_file)
   ```

 We strongly recommend trying the code snippets yourself and use these snippets as a reference. You will learn a lot by making mistakes and possibly arrive with a better solution than the one discussed here.

When the preceding code snippet is executed, a config file called `raspi.cfg` is created. The contents of the config file would include the contents shown as follows:

```
[AppInfo]
id = 123
gpio = 2
debug_switch = True
sensor_address = 0x62

[Credentials]
token = abcxyz123
```

Example 2:

Let's discuss an example where we read config parameters from a config file created in the previous example:

```python
import configparser

if __name__ == "__main__":
    # initialize ConfigParser
    config_parser = configparser.ConfigParser()

    # Let's read the config file
    config_parser.read('raspi.cfg')

    # Read config variables
    device_id = config_parser.get('AppInfo', 'id')
    debug_switch = config_parser.get('AppInfo', 'debug_switch')
    sensor_address = config_parser.get('AppInfo', 'sensor_address')

    # execute the code if the debug switch is true
    if debug_switch == "True":
        print("The device id is " + device_id)
        print("The sensor_address is " + sensor_address)
```

If the config files are created in the format shown, the `ConfigParser` class should be able to parse it. It is not really necessary to create config files using a Python program. We just wanted to show programmatic creation of config files as it is easier to programmatically create config files for multiple devices at the same time.

The preceding example is available for download along with this chapter (`config_parser_read.py`). Let's discuss how this code sample works:

1. The first step is initializing an instance of the `ConfigParser` class called `config_parser`.

2. The second step is loading and reading the config file using the instance method `read`.

3. Since we know the structure of the config file, let's go ahead and read some constants available under the section `AppInfo`. The config file parameters can be read using the `get` method. The required arguments include the section under which the config parameter is located and the name of the parameter. For example: The config `id` parameter is located under the `AppInfo` section. Hence, the required arguments to the method include `AppInfo` and `id`:

```
device_id = config_parser.get('AppInfo', 'id')
```

4. Now that the config parameters are read into variables, let's make use of it in our program. For example: Let's test if the `debug_switch` variable (a switch to determine if the program is in debug mode) and print the other config parameters that were retrieved from the file:

```
if debug_switch == "True":
    print("The device id is " + device_id)
    print("The sensor_address is " + sensor_address)
```

Example 3:

Let's discuss an example where we would like to modify an existing config file. This is especially useful in situations where we need to update the firmware version number in the config file after performing a firmware update.

The following code snippet is available for download as `config_parser_modify.py` along with this chapter:

```
import configparser

if __name__ == "__main__":
    # initialize ConfigParser
    config_parser = configparser.ConfigParser()

    # Let's read the config file
    config_parser.read('raspi.cfg')
```

```
# Set firmware version
config_parser.set('AppInfo', 'fw_version', 'A3')

# write the updated config to the config file
with open('raspi.cfg', 'w') as config_file:
    config_parser.write(config_file)
```

Let's discuss how this works:

1. As always, the first step is initializing an instance of the `ConfigParser` class. The config file is loaded using the method `read`:

   ```
   # initialize ConfigParser
   config_parser = configparser.ConfigParser()

   # Let's read the config file
   config_parser.read('raspi.cfg')
   ```

2. The required parameter is updated using the `set` method (discussed in a previous example):

   ```
   # Set firmware version
   config_parser.set('AppInfo', 'fw_version', 'A3')
   ```

3. The updated config is saved to the config file using the `write` method:

   ```
   with open('raspi.cfg', 'w') as config_file:
       config_parser.write(config_file)
   ```

Challenge to the reader

Using example 3 as a reference, update the config parameter `debug_switch` to the value `False`. Repeat example 2 and see what happens.

Reading/writing to CSV files

In this section, we are going to discuss reading/writing to CSV files. This module (https://docs.python.org/3.4/library/csv.html) is useful in data logging applications. Since we will be discussing data logging in the next chapter, let's review reading/writing to CSV files.

Writing to CSV files

Let's consider a scenario where we are reading data from different sensors. This data needs to be recorded to a CSV file where each column corresponds to a reading from a specific sensor. We are going to discuss an example where we record the value 123, 456, and 789 in the first row of the CSV file and the second row is going to consist of values including Red, Green, and Blue:

1. The first step in writing to a CSV file is opening a CSV file using the `with` keyword:

   ```
   with open("csv_example.csv", 'w') as csv_file:
   ```

2. The next step is initializing an instance of the `writer` class of the CSV module:

   ```
   csv_writer = csv.writer(csv_file)
   ```

3. Now, each row is added to the file by creating a list that contains all the elements that need to be added to a row. For example: The first row can be added to the list as follows:

   ```
   csv_writer.writerow([123, 456, 789])
   ```

4. Putting it altogether, we have:

   ```
   import csv
   if __name__ == "__main__":
       # initialize csv writer
       with open("csv_example.csv", 'w') as csv_file:
           csv_writer = csv.writer(csv_file)
           csv_writer.writerow([123, 456, 789])
           csv_writer.writerow(["Red", "Green", "Blue"])
   ```

5. When the above code snippet is executed (available for download as `csv_write.py` along with this chapter), a CSV file is created in the local directory with the following contents:

   ```
   123,456,789
   Red,Green,Blue
   ```

Reading from CSV files

Let's discuss an example where we read the contents of the CSV file created in the previous section:

1. The first step in reading a CSV file is opening it in read mode:

   ```
   with open("csv_example.csv", 'r') as csv_file:
   ```

2. Next, we initialize an instance of the `reader` class from the CSV module. The contents of the CSV file are loaded into the object `csv_reader`:

   ```
   csv_reader = csv.reader(csv_file)
   ```

3. Now that the contents of the CSV file are loaded, each row of the CSV file could be retrieved as follows:

   ```
   for row in csv_reader:
       print(row)
   ```

4. Put it all together:

   ```
   import csv

   if __name__ == "__main__":
       # initialize csv writer
       with open("csv_example.csv", 'r') as csv_file:
           csv_reader = csv.reader(csv_file)

           for row in csv_reader:
               print(row)
   ```

5. When the preceding code snippet is executed (available for download along with this chapter as `csv_read.py`), the contents of the file are printed row-by-row where each row is a list that contains the comma separated values:

   ```
   ['123', '456', '789']
   ['Red', 'Green', 'Blue']
   ```

Python utilities

Python comes with several utilities that enables interacting with other files and the operating system itself. We have identified all those Python utilities that we have used in our past projects. Let's discuss the different modules and their uses as we might use them in the final project of this book.

The os module

As the name suggests, this module (https://docs.python.org/3.1/library/os.html) enables interacting with the operating system. Let's discuss some of its applications with examples.

Checking a file's existence

The os module could be used to check if a file exists in a specific directory. For example: We extensively made use of the write_file.txt file. Before opening this file to read or write, we could check the file's existence:

```
import os
if __name__ == "__main__":
    # Check if file exists
    if os.path.isfile('/home/pi/Desktop/code_samples/write_file.txt'):
        print('The file exists!')
    else:
        print('The file does not exist!')
```

In the preceding code snippet, we make use of the isfile() function, available with the os.path module. When a file's location is passed an argument to the function, it returns True if the file exists at that location. In this example, since the file write_file.txt exists in the code examples directory, the function returns True. Hence the message, The file exists is printed to the screen:

```
if os.path.isfile('/home/pi/Desktop/code_samples/write_file.txt'):
    print('The file exists!')
else:
    print('The file does not exist!')
```

Checking for a folder's existence

Similar to `os.path.isfile()`, there is another function called `os.path.isdir()`. It returns `True` if a folder exists at a specific location. We have been reviewing all code samples from a folder called `code_samples` located on the Raspberry Pi's desktop. It's existence could be confirmed as follows:

```
# Confirm code_samples' existence
if os.path.isdir('/home/pi/Desktop/code_samples'):
    print('The directory exists!')
else:
    print('The directory does not exist!')
```

Deleting files

The `os` module also enables deleting files using the `remove()` function. Any file that is passed as an argument to the function is deleted. In the *File I/O* section, we discussed reading from files using the text file, `read_file.txt`. Let's delete the file by passing it as an argument to the `remove()` function:

```
os.remove('/home/pi/Desktop/code_samples/read_file.txt')
```

Killing a process

It is possible to kill an application running on the Raspberry Pi by passing process `pid` to the `kill()` function. In the previous chapter, we discussed the `light_scheduler` example that runs as a background process on the Raspberry Pi. To demonstrate killing a process, we are going to attempt killing that process. We need to determine the process `pid` of the `light_scheduler` process (you may pick an application that was started by you as a user and not do not touch root processes). The process `pid` could be retrieved from the command-line terminal using the following command:

```
ps aux
```

It spits out the processes currently running on the Raspberry Pi (shown in the following figure). The process `pid` for the `light_scheduler` application is **1815**:

```
pi      822   0.0  1.1   6916  5000 pts/0    Ss   Jul10   0:02 -bash
root    1548  0.0  0.0      0     0 ?         S    Jul10   0:00 [kworker/u2:1]
pi      1815  0.1  1.9  12636  8804 pts/0    S+   Jul10   0:01 python3 light_scheduler.py
root    1817  0.0  1.1  12064  5280 ?         Ss   Jul10   0:00 sshd: pi [priv]
pi      1827  0.0  0.7  12064  3504 ?         S    Jul10   0:00 sshd: pi@pts/1
pi      1830  0.0  1.0   6320  4476 pts/1    Ss   Jul10   0:00 -bash
```

light_scheduler daemon's PID

Assuming we know the process `pid` of the application that needs to be killed, let's review killing the function using `kill()`. The arguments required to kill the function include the process `pid` and signal (`signal.SIGKILL`) that needs to be sent to the process to kill the application:

```
import os
import signal
if __name__ == "__main__":
    #kill the application
    try:
        os.kill(1815, signal.SIGKILL)
    except OSError as error:
        print("OS Error " + str(error))
```

The `signal` module (`https://docs.python.org/3/library/signal.html`) contains the constants that represents the signals that could be used to stop an application. In this code snippet, we make use of the `SIGKILL` signal. Try running the `ps` command (`ps aux`) and you will notice that the `light_scheduler` application has been killed.

Monitoring a process

In the previous example, we discussed killing an application using the `kill()` function. You might have noticed that we made use of something called the `try/except` keywords to attempt killing the application. We will discuss these keywords in detail in the next chapter.

It is also possible to monitor whether an application is running using the `kill()` function using the `try/except` keywords. We will discuss monitoring processes using the `kill()` function after introducing the concept of trapping exceptions using `try/except` keywords.

All examples discussed in the `os` module are available for download along with this chapter as `os_utils.py`.

The glob module

The `glob` module (`https://docs.python.org/3/library/glob.html`) enables identifying files of a specific extension or files that have a specific pattern. For example, it is possible to list all Python files in a folder as follows:

```
# List all files
for file in glob.glob('*.py'):
    print(file)
```

The `glob()` function returns a list of files that contains the `.py` extension. A `for` loop is used to iterate through the list and print each file. When the preceding code snippet is executed, the output contains the list of all code samples belonging to this chapter (output truncated for representation):

```
read_from_file.py
config_parser_read.py
append_to_file.py
read_line_from_file.py
config_parser_modify.py
python_utils.py
config_parser_write.py
csv_write.py
```

This module is especially helpful with listing files that have a specific pattern. For example: Let's consider a scenario where you would like to upload files that were created from different trials of an experiment. You are only interested in files that are of the following format: `file1xx.txt` where x stands for any digit between 0 and 9. Those files could be sorted and listed as follows:

```
# List all files of the format 1xx.txt
for file in glob.glob('txt_files/file1[0-9][0-9].txt'):
    print(file)
```

In the preceding example, `[0-9]` means that the file name could contain any digit between 0 and 9. Since we are looking for files of the `file1xx.txt` format, the search pattern that is passed an argument to the `glob()` function is `file1[0-9][0-9].txt`.

When the preceding code snippet is executed, the output contains all text files of the specified format:

```
txt_files/file126.txt
txt_files/file125.txt
txt_files/file124.txt
txt_files/file123.txt
txt_files/file127.txt
```

We came across this article that explains the use of expressions for sorting files: http://www.linuxjournal.com/content/bash-extended-globbing. The same concept can be extended to searching for files using the glob module.

Challenge to the reader

The examples discussed with the glob module are available for download along with this chapter as glob_example.py. In one of the examples, we discussed listing files of a specific format. How would you go about listing files that are of the following format: filexxxx.*? (Here x represents any number between 0 and 9. * represents any file extension.)

The shutil module

The shutil module (https://docs.python.org/3/library/shutil.html) enables moving and copying files between folders using the move() and copy() methods. In the previous section, we listed all text files within the folder, txt_files. Let's move these files to the current directory (where the code is being executed) using move(), make a copy of these files once again in txt_files and finally remove the text files from the current directory:

```python
import glob
import shutil
import os
if __name__ == "__main__":
    # move files to the current directory
    for file in glob.glob('txt_files/file1[0-9][0-9].txt'):
        shutil.move(file, '.')
    # make a copy of files in the folder 'txt_files' and delete them
    for file in glob.glob('file1[0-9][0-9].txt'):
        shutil.copy(file, 'txt_files')
        os.remove(file)
```

In the preceding example (available for download along with this chapter as `shutil_example.py`), the files are being moved as well as copied from the origin to the destination by specifying the source and the destination as the first and second arguments respectively.

The files to be moved (or copied) are identified using the `glob` module. Then, each file is moved or copied using their corresponding methods.

The subprocess module

We briefly discussed this module in the previous chapter. The `subprocess` module (`https://docs.python.org/3.2/library/subprocess.html`) enables launching another program from within a Python program. One of the commonly used functions from the `subprocess` module is `Popen`. Any process that needs to be launched from within the program needs to be passed as a list argument to the `Popen` function:

```python
import subprocess
if __name__ == "__main__":
    subprocess.Popen(['aplay', 'tone.wav'])
```

In the preceding example, `tone.wav` (WAVE file that needs to be played) and the command that needs to be run are passed as a list argument to the function. There are several other commands from the `subprocess` module that serve a similar purpose. We leave it to your exploration.

The sys module

The `sys` module (`https://docs.python.org/3/library/sys.html`) allows interacting with the Python run-time interpreter. One of the functions of the `sys` module is parsing command-line arguments provided as inputs to the program. Let's write a program that reads and prints the contents of the file that is passed as an argument to the program:

```python
import sys
if __name__ == "__main__":
    with open(sys.argv[1], 'r') as read_file:
        print(read_file.read())
```

Try running the preceding example as follows:

```
python3 sys_example.py read_lines.txt
```

The preceding example is available for download along with this chapter as `sys_example.py`. The list of command-line arguments passed while running the program are available as a `argv` list in the `sys` module. `argv[0]` is usually the name of the Python program and `argv[1]` is usually the first argument passed to the function.

When `sys_example.py` is executed with `read_lines.txt` as an argument, the program should print the contents of the text file:

```
I am learning Python Programming using the Raspberry Pi Zero.
This is the second line.
Line 3.
Line 4.
Line 5.
Line 6.
Line 7.
```

Summary

In this chapter, we discussed file I/O – reading and writing to files, different flags used to read, write, and append to files. We talked about moving file pointers to different points in a file to retrieve specific content or overwrite the contents of a file at a specific location. We discussed the `ConfigParser` module in Python and its application in storing/retrieving config parameters for applications along with reading and writing to CSV files.

Finally, we discussed different Python utilities that have a potential use in our project. We will be extensively making use of file I/O and the discussed Python utilities in our final project. We strongly recommend familiarizing yourself with the concepts discussed in this chapter before moving onto the final projects discussed in this book.

In the upcoming chapters, we will discuss uploading sensor data stored in CSV files to the cloud and logging errors encountered during the execution of an application. See you in the next chapter!

15
Requests and Web Frameworks

The main topics of this chapter are requests and web frameworks in Python. We are going to discuss libraries and frameworks that enable retrieving data from the Web (for example, get weather updates), upload data to a remote server (for example, log sensor data), or control appliances on a local network. We will also discuss topics that will help with learning the core topics of this chapter.

The try/except keywords

So far, we have reviewed and tested all our examples assuming the ideal condition, that is, the execution of the program will encounter no errors. On the contrary, applications fail from time to time either due to external factors, such as invalid user input and poor Internet connectivity, or program logic errors caused by the programmer. In such cases, we want the program to report/log the nature of error and either continue its execution or clean up resources before exiting the program. The try/except keywords offer a mechanism to trap an error that occurs during a program's execution and take remedial action. Because it is possible to trap and log an error in crucial parts of the code, the try/except keywords are especially useful while debugging an application.

Let's understand the try/except keywords by comparing two examples. Let's build a simple guessing game where the user is asked to guess a number between 0 and 9:

1. A random number (between 0 and 9) is generated using Python's random module. If the user's guess of the generated number is right, the Python program declares the user as the winner and exits the game.
2. If the user input is the letter x, the program quits the game.

3. The user input is converted into an integer using the int() function. A sanity check is performed to determine whether the user input is a number between 0 and 9.

4. The integer is compared against a random number. If they are the same, the user is declared the winner and the program exits the game.

Let's observe what happens when we deliberately provide an erroneous input to this program (the code snippet shown here is available for download along with this chapter as guessing_game.py):

```
import random

if __name__ == "__main__":
    while True:
        # generate a random number between 0 and 9
        rand_num = random.randrange(0,10)

        # prompt the user for a number
        value = input("Enter a number between 0 and 9: ")

        if value == 'x':
            print("Thanks for playing! Bye!")
            break

        input_value = int(value)

        if input_value < 0 or input_value > 9:
            print("Input invalid. Enter a number between 0 and 9.")


        if input_value == rand_num:
            print("Your guess is correct! You win!")
            break
        else:
            print("Nope! The random value was %s" % rand_num)
```

Let's execute the preceding code snippet and provide the input hello to the program:

```
Enter a number between 0 and 9: hello
Traceback (most recent call last):
    File "guessing_game.py", line 12, in <module>
        input_value = int(value)
ValueError: invalid literal for int() with base 10: 'hello'
```

In the preceding example, the program fails when it is trying to convert the user input `hello` to an integer. The program execution ends with an exception. An exception highlights the line where the error has occurred. In this case, it has occurred in line 10:

```
File "guessing_game.py", line 12, in <module>
input_value = int(value)
```

The nature of the error is also highlighted in the exception. In this example, the last line indicates that the exception thrown is `ValueError`:

```
ValueError: invalid literal for int() with base 10: 'hello'
```

Let's discuss the same example (available for download along with this chapter as `try_and_except.py`) that makes use of the `try`/`except` keywords. It is possible to continue playing the game after trapping this exception and printing it to the screen. We have the following code:

```python
import random

if __name__ == "__main__":
    while True:
        # generate a random number between 0 and 9
        rand_num = random.randrange(0, 10)

        # prompt the user for a number
        value = input("Enter a number between 0 and 9: ")

        if value == 'x':
            print("Thanks for playing! Bye!")

        try:
            input_value = int(value)
        except ValueError as error:
            print("The value is invalid %s" % error)
            continue

        if input_value < 0 or input_value > 9:
            print("Input invalid. Enter a number between 0 and 9.")
            continue

        if input_value == rand_num:
            print("Your guess is correct! You win!")
            break
        else:
            print("Nope! The random value was %s" % rand_num)
```

Let's discuss how the same example works with the `try`/`except` keywords:

1. From the previous example, we know that when a user provides the wrong input (for example, a letter instead of a number between 0 and 9), the exception occurs at line 10 (where the user input is converted into an integer), and the nature of the error is named `ValueError`.

2. It is possible to avoid interruption of the program's execution by wrapping this in a `try...except` block:

```
try:
    input_value = int(value)
except ValueError as error:
    print("The value is invalid %s" % error)
```

3. On receiving a user input, the program attempts converting the user input into an integer under the `try` block.

4. If `ValueError` has occurred, `error` is trapped by the `except` block, and the following message is printed to the screen along with the actual error message:

```
except ValueError as error:
    print("The value is invalid %s" % error)
```

5. Try executing the code example and try providing an invalid input. You will note that the program prints the error message (along with the nature of the error) and goes back to the top of the game loop and continues seeking valid user input:

```
Enter a number between 0 and 9: 3
Nope! The random value was 5
Enter a number between 0 and 9: hello
The value is invalid invalid literal for int() with
base 10: 'hello'
Enter a number between 0 and 10: 4
Nope! The random value was 6
```

The `try...except` block comes with a substantial processing power cost. Hence, it is important to keep the `try...except` block as short as possible. Because we know that the error occurs on the line where we attempt converting the user input into an integer, we wrap it in a `try...except` block to trap an error.

Thus, the `try`/`except` keywords are used to prevent any abnormal behavior in a program's execution due to an error. It enables logging the error and taking remedial action. Similar to the `try...except` block, there are also `try...except...else` and `try...except...else` code blocks. Let's quickly review those options with a couple of examples.

try...except...else

The `try...except...else` block is especially useful when we want a certain block of code to be executed only when no exceptions are raised. In order to demonstrate this concept, let's rewrite the guessing game example using this block:

```
try:
    input_value = int(value)
except ValueError as error:
    print("The value is invalid %s" % error)
else:
    if input_value < 0 or input_value > 9:
        print("Input invalid. Enter a number between 0 and 9.")
    elif input_value == rand_num:
        print("Your guess is correct! You win!")
        break
    else:
        print("Nope! The random value was %s" % rand_num)
```

The modified guessing game example that makes use of the `try...except...else` block is available for download along with this chapter as `try_except_else.py`. In this example, the program compares the user input against the random number only if a valid user input was received. It otherwise skips the `else` block and goes back to the top of the loop to accept the next user input. Thus, `try...except...else` is used when we want a specific code block to be executed when no exceptions are raised due to the code in the `try` block.

try...except...else...finally

As the name suggests, the `finally` block is used to execute a block of code on leaving the `try` block. This block of code is executed even after an exception is raised. This is useful in scenarios where we need to clean up resources and free up memory before moving on to the next stage.

Let's demonstrate the function of the `finally` block using our guessing game. To understand how the `finally` keyword works, let's make use of a counter variable named `count` that is incremented in the `finally` block, and another counter variable named `valid_count` that is incremented in the `else` block. We have the following code:

```
count = 0
valid_count = 0
while True:
    # generate a random number between 0 and 9
    rand_num = random.randrange(0,10)

    # prompt the user for a number
    value = input("Enter a number between 0 and 9: ")

    if value == 'x':
        print("Thanks for playing! Bye!")

    try:
        input_value = int(value)
    except ValueError as error:
        print("The value is invalid %s" % error)
    else:
        if input_value < 0 or input_value > 9:
            print("Input invalid. Enter a number between 0 and 9.")
            continue

        valid_count += 1
        if input_value == rand_num:
            print("Your guess is correct! You win!")
            break
        else:
            print("Nope! The random value was %s" % rand_num)
    finally:
        count += 1

print("You won the game in %d attempts "\
        "and %d inputs were valid" % (count, valid_count))
```

The preceding code snippet is from the `try_except_else_finally.py` code sample (available for download along with this chapter). Try executing the code sample and playing the game. You will note the total number of attempts it took to win the game and the number of inputs that were valid:

```
Enter a number between 0 and 9: g
The value is invalid invalid literal for int() with
base 10: 'g'
Enter a number between 0 and 9: 3
Your guess is correct! You win!
You won the game in 9 attempts and 8 inputs were valid
```

This demonstrates how the `try-except-else-finally` block works. Any code under the `else` keyword is executed when the critical code block (under the `try` keyword) is executed successfully, whereas the code block under the `finally` keyword is executed while exiting the `try...except` block (useful for cleaning up resources while exiting a code block).

Try providing invalid inputs while playing the game using the previous code example to understand the code block flow.

Connecting to the Internet – web requests

Now that we discussed the `try`/`except` keywords, let's make use of it to build a simple application that connects to the Internet. We will write a simple application that retrieves the current time from the Internet. We will be making use of the `requests` library for Python (http://requests.readthedocs.io/en/master/#).

The `requests` module enables connecting to the Web and retrieving information. In order to do so, we need to make use of the `get()` method from the `requests` module to make a request:

```
import requests
response = requests.get('http://nist.time.gov/actualtime.cgi')
```

In the preceding code snippet, we are passing a URL as an argument to the `get()` method. In this case, it is the URL that returns the current time in the Unix format (`https://en.wikipedia.org/wiki/Unix_time`).

Let's make use of the `try`/`except` keywords to make a request to get the current time:

```
#!/usr/bin/python3

import requests

if __name__ == "__main__":
  # Source for link: http://stackoverflow.com/a/30635751/822170
  try:
    response = requests.get('http://nist.time.gov/actualtime.cgi')
    print(response.text)
  except requests.exceptions.ConnectionError as error:
    print("Something went wrong. Try again")
```

In the preceding example (available for download along with this chapter as `internet_access.py`), the request is made under the `try` block, and the response (returned by `response.text`) is printed to the screen.

If there is an error while executing the request to retrieve the current time, `ConnectionError` is raised (`http://requests.readthedocs.io/en/master/user/quickstart/#errors-and-exceptions`). This error could either be caused by the lack of an Internet connection or an incorrect URL. This error is caught by the `except` block. Try running the example, and it should return the current time from `time.gov`:

```
<timestamp time="1474421525322329" delay="0"/>
```

The application of requests – retrieving weather information

Let's make use of the `requests` module to retrieve the weather information for the city of San Francisco. We will be making use of the **OpenWeatherMap** API (`openweathermap.org`) to retrieve the weather information:

1. In order to make use of the API, sign up for an API account and get an API key (it is free of charge):

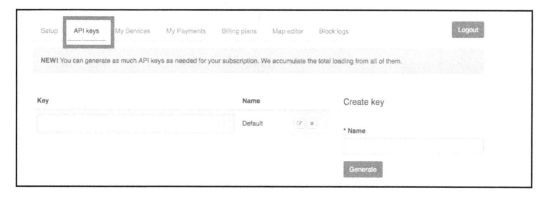

An API key from openweathermap.org

2. According to the API documentation (`openweathermap.org/current`), the weather information for a city can be retrieved using `http://api.openweathermap.org/data/2.5/weather?zip=SanFrancisco&appid=API_KEY&units=imperial` as the URL.

3. Substitute `API_KEY` with the key from your account and use it to retrieve the current weather information in a browser. You should be able to retrieve the weather information in the following format:

    ```
    {"coord":{"lon":-122.42,"lat":37.77},"weather":[{"id":800,
    "main":"Clear","description":"clear sky","icon":"01n"}],"base":
    "stations","main":{"temp":71.82,"pressure":1011,"humidity":50,
    "temp_min":68,"temp_max":75.99},"wind":
    {"speed":13.04,"deg":291},
    "clouds":{"all":0},"dt":1474505391,"sys":{"type":3,"id":9966,
    "message":0.0143,"country":"US","sunrise":1474552682,
    "sunset":1474596336},"id":5391959,"name":"San
    Francisco","cod":200}
    ```

The weather information (shown previously) is returned in the JSON format. **JavaScript Object Notation (JSON)** is a data format that is widely used to exchange data over the Web. The main advantage of JSON format is that it is in a readable format and many popular programming languages support encapsulating data in JSON format. As shown in the earlier snippet, JSON format enables exchanging information in readable name/value pairs.

Let's review retrieving the weather using the `requests` module and parsing the JSON data:

1. Substitute the URL in the previous example (`internet_access.py`) with the one discussed in this example. This should return the weather information in the JSON format.

2. The requests module provides a method to parse the JSON data. The response could be parsed as follows:

   ```
   response = requests.get(URL)
   json_data = response.json()
   ```

3. The `json()` function parses the response from the OpenWeatherMap API and returns a dictionary of different weather parameters (`json_data`) and their values.

4. Since we know the response format from the API documentation, the current temperature could be retrieved from the parsed response as follows:

   ```
   print(json_data['main']['temp'])
   ```

5. Putting it all together, we have this:

   ```
   #!/usr/bin/python3

   import requests

   # generate your own API key
   APP_ID = '5d6f02fd4472611a20f4ce602010ee0c'
   ZIP = 94103
   URL = """http://api.openweathermap.org/data/2.5/weather?zip={}
   &appid={}&units=imperial""".format(ZIP, APP_ID)

   if __name__ == "__main__":
     # API Documentation: http://openweathermap.org/
     current#current_JSON
     try:
   ```

```
# encode data payload and post it
response = requests.get(URL)
json_data = response.json()
print("Temperature is %s degrees Fahrenheit" %
json_data['main']['temp'])
except requests.exceptions.ConnectionError as error:
    print("The error is %s" % error)
```

The preceding example is available for download along with this chapter as `weather_example.py`. The example should display the current temperature as follows:

```
Temperature is 68.79 degrees Fahrenheit
```

The application of requests – publishing events to the Internet

In the previous example, we retrieved information from the Internet. Let's consider an example where we have to publish a sensor event somewhere on the Internet. This could be either a cat door opening while you are away from home or someone at your doorstep stepping on the doormat. Because we discussed interfacing sensors to the Raspberry Pi Zero in the previous chapter, let's discuss a scenario where we could post these events to *Slack*—a workplace communication tool, Twitter, or cloud services such as **Phant** (https://data.sparkfun.com/).

In this example, we will post these events to Slack using `requests`. Let's send a direct message to ourselves on Slack whenever a sensor event such as a cat door opening occurs. We need a URL to post these sensor events to Slack. Let's review generating a URL in order to post sensor events to Slack:

1. The first step in generating a URL is creating an *incoming webhook*. A webhook is a type request that can post messages that are carried as a payload to applications such as Slack.

2. If you are a member of a Slack team named *TeamX*, launch your team's application directory, namely `teamx.slack.com/apps` in a browser:

Launch your team's app directory

3. Search for `incoming webhooks` in your app directory and select the first option, **Incoming WebHooks** (as shown in the following screenshot):

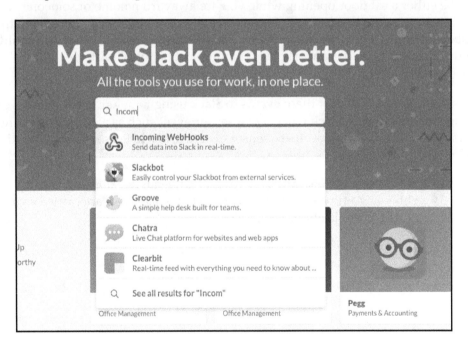

Select incoming webhooks

4. Click on **Add Configuration**:

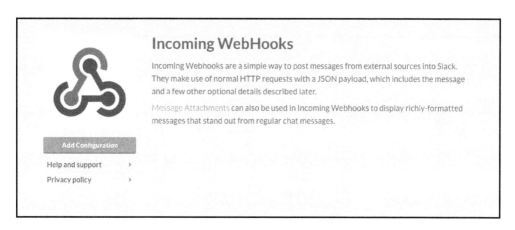

Add Configuration

5. Let's send a private message to ourselves when an event occurs. Select
   Privately to **(you)** as the option and create a webhook by clicking on
   Add Incoming WebHooks integration:

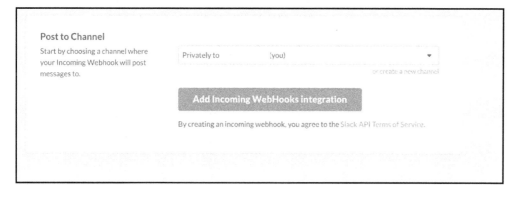

Select Privately to you

6. We have generated a URL to send direct messages about sensor events (URL partially concealed):

Webhook URL	`https://hooks.slack.com/services/`
Sending Messages	You have two options for sending data to the Webhook URL above: • Send a JSON string as the `payload` parameter in a POST request • Send a JSON string as the body of a POST request For a simple message, your JSON payload could contain a `text` property at minimum. This is the text that will be posted to the channel. A simple example: `payload={"text": "This is a line of text in a channel.\nAnd this is`

Generated URL

7. Now, we can send direct message to ourselves on Slack using the previously-mentioned URL. The sensor event can be published to Slack as a JSON payload. Let's review posting a sensor event to Slack.

8. For example, let's consider posting a message when a cat door opens. The first step is preparing the JSON payload for the message. According to the Slack API documentation (`https://api.slack.com/custom-integrations`), the message payload needs to be in the following format:

```
payload = {"text": "The cat door was just opened!"}
```

9. In order to publish this event, we will make use of the `post()` method from the `requests` module. The data payload needs to be encoded in JSON format while posting it:

```
response = requests.post(URL, json.dumps(payload))
```

10. Putting it all together, we have this:

```
#!/usr/bin/python3

import requests
import json

# generate your own URL
URL = 'https://hooks.slack.com/services/'
```

```
if __name__ == "__main__":
  payload = {"text": "The cat door was just opened!"}
  try:
    # encode data payload and post it
    response = requests.post(URL, json.dumps(payload))
    print(response.text)
  except requests.exceptions.ConnectionError as error:
    print("The error is %s" % error)
```

11. On posting the message, the request returns ok as a response. This indicates that the post was successful.

12. Generate your own URL and execute the preceding example (available for download along with this chapter as slack_post.py). You will receive a direct message on Slack:

Direct message on Slack

Now, try interfacing a sensor to the Raspberry Pi Zero (discussed in previous chapters) and post the sensor events to Slack.

It is also possible to post sensor events to Twitter and have your Raspberry Pi Zero check for new e-mails and so on. Check this book's website for more examples.

Flask web framework

In our final section, we will discuss web frameworks in Python. We will discuss the Flask framework (http://flask.pocoo.org/). Python-based frameworks enable interfacing sensors to a network using the Raspberry Pi Zero. This enables controlling appliances and reading data from sensors from anywhere within a network. Let's get started!

Installing Flask

The first step is installing the Flask framework. It can be done as follows:

```
sudo pip3 install flask
```

Building our first example

The Flask framework documentation explains building the first example. Modify the example from the documentation as follows:

```python
#!/usr/bin/python3

from flask import Flask
app = Flask(__name__)

@app.route("/")
def hello():
    return "Hello World!"

if __name__ == "__main__":
    app.run('0.0.0.0')
```

Launch this example (available for download along with this chapter as flask_example.py) and it should launch a server on the Raspberry Pi Zero visible to the network. On another computer, launch a browser and enter the IP address of the Raspberry Pi Zero along with port number, 5000, as a suffix (as shown in the following snapshot). It should take you to the index page of the server that displays the message **Hello World!**:

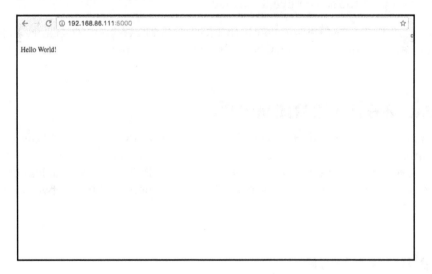

The Flask framework-based web server on the Raspberry Pi Zero

You can find the IP address of your Raspberry Pi Zero using the ifconfig command on the command-line terminal.

Controlling appliances using the Flask framework

Let's try turning on/off appliances at home using the Flask framework. In previous chapters, we made use of *PowerSwitch Tail II* to control a table lamp using the Raspberry Pi Zero. Let's try to control the same using the Flask framework. Connect PowerSwitch Tail, as shown in the following figure:

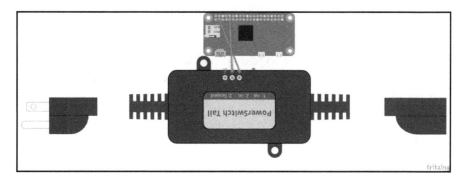

Controlling a table lamp using the Flask framework

According to the Flask framework documentation, it is possible to route a URL to a specific function. For example, it is possible to bind /lamp/<control> using route() to the control() function:

```
@app.route("/lamp/<control>")
def control(control):
  if control == "on":
    lights.on()
  elif control == "off":
    lights.off()
  return "Table lamp is now %s" % control
```

In the preceding code snippet, <control> is a variable that can be passed on as an argument to the binding function. This enables us to turn the lamp on/off. For example, <IP address>:5000/lamp/on turns on the lamp, and vice versa. Putting it all together, we have this:

```
#!/usr/bin/python3

from flask import Flask
from gpiozero import OutputDevice

app = Flask(__name__)
```

```
lights = OutputDevice(2)

@app.route("/lamp/<control>")
def control(control):
  if control == "on":
    lights.on()
  elif control == "off":
    lights.off()
  return "Table lamp is now %s" % control

if __name__ == "__main__":
    app.run('0.0.0.0')
```

The preceding example is available for download along with this chapter as `appliance_control.py`. Launch the Flask-based web server and open a web server on another computer. In order to turn on the lamp, enter `<IP Address of the Raspberry Pi Zero>:5000/lamp/on` as URL:

This should turn on the lamp:

Thus, we have built a simple framework that enables controlling appliances within the network. It is possible to include buttons to an HTML page and route them to a specific URL to perform a specific function. There are several other frameworks in Python that enable developing web applications. We have merely introduced you to different applications that are possible with Python. We recommend that you check out this book's website for more examples, such as controlling Halloween decorations and other holiday decorations using the Flask framework.

Summary

In this chapter, we discussed the `try/except` keywords in Python. We also discussed developing applications that retrieves information from the Internet, as well as publishing sensor events to the Internet. We also discussed the Flask web framework for Python and demonstrated the control of appliances within a network. In the next chapter, we will discuss some advanced topics in Python.

16
Awesome Things You Could Develop Using Python

In this chapter, we will discuss some advanced topics in Python. We will also discuss certain unique topics (such as image processing) that let you get started with application development in Python.

Image processing using a Raspberry Pi Zero

The Raspberry Pi Zero is an inexpensive piece of hardware that is powered by a 1 GHz processor. While it is not powerful to run certain advanced image processing operations, it can help you learn the basics on a $25 budget (the cost of Raspberry Pi Zero and a camera).

We recommend using a 16 GB card (or higher) with your Raspberry Pi Zero in order to install the image processing tool set discussed in this section.

For example, you could use a Raspberry Pi Zero to track a bird in your backyard. In this chapter, we are going to discuss different ways to get started with image processing on the Raspberry Pi Zero.

In order to test some examples using the camera in this section, a Raspberry Pi Zero v1.3 or later is required. Check the back of your Raspberry Pi Zero to verify the board version:

Identifying your Raspberry Pi Zero's version

OpenCV

OpenCV is an open source toolbox that consists of different software tools developed for image processing. OpenCV is a cross-platform toolbox that has been developed with support for different operating systems. Because OpenCV is available under an open source license, researchers across the world have contributed to its growth by developing tools and techniques. This has made developing applications with relative ease. Some applications of OpenCV include face recognition and license plate recognition.

Due to its limited processing power, it can take several hours to complete the installation of the framework. It took us approximately 10 hours at our end.

We followed the instructions to install OpenCV on the Raspberry Pi Zero from
`http://www.pyimagesearch.com/2015/10/26/how-to-install-opencv-3-on-raspbia`
`n-jessie/`.We specifically followed the instructions to install OpenCV with Python
3.x bindings and verified the installation process. It took us approximately 10 hours to
finish installing OpenCV on the Raspberry Pi Zero. We are not repeating the
instructions in the interest of not reinventing the wheel.

The verification of the installation

Let's make sure that the OpenCV installation and its Python bindings work. Launch
the command-line terminal and make sure that you have launched the cv virtual
environment by executing the `workon cv` command (you can verify that you are in
the cv virtual environment):

Verify that you are in the cv virtual environment

Now, let's make sure that our installation works correctly. Launch the Python
interpreter from the command line and try to import the cv2 module:

```
>>> import cv2
>>> cv2.__version__
'3.0.0'
```

This proves that OpenCV is installed on the Raspberry Pi Zero. Let's write a *hello
world* example involving OpenCV. In this example, we are going to open an image
(this can be any color image on your Raspberry Pi Zero's desktop) and display it after
converting it to grayscale. We will be using the following documentation to write our
first example:
`http://docs.opencv.org/3.0-beta/doc/py_tutorials/py_gui/py_image_display/p`
`y_image_display.html`.

According to the documentation, we need to make use of the imread() function to read the contents of the image file. We also need to specify the format in which we would like to read the image. In this case, we are going to read the image in grayscale format. This is specified by cv2.IMREAD_GRAYSCALE that is passed as the second argument to the function:

```
import cv2

img = cv2.imread('/home/pi/screenshot.jpg',cv2.IMREAD_GRAYSCALE)
```

Now that the image is loaded in grayscale format and saved to the img variable, we need to display it in a new window. This is enabled by the imshow() function. According to the documentation, we can display an image by specifying the window name as the first argument and the image as the second argument:

```
cv2.imshow('image',img)
```

In this case, we are going to open a window named image and display the contents of img that we loaded in the previous step. We will display the image until a keystroke is received. This is achieved using the cv2.waitKey() function. According to the documentation, the waitkey() function listens for keyboard events:

```
cv2.waitKey(0)
```

The 0 argument indicates that we are going to wait indefinitely for a keystroke. According to the documentation, when the duration, in milliseconds, is passed as an argument, the waitkey() function listens to keystrokes for the specified duration. When any key is pressed, the window is closed by the destroyAllWindows() function:

```
cv2.destroyAllWindows()
```

Putting it all together, we have this:

```
import cv2

img = cv2.imread('/home/pi/screenshot.jpg',cv2.IMREAD_GRAYSCALE)
cv2.imshow('image',img)
cv2.waitKey(0)
cv2.destroyAllWindows()
```

The preceding code sample is available for download along with this chapter as `opencv_test.py`. Once you are done installing OpenCV libraries, try loading an image as shown in this example. It should load an image in grayscale, as shown in the following figure:

The Raspberry Pi desktop loaded in grayscale

This window would close at the press of any key.

A challenge to the reader

In the preceding example, the window closes at the press of any key. Take a look at the documentation and determine if it is possible to close all windows at the press of a mouse button.

Installing the camera to the Raspberry Zero

A camera connector and a camera is required for testing our next example. One source to buy the camera and the adapter is provided here:

Name	Source
Raspberry Pi Zero camera adapter	https://thepihut.com/products/raspberry-pi-zero-camera-adapter
Raspberry Pi camera	https://thepihut.com/products/raspberry-pi-camera-module

Perform the following steps to install a camera to the Raspberry Pi Zero:

1. The first step is interfacing the camera to the Raspberry Pi Zero. The camera adapter can be installed as shown in the following figure. Lift the connector tab and slide the camera adapter and press the connector gently:

2. We need to enable the camera interface on the Raspberry Pi Zero. On your desktop, go to **Preferences** and launch **Raspberry Pi Configuration**. Under the **Interfaces** tab of the Raspberry Pi configuration, enable the camera, and save the configuration:

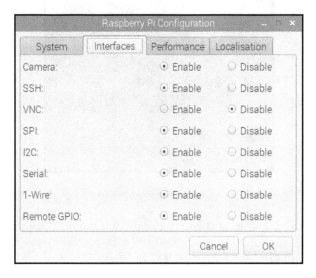

Enable the camera interface

3. Let's test the camera by taking a picture by running the following command from the command-line terminal:

```
raspistill -o /home/pi/Desktop/test.jpg
```

4. It should take a picture and save it to your Raspberry Pi's desktop. Verify that the camera is functioning correctly. If you are not able to get the camera working, we recommend the troubleshooting guide published by the Raspberry Pi Foundation:
https://www.raspberrypi.org/documentation/raspbian/applications/camera.md.

The camera cable is a bit unwieldy, and it can make things difficult while trying to take a picture. We recommend using a camera mount. We found this one to be useful (shown in the following image) at `http://a.co/hQolR7O`:

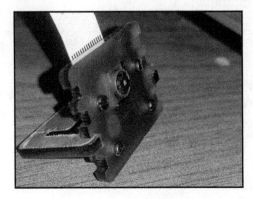

Use a mount for your Raspberry Pi's camera

Let's take the camera for a spin and use it alongside OpenCV libraries:

1. We are going to take a picture using the camera and display it using the OpenCV framework. In order to access the camera in Python, we need the `picamera` package. This can be installed as follows:

```
pip3 install picamera
```

2. Let's make sure that the package works as intended with a simple program. The documentation for the `picamera` package is available at `https://picamera.readthedocs.io/en/release-1.12/api_camera.html`.

3. The first step is initializing the `PiCamera` class. This is followed by flipping the image across the vertical axis. This is only required because the camera is mounted upside down on the mount. This may not be necessary with other mounts:

```
with PiCamera() as camera:
camera.vflip = True
```

4. Before taking a picture, we can preview the picture that is going to be captured using the `start_preview()` method:

```
camera.start_preview()
```

5. Let's preview for `10` seconds before we take a picture. We can take a picture using the `capture()` method:

```
sleep(10)
camera.capture("/home/pi/Desktop/desktop_shot.jpg")
camera.stop_preview()
```

6. The `capture()` method requires the file location as an argument (as shown in the preceding snippet). Once we are done, we can close the camera preview using `stop_preview()`.

7. Putting it altogether, we have this:

```
from picamera import PiCamera
from time import sleep

if __name__ == "__main__":
    with PiCamera() as camera:
        camera.vflip = True
        camera.start_preview()
        sleep(10)
        camera.capture("/home/pi/Desktop/desktop_shot.jpg")
        camera.stop_preview()
```

The preceding code sample is available for download along with this chapter as `picamera_test.py`. A snapshot taken using the camera is shown in the following figure:

Image captured using the Raspberry Pi camera module

8. Let's combine this example with the previous one—convert this image to grayscale and display it until a key is pressed. Ensure that you are still within the `cv` virtual environment workspace.

9. Let's convert the captured image to grayscale as follows:

```
img = cv2.imread("/home/pi/Desktop/desktop_shot.jpg",
cv2.IMREAD_GRAYSCALE)
```

The following is the image converted upon capture:

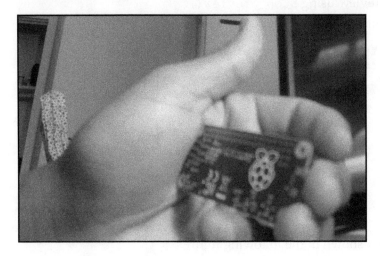

Image converted to grayscale upon capture

10. Now we can display the grayscale image as follows:

```
cv2.imshow("image", img)
cv2.waitKey(0)
cv2.destroyAllWindows()
```

The modified example is available for download as `picamera_opencvtest.py`.

So far, we have demonstrated developing image processing applications in Python. We also recommend checking out examples available with the OpenCV Python binding documentation (link provided in the introduction part of this section).

Speech recognition

In this section, we will discuss developing a speech recognition example in Python involving speech recognition. We will make use of the `requests` module (discussed in the previous chapter) to transcribe audio using `wit.ai` (`https://wit.ai/`).

 There are several speech recognition tools, including Google's Speech API, IBM Watson, Microsoft Bing's speech recognition API. We are demonstrating `wit.ai` as an example.

Speech recognition can be useful in applications where we would like to enable the Raspberry Pi Zero responses to voice commands.

Let's review building the speech recognition application in Python using `wit.ai` (its documentation is available here at `https://github.com/wit-ai/pywit`). In order to perform speech recognition and recognize voice commands, we will need a microphone. However, we will demonstrate using a readily available audio sample. We will make use of audio samples made available by a research publication (available at `http://ecs.utdallas.edu/loizou/speech/noizeus/clean.zip`).

 The `wit.ai` API license states that the tool is free to use, but the audio uploaded to their servers are used to tune their speech transcription tool.

We will now attempt transcribing the `sp02.wav` audio sample performing the following steps:

1. The first step is signing up for an account with `wit.ai`. Make a note of the API as shown in the following screenshot:

2. The first step is installing the requests library. It could be installed as follows:

   ```
   pip3 install requests
   ```

3. According to the `wit.ai` documentation, we need to add custom headers to our request that includes the API key (replace `$TOKEN` with the token from your account). We also need to specify the file format in the header. In this case, it is a `.wav` file, and the sampling frequency is 8000 Hz:

   ```python
   import requests

   if __name__ == "__main__":
       url = 'https://api.wit.ai/speech?v=20161002'
       headers = {"Authorization": "Bearer $TOKEN",
                   "Content-Type": "audio/wav"}
   ```

4. In order to transcribe the audio sample, we need to attach the audio sample in the request body:

   ```python
   files = open('sp02.wav', 'rb')
   response = requests.post(url, headers=headers, data=files)
   print(response.status_code)
   print(response.text)
   ```

5. Putting it all together, gives us this:

```
#!/usr/bin/python3

import requests

if __name__ == "__main__":
  url = 'https://api.wit.ai/speech?v=20161002'
  headers = {"Authorization": "Bearer $TOKEN",
             "Content-Type": "audio/wav"}
  files = open('sp02.wav', 'rb')
  response = requests.post(url, headers=headers, data=files)
  print(response.status_code)
  print(response.text)
```

The preceding code sample is available for download along with this chapter as wit_ai.py. Try executing the preceding code sample, and it should transcribe the audio sample: sp02.wav. We have the following code:

```
200
{
  "msg_id" : "fae9cc3a-f7ed-4831-87ba-6a08e95f515b",
  "_text" : "he knew the the great young actress",
  "outcomes" : [ {
    "_text" : "he knew the the great young actress",
    "confidence" : 0.678,
    "intent" : "DataQuery",
    "entities" : {
      "value" : [ {
        "confidence" : 0.7145905790744499,
        "type" : "value",
        "value" : "he",
        "suggested" : true
      }, {
        "confidence" : 0.5699616515542044,
        "type" : "value",
        "value" : "the",
        "suggested" : true
      }, {
        "confidence" : 0.5981701138805214,
        "type" : "value",
        "value" : "great",
        "suggested" : true
      }, {
        "confidence" : 0.8999612482250062,
        "type" : "value",
        "value" : "actress",
        "suggested" : true
```

```
        } ]
      }
    } ],
    "WARNING" : "DEPRECATED"
  }
```

The audio sample contains the following recording: *He knew the skill of the great young actress*. According to the `wit.ai` API, the transcription is *He knew the the great young actress*. The word error rate is 22% (`https://en.wikipedia.org/wiki/Word_error_rate`).

Automating routing tasks

In this section, we are going to discuss automating routing tasks in Python. We took two examples such that they demonstrate the ability of a Raspberry Pi Zero acting as a personal assistant. The first example involves improving your commute, whereas the second example serves as an aid to improve your vocabulary. Let's get started.

Improving daily commute

Many cities and public transit systems have started sharing data with the public in the interest of being transparent and improving their operational efficiency. Transit systems have started sharing advisories and transit information to the public through an API. This enables anyone to develop mobile applications that provide information to commuters. At times, it helps with easing congestion within the public transit system.

This example was inspired by a friend who tracks bicycle availability in San Francisco's bike share stations. In the San Francisco Bay Area, there is a bicycle sharing program that enables commuters to rent a bike from a transit center to their work. In a crowded city like San Francisco, bike availability at a given station fluctuates depending on the time of day.

This friend wanted to plan his day based on bike availability at the nearest bike share station. If there are very few bikes left at the station, this friend preferred leaving early to rent a bike. He was looking for a simple hack that would push a notification to his phone when the number of bikes is below a certain threshold. San Francisco's bike share program makes this data available at
`http://feeds.bayareabikeshare.com/stations/stations.json`.

Let's review building a simple example that would enable sending a push notification to a mobile device. In order to send a mobile push notification, we will be making use of **If This Then That (IFTTT)**—a service that enables connecting your project to third-party services.

In this example, we will parse the data available in JSON format, check the number of available bikes at a specific station, and if it is lower than the specified threshold, it triggers a notification on your mobile device.

Let's get started:

1. The first step is retrieving the bike availability from the bike share service. This data is available in JSON format at
    `http://feeds.bayareabikeshare.com/stations/stations.json`. The data includes bike availability throughout the network.
2. The bike availability at each station is provided with parameters, such as station ID, station name, address, number of bikes available, and so on.
3. In this example, we will retrieve the bike availability for the `Townsend at 7th` station in San Francisco. The station ID is `65` (open the earlier-mentioned link in a browser to find `id`). Let's write some Python code to retrieve the bike availability data and parse this information:

    ```
    import requests

    BIKE_URL = http://feeds.bayareabikeshare.com/stations
    /stations.json

    # fetch the bike share information
    response = requests.get(BIKE_URL)
    parsed_data = response.json()
    ```

The first step is fetching the data using a `GET` request (via the `requests` module). The `requests` module provides an inbuilt JSON decoder. The JSON data can be parsed by calling the `json()` function.

4. Now, we can iterate through the dictionary of stations and find the bike availability at `Townsend at 7th`, by performing the following steps:

1. In the retrieved data, each station's data is furnished with an ID. The station ID in question is `65` (open the data feed URL provided earlier in a browser to understand the data format; a snippet of the data is shown in the following screenshot):

```
{"id":65,"stationName":"Townsend at 7th","availableDocks":7,"totalDocks"
```

A snippet of the bike share data feed fetched using a browser

2. We need to iterate through the values and determine if the station `id` matches that of `Townsend at 7th`:

```
station_list = parsed_data['stationBeanList']
for station in station_list:
  if station['id'] == 65 and
    station['availableBikes'] < 2:
    print("The available bikes is %d" % station
    ['availableBikes'])
```

If there are less than `2` bikes available at the station, we push a mobile notification to our mobile device.

5. In order to receive mobile notifications, you need to install *IF by IFTTT* app (available for Apple and Android devices).
6. We also need to set up a recipe on IFTTT to trigger mobile notifications. Sign up for an account at `https://ifttt.com/`.

IFTTT is a service that enables creating recipes that connecting devices to different applications and automating tasks. For example, it is possible to log events tracked by the Raspberry Pi Zero to a spreadsheet on your Google Drive.

All recipes on IFTTT follow a common template—*if this then that*, that is, if a particular event has occurred, then a specific action is triggered. For this example, we need to create an applet that triggers a mobile notification on receiving a web request.

7. You can start creating an applet using the drop-down menu under your account, as shown in the following screenshot:

Start creating a recipe on IFTTT

8. It should take you to a recipe setup page (shown as follows). Click on **this** and set up an incoming web request:

Click on this

9. Select the **Maker Webhooks** channel as the incoming trigger:

Select the Maker Webhooks channel

10. Select **Receive a web request**. A web request from the Raspberry Pi would act as a trigger to send a mobile notification:

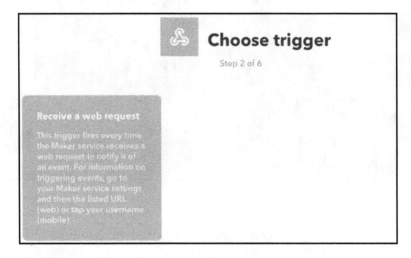

Select Receive a web request

11. Create a trigger named `mobile_notify`:

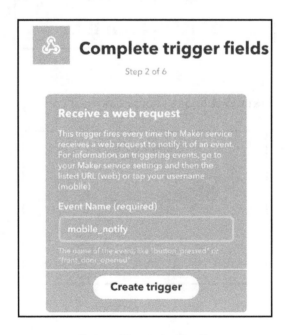

Create a new trigger named mobile_notify

12. It is time to create an action for the incoming trigger. Click on **that**.

Click on that

13. Select **Notifications**:

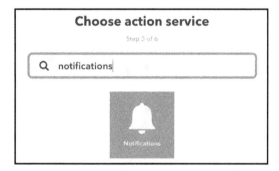

Select Notifications

14. Now, let's format the notification that we would like to receive on our
     devices:

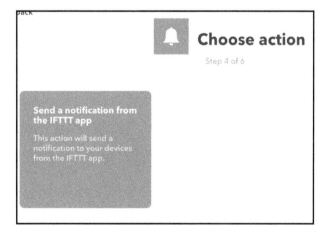

Setup notification for your device

15. In the mobile notification, we need to receive the number of bikes available at the bike share station. Click on the **+ Ingredient** button and select `Value1`.

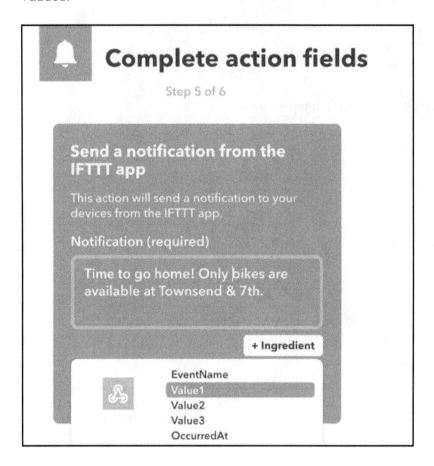

Format the message to suit your needs. For example, when a notification is triggered by the Raspberry Pi, it would be great to receive a message in the following format: `Time to go home! Only 2 bikes are available at Townsend & 7th!`

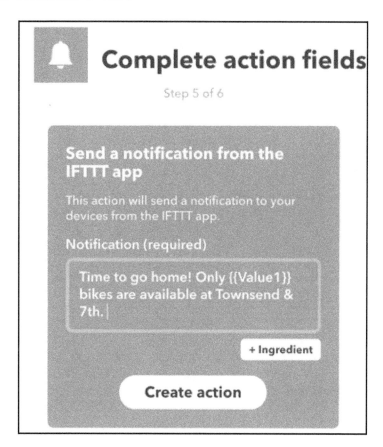

16. Once you are satisfied with the message format, select **Create action** and your recipe should be ready!

Create a recipe

17. In order to trigger a notification on our mobile device, we need a URL to make the POST request and a trigger key. This is available under **Services | Maker Webhooks | Settings** in your IFTTT account.

The trigger can be located here:

Open the URL listed in the preceding screenshot in a new browser window. It provides the URL for the `POST` request as well as an explanation on (shown in the following screenshot) how to make a web request:

Your key is:

◀ Back to service

To trigger an Event

Make a POST or GET web request to:

```
https://maker.ifttt.com/trigger/ {event} /with/key/
```

With an optional JSON body of:

```
{ "value1" : "          ", "value2" : "          ", "value3" : "          " }
```

The data is completely optional, and you can also pass `value1`, `value2`, and `value3` as query parameters or form variables. This content will be passed on to the Action in your Recipe.

You can also try it with `curl` from a command line.

```
curl -X POST https://maker.ifttt.com/trigger/{event}/with/key/
```

Test It

Making a POST request using the earlier-mentioned URL (key concealed for privacy)

18. While making a request (as explained in the IFTTT documentation), if we include the number of bikes in the JSON body of request (using `Value1`), it can be shown on the mobile notification.

19. Let's revisit the Python example to make a web request when the number of bikes is below a certain threshold. Save the `IFTTT` URL and your IFTTT access key (retrieved from your IFTTT account) to your code as follows:

```
IFTTT_URL = "https://maker.ifttt.com/trigger/mobile_notify/
with/key/$KEY"
```

20. When the number of bikes is below a certain threshold, we need to make a `POST` request with the bike information encoded in the JSON body:

```
for station in station_list:
  if station['id'] == 65 and
     station['availableBikes'] < 3:
     print("The available bikes is %d" %
     station['availableBikes'])
```

```
payload = {"value1": station['availableBikes']}
response = requests.post(IFTTT_URL, json=payload)
if response.status_code == 200:
  print("Notification successfully triggered")
```

21. In the preceding code snippet, if there are less than three bikes, a POST request is made using the `requests` module. The number of available bikes is encoded with the key `value1`:

```
payload = {"value1": station['availableBikes']}
```

22. Putting it all together, we have this:

```
#!/usr/bin/python3

import requests
import datetime

BIKE_URL = "http://feeds.bayareabikeshare.com/stations/
stations.json"
# find your key from ifttt
IFTTT_URL = "https://maker.ifttt.com/trigger/mobile_notify/
with/key/$KEY"

if __name__ == "__main__":
  # fetch the bike share information
  response = requests.get(BIKE_URL)
  parsed_data = response.json()
  station_list = parsed_data['stationBeanList']
  for station in station_list:
    if station['id'] == 65 and
       station['availableBikes'] < 10:
      print("The available bikes is %d" % station
      ['availableBikes'])
  payload = {"value1": station['availableBikes']}
      response = requests.post(IFTTT_URL, json=payload)
      if response.status_code == 200:
        print("Notification successfully triggered")
```

The preceding code sample is available for download along with this chapter as `bike_share.py`. Try executing it after setting up a recipe on IFTTT. If necessary, adjust the threshold for the number of available bikes. You should receive a mobile notification on your device:

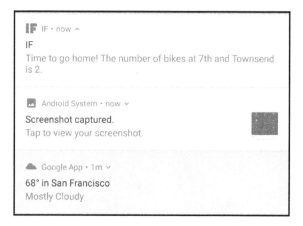

Notification on your mobile device

A challenge to the reader

In this example, the bike information is fetched and parsed and if necessary, a notification is triggered. How would you go about modifying this code example to make sure that it is executed between a given time of the day? (hint: make use of `datetime` module).

How would you go about building a desktop display that serves as a visual aid?

Project challenge

Try to find out if the transit systems in your area provide such data to its users. How would you make use of the data to help commuters save time? For example, how would you provide transit system advisories to your friends/colleagues using such data?

On completion of the book, we will post a similar example using the data from San Francisco **Bay Area Rapid Transit** (**BART**).

Improving your vocabulary

It is possible to improve your vocabulary using Python! Imagine setting up a large display that is installed somewhere prominently and updated on a daily basis. We will be making use of the wordnik API (sign up for an API key at https://www.wordnik.com/signup):

1. The first step is to install the wordnik API client for python3:

   ```
   git clone https://github.com/wordnik/wordnik-python3.git
   cd wordnik-python3/
   sudo python3 setup.py install
   ```

    There are restrictions on the wordnik API usage. Refer to the API documentation for more details.

2. Let's review writing our first example using the wordnik Python client. In order to fetch the word of the day, we need to initialize the WordsApi class. According to the API documentation, this could be done as follows:

   ```
   # sign up for an API key
   API_KEY = 'API_KEY'
   apiUrl = 'http://api.wordnik.com/v4'
   client = swagger.ApiClient(API_KEY, apiUrl)
   wordsApi = WordsApi.WordsApi(client)
   ```

3. Now that the WordsApi class is initialized, let's go ahead and fetch the word of the day:

   ```
   example = wordsApi.getWordOfTheDay()
   ```

4. This returns a WordOfTheDay object. According to the wordnik Python client documentation, this object consists of different parameters including the word, its synonym, source, usage, and so on. The word of the day and its synonym could be printed as follows:

   ```
   print("The word of the day is %s" % example.word)
   print("The definition is %s" %example.definitions[0].text)
   ```

5. Putting it all together, we have this:

```python
#!/usr/bin/python3

from wordnik import *

# sign up for an API key
API_KEY = 'API_KEY'
apiUrl = 'http://api.wordnik.com/v4'

if __name__ == "__main__":
    client = swagger.ApiClient(API_KEY, apiUrl)
    wordsApi = WordsApi.WordsApi(client)
    example = wordsApi.getWordOfTheDay()
    print("The word of the day is %s" % example.word)
    print("The definition is %s" %example.definitions[0].text)
```

The preceding code snippet is available for download along with this chapter as wordOfTheDay.py. Sign up for an API key, and you should be able to retrieve the word of the day:

```
The word of the day is transpare
The definition is To be, or cause to be, transparent; to appear,
or cause to appear, or be seen, through something.
```

A challenge to the reader

How would you daemonize this application such that the word of the day is updated every day? (hint: cronjob or datetime).

Project challenge

It is possible to build a word game using the wordnik API. Think of a word game that is entertaining as well as helps improve your vocabulary. How would you go about building something that prompts questions to the player and accepting answer inputs?

Try displaying the word of the day on a display. How would you implement this?

Logging

Logging (`https://docs.python.org/3/library/logging.html`) helps with troubleshooting a problem. It helps with determining the root cause of a problem by tracing back through the sequence of events logged by the application. Let's review logging using a simple application. In order to review logging, let's review it by making a `POST` request:

1. The first step in logging is setting the log file location and the log level:

   ```
   logging.basicConfig(format='%(asctime)s : %(levelname)s :
   %(message)s', filename='log_file.log', level=logging.INFO)
   ```

   While initializing the `logging` class, we need to specify the format for logging information, errors, and so on to the file. In this case, the format is as follows:

   ```
   format='%(asctime)s : %(levelname)s : %(message)s'
   ```

   The log messages are in the following format:

   ```
   2016-10-25 20:28:07,940 : INFO : Starting new HTTPS
   connection (1):
   maker.ifttt.com
   ```

   The log messages are saved to a file named `log_file.log`.

   The logging level determines the level of logging needed for our application. The different log levels include `DEBUG`, `INFO`, `WARN`, and `ERROR`.

   In this example, we have set the logging level to `INFO`. So, any log message belonging to `INFO`, `WARNING`, or `ERROR` levels are saved to the file.

   If the logging level is set to `ERROR`, only those log messages are saved to the file.

2. Let's log a message based on the outcome of the `POST` request:

   ```
   response = requests.post(IFTTT_URL, json=payload)
   if response.status_code == 200:
     logging.info("Notification successfully triggered")
   else:
     logging.error("POST request failed")
   ```

3. Putting it all together, we have this:

```python
#!/usr/bin/python3

import requests
import logging

# find your key from ifttt
IFTTT_URL = "https://maker.ifttt.com/trigger/rf_trigger/
with/key/$key"

if __name__ == "__main__":
  # fetch the bike share information
  logging.basicConfig(format='%(asctime)s : %(levelname)s
  : %(message)s', filename='log_file.log', level=logging.INFO)
  payload = {"value1": "Sample_1", "value2": "Sample_2"}
  response = requests.post(IFTTT_URL, json=payload)
  if response.status_code == 200:
    logging.info("Notification successfully triggered")
  else:
    logging.error("POST request failed")
```

The preceding code sample (`logging_example.py`) is available for download along with this chapter. This is a very soft introduction to the concept of logging in Python.

Threading in Python

In this section, we are going to discuss the concept of threading in Python. Threads enable running multiple processes at the same time. For example, we can run motors while listening to incoming events from sensors. Let's demonstrate this with an example.

We are going to emulate a situation where we would like to process events from sensors of the same type. In this example, we are just going to print something to the screen. We need to define a function that listens to events from each sensor:

```python
def sensor_processing(string):
  for num in range(5):
    time.sleep(5)
    print("%s: Iteration: %d" %(string, num))
```

We can make use of the preceding function to listen for sensor events from three different sensors at the same time using the `threading` module in Python:

```
thread_1 = threading.Thread(target=sensor_processing, args=("Sensor
1",))
thread_1.start()

thread_2 = threading.Thread(target=sensor_processing, args=("Sensor
2",))
thread_2.start()

thread_3 = threading.Thread(target=sensor_processing, args=("Sensor
3",))
thread_3.start()
```

Putting it all together, we have this:

```
import threading
import time

def sensor_processing(string):
  for num in range(5):
    time.sleep(5)
    print("%s: Iteration: %d" %(string, num))

if __name__ == '__main__':
  thread_1 = threading.Thread(target=sensor_processing, args=("Sensor
1",))
  thread_1.start()

  thread_2 = threading.Thread(target=sensor_processing, args=("Sensor
2",))
  thread_2.start()

  thread_3 = threading.Thread(target=sensor_processing, args=("Sensor
3",))
  thread_3.start()
```

The preceding code sample (available for download as `threading_example.py`) starts three threads that listens to events from three sensors at the same time. The output looks something like this:

```
Thread 1: Iteration: 0
Thread 2: Iteration: 0
Thread 3: Iteration: 0
Thread 2: Iteration: 1
Thread 1: Iteration: 1
Thread 3: Iteration: 1
```

```
Thread 2: Iteration: 2
Thread 1: Iteration: 2
Thread 3: Iteration: 2
Thread 1: Iteration: 3
Thread 2: Iteration: 3
Thread 3: Iteration: 3
Thread 1: Iteration: 4
Thread 2: Iteration: 4
Thread 3: Iteration: 4
```

PEP8 style guide for Python

PEP8 is a style guide for Python that helps programmers write readable code. It is important to follow certain conventions to make our code readable. Some examples of coding conventions include the following:

- Inline comments should start with a # and be followed by a single space.
- Variables should have the following convention: `first_var`.
- Avoiding trailing whitespaces on each line. For example, `if name == "test":` should not be followed by whitespaces.

> You can read the entire PEP8 standards at
> `https://www.python.org/dev/peps/pep-0008/#block-comments`.

Verifying PEP8 guidelines

There are tools to verify PEP8 standards of your code. After writing a code sample, ensure that your code adheres to PEP8 standards. This can be done using the `pep8` package. It can be installed as follows:

```
pip3 install pep8
```

Let's check whether one of our code samples has been written according to the PEP8 convention. This can be done as follows:

```
pep8 opencv_test.py
```

The check indicated the following errors:

```
opencv_test.py:5:50: E231 missing whitespace after ','
opencv_test.py:6:19: E231 missing whitespace after ','
```

As the output indicates, the following lines are missing a whitespace after a comma on lines 5 and 6:

```
5    img = cv2.imread('/home/pi/Desktop/test_shot.jpg',cv2.IMREAD_GRAYSCALE)
6    cv2.imshow('image',img)
```

Missing trailing whitespace after the comma

Let's fix the problem, and our code should adhere to PEP8 conventions. Recheck the file and the errors would have disappeared. In order to make your code readable, always run a PEP8 check before checking in your code to a public repository.

Summary

In this chapter, we discussed advanced topics in Python. We discussed topics including speech recognition, building a commuter information tool, and a Python client to improve your vocabulary. There are advanced tools in Python that are widely used in the fields of data science, AI, and so on. We hope that the topics discussed in this chapter are the first step in learning such tools.

17
Robotics 101

As soon as we say the word robot, thoughts of science fiction start to surround us. We may recall the cartoon serial *The Jetsons* or think of the movie *Terminator*. But, as a matter of fact, robots as a species do not belong to science fiction anymore. They are as real as they can get. Look around you and point out any object; it probably wouldn't have been made without a robot. The modern era has been shaped by robots.

But then, you can also take a step back and think, wait a minute, aren't the things he is talking about called machines and not robots? Well, yes, you are very correct, yet very mistaken at the same time. It is cartoons and science fiction that have imparted an image of a human-like robot that is called a **robot**. But robots are much more than that.

Unfortunately, we do not have a concrete, universally agreed definition of robots, but, as I like to say, *Any machine capable of performing physical as well as intellectual tasks can be called a robot.*

Now, you may say that, according to my definition, even an automatic washing machine can be called a robot. Well, technically, yes, and why should we not call it a robot? Think of the things it is doing for you and what kind of automation has been adapted over the years. After you feed in the type of cloth it automatically washes, rinses, and dries as you would have done yourself in the 19th century. The point I am trying to make is that there is a huge variation of robots that we can think of, which can radically change the way we live. We need to think with a wider perspective—not just limit robot to look as a human adaption in form of humanoid robots.

We live in the golden era of robotics and automation in which the development of new products is as simple as it can get. What a decade back might have taken a team of engineers, can now be done by a person sitting in bedroom in just a few minutes, thanks to the open source world. At the very same time, there is hardware horsepower available to you by which you can literally build a super computer in your own home with just a few hundred dollars. We are surrounded by problems, some simple and others complex, which are waiting to be solved. The only missing chain in the whole process is you: an innovative mind that has the capability to exploit these technologies to solve the world's problems.

To make your mind capable of doing so, we will be starting of by understanding the roots and the basics of robotics. The goal of this book is not only to make the projects that are mentioned in the book but to make you understand how to exploit the resources to build your dream projects.

Finally, I would like to congratulate you on entering this amazing and futuristic field at the correct time. I always tell my students a rule, which I would like to share with you as well:

- First is a scientist
- Second is a researcher
- Third is an engineer
- Fourth is a technician
- Last is a mechanic

What it means is that the earlier in the life cycle you enter any field, the higher in the hierarchy you can get. The later you come, the harder it is to climb to the top.

Enough talking—now let's get straight to business! We will cover the following topics in this chapter:

- The hardware arsenal
- Setting up Raspberry Pi
- Programming
- Playing with voltage

The hardware arsenal

Talking of robots, there are a few basic tangible components that they are made up of, which are as follows:

- Computing Unit
- Sensors
- Actuators
- Chassis
- Power source

Firstly, we will be discussing the microcontroller and, during the course of book, we will be discussing the rest of the tangible components in detail as and when required.

Whenever you have been to buy a laptop or a computer, you must have heard the word microprocessor. This is the primary unit that has to make all the decisions. I call it the *king*, but what is a king without an empire? For the king to work, he needs some subordinates that can do the things for him, the same way in which the microprocessor needs a few subordinates such as RAM, storage, I/O devices, and so on. Now, the problem is that when we put in all these things the overall unit gets expensive and bulky. But, as we know, subsequently weight and size are very important factors when it comes to robots, so we cannot afford to have a big bulky piece of system running a robot.

Hence, we made something called a SoC. Now, this is a one man show as this small chip, has all the necessary systems for it to work inside that small little chipset itself. So, now you don't need to add RAM or storage or any other thing for it to work. These small microcontrollers can get really powerful but a downside is, once a manufacturer has made an SoC, thereafter no changes can be done to it. The size of storage, RAM, or the I/O cannot be changed. But we generally can live with these limitations as when programming the robots, you might not be using the entire juice of the microcontroller until the time you are running some serious artificial intelligence or machine-learning code.

One such great piece of hardware is Raspberry Pi. Yes, it sounds very tasty, but there is so much more to it. This is a super small yet extremely powerful microcontroller. It is often referred to as a prototyping board because of the fact that it is used by roboticists everywhere to bring out their ideas and to make them a reality in a quick time span. It is available all across the globe and is extremely cheap. You can literally stream HD movies, surf the internet, and do much more on just a $10 device. I can't think of something as ludicrous as this. It is fairly easy to use and you can use Python to program it.

So, basically, it ticks all our boxes. This will be the primary weapon we will be using throughout the book.

So let me introduce you to Raspberry Pi! This is what it looks like:

There are various models of Raspberry Pi available on the market. But we will be using Raspberry Pi Zero W; this will cost you around $10 and it is easier to purchase than a Big Mac burger. Do make sure you buy the Raspberry Pi Zero with a W, which supposedly stands for wireless capabilities such as Wi-Fi and Bluetooth. There are a few more things that you will have to order or arrange for it to work. Here is a list of items:

- Micro USB to standard USB adapter
- Keyboard
- Mouse
- Micro SD memory card, 16 or 32 GB
- Micro SD card reader
- Micro USB power adapter (2 amp or more)
- Micro HDMI to HDMI port
- Breadboard
- Bunch of jumper wires (male to male, male to female, and female to female)
- 3V LEDs

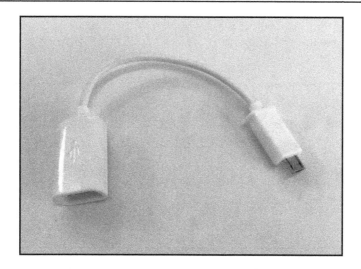

As you will instantly make out from the image, there is a micro HDMI port onboard, over which you can hook up your HD monitor or a TV screen. Second there is a micro SD card slot. This will be the primary storage device for this computer. Other than that, you will also find two USB sockets and a camera bus. You may think this is it, but the best is yet to come. Raspberry Pi has something called **GPIO**, which stands for **general purpose input/output**. These are disguised as small 40 through-hole ports on one corner of the Raspberry Pi; this is what makes it super special.

Now, conventionally you would attach things to your computer that are compatible with it. So, hooking up a mouse, keyboard or a joystick is as easy as inserting a USB port, but what if you need to connect your computer to your light bulbs or your air-conditioner? Exactly, you can't. That's where GPIO comes in to save the day. These are pins which are very useful when it comes to robotics, as these can be used to connect various components such as sensors/motors. The beauty of these pins is that they can be used as either input or output based on what we program them for. So, as we will later see, each of these pins can be defined in the program to be either input or output based on our needs.

Now, out of these 40 pins, 26 are GPIO. The rest of the pins are generic power or ground ports. There are two more ports called **ID EEPROM** which at this point of time we do not require:

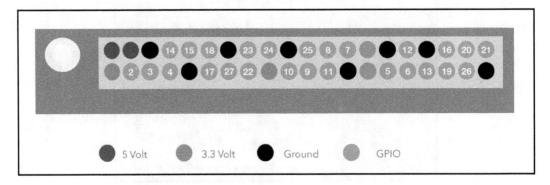

As you can see, Raspberry Pi is capable of giving us two types of power supply: 3.3V and 5V. These basically cater for most of our purposes.

Setting up Raspberry Pi

We will talk about the GPIO and other things to do with Raspberry Pi in a while. Firstly, we will understand how to set up this board for the first time.

The first thing you need to do is to make sure that the operating system of Raspberry Pi is ready. I am assuming that you are using a Windows PC, but if you are doing it on another OS as well, then there will not be much of a difference.

To install the OS, start your PC and follow these steps:

1. Go to `www.raspberrypi.org` and click on **DOWNLOADS**
2. Now click on **RASPBIAN**, you will see the following two options:
    - **RASPBIAN STRETCH WITH DESKTOP**
    - **RASPBIAN STRETCH LITE**
3. We will be downloading **RASPBIAN STRETCH WITH DESKTOP**; this will give us the GUI interface for Raspberry Pi
4. After downloading, unzip the package into a folder

Now we need to copy it to the memory card of Raspberry Pi. The memory card over which you need to copy must be formatted by low level formatting. There are basically two types of formatting. one which simply erases the index the other one which we know as low level formatting is the one in which we remove all the data from both the index and their physical memory location. There would be a button to toggle a low level format. Make sure it is clicked before you format your memory card for this function. I would recommend using the SD card formatter by `www.sdcard.org`. Now open the formatter and you simply have to format it using the 32 KB option.

 Find more details and more up-to-date information here: `https://www.raspberrypi.org/documentation/installation/installing-images/README.md`.

Once done, you have to copy the image onto the SD card. The easiest way to do that is by using WinDisk Imager. You can download it online without any problems. Then simply select the image and the location on your SD card and start copying the image.

This could take a few minutes. After it is done, your SD will be ready. Plug it into Raspberry Pi and we will be ready to power it up. But before you power it up, plug in your monitor using the Micro HDMI to HDMI wire, connect the keyboard and mouse to Raspberry Pi using the Micro USB, and power it up by using the Micro USB adapter to standard USB adapter. Now, use the other USB port on Raspberry Pi to power it up using the micro USB power adapter.

Once you start it up, you will see a boot-up screen and within a few seconds you will be able to see the desktop. So, finally, our Raspberry Pi is up and running.

Go ahead and explore a few options, surf the internet, look at some cat videos on YouTube, and get yourself familiar with this mighty device.

By now, you must already be appreciating the power of Raspberry Pi. It may be slightly slower than your average computer. But, come on, this thing costs just $10!

Let's program

In this chapter, we will get you familiar with Python and how you can use the GPIOs on this device. To do this, go ahead and click on the Raspberry icon in the top left-hand corner. You will see the Python console 3.0. There could be an older version of Python as well. We will be using the newer version in this book.

Once the window opens, you will see the playground where you would be doing the coding. So now we are ready to write the first code for Python Robotics. Now let's see how it's done.

The first thing we will write is:

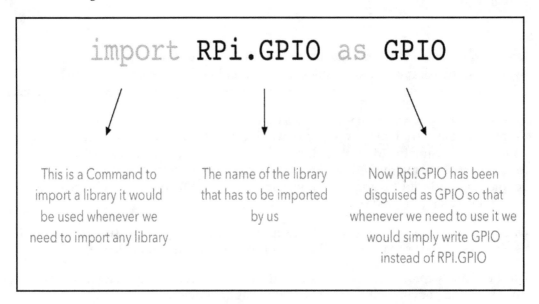

import RPi.GPIO as GPIO

This is a Command to import a library it would be used whenever we need to import any library

The name of the library that has to be imported by us

Now Rpi.GPIO has been disguised as GPIO so that whenever we need to use it we would simply write GPIO instead of RPI.GPIO

Almost all of the time when we start writing a program, we will start by writing the preceding line. Now, before we understand what it does, we need to understand libraries. Often while we are writing code, we will have to write the code again and again in multiple places. This takes a lot of time and certainly is not cool!

So, to solve this problem, we created functions. A function is a miniature program that we might think would be used over and over again. In this miniature program itself, we also mention what it would be called.

Let's say that there is a code in which we need to multiply two numbers again and again. So, what we do is we write the code once and make it a function. We also name this function `Multiply`.

So now, whenever we need to multiply two numbers, we don't have to write its code again; rather, we simply have to call the function to do it for us instead of writing the code to multiply. The problem is, how do we tell which number has to be multiplied?

There is a solution to that as well. As you might see later, whenever a function is called we put opening and closing brackets after it, such as `multiply()`.

If the brackets are empty that means no user input has been given. If, for example, we have to multiply 2 and 3 we simply write `Multiply(2,3)`.

We are giving the input as 2 and 3. The position of the input in the brackets is also important as the position in the brackets will define where in the program it will go.

Now, let's say you make functions such as:

- Add
- Subtract
- Multiply
- Divide

Say you stack them together. Then the pile of functions grouped together will be called a library. These libraries can have hundreds of functions. There are some functions which are already in the Python language so that the job is made simpler for the programmers. Others can be defined as open source or developed by you at your convenience.

Now, getting back to the point. We are calling the library `RPi.GPIO`; this is a library defined by Raspberry Pi. This will have functions that will make your life easier when it comes to programming Raspberry Pi. So, in the program, once we call the library, all the functions are at your disposal and ready to be used.

In the next line, we write `Import.time`. As you must have guessed, this is used to import a library time. What it does we will learn shortly.

The next line of code would be as follows:

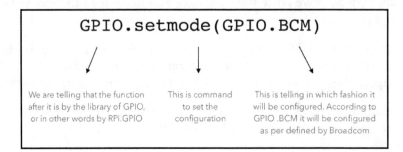

Before we understand what it does, let's learn a bit more about GPIOs. These pins are hard numbered according to their physical positions in Raspberry Pi. However, we can change the numbering of the pins in the software for our understanding and convenience. But in this code, we will not be playing around with this and will set it do the default set by Broadcom, which is the manufacturer of the microcontroller of Raspberry Pi.

This line uses a function of the `RPi.GPIO` library called `setmode`. What this function does is that it sets the pin configuration of the `setmode` to (`GPIO.BCM`)—BCM is further a function of `GPIO`.

Now we can use the base pin configuration. Further to this, a specialty of the GPIO pins is that it can be used both as input and output. But the only condition is that we have to specify whether it has to be used as input or output in the program itself. It cannot do both functions at the same time. Here is how it is done:

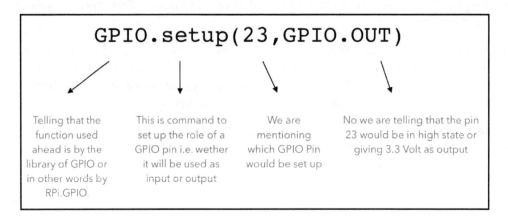

The next line of code will be as follows:

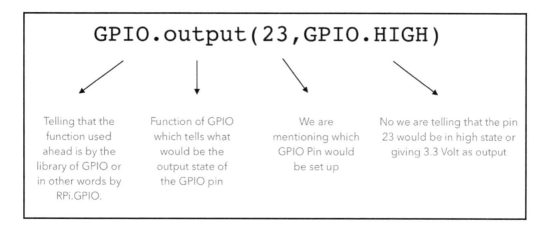

Again, we are using a function of the library `GPIO` called `output`. What this does is that it sets up a specific pin of the board in a state which we want. So, here we have mentioned that the pin number `23` has to be set high. Just for the sake of clarity, high means on and low means off.

The next line of code will be as follows:

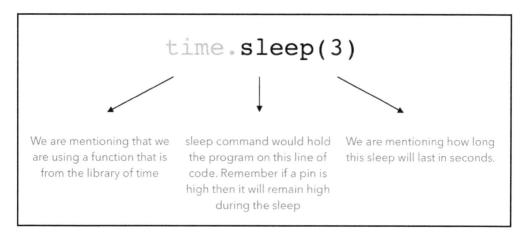

In this line, we are using a function from the library time. The function sleep basically freezes the state of all the GPIO pins. So, for example, if the pin `23` is high then it will remain high until the `time` the function `sleep` is executed. In the function `sleep`, we have defined the value as 3 seconds.

Hence, for 3 seconds, the pin state of Raspberry Pi will remain as it was before this line of code.

Finally, the last line of the code will be:

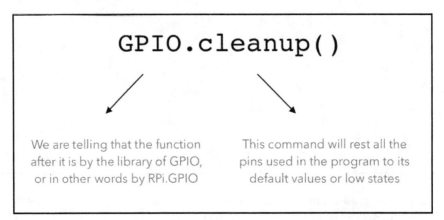

This will be a common sight after every program. This function of the GPIO library will reset the state of every pin that has been used in the program—the state of all the pins will be low. Remember, it will only affect the pins that are used in the program and not any other pins. So, for example, we have used the pin 23 in the program, so it will only affect pin 23 and not any other pin in Raspberry Pi.

Finally, your program will look something like this:

```
import RPI.GPIO as GPIO
import time

GPIO.setmode(GPIO.BCM)

GPIO.setup(23,GPIO,OUT)

GPIO.out(23,GPIO.High)

time.sleep(3)

GPIO.cleanup()
```

Now, one thing that you must remember is that whatever code we are writing will be executed one line after the other. So, let's say we keep `import RPI.GPIO as GPIO` at the bottom, then the whole program will not work. Why? Because as soon as it goes to `GPIO.setmode(GPIO.BCM)` it will not understand what `GPIO` is, neither will it understand what `setmode` is. Hence, we always import the libraries as soon as we start writing the code.

Now, working on the same concept, it will execute the program in the following way:

- `GPIO.out(23,GPIO.High)`: It will turn pin 23 high/on
- `time.sleep(3)`: It will wait for 3 seconds while pin is still high
- `GPIO.cleanup()`: Finally, it will set the state of the pin 23 to low

Now, to see whether the program is working, let's attach some hardware to check whether what we have written is actually happening.

 I am assuming that readers are already aware of how breadboard is used. If you are not familiar with it, just go ahead and google it. It will take 5 minutes to understand. It is super easy and will come in handy.

Now go ahead and connect the LED on breadboard, then connect the ground of the LED to the ground pin in Raspberry Pi, and set the positive/VCC to pin number 23 (refer the pin diagram).

You can also refer to the following diagram:

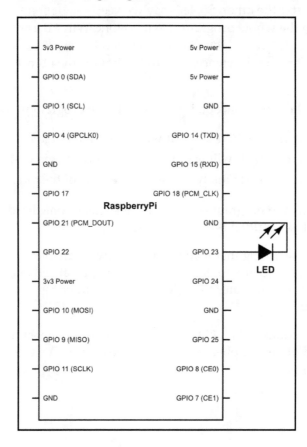

Once you are done, go ahead run the code and see what happens!

The LED will glow for 3 seconds and then turn back off again, exactly as we expected it to do. Now let's just play around with the code and do a slight modification. This time, we will add a few more lines marked in bold:

```
import RPi.GPIO as GPIO
from time
import sleep
GPIO.setmode(GPIO.BOARD)
GPIO.setup(23, GPIO.OUT)
while True:
  for i in range(3):
  GPIO.output(23, GPIO.HIGH)
sleep(.5)
```

```
GPIO.output(23, GPIO.LOW)
sleep(.5)
sleep(1)
GPIO.cleanup()
```

Before understanding what's inside the code, you will notice that not every line is aligned, they have been intended. What does this mean ?

A line indented together with other lines of code is called a block. So for example if you have a statement such as

```
while True:
  for i in range(3):
  GPIO.output(23, GPIO.HIGH)
sleep(.5)
GPIO.output(23, GPIO.LOW)
sleep(.5)
sleep(1)
GPIO.cleanup()
```

Now in this line lets see how the code will run.

- A while true loop would run, this will run the code that is inside it i.e.

```
for i in range(3):
    GPIO.output(23, GPIO.HIGH)
sleep(.5)
GPIO.output(23, GPIO.LOW)
sleep(.5)
sleep(1)
```

- Thereafter the code `for I in range (3):` would run. It will run the code inside the for loop until the value of `I` is in range, Hence the code below would run.

```
GPIO.output(23, GPIO.HIGH)
sleep(.5)
GPIO.output(23, GPIO.LOW)
sleep(.5)
```

The above code can be referred to a block of code, which is inside the `for` loop. The block of code can be made by indenting the code.

Now, let's see what it does. `While True` is a loop, it will run the `for` loop inside it again and again until the time the condition is not false. The condition we are using here is:

```
for i in range(3):
```

The maximum range is 3 and every time the statement runs it increments the value of the i by +1. So it basically acts as a counter. Let's see what the program will actually do.

It will check for the value of i and increment it by 1 thereafter. As the code progresses, it will glow the LED high for 0.5 seconds and then shut it off for 0.5 seconds. And then it will wait for 1 second. This will repeat until the while loop is false, as in the value of i becomes greater than 3 where it would get out of the program and terminate. Run the program and see if it actually happens.

By now, you understand how easy the programming is in Raspberry Pi. To go a step further, we will make another program and make some changes to the hardware.

We will be connecting five more LEDs from pin numbers 7 through to 12. We will make them switch on and off in a pattern.

Once connected, we will write the code as follows:

```
import RPi.GPIO as GPIO
from time
import sleep
GPIO.setmode(GPIO.BOARD)
GPIO.setup(7, GPIO.OUT)
GPIO.setup(8, GPIO.OUTPUT)
GPIO.setup(9, GPIO.OUTPUT)
GPIO.setup(10, GPIO.OUTPUT)
GPIO.setup(11, GPIO.OUTPUT)
while True:
   for i in range(7, 12):
   GPIO.output(i, GPIO.HIGH)
sleep(1)
GPIO.cleanup()
```

Now the code is fairly simple. Let's see what it means:

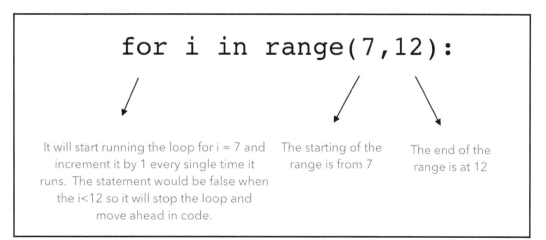

Before I tell you something more about the code, let's go ahead and run it.

When you run it, you will understand that as per the statement it is addressing the pins one by one and switching them to high after every 1 second.

Playing with voltage

So far so good! But did you notice one thing? We have been using Raspberry Pi as a switch—simply switching the various components on and off. But what if we need to vary the intensity of the LEDs that we have just programmed? Is it possible? The answer is no. But we can still get it done somehow!

Let's see how. Computers work in binary which means that they can represent either 0 or 1. This is because of the fact that the primary computing unit in any system is based on a transistor which can either be on or off representing 0 or 1. So, if we see this technically, computers are only capable of switching due to the binary architecture. However, there is a trick. This trick is called **pulse width modulation (PWM)**.

Now, before I explain any of it in detail, let's go ahead plug in an LED on pin number 18, then copy this code into Raspberry Pi and run it:

```
import RPi.GPIO as GPIO
import time
GPIO.setmode(GPIO.BCM)
```

```
GPIO.setup(18,GPIO.OUT)

pwm= GPIO.PWM(18,1)
duty_cycle = 50
pwm.start(duty_cycle)

time.sleep(10)

GPIO.cleanup()
```

What did you notice? The LED will be blinking at once a second. Now let's tweak it a bit and change the `PWM(18,1)` to `PWM(18,5)`. Let's run and see what happens.

You will have noticed that it is now blinking five times in a second. So the number 5 is basically representing the frequency as the LED is now flickering five times in a second. Now, again, rewrite the code and increase 5 to 50. Once you increase it to 50, it switches the LED on and off 50 times in a second or at 50 Hertz. So, it appears to you as if it is always on.

Now comes the interesting part. Go over to your code and change `duty_cycle = 50` to `duty_cycle = 10`.

What did you notice? You must have seen that the LED is now glowing way lower in intensity. In fact, it will be half of what it originally was.

Let's see what is actually happening:

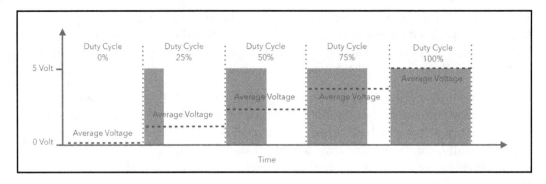

As you can make out from the diagram, the function is basically creating a pulse, the characteristics of which we are changing. The first characteristic is the frequency, the pulses generated in a second. In the code line `pwm= GPIO.PWM(18,1)`, we are basically telling the microcontroller to generate one pulse every second on pin number `1`. In the second line, duty cycle is a percent value. It determines for how much percent of the time the pulse will be high. For the rest of the time of the pulse the output of the pin will be off. So, for the following code, the below bulleted points would be the characteristics:

```
pwm= GPIO.PWM(18,1)
duty_cycle = 50
```

- Time/width of every pulse is 1 second
- Percent of time it would on is 50%
- Percent of time it would be off is 50%
- Time it would be on is 0.5 seconds
- Time it would be off is 0.5 seconds

When we increase the frequency more than 50 hertz then it is very hard for the human eye to make out if it is actually switching on or off. Theoretically, for 50% of the time the pin will remain high, and for the rest of the time it will be low. So, if we take an average then we can easily say that the overall voltage would be half of the original. Using this method, we can modulate the voltage output of any pin as per our requirements.

Summary

Now you must have understood how the GPIOs can be used as output and how, by applying conditions, we can change their behaviors.

In the next chapter, we will understand how these pins can be used as input as well. So come back, and see you there!

18

Using GPIOs as Input

In the previous chapter, we understood how GPIOs are used for output. But, as the name suggests, the GPIO can be used for both input and output purposes. In this chapter, we will see how you can go ahead and use these pins to input the data over to Raspberry Pi.

The topics which we will cover in this chapter are:

- A deeper dive into GPIOs
- Interfacing the PIR sensor
- Interfacing the ultrasonic proximity sensor
- Interfacing through I2C

A deeper dive into GPIOs

I am sure you remember this line of code from the previous chapter:

```
GPIO.setup(18,GPIO.OUT)
```

As explained earlier, this basically tells us how GPIO the pin will behave in a certain program. By now, you must have guessed that by changing this single line of code we can change the behavior of the pin and convert it from output to input. This is how you would do it:

```
GPIO.setup(18,GPIO.IN)
```

Once you write this line of code in your program, the microcontroller will know that during the time that the program is being run, the pin number 18 will only be used for input purposes.

To understand how this would actually work, let's head back to our hardware and see how it can be done. Firstly, you need to connect an LED to any of the pins; we will be using pin number 23 in this program. Secondly, you need to connect a switch on pin number 24. You can refer the diagram that follows for making the connections:

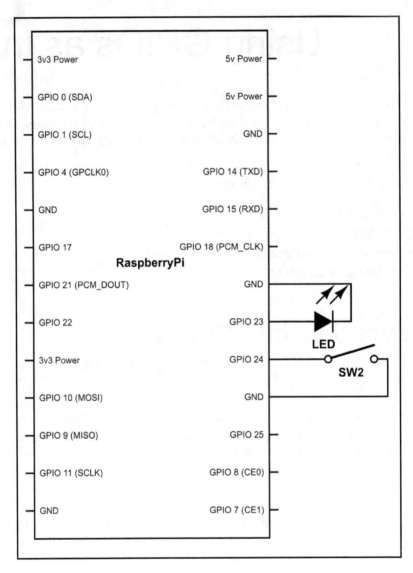

Once you connect it, you can go ahead and write this program:

```
import time import RPi.GPIO as GPIO
GPIO.setmode(GPIO.BCM)
GPIO.setup(24,GPIO.IN)
GPIO.setup(23,GPIO.OUT)
while True:
    button_state = GPIO.input(24)
        if button_state == True:
        GPIO.output(23,GPIO.HIGH)
        else:
        GPIO.output(23,GPIO.LOW)
    time.sleep(0.5)
GPIO.cleanup()
```

Once the program is uploaded, then, as soon as you press the push button, the LED will turn itself on.

Let's understand what exactly is happening. `while True:` is basically an infinite loop; once you apply this loop, the code running inside it is repeated over and over again until something breaks it, and by break I mean some interruption that causes the program to stop and exit. Now, ideally we exit the program by pressing *Ctrl + C* whenever there is an infinite loop.

```
button_state = GPIO.input(24)
```

In the above line, the program understands where it has to look; in this program. In this line we are telling the program that we are looking for GPIO 24, which is an input:

```
if button_state == True:
    GPIO.output(23,GPIO.HIGH)
```

If the button is high, in other words when the button is pressed and the current is reaching the pin number 24, then the GPIO pin number 23 will be set to high:

```
else:
    GPIO.output(23,GPIO.LOW)
```

If the pin number 24 is not true, it will follow this line of code and will keep the pin number 23 low, in other words switched off.

So, there it is, your first program for using the GPIOs for input purposes.

Interfacing the PIR sensor

So far, so good! In this unit, we will go ahead and interface out first sensor, which is a passive infrared, commonly known as a PIR sensor. This sensor is a very special sensor and is used very commonly in automation projects. Its low energy consumption makes it a superb contender for IoT projects as well. So let's see how it works.

You must have noticed that when we heat a metal to a high temperature, it slowly gets dark red in color, and when we heat it further, it gets brighter and slowly goes from red to yellow as depicted in the below diagram which shows a red hot steel tab. Now, as the temperature increases, the wavelength of the emitted radiation decreases; that is why with the increase in temperature the color changes from red to yellow, as yellow has a shorter wavelength compared to red.

But the interesting part is that even when the objects are not heated enough, they emit radiation; in fact, any object that is above the temperate of absolute zero emits some form of radiation. Some we can see with the naked eye, others we can't. So, at room temperature, objects emit infrared radiation which has a higher wavelength compared to visible light. Hence, we don't see it with our eyes. Nonetheless, it is still there.

What this PIR sensor does is that it senses the infrared light from the objects around it and whenever an object moves, it can sense the overall change in its pattern and, based on that, can detect if there is any movement that has happened in its proximity.

We assume that whenever there is someone in a room there will be some inherent movement that will happen, and hence this sensor is very commonly used as an occupancy sensor. Now, let's connect this sensor and see how we can use it:

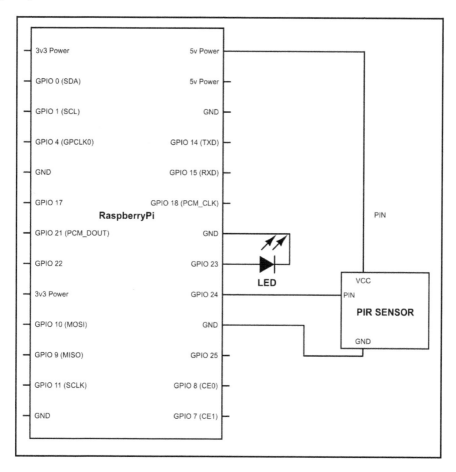

Once you have connected it as per the preceding diagram, go ahead and upload the code: :

```
import time import RPi.GPIO as GPIO
GPIO.setmode(GPIO.BCM)
GPIO.setup(23,GPIO.IN)
GPIO.setup(24,GPIO.OUT)
while True:
 if GPIO.input(23) == 1:
  GPIO.output(24,GPIO.HIGH)
 else:
  GPIO.output(24,GPIO.LOW)

 time.sleep(1)
GPIO.cleanup()
```

Now, let's see what is happening. The logic is very simple. As soon as the PIR sensor detects movement, it turns its output pin to high. All we have to do is to monitor that pin and that's basically it.

The logic is entirely similar to that of a push-button switch, and it will also work in a similar manner. So not much explaining is needed.

Interfacing the ultrasonic proximity sensor

First, the basics. A proximity sensor is a type of sensor that senses the proximity of an object from it. There is a universe full of sensors that are available to accomplish this task and numerous technologies that allow us to do so. As the name says, the ultrasonic proximity sensor works on the principal of ultrasonic sound waves. The working principle is quite easy to understand. The ultrasonic sensor sends a beam of ultrasonic sound waves; these waves are inaudible to human ears, but nonetheless it is still a sound wave and it also behaves like a sound wave.

Now, as we know, sound bounces off different surfaces and forms an echo. You must have experienced this echo when speaking in an empty room. You can hear your own sound but with a slight delay. This delay is caused by the property of sound. A sound is a wave, hence it has a speed. Sound waves have a set speed of travel. So, to cover a specific distance, they take some time. By calculating this time, we can derive how far the sound waves are going before getting bounced off from a surface.

Similarly, in this sensor, we shoot ultrasonic sound waves in a specific direction and then sense the echo which bounces back. Naturally, there would be a delay in receiving the echo; the delay would be directly proportional to the distance of the object from the sensor and, based on this delay, we could easily compute the distance.

Now, to work with the proximity sensor, we need to understand the physical architecture of the sensor to wire it correctly. There are four pins in the sensor, which are:

- VCC (positive)
- Trigger
- Echo
- GND (ground)

I obviously don't have any need to explain what VCC and ground does. So, let's move on straight to trigger. Whenever the pin is high for 10 microseconds, the ultrasonic sensor will send eight cycles of 40 kHz sound waves to the target. Once the trigger cycle is completed, the **ECHO** is set to high. Once it receives the echo signal back, the **ECHO** pin is set back to low. Here is a diagram to show how it actually happens:

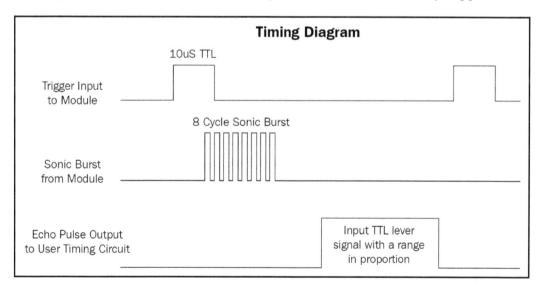

That is all we need to know for now. Subsequently, we will learn more as we move along. Now, to go ahead and make it live, connect it as per the diagram:

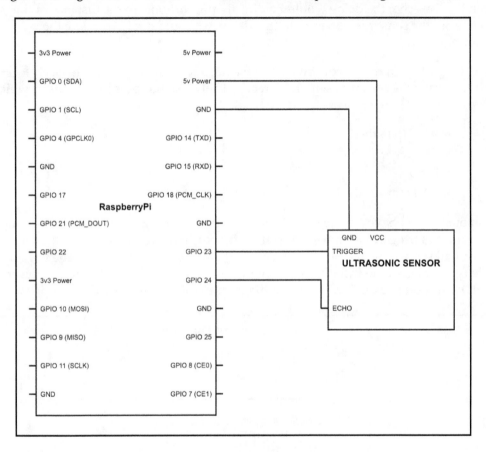

Once the connection is made, the following is the code that you need to run:

```
import RPi.GPIO as GPIO
import time

GPIO.setmode(GPIO.BCM)
GPIO.setup(23,GPIO.OUT)
GPIO.setup(24,GPIO.IN)

while True:
    pulse_start = 0
    pulse_stop = 0
    duration = 0
    distance = 0
```

```
GPIO.output(23,GPIO.LOW)
time.sleep(0.1)
GPIO.output(23,GPIO.HIGH)
time.sleep(0.000010)
GPIO.output(23,GPIO.LOW)

while GPIO.input(24)==0:
    pulse_start = time.time()

while GPIO.input(24)==1:
    pulse_stop = time.time()

duration = pulse_stop - pulse_start

distance = duration*17150.0
distance = round(distance,2)
print ("distance" + str(distance))

time.sleep(0.2)
}
```

Now, once you run this program, the output on your screen will be showing you the distance of the object once in every 0.2 seconds. Now, you must be wondering how this is communicating all these readings:

```
GPIO.setup(23,GPIO.OUT)
```

We are assigning pin 23 to give pulse to **TRIGGER** pin of the sensor when required:

```
GPIO.setup(24,GPIO.IN)
```

We are assigning pin 24 to receive the logic to confirm the receipt of the echo signal:

```
pulse_start = 0
pulse_stop = 0
duration = 0
distance = 0
```

We will be using the preceding as variables, and every time the loop starts we are assigning them a value which is 0; this is to wipe off the previous reading that we would have stored during the course of program:

```
GPIO.output(23,GPIO.HIGH)
    time.sleep(0.000010)
    GPIO.output(23,GPIO.LOW)
```

We keep the trigger pin number 23 high for 0.000010 seconds so that the ultrasonic sensor can send a brief pulse of ultrasonic waves:

```
while GPIO.input(24)==0:
    pulse_start = time.time()
```

This while statement will keep noting down the time of the `pulse_start` variable until the time pin number 24 is low. The final reading of the time will be stored in the `pulse_start` variable, as in noting down the time when the pulse was sent:

```
while GPIO.input(24)==1:
    pulse_stop = time.time()
```

The `while` statement in this loop will start noting the time when the input on pin number 24 is high and it will keep noting the time until the pin number 24 remains high. The final reading of the time will be stored in the `pulse_stop` variable, as in noting down the time when the pulse is received:

```
duration = pulse_stop - pulse_start
```

In this statement we are calculating the overall time it took for the pulse to travel from the sensor to the object and bounce back to the receiver on the sensor:

```
distance = duration*17150.0
```

This is an arithmetic formula given by the manufacturer to convert the time duration it took for the ultrasonic waves to travel into the actual distance in centimeters. You may ask how did we get to this equation?

Let me give you a brief about it. With elementary physics we would remember this simple equation: *Speed = Distance / Time.*

Now you may also recall that the speed of sound is 343 meters per second. Now 1 meter has 100 centimeters hence to convert this speed into centimeters per second, we would have to multiply the speed by 100, hence the speed would be 34,300 centimeters per second.

Now we know one element of the equation which is the speed. So lets put the value of speed into the equation. Now the equation would look something like this: *34,300 = Distance / Time*.

Now we know one thing that the distance which the sound is travelling is twice the actual distance. How ? Because the sound first goes from the sensor to the object. Then it bounces off that surface and reaches back to the sensor. So essentially it is covering twice the distance. Hence we to adapt this equation we have to make a small change: *34,300 / 2 = Distance / Time*

Now what we want out of this equation is distance So lets take all other part to the other side. Now the formula would look something like this: *17,150 * Time = Distance*

So here we have it the formula for the distance.

```
distance = round(distance,2)
```

As the distance the ultrasonic waves have traveled is twice the actual distance (once for going towards the object and second for bouncing back to the sensor), we divide it by half to get the actual distance:

```
print 'Distance = ',distance
```

Finally, we will print the measured distance via the following statement. Anything that is in the quotation marks ' . . . ' will be written the way it has been written. However, `distance` is written without quotation marks, and distance is a variable. Hence, the variable stored in the distance will be written in the final output on the screen:

```
time.sleep(0.25)
```

The code will pause on this line for a time of 0.2 seconds. If we did not have this pause, then the values would come out at an incredible speed which would be hard for us to read or understand. If you are tinkering around, I would recommend removing this statement and running the code to see what happens.

Interfacing through I2C

So far, so good. Electronic circuits can be very interesting and, while they seem very complex, often we find that the working can be very simple. In the previous section, we interfaced one sensor at a time. We can go ahead and interface multiple sensors, but we are limited by the number of GPIOs that are present. We have also seen that some sensors such as ultrasonic sensors may use more than one GPIO pin for their working. This further reduces the number of sensors that we can interface with the microcontroller. Once we move on to more complex circuits, we will also realize that the wiring can be really messy and if a problem occurs then finding what's wrong becomes one tedious task.

Now, there is an even bigger problem that we face while designing robotic systems and that's the problem of timing—all the work done in a system has to be synchronized. Most of the systems are currently sequential in nature, as in the output of one unit becomes the input of another:

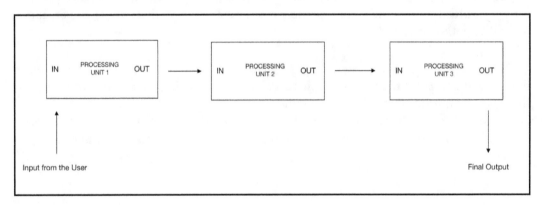

Now, for the task to be completed, the **PROCESSING UNIT 1** has to deliver the input to **PROCESSING UNIT 2** when needed, and the same goes for **PROCESSING UNIT 3**. If the data is not timed perfectly, then either the **PROCESSING UNIT 2** will keep waiting for the input from **PROCESSING UNIT 1** or, even worse, the **PROCESSING UNIT 1** will send the data to **PROCESSING UNIT 2** at a time when it does not need it. In which case, the data will get lost and the process will have some errors.

Hence, to solve this problem, the computer scientists back in the day invented a system of pulsing. The clock pulse is a very simple square wave which has a 50% duty cycle (recollect **pulse width modulation (PWM)**). The circuits are designed to do one operation at either the rising or the falling edge of the clock pulse. Due to this synchronization, every part of the circuit knows when to work. Here is what the clock pulse looks like:

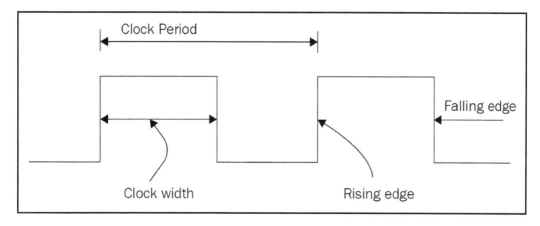

Now, coming back to the point, we have two problems:

- There is a physical limit to how many devices/sensors can be connected to the robot
- How to time the sensors and interconnected circuits to work in harmony

To solve these problems, we use a very commonly used protocol called **I2C**, which stands for **Inter-integrated Circuits**. This protocol is extremely useful when we need to connect multiple devices on the same set of GPIOs, such as when we have only one set of GPIO pins over which multiple sensors can be linked. This is made possible due to unique addresses allocated to each hardware. This address is used to identify a sensor and then to communicate with it accordingly. Now, to implement the I2C protocol we need two lines; these lines are as follows:

- Data
- Clock

As you may have guessed, the clock line is used to send a clock pulse to the devices attached to it and the data is the bus over which the data flows to and fro.

Now, the entire I2C architecture works on a master-slave configuration, wherein the master generates the clock signal all the time for the slave devices and the slave devices have to constantly look for the clock pulse and the data packets sent by the master devices. Let's see how it's done.

As mentioned earlier, there are two lines: the data line, which is referred to as **Serial Data (SDA)**, and the clock line, which is referred to as **Serial Clock (SCL)**. From now on, we will be using the terms SCL and SDA:

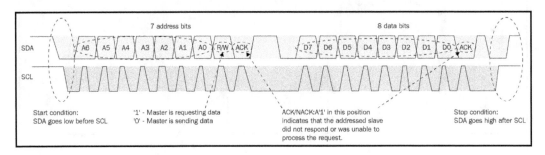

Lets look at the main pointers shown in the diagram:

- **Start condition**: To start a communication, a start condition is created indicating that the communication is about to happen. This condition is depicted by the master by keeping the SDA line low before the SCL. This indicates all the slave devices are ready for communication.

- **Address frame**: Once the communication is started the master sends the address of the device that needs to be communicated with. This is a 7-bit address. In every clock pulse, a bit is sent, hence it takes seven clock pulses to send the 7-bit address. After that 7-bit address is a read/write bit. This indicates to the device whether the master would like to write in this operation or if it wants to read some data. Hence, the total address frame is of 8 bits, which takes eight clock pulses to be sent. After these eight pulses, during the ninth clock pulse, the master waits for the acknowledgement from the device. This acknowledgement is sent by the slave device when the SDA line is pulled low by the slave device which is being addressed. With this strategy, the master knows that the address sent by it has been received and the slave device is now ready for the communication. If the acknowledgement is not sent back, then it is up to the master what has to be done.

- **Data frame**: Once the acknowledgement is sent, depending on if it is a read or write operation, the data is either written by the master onto the slave or, in read operation, the data is sent by the slave over to the master. The length of this data frame can be arbitrary.
- **Stop frame**: Once the data transfer is completed, the stop condition is made by the master to indicate that the communication has to stop. This condition is done when the SDA line goes from low to high after the SCL line goes from low to high.

So this is basically how I2C communication works. For every device we have a 7-bit address, hence we can connect up to 128 devices on a single bus. That's a lot of devices. The chances of running out of physical limits is almost negligible. Now let's go ahead and see how we can connect the sensors via this protocol. Generally, it is not required to do the core programming for the I2C, as it is lengthy and cumbersome. That's where the magic of open source comes in. There are a lot of developers across the globe who are working on these sensors and most of them are generous enough to make a library and share it for ease of programming. These libraries are available online and most of them take care of the complex process of communication.

Now is the time that we interface our first I2C device, which is an analogue to digital converter. You must be wondering why we use this converter in the first place. Recall the time when we started understanding GPIO pins. These magic pins can be used both as input and output; you may also remember that these pins can either be on or off—these are all digital pins, not only when it comes to output but also for input. But there are a huge amount of sensors that work over analogue communication. Due to the digital architecture of Raspberry Pi, it is difficult to interface these sensors directly. Hence, we use an **analogue to digital converter** (**ADC**), this converter converts the analogue value of the sensors to the digital bits that are understandable by Raspberry Pi.

We will be connecting an LDR, the resistor will change the value of resistance based on how much light is falling onto it. Hence, the voltage will be dependent upon how much light is falling over the LDR.

Now let's see how it is practically done. Take up your Pi and let's get going. To start, firstly we need to enable I2C on our Raspberry Pi; follow the steps listed here:

1. Open the terminal (*Ctrl + Shift + T*)
2. Type `sudo raspi-config`
3. Select the interfacing options:

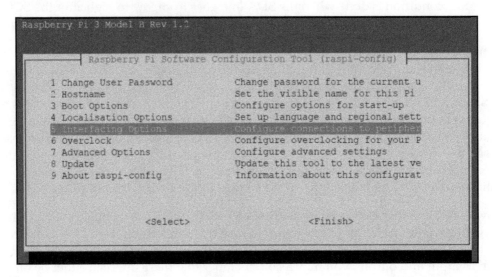

4. Then go to **Advanced Options**:

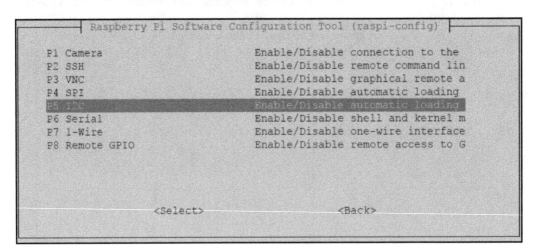

5. Then select **I2C** to enable it. Then select **Yes**:

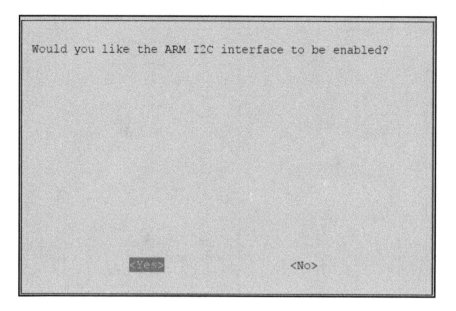

Now install the `adafruit` library to interface the ADC1115:

1. Open the terminal and copy the following command:

   ```
   sudo apt-get install build-essential python-dev python-smbus
   python-pip
   ```

   This command downloads the libraries and the dependencies over to Raspberry Pi

2. Now type the following:

   ```
   sudo pip install adafruit-ads1x15
   ```

This command installs the libraries and the dependencies over to Raspberry Pi.

Now that the software is set up, let's get the hardware ready. Connect Raspberry Pi to the ADS1115 as shown in the following diagram:

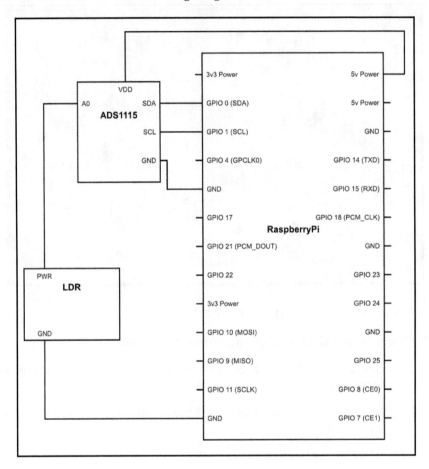

Once you are ready, go ahead and upload this code in Pi:

```
import time
import Adafruit_ADS1x15
import RPi.GPIO as GPIO
LED =14

GPIO.setmode(GPIO.BCM)
GPIO.setup(LED,GPIO.OUT)

adc = Adafruit_ADS1x15.ADS1115()
GAIN = 1
```

```
channel=0
adc.start_adc(channel, gain=GAIN)

while True:
    value = adc.get_last_result()
    print(str(value))
    time.sleep(0.1)
    if value >= 100:
        GPIO.output(LED,1)
    else :
        GPIO.output(LED,0)

adc.stop_adc()
```

Note that there can be times when this code may not work, in which case try tweaking the value of threshold:

```
if value >= 100:
```

What you might have noticed is that whenever the LDR is faced towards a light source, the LED also switches on, and whenever it is away from light, the LED switches off.

So now you have interfaced an I2C device. Let's understand how this code is actually working:

```
import Adafruit_ADS1x15
```

The preceding line of code imports the `Adafruit_ADS1x15` library in the code so that we can use all its functions during the program.

```
adc = Adafruit_ADS1x15.ADS1115()
```

The preceding line of code creates the instance of the library `Adafruit_ADS1x115`. The line `.ADS1115()` is the function for creating the instance as `adc`. Understood anything? Let me put it in English.

Now, instead of writing `Adafruit_ADS1x15` all the time, we can simply write `adc` to call the library functions. Further, you can use any word instead of `adc`; it can be your cat's name or your neighbor's name, and it would still work:

```
GAIN = 1
```

This is the value to which the sensing would be done. 1 depicts that the sensing would happen in full range. Which for our ADC is from a voltage range of 0V to +/-4.096V. Now changing the gain would result in change of the sensing range. I.e. if we change the value of gain to 2 Then the Range in which the sensing would happen would be Half of the original range i.w. 0 to +/- 2.048 Volts.

Now you must be asking what is the voltage range and why are we changing the gain ?

The reason is simple. There are different types of analog sensors. Which give output in a wide variety of voltage range. Some sensors can give you output in the range of 0.5 volt to 4 volt others can give you from 0.1 volt to 0.98 volts. Now if we set the gain to 1 then the all of these sensors could be easily interfaced. As all of them fall in between the sensing range of 0 to 4.098 Volts. However as it is a 16 bit ADC hence the total number of discrete values that the ADC can provide would be in between 2^{16} or 65,536 readings. Hence at the gain of 1 the minimum voltage change that the ADC could detect would be: *4.096 / 65536 = 0.000062*.

But if increase the gain to 4 then the sensing range would reduce to a mere 0 to +/- 1.0245. So this would be able to work with the output range between 0.1 volt to 0.98 volt. But now lets see the minimum voltage change that it could detect: *1.0245 / 65536 = 0.00001563*.

Now as you can see the minimum voltage that can be detected is very low. Which is a good thing for the compatibility with sensor.

Now, it is up to you as to what gain value you want. The LDR is working on 5V, hence it is better for us to use the entire gain reading of 1:

```
channel=0
```

When you look closely at the ADC hardware, you will notice that there are various pins including **A0, A1, A2,** and **A4** This is a four-channel ADC—it can convert four analogue inputs and convert them into digital data. As we are only using one single data stream, we will be letting Pi know which pin it is connected on. With the following line, we are telling Pi to start the process of converting the data:

```
adc.start_adc(channel, gain=GAIN)
```

In the following line, we are instructing the ADC to stop the conversion, and that's where the code ends.

```
adc.stop_adc()
```

Summary

This chapter was all about interfacing sensors with GPIOs so that the data can be retrieved by sensors.

19
Making a Gardener Robot

All right my friends, you have understood some of the basics of input and output; now it's the time to make something to which we can hand over some of our daily responsibilities. This robot might not really look like a robot, but trust me, it will make your life easier. Most of all the plants in your garden will be blessing you for making it.

We will be covering the following topics:

- Working with solenoids
- Making the robot
- Making it more intelligent
- Making it truly intelligent

Working with solenoids

What we are going to make is an automation system that will water your plants whenever they need it. So technically, once it is set up, you don't really have to worry ever about watering your green creatures. Whether you are at your home, at the office, or on a vacation, this will keep doing its job no matter what.

Now, you must be wondering how it will water the plants, so let me tell you, for every problem in this world, there exists a solution. In our case, that solution is called a solenoid valve. What it essentially does is switch the flow of liquids. There are various solenoid valves available in the market; some of the identifying features are as follows:

- **Size**: They come in various sizes such as half an inch, three quarters of an inch, 1 inch, and so on. This basically will determine the flow rate of the solenoid valve.

- **Medium**: Whether it is meant for fluid, gas, vapor, and so on.
- **Normal condition**:
    - **Normally opened**: This valve will allow the flow of liquids in the off state—when no power is supplied to the valve
    - **Normally closed**: This valve will stop the flow of liquids in the off state—when no power is supplied to the valve

- **Number of ways**: A simple valve will have an inlet and an outlet. So, when it is open, it will allow the liquid to flow from the inlet to the outlet. However, there can be other types of valve such as a three-way valve which might have two outlets and one inlet. It would regulate where the flow of the liquid would happen.

There can be some more specifics in terms of the valves as well, but for now that's all we need to know. One thing to notice about the solenoid valve is that these valves can either be opened or closed. Achieving any state in between or controlling flow via these valves is not possible. For this we can use a servo valve or motor valve. But as of now, we don't need it.

What we will be using in this chapter is a half inch valve for water/fluid, which is normally closed. When you look closely at this valve you will see that it operates at 12 volts and the current consumption is close to 1 amp. This is a lot of current for Raspberry Pi. The upper limit of current that Raspberry Pi can provide per pin is about 50 milliamp. So if we connect this valve to Raspberry Pi then it's surely not going to work.

What do we do now? The answer to this question is a relay. The basic job of a relay is to re-lay the circuits. Basically, it's an electronically controlled switch. The basic job of a relay is to switch devices that have a higher current/voltage consumption than what can be given by a controlling unit on and off. This is a fairly simple device, as you can see in the diagram. There are two circuits. One is depicted in blue, which is a low voltage and low current circuit. This circuit is powering up a coil. The other circuit is depicted in red and black. This circuit is a high voltage, high current circuit.

In the initial stages, as you can see, the high voltage high current circuit is not complete and the oven will not work:

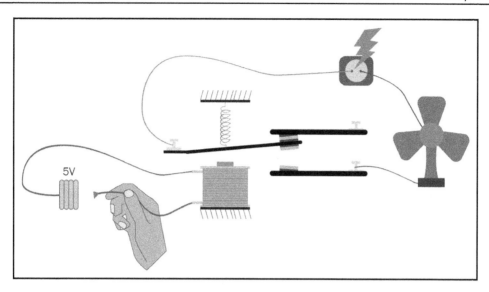

Now, in this second diagram, you can see that the blue circuit is connected to the 5V power source and that the coil is energized. Whenever a coil gets energized, it forms an electromagnet and attracts the metal leaf of the high power circuit to make the circuit complete, hence powering up the oven:

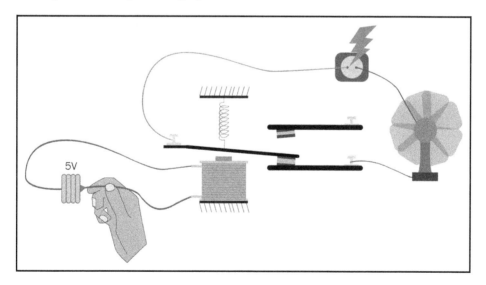

This is how a solenoid works. The consumption of the coil is hardly a few milliamps, hence it is very easy to actuate a coil via a micro-controller. This in turn makes a contact between the final circuit.

There are various kinds of relays available on the market; some of the identifying features are as follows:

- **Max output voltage**: The maximum voltage that it can handle
- **Maximum output current**: The maximum current that it can bear for any output device connected to it
- **Signal voltage**: The voltage that it requires switch the components on or off
- **Normal condition**:
    - **Normal off**: This will not allow any current to flow until the time the signal is not received
    - **Normal on**: It will allow the current to flow until the time the signal is not received

Now, coming back to our gardening robot, the solenoid attached to it will be working on 1 amp and 12V, so any relay which can supply equal to or more than 1 amp and 12V would work.

Commonly, the relays available on the market are 120V and 12 amp DC. One important thing to remember is that there will be two separate ratings for AC and DC voltage and current. As our solenoid will be working at 12V, we will only be considering the DC upper limit.

Making the robot

Now, let's get down to making the robot. Firstly, you need to make the water connection from the tap to the solenoid and from the solenoid to the sprinkler. You also have to make the connection, as follows:

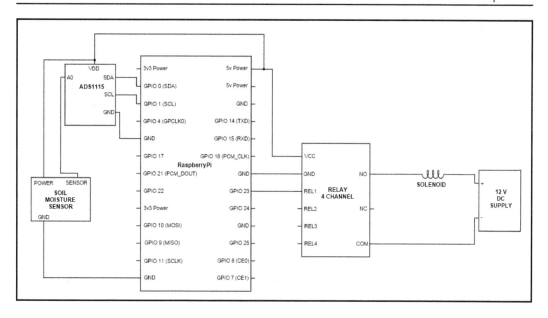

Now let's start programming. We will be interfacing a soil moisture sensor in this robot. The job of this sensor is to determine the amount of water in the soil. By determining this, we can understand if the garden needs water or not. This soil moisture sensor is an analogue sensor, hence we will be using an ADC to convert the analogue reading to Pi-understandable digital values. So let's get going:

```
import time
import RPi.GPIO as GPIO
import Adafruit_ADS1x15
water_valve_pin = 23
moisture_percentage = 20
GPIO.setmode(GPIO.BCM)
GPIO.setwarnings(False)
GPIO.setup(water_valve_pin, GPIO.OUT)
adc = Adafruit_ADS1x15.ADS1115()
channel = 0
GAIN = 1
while True:
 adc.start_adc(channel, gain=GAIN)
 moisture_value = adc.get_last_result()
 moisture_value= int(moisture_value/327)
 print moisture_value
 if moisture_value < moisture_percentage:
 GPIO.output(water_valve_pin, GPIO.HIGH)
 time.sleep(5)
 else:
 GPIO.output(water_valve_pin, GPIO.LOW)
```

Before you run this code, let's understand what it is actually doing:

```
moisture_percentage = 20
```

`moisture_percentage = 20` is the percentage that will act as a threshold; if the moisture level in the soil becomes less than 20% then your garden needs water. It is this condition that your robot will keep looking for; once this condition is met then appropriate action can be taken. This percentage can also be changed to 30, 40, or any other value as per your garden's needs:

```
moisture_value = int(moisture_value/327)
```

The ADC is a 16-bit device—there are 16 binary digits that can represent a value. Hence, the value can be between 0 and 2^{15} or, in other words, between 0 and 32768. Now, it is simple math that for every percentage of moisture the ADC will give the following reading: 32768/100, or 327.68. Hence, to find out the percentage of moisture in the soil, we would have to divide the actual value given by the ADC by 327.68.

The rest of the code is fairly simple and, once you go through it, it won't be very hard for you to understand.

Making it more intelligent

Congratulations on making your first robot! But did you notice one problem? The robot we made was continuously looking for a moisture value and, as soon as it noticed that the moisture value was low, it suddenly pumped water and made sure that the humidity of the soil was always more than 20%. However, this is not required. In general, we water the garden once or twice a day. If we water it more then it might not be good for the plants.

So, let's go ahead and make it slightly more intelligent and make it water the plants only when the moisture level is low at a certain time. This time, we won't need to make any changes to the hardware; we simply need to tweak the code.

Let's go ahead and upload the following code, and then see what exactly happens:

```
from time import sleep
from datetime import datetime
import RPi.GPIO as GPIO
import Adafruit_ADS1x15
water_valve_pin = 23
moisture_percentage = 20
GPIO.setmode(GPIO.BCM)
GPIO.setwarnings(False)
GPIO.setup(water_valve_pin, GPIO.OUT)
adc = Adafruit_ADS1x15.ADS1115()
GAIN = 1
def check_moisture():
 adc.start_adc(0,gain= GAIN)
 moisture_value = adc.get_last_result()
 moisture_value = int(moisture_value/327)
 if moisture_value < moisture_level:
 GPIO.output(water_valve_pin, GPIO.HIGH)
 sleep(5)
 GPIO.output(water_valve_pin, GPIO.LOW)
 else:
 GPIO.output(water_valve_pin, GPIO.LOW)
while True:
 H = datetime.now().strftime('%H')
 M = datetime.now().strftime('%M')
 if H == '07' and M <= '10':
 check_moisture()
 if H == '17' and M <= '01':
 check_moisture()
```

This code might look a little alien to you, but trust me, it is as simple as it can get. Let's see what's happening step by step:

```
from datetime import datetime
```

This line of code is importing daytime instances from the date time library. This is a library which is by default in Python. All we need to do is to call it. Now, what it does is that without any hustle and bustle, it helps us determine the time within our code:

```
def check_moisture():
```

There are several times when we have to do something over and over again. These sets of code can be a few repetitive lines or multiple pages of code. Hence, rewriting that code doesn't make sense at all. We can create a function. In this function, we can define what will happen whenever it is called. Here in this line, we have created a function by the name of `check_moisture()`; now, whenever this function is called within a program, there will be a set of activities that will be performed. The set of activities that will be performed is defined by the user. So, whenever we write `def`, then it means that we are defining a function; thereafter, we write the name of the function that needs to be defined.

Once done, then whatever we write in the indentation following it will be done once the function is called. Do remember that whenever we call or define a function, it is denoted by an open and a closed `()` bracket at the end of the name of the function:

```
moisture_value = adc.get_last_result()
```

`adc.get_last_result()` is a function of `adc`. The activity it does is to simply take the result from the pin defined earlier (pin number 0) and fetch the reading to a variable `moisture_value`. So, after the line `moisture_value` will be the reading of the pin number 0 of the ADC or, in other words, the reading of the moisture sensor:

```
H = datetime.now().strftime('%H')
```

The code `datetime` is an instance and a method of `.now()`. What this function does is that it updates the time. Now, the `date time.now()` has updated all the parameters of date and time which includes the hours, minutes, seconds, and even the date. It is up to us whether we want all of it or any specific part of the date and time. At present, we want to put the value of hours in the variable `H`, hence we are using a `.strftime('%H')` method. `strftime` stands for string format of time. So whatever value it outputs is in string format. `('%H')` means that it will give us the value of the hours only. Similarly, we can also get the time in minutes by using `('%M')` and `('%S')`. We can also get the value of the date, month, and year with the following syntax:

- For getting the date: `('%d')`
- For getting the month: `('%m')`
- For getting the year: `('%Y')`

```
if H == '07' and M <= '10':
```

In the preceding condition, we are checking if the time is 7 o'clock or not; further, we are also checking if the time is less than or equal to 10 minutes or not. So this piece of code will only run the statement in the `if` statement when the time is 7 hours and between 0 and 10 minutes.

One thing to particularly note is that we have used an `and` between both the conditions, hence it will only run the code inside it once both the statements are absolutely true. There are some other statements we can use inside it, as well, such as `or`, in which case it will run the code if either of the statements is true.

If we replace `and` with `or` in this `if` statement, then it will run the code for every 0 to 10 minutes of every hour and will run the code continuously for the entire time between 7:00 a.m. and 7:59 a.m.:

```
check_moisture()
```

As you may remember, previously we defined a function by the name of `check_moisture()`. While defining that function, we had also defined the set of activities that would happen every time this function is called.

Now is the time to call that function. As soon as the program reaches this end of the code, it will execute the set of activities that was earlier defined in the function.

So there we have it. Now, as soon as you run this code, it will wait for the time defined by you in the program. Once the specific time has been reached, then it will check for the moisture. If the moisture is less than the set value then it will start to water the plants until the time the moisture reaches above that threshold.

Making it truly intelligent

Amazing work! We have started building things that are smarter than us by ourselves. But now we want to take it a step further and make it even smarter than us—that's what robots are here for. Not only to do what we do but to do all that in a better way.

So, what can we improve? Well, we do not require a lot of water on a chilly winter day, but when it's summertime we need way more than what we drink in winter. The same thing happens with plants as well.

In winter, the amount of water they need is way less. Furthermore, even the rate of evaporation of water in the soil is slower. Hence, in both the conditions, we need to supply varying amounts of water to the garden. The question is, how do we do that?

Well, firstly, to know if it's hot or cold outside we require a sensor. We will be using a sensor named DHT11. It is a cheap yet robust sensor that gives us the readings of both the temperature and humidity. The best part is, it is super cheap at a rate of around $2.

It has four pins. But if you presume that it will work to I2C protocols, then you would be wrong. It has its own data transfer methodology. It is good to have one single protocol for all the sensors, but often you will also find that there are various sensors or devices which work on a different or an altogether new protocol. DHT11 is one such sensor. In this case, we have the choice of either understanding the entire methodology of communication or to simply get the library from the manufacturer and use it at our disposal. At present we will be opting for the latter.

Now let's see what the pins of the DHT11 look like:

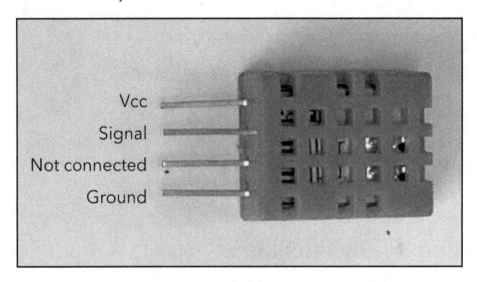

What you can see here is that there is only one signal pin which will do all the communication digitally. There are two pins for power and one of the pin is not in use. I.e. there is no significant purpose of the pin. It might be there just for soldering or for future use. This sensor works on a 5V supply and only needs a few milliamps, hence we can simply power it up by using Raspberry Pi. Now, for the data communication, we will connect the signal pin to GPIO pin number 4.

Before we start writing the code, let's first install the libraries for the communication between DHT11 and Raspberry Pi. We have done this before with the library of ADS1115, but in this one there are a few little tricks that we need to take care of. So let's get started.

Firstly, we need to make sure that the operating system of your Raspberry Pi is up to date. So connect Raspberry Pi to the internet, open the command prompt in Raspberry Pi, and type the following command:

```
sudo apt-get update
```

This command will update the raspbian OS of your Raspberry Pi automatically. Then go ahead and type in this:

```
sudo apt-get install build-essential python-dev python-openssl
```

In this command, we are installing the following packages:

- `build-essential`
- `python-dev`
- `python-openssl`

You must be wondering why we are installing all of these. Well, to cut a long story short, these are the dependencies for the library that we are about to install for the communication of DHT11. We will not be able to use the library if these packages are not installed on Raspberry Pi.

Finally, we have to install the library; this is a generic library in which the function of communicating with the DHT11 sensor is also available. This should suffice for our needs of easy communication. Here is the command to install it:

```
sudo python setup.py install
```

All right then, we are good to go. Our system is ready to talk to DHT11. Let's first just see if what we have done up until now works the way we want. To do that, connect the DHT11 as follows; you can leave the rest of the components such as the solenoid and the soil humidity sensor connected as they are. They should not interfere. Now upload the the following code in Pi:

```
from time import sleep
from datetime import datetime
import RPi.GPIO as GPIO
import Adafruit_DHT
sensor = 11
pin = 4
GPIO.setmode(GPIO.BCM)
GPIO.setwarnings(False)
while True:
  humidity, temperature = Adafruit_DHT.read_retry(sensor, pin)
  print("Temperature: " +temperature+ "C")
  print("Humidity: " +humidity+ "%")
```

```
time.sleep(2)
```

Once you upload this code, you will see readings of the sensor on your screen. This code is simply providing you with the raw readings of the sensor. This code is super simple and everything written here will be well understood by you, except for a few lines of the code, which are:

```
import Adafruit_DHT
```

In this line of the code, we are importing the `Adafruit_DHT` library in our code. This is the same library that will be used to communicate with the DHT11 sensor:

```
sensor = 11
```

There are different versions of DHT available, such as DHT11, DHT22, and so on. We need to tell the program which sensor we are using. Hence, we have allotted a value to the variable sensor. Later, you will see how we will be using it:

```
pin = 4
```

In this line, we are assigning the value 4 to a variable called `pin`. This variable will be used to tell the program on which pin of the Raspberry Pi we have connected the DHT11:

```
humidity, temperature = Adafruit_DHT.read_retry(sensor, pin)
```

In this line, we are using a method of the `Adafruit` library named `Adafruit_DHT.read_retry()`. Now, what this does is that it reads the DHT sensor and gives the reading of the sensor to the variables `humidity` and `temperature`. One thing to note is that the DHT11 gives a reading which is updated every 2 seconds. Hence, the readings that you will be receiving will be refresh after every 2 seconds.

Once this code is through, then we can be sure that the sensor is working the way we want. Finally, the time has come to integrate all of the sensors together and make an entirely intelligent robot. As the solenoid, humidity sensor, and temperature sensors are already connected, all we need to do is to upload the code over to Pi and see the magic:

```
from time import sleep
from datetime import datetime
import RPi.GPIO as GPIO
import Adafruit_ADS1x15
import Adafruit_DHT
water_valve_pin = 23
sensor = 11
```

```
pin = 4
GPIO.setmode(GPIO.BCM)
GPIO.setwarnings(False)
GPIO.setup(water_valve_pin, GPIO.OUT)
Channel =0
GAIN = 1
adc = Adafruit_ADS1x15.ADS1115()
def check_moisture(m):
 adc.start_adc(channel, gain=GAIN)
 moisture_value = adc.get_last_result()
 moisture_value = int(moisture_value/327)
 print moisture_value
 if moisture_value < m:
 GPIO.output(water_valve_pin, GPIO.HIGH)
 sleep(5)
 GPIO.output(water_valve_pin, GPIO.LOW)
 else:
 GPIO.output(water_valve_pin, GPIO.LOW)
while True:
 humidity, temperature = Adafruit_DHT.read_retry(sensor, pin)
 H = datetime.now().strftime('%H')
 M = datetime.now().strftime('%M')
 if H == '07' and M <= '10':
 if temperature < 15:
 check_moisture(20)
 elif temperature >= 15 and temperature < 28:
 check_moisture(30)
 elif temperature >= 28:
 check_moisture(40)
 if H == '17' and M <= '10':
 if temperature < 15:

 check_moisture(20)
 elif temperature >= 15 and temperature < 28:
 check_moisture(30)
 elif temperature >= 28:
 check_moisture(40)
```

Pretty long code, right? It might look so, but once you write it line by line, you will certainly understand that it might be longer than all the code we have written so far, but it's anything but complex. You might have understood most of the program, however let me explain a few new things that we have used here:

```
def check_moisture(m):
   adc.start_adc(channel, gain = GAIN)

moisture_value = adc.get_last_result()
moisture_value = int(moisture_value / 327)
```

```
print moisture_value

if moisture_value < m:
   GPIO.output(water_valve_pin, GPIO.HIGH)
   sleep(5)
   GPIO.output(water_valve_pin, GPIO.LOW)
else :
   GPIO.output(water_valve_pin, GPIO.LOW)
```

In this line, we are defining a function named check_moisture(). Previously, if you remember, while we were making the function check_moisture, we were basically checking if the moisture value was either more or less than 20%. What if we have to check the moisture for 30%, 40%, and 50%? Would we make a separate function for that?

Obviously not! What we do is we pass an argument to the function, an argument is basically a variable placed within the brackets of the function. Now we can assign values to this variable for, for example, check_moisture(30) —now the value of the m will be 30 during the time that function is executing. Then again, if you call it as check_moisture(40) then the value of that m would be 40.

Now, as you can see, we are comparing values of m throughout the function:

```
if moisture_value < m:
```

The if statement will be checking the value of the m which is assigned while calling the function. This makes our job very easy and simple.

Let's see what the rest of the program is doing:

```
if temperature < 15:
    check_moisture(20)
```

Every time the desired time is reached it will go ahead and check for the temperature. If the temperature is less than 15 it will call the function check_moisture with the value of the argument as 20. Hence, if the moisture is less than 20%, then the water will be fed to the garden:

```
elif temperature >= 15 and temperature < 28:
        check_moisture(30)
```

The `elif` or the `else` `if` statement is used after an `if` statement. This in common words means that if the previous `if` statement is not true, then it will check for this `if` statement. So, in the preceding line it will check if the temperature is between 15 and 28 degrees Celsius. If that is true, then it will check the moisture of the soil. The argument to the function is 30 in this line. Hence, it will check if the moisture is less than 30. If so, then it will supply the water to the garden:

```
elif temperature >= 28:
            check_moisture(40)
```

Similarly, in this line of code we are checking the temperature, and if it is equal to or more than 28 degrees Celsius then it will pass the value 40 as an argument to the function `check_moisture`. Hence this time it will check for moisture if it is 28 or more than that.

As you can see, now the system will be checking the ambient temperature and, based on that, the amount of water to the plants is regulated. The best part is that it is consistent and will provide the right amount of water needed by the plants.

 The values mentioned in this entire chapter are simply assumed values. I would strongly recommend to tweak it based on where you live and what kind of plants you have in your garden to get the best out of the system.

Summary

In this chapter, we covered certain topics such as solenoid integration and soil humidity sensors to build a robot that waters your backyard garden automatically. Next up, we will cover the basics of motors.

20
Basics of Motors

All right then! We have made a robot that takes care of your garden and I hope it's working fine. It's time to take things to another level.

We have always thought that robots are like WALL-E, moving around and doing things for us. Well, my friend, now that dream is not far away. In fact, in this chapter we will be going ahead and making one. Let's see how it's done.

We will be covering the following topics:

- The basics
- Getting it rolling
- Changing the speed

The basics

Whenever we talk about moving from one place to another, we think about wheels and similarly whenever we think about moving the wheels of a robot, we think about motors. There are various different types of motors that exist. So let's firstly look at the most basic type of motor, which is called a brushed DC motor. As the name suggests, it works on a direct current. You may find such motors like this:

Trust me, these things are omnipresent, from the Christmas gift you bought for your neighbor to the biggest baddest machines out there—you will find these motors hiding under the hood. These motors are common for a reason and that is because they are very, very simple. So simple that powering them up only requires a battery and two wires. Simply connect the positive to one terminal and negative to the other, and the motor will start spinning. Interchange those connections and the direction of the rotation will change. Take two cells and double the voltage and the motor will spin even faster. It is that simple.

Now you might assume that we would simply connect this motor to Raspberry Pi and that we would be good to go. But unfortunately this is not going to be the case. As you may remember from the previous chapters, Raspberry Pi can only supply around 50 milliamps, but the consumption of a motor can be much higher. Hence, to run one we need an intermediate device.

The first thing that will come to your mind will be to use a relay, and why not? They can channel a huge amount of current and can handle high voltages. This should be the ideal choice. You would be right if you thought so, but only to some extent, and that is because a relay is simply a switch we can use to turn the motor on or off. We would not be able to control the speed or the direction of rotation of the motor. Now, you would think that this problem is not new and that we can very easily solve it by using **pulse width modulation (PWM)**, right? Well, the answer is no! Because these relays are mechanical devices, and due to their mechanical nature, there are some maximum limits in terms of it being switched on or off in a second. Hence, it would not be able to cope with the frequency of PWM. Finally, we would still be left with the problem of changing the direction and the speed of the motor. So what do we do now?

As I always say, the beauty of a problem is that it always has a solution, and the solution here is called a motor driver. A motor driver is primarily a set of electronic relays—a switch that can allow high currents yet is not mechanical. Hence, we can switch it hundreds of times every second. These electronic relays are either made of simple transistors or, in high power applications, they can even use MOSFETs for switching. We can simply give PWM to these electronic switches and get the voltage to modulate while making sure that enough current is being delivered to the circuit. Further, as I mentioned earlier, the motor driver is made of a set of these electronic relays. The most common and workable fashion in which they are arranged is called a full bridge or an H Bridge. Before I explain any further, let's see what this is, exactly:

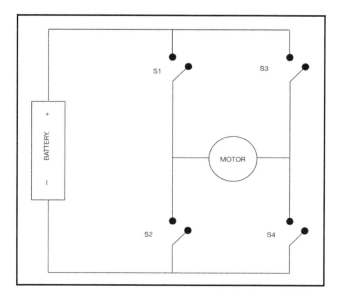

In a full bridge we have four switching circuits across the connected motor; these can be independently switched on or off based on the requirements. In the off state, all of these switching circuits are in an open state, hence keeping the motor switched off. Now, whenever we want to start the motor, we will have to switch on two switches in such a way that the circuit is complete and the motor starts working. So let's see what it would look like:

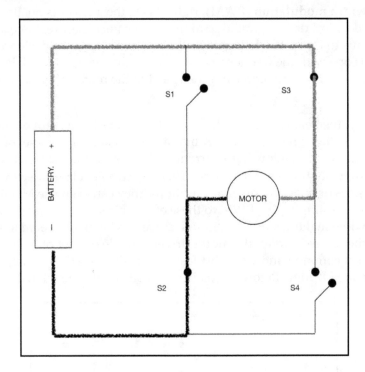

Here, we have switched on the switching circuit **S2** and **S3**; this in turn completes the circuit and lets the current flow in the motor. Now, to control the speed, these same switching circuits can be switched on and off at a very high frequency at varying duty cycles to achieve a specific mean voltage. Now that we can achieve a specific speed for the motor by changing the voltage via these two switching circuits, let's see how we are going to change the direction of rotation of the motor:

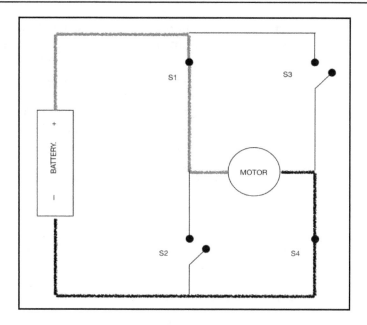

In this circuit we have switched off the previously connected **S2** and **S3** and instead switched on **S1** and **S4**, hence the polarity to the motor is reversed. As we discussed earlier, whenever the polarity of a DC-brushed motor is changed, the direction also changes subsequently. There are various types of motor drivers you can find on the market. What we have understood here is called a brushed DC H-bridge motor driver; there are other types of motor drivers as well for controlling other types of motors, but currently we will stick to the brushed motor only. While selecting a motor driver, you should examine the specification sheet of the motor driver very carefully. Some of the key specifications that will be mentioned are as follows:

- **Voltage rating**: There will be a minimum and maximum limit to the voltage that the motor driver can handle and modulate between. Make sure your motor lies in between this specific voltage range.
- **Current rating**: There will be an absolute maximum current that the motor driver can handle; going anywhere beyond it will burn or damage the motor driver. This can be a little deceptive. Let's see why. Except for the absolute maximum, there will be many other current ratings that might be specified. These might be:

- **Repetitive maximum current**: This is the current rating that can be the maximum current the motor driver can handle, but not continuously. This rating is given because at times the load on the motor might increase and there might be a higher current requirement for a brief moment. The motor driver will provide the adequate current on a repetitive basis without getting damaged. But this current requirement should not be continuous.
- **Burst maximum current**: This is the absolute maximum current that the motor driver can handle; anything beyond it will damage the motor driver. The DC motors might have a very high current requirement when it starts from a standstill. Hence, the motor drivers are designed to handle these currents. But this surge of current should not be repetitive, otherwise heating and subsequent damage can happen. Often, burst maximum current is referred to as the maximum current by the manufacturers.
- **Continuous maximum current**: This is the real deal; the continuous maximum current is the maximum continuous current that the motor driver can mange on a continuous basis.

- **Supply voltage**: This is the operating voltage of the motor driver—this voltage must be given to the motor driver for its own internal workings.
- **Logic supply voltage**: This is the control signal given to the motor driver, and can be given at various voltages such as 5V, 3.3V, and 12V. Hence, the motor driver will specify the maximum logical voltage that it can accept in the signal line.

Now, let's see what we have got. During the course of this book, we will be using the L298N motor driver module, which currently is one of the most common motor driver modules available on the market. It has two channels—you have two H-bridges and hence you can connect two motors onto it. Further, the specifications for this motor driver are also decent for the price. Here are the specifications:

- **Voltage rating**: 2.5V to 46V
- **Repetitive maximum current**: 2.5 amp
- **Burst maximum current**: 3 amp
- **Continuous maximum current**: 2 amp
- **Supply voltage**: 4.5V to 7V
- **Logic supply voltage**: 4.5V to 7V

Once you have the physical motor driver with you, you will notice the following pins:

- **Motor A**: This is channel 1 of the motor driver. You can connect the first motor to this port.
- **Motor B**: This is channel 2 of the motor driver. You can connect a second motor to this port. If you only have one motor, you can simply leave this port unconnected.
- **GND**: This is the ground of the power supply that you will attach for the motor. It is very important that you not only connect the ground of the power supply but also connect the ground of Raspberry Pi to this port so that the circuit is complete between Raspberry Pi and the motor driver.
- **VCC**: This is the positive port of the motor driver. This is where the positive terminal of your battery or power adapter will go.
- **IN 1 and IN 2**: These are the two logical inputs that we need to provide from the microcontroller for motor A. Whenever IN 1 receives the signal, one part of the H-bridge is activated—the motor starts spinning in one direction. Whenever IN 2 receives the signal, the other part of the H-bridge is activated, making the motor spin in the opposite direction.
- **IN 3 and IN 4**: This is the logical input of the motor B, which will work in exactly the same way as IN 1 and IN 2.
- **EN A and EN B**: These are the enable pins for both the channels. If these pins are not high, the respective channels will not work despite any signal that you give over the input ports. You might notice that there is a small cap on the EN ports. This is called a shunt. What it does is that it makes contact between the two pins that it has been connected on. This cap, when present over the EN pin, means that it would permanently be high as long as this shunt is connected.

Getting it rolling

OK, that's a lot of theory, so now let's fire up one of our motors via Raspberry Pi. To do that, go ahead and connect the motor and the motor driver as shown:

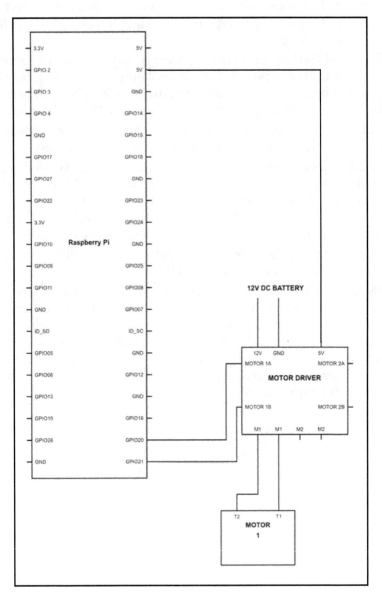

Now, once you are done with it, let's upload the code and see what happens:

```
import RPi.GPIO as GPIO
from time import sleep
GPIO.setmode(GPIO.BCM)

Motor1R = 20
Motor1L = 21

GPIO.setup(Motor1R,GPIO.OUT)
GPIO.setup(Motor1L,GPIO.OUT)


GPIO.output(Motor1R,GPIO.HIGH)
GPIO.output(Motor1L,GPIO.LOW)

sleep(5)

GPIO.output(Motor1R,GPIO.LOW)
GPIO.output(Motor1L,GPIO.HIGH)

sleep(5)

GPIO.cleanup()
```

Now, let's understand the code a bit:

```
Motor1R = 20
Motor1L = 21
```

Pin number 20 is connected to IN 1 of the motor driver. For convenience, we have changed motor 1 right to `Motor1R`; in reality, the motor can spin in any direction but we have just written this for convenience and understanding. Similarly, we have done this for `Motor1L` as well. This is connected to IN 2, hence this will lead to the motor spinning in the other direction:

```
GPIO.output(Motor1R,GPIO.HIGH)
GPIO.output(Motor1L,GPIO.LOW)
```

Here, we are making the `Motor1R` or the pin number 20 high, which means that the input motor driver is getting is:

Motor	Pin	Input	State
Motor 1R	Pin number 20 of Raspberry Pi	IN 1	HIGH
Motor 1L	Pin number 21 of Raspberry Pi	IN 2	LOW

Now, after a delay of 5 seconds, the following code will run, which will change the state of the pins as depicted in the below table:

```
GPIO.output(Motor1R,GPIO.LOW)
GPIO.output(Motor1L,GPIO.HIGH)
```

Motor	Pin	Input	State
Motor 1R	Pin number 20 of Raspberry Pi	IN 1	LOW
Motor 1L	Pin number 21 of Raspberry Pi	IN 2	HIGH

Now, let's see what happens once we run it. The motor will spin firstly in one direction and then it will go in the other direction. The code is very straightforward and I don't think there is any need for explanation. All we are doing here is simply turning either of the two GPIOs connected to the motor driver on and off. Once the input IN 1 of the motor driver is activated, a part of the H-bridge is switched on, causing the motor to spin in one direction. Whenever the IN 2 of the motor driver is high, then the opposite part of H-bridge is turned on, causing the polarity at the output end of the motor driver to change, and hence the motor turns in the other direction.

Changing the speed

Now that we have understood how to change the direction of the motor using the motor driver, it's time to take it a step further and control the speed of the motor using the motor driver. To do this, we don't really have to do much. The motor drivers are built to understand the PWM signals. Once the PWM signal to the motor driver is provided, then the motor driver in turn adjusts the output voltage for the motor and hence changes the speed of the motor driver. The PWM has to be provided on the same input ports IN 1 and IN 2 for motor A, and IN 3 and IN 4 for motor B. It is obvious that the pin on which the PWM is provided will decide the direction in which the motor will move, and the duty cycle of the PWM will decide the speed at which the motor will be spinning.

Now we have understood how speed control in motor driver works. It's time to do it by ourselves. To do so, we do not need to make any changes to the connections; all we need to do is to upload the following code:

```
import RPi.GPIO as GPIO
from time
import sleep
GPIO.setmode(GPIO.BCM)
```

```
Motor1R = 20
Motor1L = 21

GPIO.setup(Motor1R, GPIO.OUT)
GPIO.setup(Motor1L, GPIO.OUT)

pwm = GPIO.PWM(Motor1R, 100)
pwm.start(0)

try:
while True:
  GPIO.output(Motor1L, GPIO.LOW)
for i in range(0, 101):
  pwm.ChangeDutyCycle(i)
sleep(0.1)

except KeyboardInterrupt:

  pwm.stop()
GPIO.cleanup()
```

What happened after you ran this code? I'm sure the motor started slowly and then started increasing its speed and, upon reaching its top speed, it eventually stopped—exactly what we wanted it to do. If you remember, this code looks very familiar. Remember changing the brightness of the LED in the first chapter? It is almost the same; there are a few differences, though, so let's see what they are:

```
pwm = GPIO.PWM(Motor1R, 100)
```

In this line, we are simply defining the pin we have to give the PWM on—as in, on Motor1R, which corresponds to pin number 20. Also, we are are defining the frequency of the PWM as 100 hertz or 100 times in a second:

```
pwm.start(0)
```

If you remember, the preceding command from the previous chapters, pwm.start(), is primarily used for defining the duty cycle of the signal. Here, we are giving it the duty cycle as 0 that is the pin would be off:

```
GPIO.output(Motor1L,GPIO.LOW)
```

As we are running motor in one specific direction and which is `1R` hence the other half of the H bridge should be turned off. this would be done by the above line by putting the line `1L` LOW. If we don't do this then the pin `21` can be in an arbitrary state, hence it can be either on or off. This might conflict with the direction in which the motor is moving and the hardware would not work properly:

```
for i in range(0,101):
```

Here comes the real deal; this line, `for i in range(0,101):`, will keep on running the program contained in it until the time the value of `i` is between 0 to `101`. It will also increment the value of `i` every time this loop runs. Here, every time, the value will increase by one:

```
pwm.ChangeDutyCycle(i)
```

Now, this is a slightly new command. Previously, we have used the line `pwm.start(0)` to assign a duty cycle to the PWM. As we have already assigned a duty cycle value to the PWM, to change it we would use the previously mentioned command. The duty cycle would be the same as the value of `i`.

Hence, every time the code passes through the `for` loop, the value or the duty cycle will increase by one. Super easy, isn't it?

Everything in robotics is very easy if you do it right. The idea is to break your problem into small pieces and solve them one by one; trust me, once you do that, nothing will look difficult to you.

Summary

In this chapter, we worked on the various aspects of a motor. Moving on, by using all the basics, we will study the interaction of Bluetooth with mobile devices and build a Bluetooth-controlled robotic car.

21
Bluetooth-Controlled Robotic Car

We have come a long way; now it's time to go ahead and make something even better. The world is going all gaga over the inception of autonomous cars and within this decade this will become the new normal. There is so much going on in these vehicles. Multiple sensors, GPS, and telemetry are all calculated in real time to make sure that the car is on the right course and is being driven by the system safely on the road, so making a robotic vehicle proves to be an ideal way to learn robotics and future technologies. In this book, we will always try to make technologies that are not only as good as the present technologies but in some ways even better. So, let's go ahead and get to making this autonomous vehicle one step at a time.

This chapter will cover the following topics:

- Basics of the vehicle
- Getting the vehicle ready
- Controlling the vehicle by Bluetooth

Basics of the vehicle

You must be thinking: what can we possibly learn about the vehicle that we don't already know? This may be true, but there are a few that we must make sure we understand before taking on this chapter. So, let's get started.

First is the chassis, which we will be using: it's is a four-wheel drive chassis and all the four wheels are independently controlled by a dedicated motor. Hence, we can change the speed of every single wheels as per our needs. We have chosen a four-wheel drive drivetrain as it is harder for it to get stuck on carpets and uneven surfaces. You can also opt for a two-wheel drive drivetrain if you want to do so, as it won't make a huge difference.

Now, once you assemble the chassis you might see that it does not have a steering mechanism. Does this mean that the car will only go straight? Well, obviously not. There are many ways by which we can steer the direction of a car while making small vehicles. The best one is called differential turning.

In conventional cars, there is one engine and that engine powers up the wheels; hence in principal all the wheels turn at the same speed. Now this works fine when we are going straight but whenever the car wants to turn there comes a new problem. Refer to the following diagram:

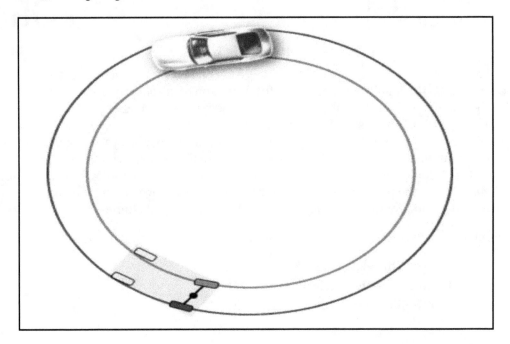

You will see that the wheels, which are on the inner curve, have a smaller diameter and the one on the outer edge has a larger diameter. You may remember a fact from elementary school: the larger the diameter the more the circumference, and vice a versa. Hence, the wheel towards the inner edge will be covering a shorter distance compared to the wheels on the outer edge at the same time, or in simple words, the inner wheels will be spinning slower and the outer wheels will be spinning faster.

This problem leads to the discovery of differentials in cars, which is a round lump at the center of the axle of the car. What this does is that it varies the rate at which the wheels are spinning based on the turning radius. Genius, isn't it? Now, you must be thinking: this is all right, but why are you telling me all this? Well, because we will do the exact opposite to turn the robot. If we change the speed of the motors on the inner and outer edge of the turning circle, then the car will try to turn towards inside and similarly if we do it for the other end then it will try to turn in the other direction. While making wheeled robot this strategy is not new at all. Steering mechanisms are complicated and implementing them on small robot is simply a challenge. Hence this is a far simpler and easy way to turn your vehicle around.

Not only is this way simple but it is a very efficient and simple strategy that requires minimal components. It is also better as the turning radius of the vehicle is also reduced. In fact, if we spin the opposite sides of the wheels in the opposite direction at the same speed then the vehicle will turn completely on its own axis, making the turning radius entirely zero. this type of configuration is called skid-steer drive. For a robot that is wheeled and works indoors, this is a killer feature.

 To know more about it read more here: `https://groups.csail.mit.edu/drl/courses/cs54-2001s/skidsteer.html`

Getting the vehicle ready

Now is the time to go ahead and make the robotic vehicle a reality. So let's unbox the vehicle chassis and screw every part together. The assembly manual generally comes along with the kit, so it won't take long for you to complete it.

Once you have completed building the kit, go ahead and segregate the wires for each of the motors. This is going to be a very important part of making the vehicle ready. So, once you have all the wires coming out of the vehicle, take a cell and power up each of the wheels. Notice the polarity of connection in which the wheels spin in the forward direction. All you have to do is to take a permanent marker or perhaps a nail paint and mark the wire which goes to the positive terminal when the motor is spinning in the forward direction. As all of these motors are entirely dependent on polarity for the direction, this step is key to ensure that whenever we power them up they always spin in the same direction. Trust me, this will save you a lot of headaches.

Now, once this is all done, connect the wires to the motor driver as shown in the following diagram (the wire marked by red is the wire that you marked earlier):

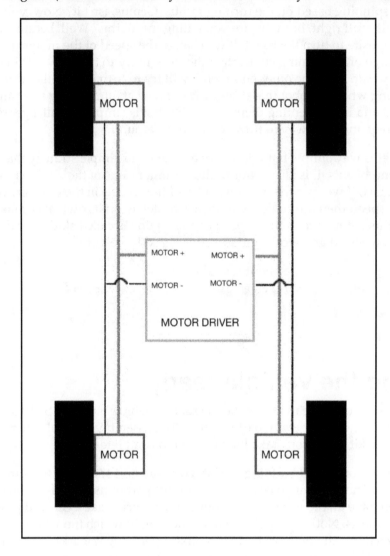

Perfect! Now everything seems sorted, except for the connection of the motor driver with the power source and Raspberry Pi. So let's see how we are going to do it:

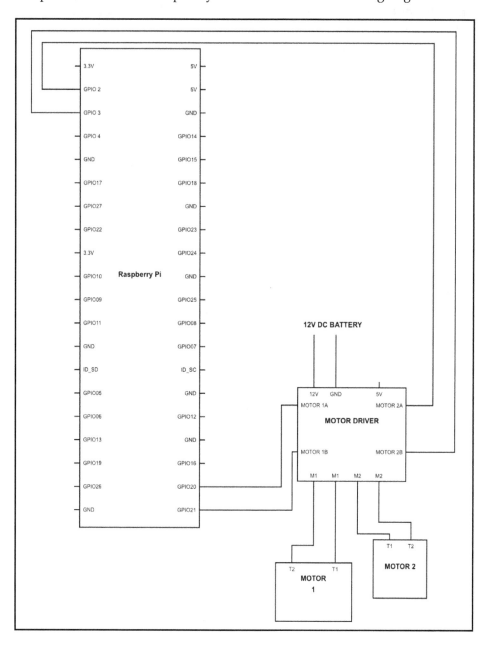

All right then! Time for the real deal! So the first thing we want to make sure is that all the connections are working exactly the way we planned them to. For this, we will start off with a dummy code which will simply switch all the motors on and in forward direction. So here is the code:

```
import RPi.GPIO as GPIO
import time
GPIO.setmode(GPIO.BCM)
Motor1a = 20
Motor1b = 21
Motor2a = 2
Motor2b = 3
GPIO.setup(Motor1a,GPIO.OUT)
GPIO.setup(Motor1b,GPIO.OUT)
GPIO.setup(Motor2a,GPIO.OUT)
GPIO.setup(Motor2b,GPIO.OUT)
GPIO.output(Motor1a,1)
GPIO.output(Motor1b,0)
GPIO.output(Motor2a,1)
GPIO.output(Motor2b,0)
time.sleep(10)
GPIO.cleanup()
```

The program can't be more simple than this; all we are doing here is giving the motor driver the command to spin the motor in one single direction. There might be a chance that a set of motors will be rotating in the reverse direction, in which case you should change the polarity of connections on the motor driver. This should solve the problem. Some people might think that we can make a change to the code as well to do this, but as per my experience it starts getting complicated from there and would cause you trouble if you chose the other path.

All right then, everything is set and all is working well. Go ahead, try some other output permutations and combinations and see what happens to the car. Don't worry, whatever you do, you won't be able to damage the car unless it runs off the roof!

Controlling the vehicle by Bluetooth

Had some fun trying those combinations? Now is the time that we take this journey a step ahead and see what else is possible. We have all played with remote-controlled cars and I'm sure everyone will have had fun with those zippy little toys. We are going to do something similar but in a much more sophisticated way.

We all are aware of Bluetooth: this is one of the best ways to communicate with devices in close proximity. Bluetooth communication is a medium data rate, low power communication method. This is almost omnipresent in mobile devices, hence it is an ideal way to start. What we will be doing in this chapter is controlling the car via your mobile phone using Bluetooth. Now let's see how we can do it.

The first thing we want to do is pair up the smartphone to the robotic vehicle, and to do so we need to open the terminal on Raspberry Pi and perform the following steps:

1. Type in the command ~ $ `bluetoothctl`; this is a Bluetooth agent which allows two Bluetooth devices to communicate. Without the Bluetooth agent, the two devices will not be able to communicate with each other in the first place.
2. The `[Bluetooth]` # `power on` command simply powers up the Bluetooth on board the Raspberry.
3. The `[Bluetooth]` # `agent on` command starts up the agent which can then initiate the connection for us.
4. The `[Bluetooth]` # `discoverable on` command makes Raspberry Pi's Bluetooth discoverable. The Bluetooth might be on, but we must make it discoverable to make sure that the other device can find it and connect to it.
5. The `[Bluetooth]` # `pairable on` command makes the device pairable. If the Bluetooth is on, this doesn't mean your device will be able to connect, hence we need to make it pairable and this command does exactly that.
6. The `[Bluetooth]` # `scan on` command starts scanning for nearby Bluetooth devices. The output of this command will be a couple of MAC addresses along with the Bluetooth name. The MAC address is a physical address of the device; this is a unique address, hence it will never ever be the same for two devices.
7. The `[Bluetooth]` # `pair 94:65:2D:94:9B:D3` command helps you to pair up with the device you want. You simply need to type the mentioned command with the MAC address.

Just to be clear, this what your screen should look like:

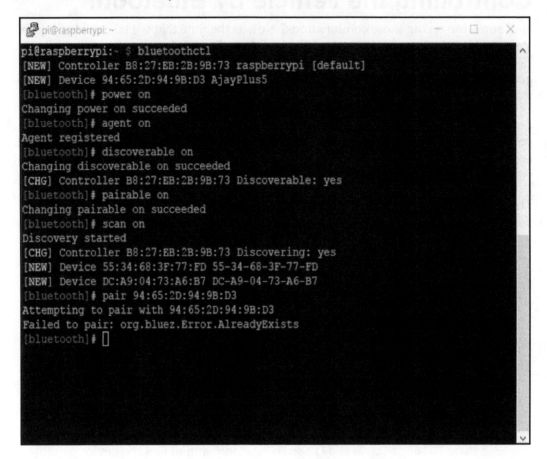

Once you have done this process, you should be able to connect Raspberry Pi to your mobile devices. Now that you are connected, it's time to go ahead and write the code through which we will be able to control the Bluetooth car just using our mobile devices. So here is the code. Go ahead, have a look, then we will get to the explanation:

```
import bluetooth
import time
import RPi.GPIO as GPIO
Motor1a = 20
Motor1b = 21
Motor2a = 2
Motor2b = 3
GPIO.setmode(GPIO.BCM)
GPIO.setwarnings(False)
GPIO.setup(Motor1a,GPIO.OUT)
GPIO.setup(Motor1b,GPIO.OUT)
GPIO.setup(Motor2a,GPIO.OUT)
GPIO.setup(Motor2b,GPIO.OUT)
server_socket=bluetooth.BluetoothSocket( bluetooth.RFCOMM )
port = 1
server_socket.bind(("",port))
server_socket.listen(1)
client_socket,address = server_socket.accept()
print ("Accepted connection from "+str(address))
def stop_car():
  GPIO.output(Motor1a,0)
  GPIO.output(Motor1b,0)
  GPIO.output(Motor2a,0)
  GPIO.output(Motor2b,0)

while True:
  data = client_socket.recv(1024)
  if (data == "B" or data== "b"):
    GPIO.output(Motor1a,1)
    GPIO.output(Motor1b,0)
    GPIO.output(Motor2a,1)
    GPIO.output(Motor2b,0)
    time.sleep(1)
    stop_car()

  if (data == "F" or data == "f"):
    GPIO.output(Motor1a,0)
    GPIO.output(Motor1b,1)
    GPIO.output(Motor2a,0)
    GPIO.output(Motor2b,1)
    time.sleep(1)
```

```
    stop_car()

if (data == "R" or data == "r"):
    GPIO.output(Motor1a,0)
    GPIO.output(Motor1b,1)
    GPIO.output(Motor2a,1)
    GPIO.output(Motor2b,0)
    time.sleep(1)
    stop_car()

if (data == "L" or data == "l"):
    GPIO.output(Motor1a,1)
    GPIO.output(Motor1b,0)
    GPIO.output(Motor2a,0)
    GPIO.output(Motor2b,1)
    time.sleep(1)
    stop_car()

if (data == "Q" or data =="q"):
    stop_car()
if (data =='Z' or data == "z"):
    client_socket.close()
    server_socket.close()
```

Now let's see what this code is actually doing:

```
import bluetooth
```

We will be using some generic functions of Bluetooth during this program, hence we are calling the library `bluetooth` so that we are able to call those methods:

```
server_socket=bluetooth.BluetoothSocket( bluetooth.RFCOMM )
```

Now, whenever we connect two Bluetooth devices, we have various methods of communication; the easiest among them is radio frequency communication, herein referred to as RFCOMM. Now, in this line, we are using the `BluetoothSocket` method of the `bluetooth` library to define what communication protocol we are using in our program, which by now you know is RFCOMM. We are further storing this data in a variable called `server_socket` so that we don't have to repeat this step over and over again. Rather, whenever we need this data it will already be stored in the variable called `server_socket`:

```
port = 1
```

Now, Bluetooth has multiple ports; this is a very useful concept as through one single Bluetooth connection we can have various streams of data being transferred to various devices and programs. This avoids the clash of data and also makes sure that the data is securely communicated to exactly the right receiver. The program which we are using right now is extremely simple and we do not need multiple ports for data communication. Hence, we can use any of the 1 to 60 ports available to us for the communication. In this part of the program, you can write any port and your program will run just fine:

```
server_socket.bind(("",port))
```

Now, whenever we are connecting two devices we need to make sure that they stay connected throughout the communication. Hence, here we are writing this command: `server_socket.bind`. What this will do is that it will make sure that your Bluetooth connection is maintained during the entire communication.

As you can see, the first parameter inside the argument is empty. Here, we generally write the MAC address which it has to be bound with. However, as we have set this as empty it will automatically bind to the MAC address we are already paired with. The second argument we have is the port on which it has to be connected. As we know, the value of the `port` variable is set to be 1. Hence, it will automatically connect to port number 1:

```
server_socket.listen(1)
```

This is a very interesting line. As we know, we might not be the only person trying to connect to the Bluetooth device of Raspberry, hence what should Raspberry do when it receives another connection request?

In this line, we are defining just that: we are calling a method called `listen(1)`. In this function, we have defined the value of argument as 1. What it means is that it will be connected to one device only. Any other device that tries to connect will not get through. If we change this argument to 2 then it will be connected to two devices, however it would stay in the queue and hence it is called **queue connection**:

```
client_socket,address = server_socket.accept()
```

Now that most of the things for the connection have been done, we also need to know if we are connected to the right address. What the method `server_socket.accept()` does is that it returns the socket number and the address it is serving to. Hence, we are storing it within two variables called `client_socket` and `address`. However, as we know, the socket will remain only as 1, hence we will not be using it any further:

```
print ("Accepted connection from "+str(address))
```

In this line we are simply telling the user that the connection has been made successfully with the sue of the function `str(address)` we are printing the value of the address to which it is connected to. This way we can be double sure that the connection has been made to the right device.

```
data = client_socket.recv(1024)
```

In this line, we are receiving the data from the client; also, we are defining how long that data will be. Hence, in the method `client_socket.recv(1024)` we have passed on a parameter in the argument as `1024` which basically denotes that the maximum length of the data packet will be `1024` bytes. Once the data is received, it is then passed on to the variable `data` for further use.

After this, the rest of the program is pretty simple. We simply need to compare the value received by the mobile device and make the car do whatever we want to do. Here, we have made the car go in all four directions, that is, forward, backward, right, and left. You may also add specific conditions as per your needs:

```
client_socket.close()
```

In this line, we are closing the connection of the client socket so that the client can be disconnected and the data transfer can be terminated:

```
server_socket.close()
```

In the preceding line, we are closing the connection of the server socket so that the server connection can be disconnected.

Summary

This chapter taught us to automate and control a car using Bluetooth interfacing via data grabbing and sharing. Next up, we will develop what we have learned so far to interface IR sensors for obstacle avoidance and patch planning.

22
Sensor Interface for Obstacle Avoidance

To make a robotic vehicle that drives itself, we need to first understand how humans drive a vehicle. When we drive a car, we constantly analyze the space and the distance to other objects. Thereafter, we make a decision if we can go through it or not. This happens constantly with our brain – eye coordination. Similarly, a robot would have to do the same sort of thing.

In our previous chapters, you learned that we can find the proximity of objects around us, using sensors. These sensors can tell us how far an object is, and based on it, we can make decisions. We have done using an ultrasonic sensor primarily because it is extremely cheap. However, as you remember, it was slightly cumbersome to attach ultrasonic sensors and to run its code. It's time that we take a much simpler sensor and attach it to the car.

This chapter will cover the following topics:

- Infrared proximity sensor
- Autonomous emergency braking
- Giving it self-steering capabilities
- Making it fully autonomous

Infrared proximity sensor

The following photo depicts an infrared proximity sensor:

It consists of two major parts—the sensor and the transmitter. The transmitter emits IR waves; these **Infrared** (**IR**) waves then hit the object and come back to the sensor, as depicted in the following diagram..

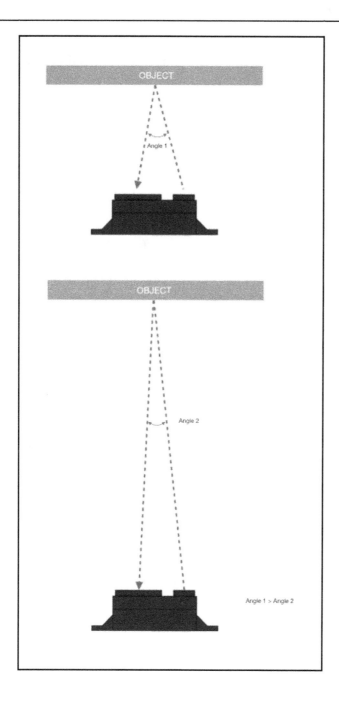

Now, as you can see in the preceding diagram, the emitted IR waves bounces back from a surface at a different distance from the sensor, then they makes an angular approach to the sensor. Now, because the distance between the transmitter and the sensor is fixed at all points of time, the angle corresponding to reflected IR waves would be proportional to the distance it has traveled before bouncing off. There are ultraprecise sensors in the IR proximity sensors that are capable of sensing the angle at which the IR waves approach it. By this angle, it gives the user a value of distance corresponding to it. This method of finding distance is named **triangulation**, and it has been used widely in the industry. One more thing we need to keep in mind is that we are all surrounded by IR radiation as we mentioned earlier in the chapters; any object above absolute zero temperature would have corresponding waves emitted to it. Also, the sunlight around us is having ample amount of IR radiations. Hence, these sensors have a built-in circuitry to compensate for it; however, there is only so much it can do. That's why, this solution might have some trouble when dealing with direct sunlight.

Now, enough of the theory, let's see how the car actually works. The IR proximity sensor we are using in this example is an analog sensor by Sharp with part code GP2D12. It has an effective sensing range of 1000-800 mm. The range is also dependent on the reflectivity of the surface of the object in question. The darker the object, the shorter the range. This sensor has three pins. As you might have guessed, there is one for VCC, another for ground, and the last for the signal. This is an analog sensor; hence, the distance reading would be given based on the voltage. Generally with most analog sensors you would get a graph which will depict the various voltages at various sensing ranges. The output is basically depending on the internal hardware of the sensor and its construction so it can be vastly different. Below is a graph for our sensor and its output :

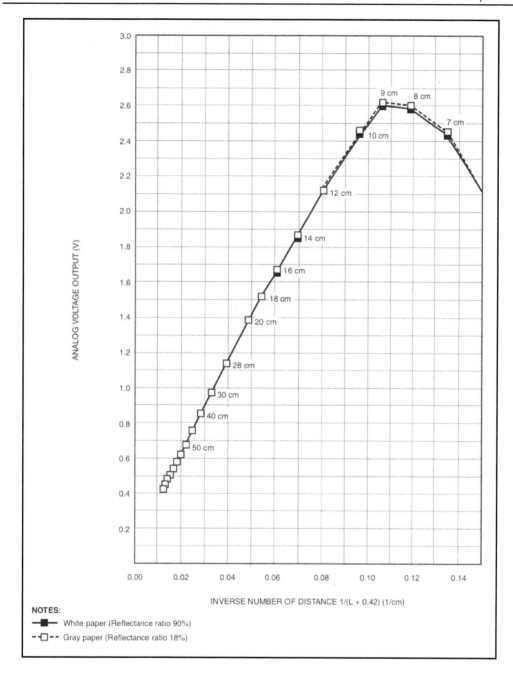

ANALOG VOLTAGE OUTPUT (V)

INVERSE NUMBER OF DISTANCE 1/(L + 0.42) (1/cm)

NOTES:

■ White paper (Reflectance ratio 90%)

□ Gray paper (Reflectance ratio 18%)

Okay then, so far so good. As we know that Raspberry Pi does not accept analog input; hence, we will go ahead and use what we have used earlier as well, an ADC. We will be using the same ADC we have used before.

Autonomous emergency braking

There is a new technology that newer cars are equipped with. It's called **autonomous emergency braking**; no matter how serious we are while driving, we do get distractions, such as Facebook or WhatsApp notifications, which tempt us to look away from the road onto the screen of our phones. This can be a leading cause of road accidents; hence, car manufacturers are using autonomous braking technology. This generally relies on long range and short range radars and it detects the proximity of other objects around the car, and in the case of an eminent collision, it applies the brakes to the car autonomously preventing them from colliding from other cars or pedestrians. This is a really cool technology, but what's interesting is that we would be making it today with our own bare hands.

To make this, we will be using the IR proximity sensor to sense the proximity of objects around it. Now go ahead, grab a double-sided tape, and attach the IR distance sensor at the front of the car. Once this is done, connect the circuit as shown here:

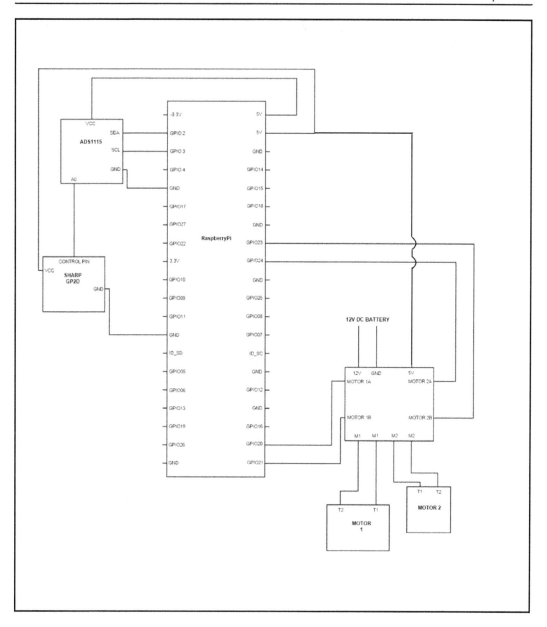

All right then, we are all set up to code it up. The following is the code, and just copy it into your Pi:

```python
import RPi.GPIO as GPIO
import time
GPIO.setmode(GPIO.BCM)

import Adafruit_ADS1x15
adc0 = Adafruit_ADS1x15.ADS1115()

GAIN = 1

adc0.start_adc(0, gain=GAIN)

Motor1a = 20
Motor1b = 21
Motor2b = 23
Motor2a = 24

GPIO.setup(Motor1a,GPIO.OUT)
GPIO.setup(Motor1b,GPIO.OUT)
GPIO.setup(Motor2a,GPIO.OUT)
GPIO.setup(Motor2b,GPIO.OUT)

def forward():
        GPIO.output(Motor1a,0)
        GPIO.output(Motor1b,1)
        GPIO.output(Motor2a,0)
        GPIO.output(Motor2b,1)

def stop():
        GPIO.output(Motor1a,0)
        GPIO.output(Motor1b,0)
        GPIO.output(Motor2a,0)
        GPIO.output(Motor2b,0)

while True:
    F_value = adc0.get_last_result()
    F =    (1.0 / (F_value / 13.15)) - 0.35
    forward()

    min_dist = 20
    if F < min_dist:
        stop()
```

Now, let's see what's actually happening in this code. Everything is very much elementary; the IR proximity sensor is sensing the proximity of objects in front of it and gives the corresponding distance value in the form of analog signals. These signals are then taken by the ADC, and they are converted into digital values. These digital values are finally transferred to Raspberry Pi via the I2C protocol.

So far, so good. But you must be wondering what this line is doing?

```
F =     (1.0 / (F_value / 13.15)) - 0.35
```

There is not much we are doing here, we are simply taking the digital values given by ADC, and using this formula, we are covering that digital value to understandable distance values in the unit of centimeters. This calculation is provided by the manufacturer, and we really don't have to get our head into this. Most of the sensors have these calculations provided. However, if you want to go and understand how and why we are using this formula, then I would recommend you go through the data sheet of the sensor. The data sheet is available easily online on the following link: https://engineering.purdue.edu/ME588/SpecSheets/sharp_gp2d12.pdf.

Moving on, the main part of the code is as follows:

```
min_dist = 20
If F < min_dist:
    stop()
```

It is again very simple. We have entered a distance value, which in this program, we have set to 20. So, whenever the value of F (the distance accrued by IR proximity sensor) is smaller than 20, then a stop() function is called. The stop function simply stalls the car and stops it from colliding with anything.

Let's upload the code and see if it actually works! Make sure that you run this car indoors; otherwise, you would have a tough time trying to stop this car if it does not get any obstacles. Have fun!

Giving the car self-steering capabilities

I hope that you are having fun with this little zippy thing. It is interesting how simple the application of sensors can be and how much difference it can make. As you have learned the basics, it's now time to move ahead and give the car some more powers.

In the previous code, we just made the robot stop in front of the obstacles, why don't we make it steer around the car? It's going to be super simple yet super fun. All we need to do is to tweak the function stop() and make it able to turn. Obviously, we will also change the name of the function from stop() to turn() just for the sake of clarity. One thing to remember that you won't have to rewrite the code; all we need to do is some minor tweaking. So, let's see the code and then I will tell you what exactly has changed and why:

```
import RPi.GPIO as GPIO
import time
GPIO.setmode(GPIO.BCM)

import Adafruit_ADS1x15
adc0 = Adafruit_ADS1x15.ADS1115()

GAIN = 1

adc0.start_adc(0, gain=GAIN)

Motor1a = 20
Motor1b = 21
Motor2a = 23
Motor2b = 24

GPIO.setup(Motor1a,GPIO.OUT)
GPIO.setup(Motor1b,GPIO.OUT)
GPIO.setup(Motor2a,GPIO.OUT)
GPIO.setup(Motor2b,GPIO.OUT)

def forward():
        GPIO.output(Motor1a,0)
        GPIO.output(Motor1b,1)
        GPIO.output(Motor2a,0)
        GPIO.output(Motor2b,1)

def turn():
        GPIO.output(Motor1a,0)
        GPIO.output(Motor1b,1)
        GPIO.output(Motor2a,1)
        GPIO.output(Motor2b,0)
```

```
)

while True:
    forward()

    F_value = adc0.get_last_result()
    F =    (1.0 / (F_value / 13.15)) - 0.35

    min_dist = 20

    while F < min_dist:
        turn()
```

As you would have noted, everything remains pretty much the same except for the following:

```
def turn():
        GPIO.output(Motor1a,0)
        GPIO.output(Motor1b,1)
        GPIO.output(Motor2a,1)
        GPIO.output(Motor2b,0)
```

This part of the code is defining the turn() function in which the opposite side wheels of the vehicles would be spinning in the opposite direction; hence, making the car turn on its own axis:

```
    min_dist = 20

    while F < min_dist:
        turn()
```

Now this is the main part of the program; in this part, we are defining what the car would do if it encounters any sort of obstacle in front of it. In our previous programs, we were primarily just telling the robot to stop as soon as it encounters any obstacle; however, now we are chaining the stop function with a turn function, which we have defined previously in the program.

We simply put in a condition as follows:

```
    min_dist = 20
    If F < min_dist:
        turn()
```

Then, it would turn just for a fraction of seconds, as the microcontroller would parse through the code and execute it and get out of the condition. To do this, our Raspberry Pi would hardly take a couple of microseconds. So, we might not even able to see what has happened. Hence, in our program, we have used a `while` loop. This essentially keeps the loops running till the time condition is fulfilled. Our condition is `while F < min_dist:`, so till the time the robot is detecting an object in front of it, it will keep executing the function inside it, which in our case is, the `turn()` function. So in simple words, till the time it has not turned enough to avoid the obstacle, the vehicle would keep turning and then once the loop is executed, it will again jump back to the main program and keep going straight.

Simple isn't it? That's the beauty about programming!

Making it fully autonomous

Now, you must have understood the basics of autonomous driving using a simple proximity sensor. Now is the time when we make it fully autonomous. To make it fully autonomous, we must understand and map our surroundings rather than to just turn the vehicle till the time it encounters an obstacle. We basically need to divide this whole activity in the following two basic parts:

- Scanning the environment
- Deciding what to do with the perceived data

Now, let's first write the code and then see what we need to do:

```
import RPi.GPIO as GPIO
import time

GPIO.setmode(GPIO.BCM)

import Adafruit_ADS1x15
adc0 = Adafruit_ADS1x15.ADS1115()

GAIN = 1
adc0.start_adc(0, gain=GAIN)

Motor1a = 20
Motor1b = 21
Motor2a = 23
Motor2b = 24

GPIO.setup(Motor1a,GPIO.OUT)
```

```
GPIO.setup(Motor1b,GPIO.OUT)
GPIO.setup(Motor2a,GPIO.OUT)
GPIO.setup(Motor2b,GPIO.OUT)

def forward():
        GPIO.output(Motor1a,0)
        GPIO.output(Motor1b,1)
        GPIO.output(Motor2a,0)
        GPIO.output(Motor2b,1)

def right():
        GPIO.output(Motor1a,0)
        GPIO.output(Motor1b,1)
        GPIO.output(Motor2a,1)
        GPIO.output(Motor2b,0)

def left():
        GPIO.output(Motor1a,1)
        GPIO.output(Motor1b,0)
        GPIO.output(Motor2a,0)
        GPIO.output(Motor2b,1)

def stop():
        GPIO.output(Motor1a,0)
        GPIO.output(Motor1b,0)
        GPIO.output(Motor2a,0)
        GPIO.output(Motor2b,0)

while True:

    forward()

    F_value = adc0.get_last_result()
    F =    (1.0 / (F_value / 13.15)) - 0.35

    min_dist = 20
    if F< min_dist:

        stop()

     right()
     time.sleep(1)

    F_value = adc0.get_last_result()
    F =    (1.0 / (F_value / 13.15)) - 0.35
    R = F

    left()
```

```
time.sleep(2)

F_value = adc0.get_last_result()
F =     (1.0 / (F_value / 13.15)) - 0.3

L = F

if L < R:
    right()
    time.sleep(2)

else:
    forward()
```

Now most of the program is just like all of our previous programs; in this program, we have defined the following functions:

- forward()
- right()
- left()
- stop()

There is not much I need to tell you about defining the functions, so let's move ahead and see what else do we have in stock for us.

The main action is going on in our infinite loop while True:. Let's see what exactly is happening:

```
while True:

    forward()

    F_value = adc0.get_last_result()
    F =     (1.0 / (F_value / 13.15)) - 0.35

    min_dist = 20
    if F< min_dist:

        stop()
```

Let's see what this part of code is doing:

- The first thing that is executed as soon as our program enters the infinite loop is the `forward()` function; that is, as soon as the infinite loop is executed, the vehicle will start to go forward
- Thereafter, `F_value = adc.get_last_result()` is taking the reading from ADC and storing it in a variable named `F_value`
- `F = (1.0/(F-value/13.15))-0.35` is calculating the distance into understandable metric distance value
- `min_dist = 20`, we have simply defined the minimum distance that we will be using later

Once this part of code is done, then the `if` statement will check whether `F < min_dist:`. If it is so, then the code that is under the `if` statement will start to execute. The first line of this will be the `stop()` function. So whenever the vehicle encounters any obstacle in front of it, the first thing it will do is stop.

Now, as I mentioned, the first part of our code is to understand the environment, so let's go ahead and see how we do it :

```
right()
    time.sleep(1)

    F_value = adc0.get_last_result()
    F =    (1.0 / (F_value / 13.15)) - 0.35
    R = F

    left()
    time.sleep(2)

    F_value = adc0.get_last_result()
    F =    (1.0 / (F_value / 13.15)) - 0.35

    L = F
```

After the vehicle has stopped, it will immediately turn right. As you can see, the next line of code is `time.sleep(1)`, so for another 1 second, the vehicle will keep turning right. We have randomly picked a time of 1 second, you can tweak it later.

Once it has turned right, it will again take the reading from the proximity sensor, and in using this code R=F, we are storing that value in a variable named R.

After it has done that, the car will turn to the other side, that is, toward left side using the `left()` function, and it will keep turning left for 2 seconds as we have `time.sleep(2)`. This will turn the car toward left of the obstacle. Once it has turned left, it will again take in the value of proximity sensor and store the value in a variable L using the code `L = F`.

So essentially what we have done is that we have scanned the areas around us. In the center, we have an obstacle. It will first turn right and take the distance value of the right side; thereafter, we will turn left and take the distance value of the left side. So we essentially know the environment around the obstacle.

Now we come to the part where we have to make a decision, in which direction we have to go forward. Let's see how we will do it:

```
if L < R:
        right()
        time.sleep(2)

    else:
        forward()
```

Using an `if` statement, we are comparing the values of the proximity sensor for the right and left of the obstacle by this code `if L < R:`. If L is smaller than R, then the vehicle will turn right for 2 seconds. If the condition is not true, then the `else:` statement would come into action, which will in turn make the vehicle go forward.

Now if we see the code in a larger picture, the following things are happening:

- The vehicle would go forward until it encounters an obstacle
- Upon encountering an obstacle, the robot will stop
- It will first turn right and measure the distance to objects in front of it
- Then, it will turn left and measure the distance to objects in front of it
- After this, it will compare the distance of both left and right and choose which direction it has to go in
- If it has to go right, it will turn right and then go forward
- If it has to go left, then it would already be in the left turned orientation, so it simply has to go straight

Let's upload the code and see whether things happen according to plan or not. Remember this, though every environment is different and every vehicle is different, so you may have to tweak the code to make it work smoothly.

Now I will leave you with a problem. What if in both case the reading of the sensor is infinity or the maximum possible value that it can give? What will the robot do?

Go ahead, do some brainstorming and see what we can do to solve this problem!

Summary

In this chapter, using all basics that you learned so far and also by introducing IR proximity sensor, we were able to take an advanced step of developing our robotic car to detect obstacles and accordingly change the directions. In the next chapter, we will study how to make our own area scanner—see you there!

23
Making Your Own Area Scanner

Motors are amazing things; they come in all shapes and sizes. Primarily, they can be considered the backbone of most robots. However, nothing is perfect in this world. There must be some drawbacks to these motors as well. By now, you might have figured out some by yourself. In the previous chapter, when we made the car turn, you might have seen that the angle of turn was never really the same. Also when the vehicle was given the command to go straight, it really would not do so. Rather it would try to run slight, toward one side.

Say hello to the first problem—precision. The motors are exceptionally simple to control, but the problem with these motors come when we have to rotate the motors only till a specific angle. If you need to rotate the motor of your robotic vehicle only by 90 degrees, then how would you do it? The first and foremost thing that might come to your mind would be to fiddle with the timings of the motors. You might be right here. But still, it would be impossible to make sure that it is exactly 90 degrees every single time.

But when we talk about robots, accuracy of even 1 degree may not be enough. Roboticists these days are looking forward to accuracy within the magnitude of two decimal digits. So, the precision we are talking about is close to 0.01 degrees. What do you think now? How do we achieve this level of accuracy with motors?

The answers to all these questions will be answered in this chapter through the following topics:

- Servo motor
- Lists
- LIDAR

Servo motor

So, let me introduce you to *servo motor*. Servo motor is basically a motor with a few added components. Now to understand what those added components, let's first go through this example. Let's say that you want to go to London. Now to see how you have to go there and what would be the route to reach London, the first thing you need to know is that where exactly you are now. If you don't know where you are currently, it is impossible to calculate a route. Similarly, if we want to reach a certain position of motor, we need to know where the shaft of the motor is standing right now. To do this, we use a **potentiometer**. A potentiometer is basically a variable resistor that essentially has a shaft that when rotated changes the value of resistance. A variable resistor looks like this:

When the value of resistor change, then the output voltage from the resistor will also change. The interesting thing is that if the input voltage to the potentiometer is well known, then the output voltage from it can be used to infer where the shaft is. Let's see how:

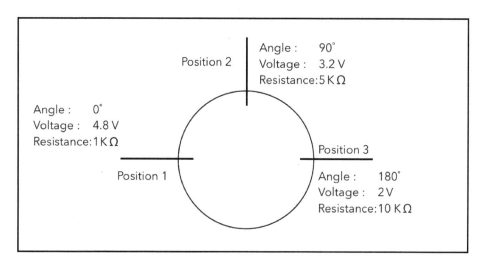

Now, let's say at a position of 0 degrees, the output voltage for the potentiometer is 4.8V; when we move it up to 90 degrees, the value changes to around 3.2V, and upon turning entirely 180 degrees, the voltage reduces to a mere 2V due to the change in resistance.

Without really looking at the shaft of the potentiometer, we can easily derive that if the voltage output from the resistor is 4.8V, then the shaft must be at a position of 0 degrees. Similarly, we can say that it is at 90 degrees if the voltage is 3.2V and at 180 degrees when the voltage is 2V.

Here, we have just plotted three points, but for any given point on the potentiometer, there would be a very specific resistance corresponding to it. Through this we can precisely calculate where the shaft of the potentiometer would be. Now, let's put it in an interesting combination:

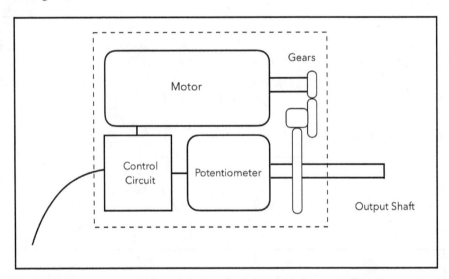

Now what we have is a motor coupled with potentiometer through multiple reducing gears that will reduce the speed of the motor and increase the torque. Further at the final gear, a shaft is mounted outward to the body coupled with a potentiometer.

So as you learned, the potentiometer will be able to sense at which angle the output shaft is pointing. The potentiometer is then connected to a control circuit that takes the reading from the potentiometer and further guides the motor on how much more to move to reach the goal position. Due to this closed loop arrangement in which the control circuit knows where the shaft is, it could calculate how much it has to move the motor to reach the goal position. Hence, this arrangement is able to turn the output shaft to any given position precisely.

This arrangement is typically known as a **servo motor**. Throughout the robotics industry, it is one of the most widely used hardware to control precise movements. Essentially, there are three wires going into the control circuit—VCC, ground, and signal. The signal line will receive the data from our Raspberry Pi, and upon receiving, it will do the necessary motor movement to make the shaft reach the desired position. An image of a servo motor is as follows:

These can start from being extremely inexpensive, around $4 to $5, but they can go up to thousands of dollars. But what really decides the pricing of these servo motors? There are several factors that we need to keep in mind while choosing a servo motor, but the most important of it is **torque**.

Torque is a basically a turning force by which a motor can turn the output shaft. This is measured usually in kg·cm or N·m. Now what does this actually mean? Let's see the following diagram:

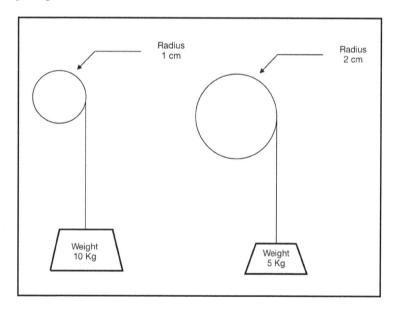

Let's say in the preceding diagram, we have a motor that has a torque of 10 kg·cm and the rotor attached to it is of 1 cm. So, it should be able to pull up a weight of 10 kg perpendicularly up from the ground. However, when we change the radius of the rotor to 2 cm, then the weight that can be lifted gets halved. Similarly, if the radius increases to 10 cm, then the weight that can be lifted would only reduce to 1 kg. So basically, the weight that can be lifted would be torque/radius.

But for most of our purposes, we would not be using a mechanism as shown previously, so let's look at the next diagram to see how the calculations can be made:

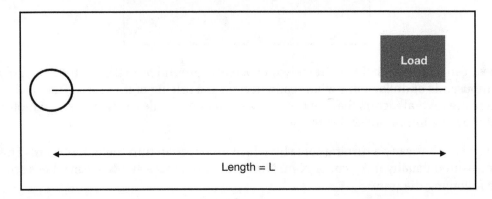

Now, let's say we have a shaft of length **L** and a load at the extreme edge of the shaft. For ease of calculation purposes, we would consider the weight of shaft to be negligible. Now if the servo is having a torque of 100 kg·cm and the length of shaft (**L**) is 10 cm, then by simple calculation, the load that we can pick up would be 100/10 = 10 kg. Similarly, if the length increases to 100 cm, the load that can be lifted would reduce to a mere 1 kg.

OK then; we have had a good amount of exposure to servo motors. Now the question is how do we control a servo motor? As I mentioned, there are different types of servo motors that are available that can be addressed by various means. However, the most common one used for hobby purposes is a digital servo motor. These servo motors require **PWM**, and based on the duty cycle of PWM, the angle of the shaft changes. So, let's see how it happens.

Typically, most of these servos have a frequency of 50 Hz. So basically the length of every pulse would be 1/50 = 0.02 seconds or in other words 20 ms. Further, the duty cycle that can be given to theses servo motors can be 2.5% to 12.5%, which basically means pulse width of 0.5 ms to 2.5 ms. Now let's see how it works:

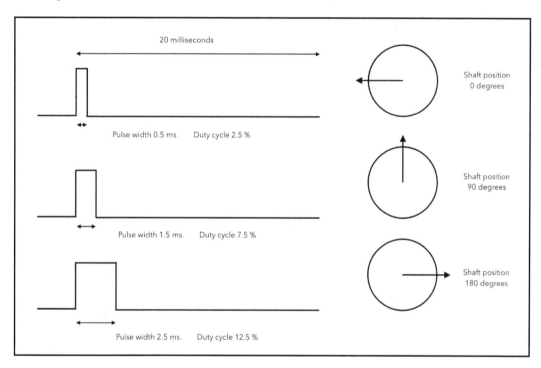

As you can see, when given a duty cycle of 2.5%, the shaft gets down to the minimum position of 0 degrees, and when the duty cycle is increased to 7.5%, the shaft goes to the middle position of 90 degrees. Finally, when the duty cycle is increased to 12.5%, the shaft goes to the maximum position of 180 degrees. If you want any position in between, then you can simply choose the PWM corresponding to it, and it will change the position of servo to the desired angle.

But you may be thinking what if we want to take it beyond 180 degrees? Well, good question, but most of the digital servos only come with a range of 180 degrees of rotation. There are servos that can rotate completely its axis, that is, 360 degrees; however, their addressing is slightly different. After this chapter, you can pretty much go ahead check out any digital servo motor's data sheet and control it the way you want.

All right, enough of theory; it's time to do some fun. So, let's go ahead and set up the hardware and control a servo by our bare hands! Connect the servo to Raspberry Pi as follows:

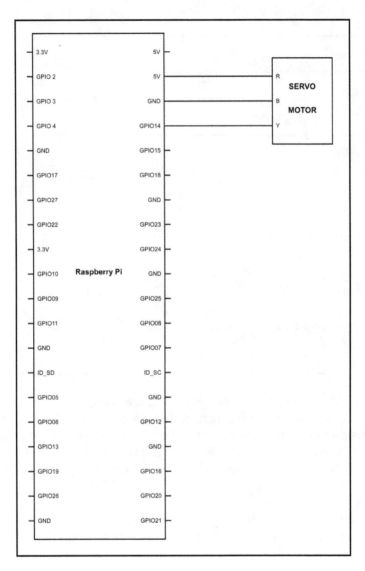

The color coding of the wires is as follows:

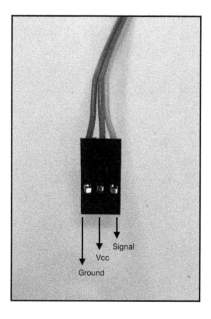

Next, we need to upload the following code and see what happens:

```python
import RPi.GPIO as GPIO
import time

GPIO.setmode(GPIO.BCM)
GPIO.setup(14,GPIO.OUT)

pwm = GPIO.PWM(14, 50)
pwm.start(0)

while 1:

        pwm.ChangeDutyCycle(2.5)
        time.sleep(2)

        pwm.ChangeDutyCycle(5)
        time.sleep(2)

        pwm.ChangeDutyCycle(7.5)
        time.sleep(2)

        pwm.ChangeDutyCycle(10)
        time.sleep(2)
```

```
pwm.ChangeDutyCycle(12.5)
time.sleep(2)
```

As soon as you run this program, you will see the shaft of the servo moving from left to right, making steps at 0 degrees, 45 degrees, 90 degrees, 135 degrees, and finally 180 degrees.

Let's see what we have done in the program to achieve it:

```
pwm = GPIO.PWM(14, 50)
pwm.start(0)
```

With the line `pwm = GPIO.PWM(14, 50)`, we have defined that GPIO pin number `14` will be used for PWM and the frequency of PWM will be `50`. We have used the line `pwm.start(0)` in earlier chapters as well. It basically sets the PWM pin to `0` that is no duty cycle:

```
pwm.ChangeDutyCycle(2.5)
time.sleep(2)

pwm.ChangeDutyCycle(5)
time.sleep(2)

pwm.ChangeDutyCycle(7.5)
time.sleep(2)

pwm.ChangeDutyCycle(10)
time.sleep(2)

pwm.ChangeDutyCycle(12.5)
time.sleep(2)
```

No all the earlier program is in the `while` loop, that is, it will be executed over and over until the program is forced to quit. Now the line `pwm.ChangeDutyCycle(2.5)` sends a PWM of 2.5% duty cycle to the servo motor. This will simply turn the servo motor to 0 degree angle. Next, we use the good old `time.sleep(2)`, which we all know would halt the program that line for two seconds.

The same cycle is being repeated with different PWM values of 5%, which would turn the shaft to 45 degrees, 7.5% for 90 degrees, 10% for 135 degrees, 12.5 % for 180 degrees. It's a very simple program that would clear out our basics of the servo motor.

So by now, you have learned how to control servo motor and move it in the direction in which we want. Now, let's go a step ahead and change the code slightly to make the servo run smoothly:

```
import RPi.GPIO as GPIO
import time

GPIO.setmode(GPIO.BCM)
GPIO.setup(14,GPIO.OUT)

pwm = GPIO.PWM(14, 50)
pwm.start(0)

i=2.5
j=12.5

while 1:
        while i<=12.5:
                pwm.ChangeDutyCycle(i)
                time.sleep(0.1)
                i = i + 0.1

        while j>=2.5:
                pwm.ChangeDutyCycle(j)
                time.sleep(0.1)
                j = j - 0.1
```

What happened when you uploaded this code in your Pi? You would have noted that the servo is swiping from left to right very smoothly and then right to left. We have done a very simple trick; let's see what it is:

```
        while i<=12.5:
                pwm.ChangeDutyCycle(i)
                time.sleep(0.1)
                i = i + 0.1
```

Here, we are running a loop that will run till the time the value of i<=12.5, as we have defined earlier in the program the value of i has been set to 2.5 as default in the starting of the program. Thereafter every time the code runs, the duty cycle is set to the value of I, the program halts for 0.1 seconds and then the value of i is incremented by a value of 0.1. This is increasing the duty cycle of the PWM. Once the value reaches 12.5, the loop exits.

The entire PWM range we have is 2.5% to 12.5%, so we have a space of 10% to play with. Now if we map it to the angular rotation of the servo motor, then every percent of PWM corresponds to a change of 180/10 = 18 degrees. Similarly, every 0.1% of the change would result in a change of 180/100 = 1.8 degrees. Hence, with every 0.1 seconds, we are adding duty cycle by 0.1%, or in other words, we are increasing the angle by 1.8 degrees. Hence, we find this action extremely smooth.

We are doing the similar thing in the next portion of the program; however, we are doing it for the reverse motion.

Lists

All right then, we are quite sure on how to use the servo and have a controlled motion as per our needs. Now it's time to move forward and understand another concept that we would be using greatly. It's named **arrays**. If you have programmed in any other language, you must be familiar with it. But we need to understand a few basics concepts of it, which will make our lives a lot easier. So, let's get started.

First things, first. Arrays in Python are not named arrays, rather it is named as **lists**. List is basically a data structure that can store multiple elements at the same time. The only limitation being is that the elements must be of the same data type. Such as if you are storing integers, then all the values should be int. Similarly, if you are storing a character, then every element of the list should be char. To define a list, all you need to do is name the list such as we have done by doing myList; the name of the list could be anything next we need to tell the compiler that it is actually a list. To do that, we need to put values inside square brackets. It would look like:

```
myList = [14,35,108,64,9]
```

One thing to keep in mind is that every value should be separated with commas. Whenever we want to address any single element of the list, we can simply use it by calling their index number. This is based on the position of the element in the list. The index value in Python list starts from 0. So as per the preceding declaration at the index 0, the value would be 14, and at the address 4, the value would be 9. Now when we need to print these elements in between our program, we need to write the following code:

```
print myList[2]
```

Once we write this, the program will print the value of the second value in the list. In our case, it would be 35.

Now, this is one way to access the elements of the list; we can however access it in reverse order as well. So, let's say you want to access the last item of the array. Then, we can write the following code:

```
print myList[-1]
```

This code will return the value of the last element of the array. Now whenever we use the negative values in the lists, then it would start the indexing in the reverse order. So, let's say if we type in print myList [-2], this will give us the value of the second last value in the array. One thing to remember in this whole schematic is that the numbering would start from 0, whereas when we start it in the reverse order, then the numbering would start from -1.

Python is really interesting and quite simple if you know the right tools. The developers of Python have included some really helpful functions that can be used over lists. So, let's go and explore them a bit.

The first one is to add elements to the array. For this, we use a function named append(). What the append() function does is that it adds the value, which would want at the end of the array. So, write the following:

```
myList.append(45)
```

What this would do is that it would add the element 45 at the end of myList. So now the list would be as follows:

```
myList = [14,35,108,64,9, 45]
```

Easy, isn't it ? But what if you want to add an element in between the list? Obviously, the developer won't leave you dry. They have included a function for that as well; it's named insert(index, element). Now whenever you are using this function, you need to make sure that you mention the index where you want this element to be and second, the element that you want to put. So it looks something like this:

```
myList.insert(3,23)
```

When you have used this function, the array will look as follows:

```
myList = [14,35,108,23,64,9,45]
```

Obviously, whenever the developer has given the function to add an element, then they would have certainly given a function to remove the elements as well. But the trick is that you can do it two ways. First, the common way. We simply select the index number and delete it. We are going to do it now:

```
del myList[2]
```

Now what this will do is that it would delete the second element of the array, so after doing this operation, the array will look like this:

```
myList = [14,35,108,64,9,45]
```

But now here comes the real trick; you can also delete the element by simply specifying the element. This is how it's done:

```
myList.remove(9)
```

Now the moment you do this, it will find wherever the element 9 is in your list and delete it from the positions. So you don't have to care about where the element is; this function will say, I will find you and I will kill you!

Looking around

Okay then enough of movie quotes. We can talk about many other functions that we can use over lists, but what we have done is enough for now. We will see the rest of them as the need arise. But for now let's take the things a step further in robotics. You might have seen a rotating object on top of many autonomous cars. The production cars generally don't tend to have primarily due to its high price, but research purpose cars are always loaded with it.

So what is this device? It's named **LIDAR**; it is an acronym for **Light Detection and Ranging**. I know bad acronym. There is a reason for LIDAR to be very common. It gives distance reading of the areas around it in a very precise way. However, buying it for our projects would slightly overkill as a good one would cost you close $500 to $10,000. If you still think that it's in your budget, then you would be very lucky! But for those who don't want to buy it. I have a good news for you. Today, we are going to build our own LIDAR scanner. So to make an area scanner, we need a servo over which we will mount our IR proximity sensor. Now to do this, we would need a slight makeshift arrangement. You can take a cardboard and fix it like we have done in the picture here, or otherwise, you can also use a right-angled aluminum and drill it to fix the components if you want it to do the pro way. The one thing to remember that the sensor must be facing exactly parallel to the ground and not up or down.

Once the mounting is done, then it's time to connect the rest of the hardware. So go ahead and connect the hardware, as shown in the following diagram:

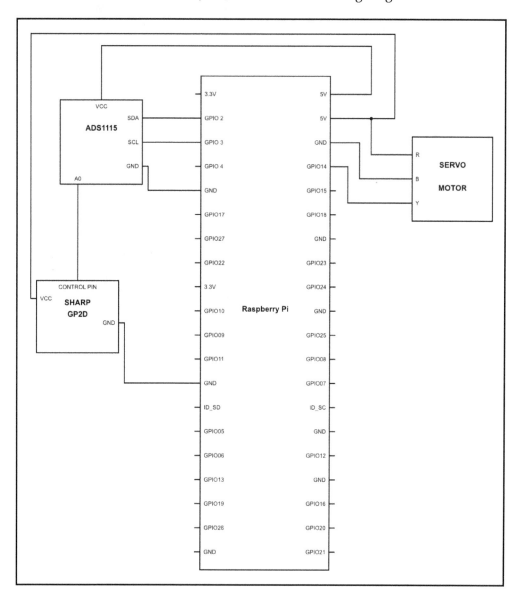

OK, so let's see what this thing can do, so get ready and upload this code:

```
import RPi.GPIO as GPIO
import time
import Adafruit_ADS1x15

adc = Adafruit_ADS1x15.ADS1115()
GAIN = 1

adc.start_adc(0, gain=GAIN)
GPIO.setmode(GPIO.BCM)
GPIO.setup(14,GPIO.OUT)
GPIO.setwarnings(False)

servo = GPIO.PWM(14, 50)

servo.start(0)

Def Distance():
    D_value = adc0.get_last_result()
    D =     (1.0 / (F_value / 13.15)) - 0.35
    Return D

j=12.5
k=2.5
i=0

distLR=[]
distRL=[]

while True:
        while k<=12.5:
                servo.ChangeDutyCycle(k)
                time.sleep(.1)
                distLR.insert(i,Distance())
                k = k + 2.5
                i = i + 1
        print distLR

        i=0
        k=0

        del distLR[:]

        while j>=2.5:
                servo.ChangeDutyCycle(j)
                time.sleep(.1)
                j = j - 2.5
```

```
        distRL.insert(i,Distance())
        i = i + 1

    print distRL

    i=0
    k=2.5
    j=12.5

    del distRL[:]
```

What did the code do? If it ran fine, then it should return you the scanned readings entire 180 degree broken down into 10 even steps. Go ahead—try it out and then return to see what actually is happening.

Now most of the code is elementary, and you must have also got an idea of what this code is actually doing. However, let's get deeper into it and see the specifics:

```
Def Distance():
    D_value = adc0.get_last_result()
    D =    (1.0 / (F_value / 13.15)) - 0.35
    Return D
```

In this part of the program, we have defined a function named `Distance()`. As you can see, it is simply getting the reading from the ADC in the step `D_value = adc0.get_last_result()`; thereafter, this is the value procured that is stored in a variable `D` is then computed in the line `D = (1.0/F-value/13.15)) - 0.35` to get the metric reading from the ADC reading. Finally, using the line `Return D`, we are returning the value `D` from the function:

```
distLR=[]
distRL=[]
```

We have declared two lists: `distLR`, namely for distance for left to right swipe of the servo and `distRL` for the distance received in right to left swipe of the servo. You might be wondering how is it that there is nothing inside these brackets. It is completely normal to have an empty array declared. There is no need for them to have value initially:

```
        while k<=12.5:
            servo.ChangeDutyCycle(k)
            time.sleep(.1)
            distLR.insert(i,Distance())
            k = k + 1
            i = i + 1
        print distLR
```

Now this is where the real action is happening. The `while` loop will be executed only till the time the value of `k` is less than or equal to `12.5`. In the next line `servo.ChangeDutyCycle(k)`, the value of the duty cycle will be whatever the value of `k` would be. Initially, the value of `k` would be `2.5` as we have already defined in the beginning of the program. Now we add another line `time sleep(.1)`, which will make the program halt for `.1` second. This is necessary; otherwise, the program would parse through this loop within milliseconds and the servo would not be able to cope up with it. Hence, this is a short delay. In the next line, we have `distLR.insert(I,Distance())`. This line of program is doing a lot of things. First, as we have named a `Distance()` function inside this line. As we defined, it would calculate the distance using the ADC and the IR proximity sensor. Thereafter, it would insert that distance value inside an the list `distLR` at the position `I`. Previously in our program, we have already assigned the value `i = 0`; hence, the distance value would be put up in the first position in the array. Once this entire process is done, then we move forward and increment the value by one in this line `k = k + 1`; thereafter, we do the same thing in `I = I + 1`. Now finally, once this loop's executed, the values of the list is printed using the line `print distLR`:

```
i=0
k=0
```

In this line, we are simply resetting the values of `i = 0` and `k = 0` for the next loop:

```
del distLR[:]
```

This may be slightly new for you. Whenever we use a colon inside a bracket, that basically means that the entire elements of the array would be deleted:

```
while j>=2.5:
                servo.ChangeDutyCycle(j)
                time.sleep(.1)
                j = j - 2.5
                distRL.insert(i,Distance())
                i = i + 1

        print distRL
```

In this code, the same thing is happening that we did for the left to right swipe; the only difference being is that we are saving it a new list named `distRL`, and the swipe starts from 12.5% duty cycle and ends at 2.5%:

```
i=0
    k=2.5
    j=12.5

del distRL[:]
```

When we have printed all the values, we again reset the values of `i = 1`, `k = 2.5`, and `j = 12.5` so that our first loop can start seamlessly further to it we are also making sure that there is nothing left inside the list `distRL`.

So this is how our code was working, straight and simple!

LIDAR on an autonomous vehicle

Remember the last time we made autonomous car. It was cool, and surely it might be something you can show off to your friends. However, now what we are about to make is surely cooler than anything we have ever done till now.

We are going to put this area scanner over our robotic vehicle. But wait, didn't we scan the area earlier using the same sensor and turning the car to other sides. We did it and it worked fine, almost fine. I bet sometimes it wasn't as accurate as you thought it would be. But that's not the real problem. The main problem is that it was not seamless. It has to stop in between check for spaces and then move in either direction. What we are going to do now is something that is a step ahead. So before doing any more explanation, let's go ahead and make this new robotic vehicle and then you be the judge to decide whether it is cooler.

So, to make it, you need to mount the area scanner on the vehicle. It's advisable that you set it up at the frontend of the vehicle and make sure that the arm of the servo is able to rotate 180 degrees. You can use the similar method that we did to fix the IR sensor on top of the servo. While you are doing all of this, try using cable ties to make sure the cables are not messy and also make sure to leave some slack for the movement of the shaft and the sensor on top of it. These cable ties can make your life really simple. Once we are all set up, you should connect the IR proximity using an ADS1115 to the Raspberry Pi and then connect the motor driver, as shown in the following diagram:

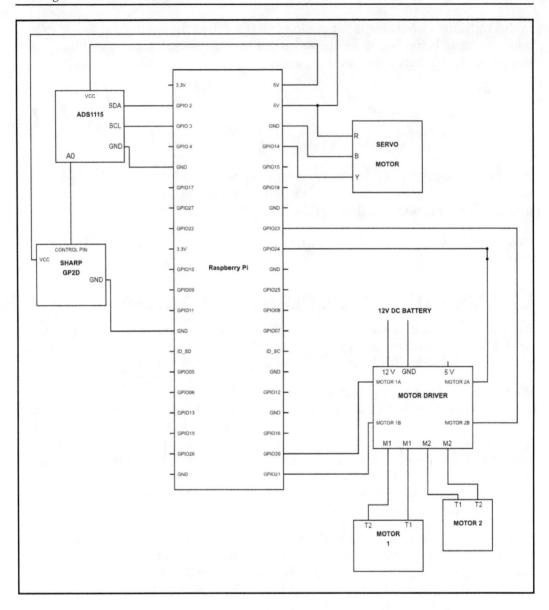

Once we are done go ahead and upload the following code:

```
import RPi.GPIO as GPIO
import time
import Adafruit_ADS1x15

adc0 = Adafruit_ADS1x15.ADS1115()
GAIN = 1
adc0.start_adc(0, gain=GAIN)

GPIO.setmode(GPIO.BCM)
GPIO.setup(14,GPIO.OUT)

servo = GPIO.PWM(14, 50)
servo.start(0)

def Distance():
    D_value = adc0.get_last_result()
    D =    (1.0 / (F_value / 13.15)) - 0.35
    Return D

GPIO.setup(20,GPIO.OUT)
GPIO.setup(21,GPIO.OUT)
GPIO.setup(23,GPIO.OUT)
GPIO.setup(24,GPIO.OUT)

LForward = GPIO.PWM(20, 50)
LReverse = GPIO.PWM(21, 50)
RForward = GPIO.PWM(23,50)
RReverse = GPIO.PWM(24,50)

def stop():
    LForward.changeDutyCycle(0)
    LReverse.changeDutyCycle(0)
    RForward.changeDutyCycle(0)
    RReverse.changeDutyCycle(0)


def direction(index):

  if index == 0 :
    LForward.changeDutyCycle(0)
    LReverse.changeDutyCycle(30)
    RForward.changeDutyCycle(30)
    RReverse.changeDutyCycle(0)

elif index == 1
```

```
        LForward.changeDutyCycle(20)
        LReverse.changeDutyCycle(0)
        RForward.changeDutyCycle(50)
        RReverse.changeDutyCycle(0)

    elif index == 2 :

        LForward.changeDutyCycle(50)
        LReverse.changeDutyCycle(0)
        RForward.changeDutyCycle(50)
        RReverse.changeDutyCycle(0)

   elif index == 3 :

        LForward.changeDutyCycle(50)
        LReverse.changeDutyCycle(0)
        RForward.changeDutyCycle(20)
        RReverse.changeDutyCycle(0)


    elif index == 4 :

        LForward.changeDutyCycle(20)
        LReverse.changeDutyCycle(0)
        RForward.changeDutyCycle(0)
        RReverse.changeDutyCycle(20)

    else:
    stop()

j=12.5
k=2.5
i=0

dist1=[]
dist2=[]

while True:

        while k<=12.5:
        servo.ChangeDutyCycle(k)
        time.sleep(.2)
        dist1.insert(i,Distance())
        k = k + 2.5
        i = i + 1

    print dist1
```

```
i=0
k=2

max_dist1 = max(dist1)
max_dist1_index = dist1.index(max_dist1)

direction(max_dist1_index)

del dist1[:]

print max_dist1
print max_dist1_index

while j>=2.5:
    servo.ChangeDutyCycle(j)
    time.sleep(.2)
    j = j - 2.5
    dist2.insert(i,Distance())
    i = i + 1

print dist2

i=0
j=12

max_dist2 = max(dist2)
max_dist2_index = dist2.index(max_dist2)

direction(max_dist2_index)

del dist2[:]

print max_dist2
print max_dist2_index
```

Phew! That was long wasn't it? But trust me it might be long, but not tough. So let's see what this code is doing:

```
LForward = GPIO.PWM(20, 50)
LReverse = GPIO.PWM(21, 50)
RForward = GPIO.PWM(23,50)
RReverse = GPIO.PWM(24,50)
```

This stuff might look pretty new to you. Though it isn't. What we are doing is that we are defining which pin number will be operating at what PWM frequency. Also, we have named every GPIO pins that is being used for motor control. OK then, it is fine that we are doing all this, but why have we suddenly started to give PWM to motor drivers. Were we not happy giving a simple high pulse?

The answer is very straightforward. With the use of PWM, we were able to change the brightness of an LED in previous chapters. Similarly, by changing the PWM output to the control pins of the motor driver, you cannot only define which direction to spin in. But also the speed at which it can spin. This is all done with PWM. So let's say pin number 20 is getting a PWM at 50% duty cycle. So it basically means that the motor which is attached to it will get half the input voltage that the motor driver is receiving. So now we can not only control which direction we want the motor to spin but also at what speed we can do so:

```
def direction(index):

  if index == 0 :
      LForward.changeDutyCycle(0)
      LReverse.changeDutyCycle(30)
      RForward.changeDutyCycle(30)
      RReverse.changeDutyCycle(0)

  elif index == 1
      LForward.changeDutyCycle(20)
      LReverse.changeDutyCycle(0)
      RForward.changeDutyCycle(50)
      RReverse.changeDutyCycle(0)
```

In this statement, we have defined a function direction(index). What this does is that it compares the value of index and based on it. The power will be given to the motors. So lets say that the index is 0. In this case the wheel on the left side would move in reverse direction whereas the right wheel would move in the reverse direction this will turn the robot on its axis.

In the next statement, we have written an elif statement, so if the else statement is not true, then it will check for the rest else if statement in the body. There are four elif statements in the entire definition of direction(index), which basically means that it will check for each one of it and do either of the activities based on the value of the argument. In this case, it is the index. Further, there is a final else statement, which would be done if none of the cases are true. So according to the statement, it will call a function of stop. That would stop the vehicle:

```
max_dist1 = max(dist1)
```

This line is pretty interesting as we are using another fun part of the lists that we have used. So, with the `max()` method, we can find the largest value inside a list. So, in this line, we are simply finding the max value and putting it in a variable named `max_dist1`:

```
max_dist1_index = dist1.index(max_dist1)
```

The beauty of lists just doesn't seem to end. In this line, we are using another method named `index()`; this method gives us the index of the value inside the list. So, we can know where the value exists in the list. Hence, in this line, we are proving the value of `max_dist1`. The method `index()` searches the index number and stores that value down into a variable named `max_dist1_index`:

```
direction(max_dist1_index)
```

As we have already defined the function `Direction()`, now all we are doing is calling the function to decide which direction to go in. Prefect then, power up your vehicles and see how well they are driving and do not forget to shoot a video and post it online.

Have fun!

Summary

Professional laser scanners are super expensive, so, in this chapter, we went on to build an alternative by ourselves and mounted it on our vehicle. In the next chapter, we will cover topics such as vision processing, and object detection, object tracking, which will enable us to do basic vision processing and to make the car move in the direction of a specific object such as a ball.

24
Basic Switching

It must have been an epic journey so far! Recollect the time when you would have started reading this book, did you ever imagine that things could be this simple? It is worth noting that everything starts off very simple and, slowly and steadily, with the need for more sophisticated systems, the complexity of the technology also increases. Go back to the time when personal computing was not really a thing. It was only used in business and companies such as IBM were only servicing business clients. At that time, people who wanted a personal computer had only one option. They needed to build it from scratch, and to be honest, a lot of people used to do that. It really wasn't that hard either at least from my perspective. But, in contrast to that time, think about what they have become right now. Ever thought of building a computer at home? By building, I mean designing everything and not just assembly of the CPU. It is not very easy.

What I am trying to tell you here is that there was a time when computers were exotic; they were not very common, and they had very limited functionalities. However, with time and the brains of people, such as Steve Jobs, Bill Gates, and Hewlett and Packard, computers became more user-friendly, more easily available, and a desirable commodity. Think of the same thing with robots. They are expensive; for most people, there is not much they can do with them and also they are rare in the public space. But, as you have learned, it is not very hard to build a robot for our personal use, and with some tweaking here and there and with inventive minds such as yours, things can be taken in an altogether different direction. You could be the next Steve Jobs or Bill Gates. All we need is zeal, passion, and out-of-the-box thinking. You may be ridiculed for your vision. But do remember every inventor has been called mad at some point in time. So the next time someone calls you mad, you can be very sure that you are progressing!

Well, I'm quite sure that, if you are a robotic enthusiast, then you must have seen the movie *Iron Man*. If you haven't seen it yet, then take a break from reading this book and go ahead and open Netflix and see that movie.

Once I saw that movie, there were two main things that I wanted to build: one, the suit of Iron Man and other his personal assistant Jarvis, who takes care of all his needs. Though suits seem to be something that I may have to work on for a while, but, by that time, you can go ahead and build the personal assistant for yourself.

Imagine your home doing things for itself. How cool would it be? It knows what you like, what time you wake up, when you come back home, and, based on that, it automatically does things for you. Best of all, it would not be something you buy off the shelf, rather you would be making it with your own hands.

Before you do any of this, I must tell you that you will be dealing with high voltages and considerable currents. Electricity is no joke, and you must take care at all times and wear all the safety equipment. If you are not sure of it, then it would be a good idea to get an electrician to help you. Before you touch or open any of the electrical boards, make sure that you are wearing non-conductive shoes; also inspect whether the tools such as screwdrivers, pliers, nose pliers, cutters, and other tools are well insulated and in good condition. It is a good idea to wear gloves for added safety. If you are under 18, then you must have an adult with you all times to help you.

Now that that's said, let's get started and see what we have got here.

Making Jarvis wake you up

Now, this one is very interesting, as you all know our human body is programmed in a certain way. Hence, we react to different stimuli in a very known way. Like when it gets dark, our brain produces hormones that trigger sleep. Once the sunlight falls on our eyes, we tend to wake up. Well, at least this should be the case! In recent times, our lifestyle has changed enormously, which has started to defy this cycle. That's why, we are seeing more and more cases of insomnia. Waking up by an alarm is certainly not natural. Hence, you are never happy listening to an alarm in the morning, even if it has your favorite song as its tone. Our sleep cycle is supposed to be synchronized with the sunlight, but nowadays hardly anyone wakes up by this method. So, in this chapter, let's first make a smart alarm that will replicate the natural way we wake up.

Working with relay and PIR sensor

As we are dealing with high voltage and higher currents, we would be using a relay. To do this, connect the wires as follows:

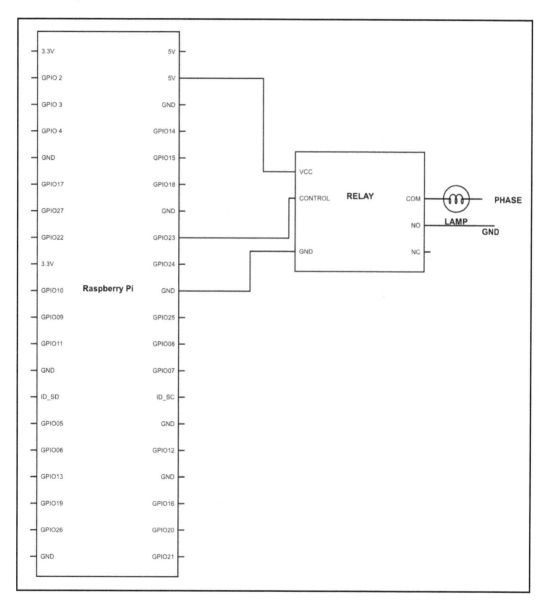

Once you are done connecting it, upload the following code and let's see what happens:

```
import RPi.GPIO as GPIO
import time

LIGHT = 23

GPIO.setmode(GPIO.BCM)
GPIO.setwarnings(False)
GPIO.setup(LIGHT,GPIO.OUT)

import datetime

H = datetime.datetime.now().strftime('%H')
M = datetime.datetime.now().strftime('%M')

while True:

    if H = '06'and M < 20 :
        GPIO.output(LIGHT,GPIO.HIGH)

    else:
        GPIO.output(LIGHT,GPIO.LOW)
```

OK, then it is a fairly simple code with not much explanation needed. We have done a very similar code before as well. Do you remember when? It was in the first few chapters when we were making a gardening robot where we had to fetch water to the plants at a certain time. All it is doing at this time is to check the time and whether the time is 06 hours and the minute is less than 20. That is, the light would be switched on between 07:00 hours to 07:19 hours. Thereafter, it would switch off.

Making the alarm irritating

But there is a problem. The problem is that the lights will be switched on and, no matter whether you get up, the light would automatically switch itself off within 20 minutes. That is a bit of problem because not every time will you wake up in just 20 minutes. So, in that case, what should we do? The first thing we need to do is to detect whether you have woken up. This is very simple and not much needs to be told here. If you wake up in the morning, it is very certain that you will move out of the bed. Once you do, we can detect the motion that can tell our automated system whether you have really woken up.

Now, what we can do here is something very simple. We can detect your motion, and based on that detection, we can be decisive on whether you have really woken up. This doesn't seem much of a task. All we need to do is to add a motion detection sensor. For this purpose, we can use a PIR sensor, which can tell us whether the motion has been detected. So, let's go ahead, add another layer of sensor on top of our system, and see what happens.

So, first, connect the circuit as follows. While mounting the PIR sensor, do make sure that it is facing the bed and detecting any motion on and around it. Once the PIR is set up, wire the sensors as shown in the following diagram and see what happens:

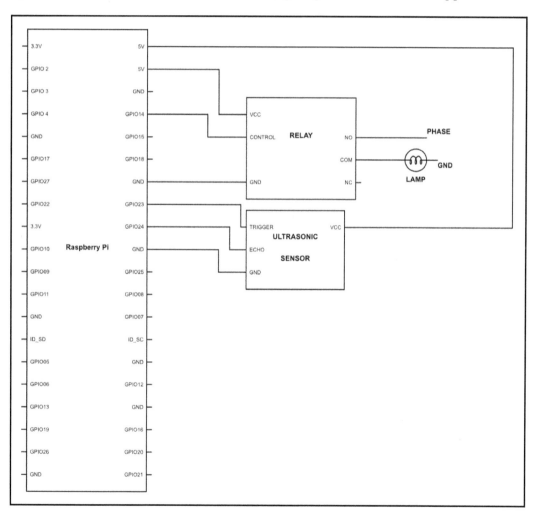

Once done, then go ahead and write the following code:

```
import RPi.GPIO as GPIO
import time

LIGHT = 23
PIR = 24
Irritation_flag = 3

GPIO.setmode(GPIO.BCM)
GPIO.setwarnings(False)

GPIO.setup(LIGHT,GPIO.OUT)
GPIO.setup(PIR,  GPIO.IN)

import datetime

H = datetime.datetime.now().strftime('%H')
M = datetime.datetime.now().strftime('%M')


    while True:

        if H = '07' and M <= '15' and Iriitation_Flag > 0 and
GPIO.input(PIR)  == 0:

            GPIO.output(LIGHT,GPIO.HIGH)


        if H = '07'and GPIO.input(PIR)==1:

            GPIO.output(LIGHT,GPIO.LOW)
            time.sleep(10)
            Irritation_Flag = Irritation_Flag - 1


        for H = '07'and M > '15' and Irritation_Flag > 0 and
GPIO.input(PIR) = 0:

            GPIO.output(LIGHT,GPIO.HIGH)
            time.sleep(5)
            GPIO.output(LIGHT,GPIO.LOW)
            time.sleep(5)

        if H != '07':
            Irritation_flag = 3
            GPIOP.output(LIGHT,  GPIO.LOW)
```

OK, let's see what we have done. The code is extremely simple, but we had a small twist in it, that is, `Irritation_Flag`:

```
Irritation_flag = 3
```

Now this variable works something like a snooze button. As we know, when we wake up sometimes, or in fact, most of the time, we again go back to sleep only to wake up much later to realize that we are late. To prevent this, we have this `Irritation_flag`, and what this basically would be used for is to detect the number of times you have performed the action to stop the alarm. How it would be used we will see later:

```
        if H = '07' and M <= '15' and Irritation_Flag > 0 and
GPIO.input(PIR) == 0:

            GPIO.output(LIGHT,GPIO.HIGH)
```

In this line, we are simply comparing time values by hours and minutes. If the hours is `07` and minutes are fewer than or equal to `15`, then the lights would be switched off. There is also a condition that says `Irritation_Flag > 0` as we have already declared in the beginning that the value of `Irritation_flag = 3`; hence, initially this condition will always be true. The last condition is `GPIO.input(PIR) == 0`; which means that the condition will only be satisfied when the PIR has not detected any motion. In very simple words, the alarm will go off every time between 07:00 and 07:15 if the PIR does not detect any motion:

```
     if H = '07'and GPIO.input(PIR)==1:

         GPIO.output(LIGHT,GPIO.LOW)
         time.sleep(10)
         Irritation_Flag = Irritation_Flag - 1
```

In this part of the program, the condition will only be true if the hours or `H` is equal to `7` and when the PIR is detecting some motion. Hence, every time when the time is between 07:00 and 07:59 and whenever the motion is detected, the condition will be true. Once true, the program will first switch off the light using the line `GPIO.output*LIGHT,GPIO.LOW`. Once it is turned off, it waits for `10` seconds using `time.sleep(10)`. Once the time is over, it will implement the following operation: `Irritation_Flag - Irritation_Flag - 1`. Now what it does is that it decrements the value of `Irritation_Flag` by 1 every time it detects a motion. So the first time a motion happens, the value of `Irritation_Flag` would be 2; thereafter, it would be 1, and finally, it would be 0.

If you look at the previous part of the code, you will be able to make out that the light would be switched on if the value of `Irritation_Flag` was greater than 0. So if you want to turn off the light, you would have to move at least three times. Why three times? Because then the code `Irritation_Flag = Irritation - 1` would be executed three times so as to make the value get down to 0, which obviously makes the condition `GPIO.input(PIR) > 0` false:

```
for H = '07'and M > '15' and Irritation_Flag > 0 and
GPIO.input(PIR) = 0:

        GPIO.output(LIGHT,GPIO.HIGH)
        time.sleep(5)
        GPIO.output(LIGHT,GPIO.LOW)
        time.sleep(5)
```

Now, let's say even after of all this, you still do not wake up. Then what should happen? We have something special for you here. Now, instead of an `if` condition, we have a `for` loop. What this will check for is that the time should be `07` hours, and minutes should be greater than 15, `Irritation_Flag > 0`, and obviously no motion is being detected. Till the time all of these are true, the light would be switched on thereafter for 5 seconds, it would be kept switched on using the `time.sleep(5)`. The lights would be again switched on. Now this will keep on happening till the time the conditions are true or in other words, till the time is between 07:15 and 07:59. `Irritation)_Flag > 0`, that is, the motion is not detected for three times and there is no motion detected. Till that time, the for loop would keep on the switch on and off of the light in action. Due to frequent biking of light, there is a very higher chance of you waking up. This may be very effective, but surely not the most convenient. Well, however inconvenient it is, it will still be better than the conventional alarm:

```
if H != '07':
    Irritation_flag = 3
```

We have the entire light-based alarm ready for us to wake us up every morning. However, there is a problem. Once it is turned off, the value of `Irritation_Flag` will be 0. Once it is turned to 0, then no matter what the time is, the light would never start up. Hence, to make sure that the alarm is always operational at the same time every single day, we would need to set the value of the flag to any number more than 0.

Now in the preceding line, if `H != '07'`, then the `Irritation_flag` would be 3. That is whenever the time is anything other than 07 hours, then the value of `Irritation_Flag` would be 3.

It was simple, wasn't it? But I'm sure that it would do a good job to make sure you wake up on time.

Making it even more irritating

Can you completely rely on the preceding system? If you really have control over your morning emotions of not getting out of the bed, then, yes, sure you can. But for those who just love to be in bed and sleep again after hitting the snooze button, then I am sure you would be able to find a way to switch off the light without properly waking up. So as in the code, the light would switch off whenever the motion was detected three times. But the motion can be anything. You can simply wave your hand while still being in the bed, and the system would detect it as a motion, which would defy the whole purpose. So what should we do now?

We have a solution for it! We can use a way by which we can be sure that you have to get out of bed. For this very purpose, we will be using our IR proximity sensor, which we have used earlier in our projects, and based on the distance reading of the sensor, we can detect whether you have gone past any specific area. This can be really interesting as you can fit this sensor pointing away from the bed or maybe on the gate of the bathroom, and till the time, you do not cross that specific line. The system would not switch off the alarm. So let's see how we would do it. First, connect the hardware, as shown in the following diagram:

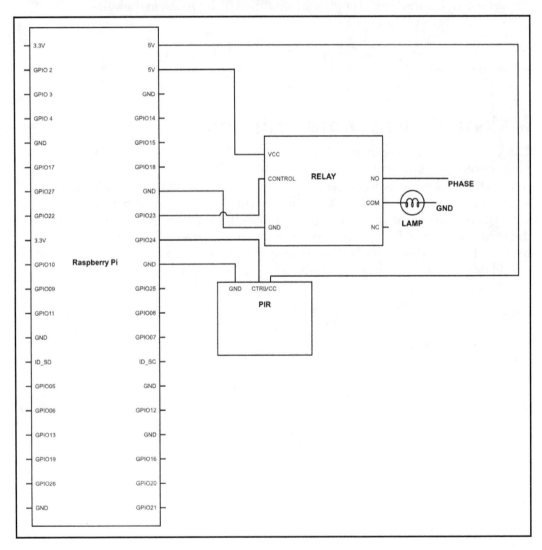

Once you are done with the diagram, go ahead and upload the following code:

```
import RPi.GPIO as GPIO
import time

import Adafruit_ADS1x15
adc0 = Adafruit_ADS1x15.ADS1115()

GAIN = 1

adc0.start_adc(0, gain=GAIN)

LIGHT = 23
PIR = 24
Irritation_flag = 1
IR = 2

GPIO.setmode(GPIO.BCM)
GPIO.setwarnings(False)

GPIO.setup(LIGHT,GPIO.OUT)
GPIO.setup(PIR, GPIO.IN)
GPIO.setup(IR. GPIO.IN)

import datetime

H = datetime.datetime.now().strftime('%H')
M = datetime.datetime.now().strftime('%M')


  while True:

  if H = '07' and M <= '15' and Iriitation_Flag > 0 and
GPIO.input(PIR) == 0:

     GPIO.output(LIGHT,GPIO.HIGH)


  if H = '07'and GPIO.input(PIR)==1:
   M_snooze = datetime.datetime.now().strftime('%M')
   M_snooze = M_snooze + 5
   for M <= M_snooze
     GPIO.output(LIGHT,GPIO.LOW)

     F_value = adc0.get_last_result()
     F1 =    (1.0 / (F_value / 13.15)) - 0.35

     time.sleep(0.1)
```

```
F_value = adc0.get_last_result()
F2 =    (1.0 / (F_value / 13.15)) - 0.35

F_final = F1-F2

M = datetime.datetime.now().strftime('%M')

if F_final > 25

    Irritation_flag = 0



for H = '07'and M > '15' and Irritation_Flag > 0 and GPIO.input(PIR)
= 0:

GPIO.output(LIGHT,GPIO.HIGH)
time.sleep(5)
GPIO.output(LIGHT,GPIO.LOW)
time.sleep(5)

if H != '07':

Irritation_flag = 1
```

Mind blown? This code seems quite complex, having conditions inside conditions and again some more conditions. Say hello to robotics! These conditions make up a lot of robot's programming. A robot has to see continuously what is happening around and make decisions according to it. It's also the way humans work, don't we?

So, that being said, let's see what we are actually doing here. Most of the code is pretty much the same as the last one. The main difference comes somewhere around the middle of the programming section:

```
if H = '07' and M <= '15' and Iriitation_Flag > 0 and
GPIO.input(PIR) == 0:

    GPIO.output(LIGHT,GPIO.HIGH)
```

We are switching on the lights as soon as the time is between 07:00 and 07:15:

```
if H = '07'and GPIO.input(PIR)==1:
  M_snooze = datetime.datetime.now().strftime('%M')
  M_snooze = M_snooze + 5
```

In the hour of `07` whenever the PIR sensor is triggered or in other words, the PIR sensor detects any motion, then it will do a set of activities inside the `if` condition, which includes noting down the time by the function `datetime.datetime.now().strftime('%M')` and then storing it down in a variable named `M_snooze`.

In the next line, we are taking the value of that minute stored in `M_snooze` and adding another 5 minutes to it. So the value of `M_snooze` is now incremented by 5:

```
for M <= M_snooze
```

Now, in the same `if` condition that we used previously, we have placed a `for` loop, which looks like this: `for M <= M_snooze`. But what does this mean? Here, what we are doing is pretty simple. The program inside the `for` loop will keep on running and will stay in the loop till the time the condition that we have stated is true. Now, the condition here states that till the time `M` is smaller or equal to `M_snooze`, the condition will stay true. As you have learned earlier, `M` is the current minute value and `M_snooze` is the value of `M` at the time of starting of this loop, which is incremented by 5. Hence, the loop would be true for 5 minutes from the time of starting:

```
GPIO.output(LIGHT,GPIO.LOW)

F_value = adc0.get_last_result()
F1 =    (1.0 / (F_value / 13.15)) - 0.35

time.sleep(0.1)
F_value = adc0.get_last_result()
F2 =    (1.0 / (F_value / 13.15)) - 0.35

F_final = F1-F2
```

Now, this is the most interesting part of the program. Till the time, the `for` loop for `M <= M_snooze` is true, the preceding lines of code will run. Let's see what it is doing. In the line, `F-value = adc0.get_last_result()`, it is taking the value of the IR proximity sensor and storing it in `F_value`. Thereafter, in the line `F1 = (1.0/(F_value/13.15))-0.35`, we are simply calculating the distance in centimeters. We have already studied how this is happening, so not much explanation needs to be done here. The value of distance is stored in a variable named `F1`. Thereafter, using the function `time.sleep(0.1)`, we are pausing the program for `0.1` seconds. Thereafter, we are again repeating the same task again; that is, we are again taking the value of distance. But this time, the distance value calculated is stored in an another variable named `F2`. Finally, after all of this is done, we are calculating `F_final`, which is `F_final = F1 - F2`. So we are simply calculating the difference in distance between the first and the second reading. But, you must be asking why are we doing this. What good does it do?

Well, as you remember, we have placed the IR proximity sensor in front of our bathroom gate. Now, if no one is passing in front of it, the value will remain fairly constant. But whenever a person passes through it, there will be a change in distance. So if there is a change in the overall distance from first to last reading, then we can say that someone has passed through the IR sensor.

That is pretty cool, but why don't we simply keep a threshold value like we have done previously? The answer to this is simple. That is because if you need to change the position of the sensor, then you again need to recalibrate the sensor according to the position. So this is a simple yet robust solution that can be used anywhere:

```
if F_final > 10
    Irritation_flag = 1
```

Now we have got the reading, which can tell us whether a person has passed in front of it. But this data will not be useful until we put it somewhere.

So, here in the condition `if F_final > 10`, whenever the distance change is more than `10` cm, then the condition would be true and the line `Irritation_flag` would be set to `1`.

If you go back to the previous lines, then you will be able to make out that the lights will only be on when the time is between 07:00 and 07:15 and the `Irritation_flag` must be `0`. As with this condition, we have set a part of the condition false by making the `Irritation_flag = 1`; hence, the program to switch on the lights will not work.

Now, let's look back and see what we have done so far:

- Whenever the time is 07:00–07:15, the lights would be switched on
- If a movement is detected, then the lights would be switched off
- A condition will be true for another five minutes, which will wait for detection of human motion through the IR proximity sensor
- If a person crosses that within five minutes, then the alarm would be deactivated or else the alarm will again start to switch on the light

Pretty cool, huh? That being said, let's add another added functionality from the previous program:

```
for H = '07'and M > '15' and Irritation_Flag = 0 and GPIO.input(PIR)
= 0:

    GPIO.output(LIGHT,GPIO.HIGH)
    time.sleep(5)
    GPIO.output(LIGHT,GPIO.LOW)
    time.sleep(5)
```

You know what this does. If you do not move around in the first 15 minutes, that is from 07:00 to 07:15, then it will start blinking the lights every five seconds, forcing you to wake up:

```
if H != '07':
    Irritation_flag = 0
```

Finally, we use the condition if H != '07':. So, whenever the value of H is anything other than 07, then the condition would be true, and this will reset the Irritation_flag to 0. By now, you know what turning Irritation_flag to 0 does.

Summary

So, finally, we have made our first mini Jarvis, which wakes you up in the morning and even irritates you if you don't wake up on time. I hope you have really enjoyed this chapter by learning about two-motion sensors and their application in automating the electrical appliance. So, go ahead and try one at home, modify the code according to your needs, and bring out some really cool stuff. Next up, we will make our Jarvis do some more cool stuff, and we will cover some more exciting stuff on human detection.

25

Recognizing Humans with Jarvis

By now we have understood in the last chapter how multiple layers of conditions can be clubbed together to get the functionality that is desired. We have just completed the first step in making Jarvis work for you. Now, it's time to make it even more capable.

In this chapter, we will make it control more electronics at your home, which can be controlled autonomously without you telling anything to the system. So without delay, let's get straight into it and see what we have in our bucket.

Turn on the light Jarvis

One of the basic functionalities of a smart home is to turn on the lights for you whenever you are around. It is one of the most basic things that any system can do for you. We will start off by turning on the light as soon as you come inside the room, thereafter, we will make the system more and more intelligent.

So, the first thing we need to do is recognize whether you are in a room or not. There are multiple ways to do that. One important characteristic of life is the presence of movement. You may say plants don't move, well they do; they grow, don't they? So detecting movement can be a key step in detecting whether someone is there or not!

This step will not be so difficult for you, as we have already interfaced this sensor previously. We are talking about the good old PIR sensor. So the sensor will sense any movement in the area. If there is any movement, then Jarvis will switch on the lights. I am sure this is something you can do by yourself by now. You can still refer to the code and the circuit diagram here:

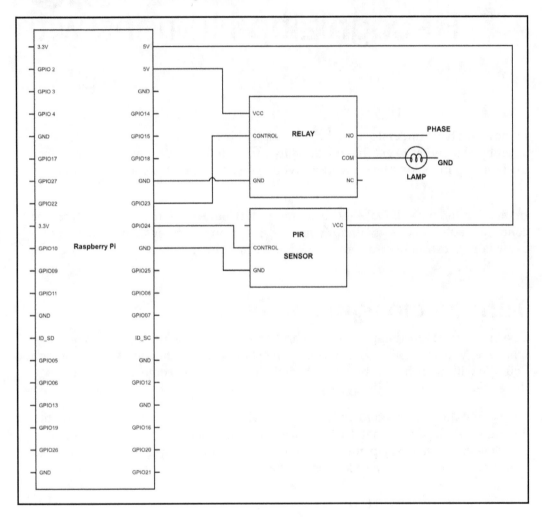

Now upload the following code:

```
import RPi.GPIO as GPIO
import time
GPIO.setmode(GPIO.BCM)
GPIO.setwarnings(False)
PIR = 24
LIGHT = 23
GPIO.setup(DOPPLER,GPIO.IN)
GPIO.setup(BUZZER,GPIO.OUT)
While True:
    if GPIO.input(PIR) == 1:
        GPIO.output(LIGHT,GPIO.HIGH)
    if GPIO.input(PIR) == 0:
        GPIO.output(LIGHT,GPIO.LOW)
```

In the preceding code, we are simply turning on the light as soon as the motion is detected, but the problem is that it will only switch on the light for the time the motion is there. What does that mean? Simple, while there is some movement, will keep the lights on and as soon as the movement stops, it will switch off the light.

This can be a very good code for a person who wants to lose weight, but for most of us, it will be annoying. So, let's include a small loop, which we have used in the previous chapter and make this a little better:

```
import RPi.GPIO as GPIO
import time

GPIO.setmode(GPIO.BCM)
GPIO.setwarnings(False)

PIR = 24
LIGHT = 23
TIME = 5

GPIO.setup(PIR,GPIO.IN)
GPIO.setup(BUZZER,GPIO.OUT)

While True:

    If GPIO.input(PIR) == 1:
        M = datetime.datetime.now().strftime('%M')
        M_final= M + TIME

        for M < M_final:

            GPIO.output(LIGHT,GPIO.HIGH)
```

```
M = datetime.datetime.now().strftime('%M')

if GPIO.input(PIR) == 1:
    M_final = M_final + 1


if GPIO.input(PIR) = 0:

    GPIO.output(LIGHT, GPIO.LOW) }
```

So, in this program, all we have done is we have added a `for` loop, which switches on the light for a set amount of time. How long that time will be can be toggled by changing the value of the variable `TIME`.

There is one more interesting part in that loop which is as follows:

```
if GPIO.input(PIR) == 1
    M_final = M_final + 1
```

Why did we do this you might wonder? Whenever the light will be switched on, it will remain on for 5 minutes. Then, it will switch off and wait for movement to occur. So, essentially, the problem with this code will be that if you are in the room and the light switches on, then for 5 minutes it will see if there is any motion detected or not. There is a chance that you will be in motion when it searches for the motion after 5 minutes. But for most of the time, it won't be the case. So we are detecting the movement using the PIR sensor. Whenever movement is detected, the value of `M_final` is incremented using the line `M_final = M_final + 1`, thereby increasing the time until which the light will be switched on.

Understanding motion

By now you must have figured that the PIR sensor is not the most idealistic sensor for us to switch the lights on or off. Mostly because, although the motion is one of the best indicators of presence, there can be times when you might not move at all, for example, while resting, reading a book, watching a movie, and so on.

What do we do now? Well, we can do a little trick. Remember in the last chapter we used our proximity sensor to sense whether a person has crossed a specific area or not? We will implant a similar logic here; but rather than just copy pasting the code, we will improve it and make it even better.

So rather than using one single IR proximity sensor, we will be using two of these things. The mounting will be as shown in the following diagram:

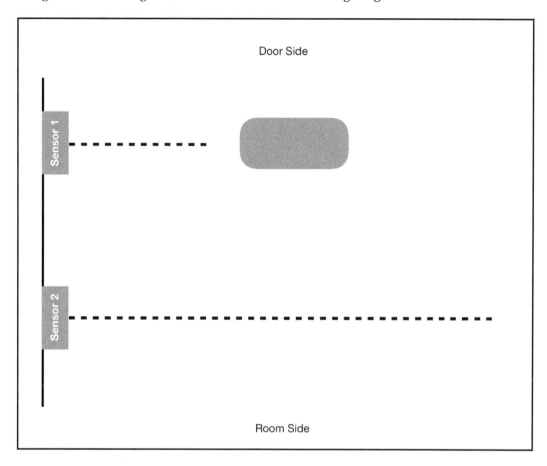

Now it is very evident that whenever a person walks in from the door side to the room side the **Sensor 1** will show a lower reading when detecting a body. Then, while he is walking towards the room side, **Sensor 2** will show a similar reading.

If first **Sensor 1** is triggered and thereafter **Sensor 2** is triggered, then we can safely assume that the person is travelling from the door side to the room side. Similarly, if the opposite is happening, then it is understood that the person is walking out of the room.

Now, this is fairly simple. But how do we implement it in a real-life situation? Firstly, we need to connect the circuit as follows:

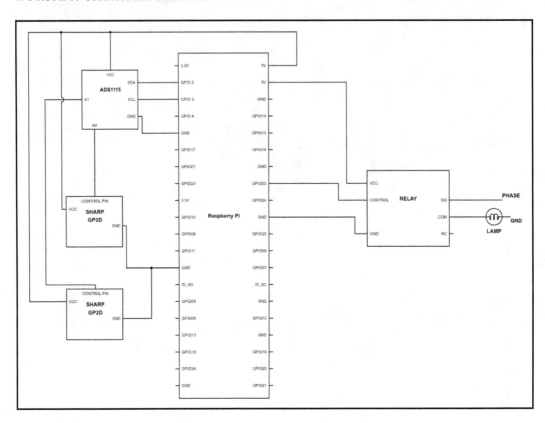

Once that is done, upload the following code:

```
import GPIO library
import RPi.GPIO as GPIO
import time

import Adafruit_ADS1x15
adc0 = Adafruit_ADS1x15.ADS1115()

GAIN = 1
LIGHT = 23

adc0.start_adc(0, gain=GAIN)
adc1.start_adc(1, gain=GAIN)

GPIO.setmode(GPIO.BCM)
```

```
GPIO.setwarnings(False)


while True:


    F_value = adc0.get_last_result()
    F1 =    (1.0 / (F_value / 13.15)) - 0.35

    time.sleep(0.1)

    F_value = adc0.get_last_result()
    F2 =    (1.0 / (F_value / 13.15)) - 0.35

    F0_final = F1-F2

    if F0 > 10 :
         Time0 =  time.time()

    F_value = adc1.get_last_result()
    F1 =    (1.0 / (F_value / 13.15)) - 0.35

    time.sleep(0.1)

    F_value = adc1.get_last_result()
    F2 =    (1.0 / (F_value / 13.15)) - 0.35

    F1_final = F1-F2

    if F1 > 10:

         Time1 =  time.time()

     if Time1 > Time0:

         GPIO.output(LIGHT, GPIO.HIGH)


     if Time1 < Time0:

         GPIO.output(LIGHT, GPIO.LOW)        }
```

Now, let's see what are we doing here. As always, most of the syntax is very simple and straightforward. The most important part is the logic. So, let's understand in proper steps as to what we are doing.

```
F_value = adc0.get_last_result()
F1 =    (1.0 / (F_value / 13.15)) - 0.35

time.sleep(0.1)

F_value = adc0.get_last_result()
F2 =    (1.0 / (F_value / 13.15)) - 0.35
```

In the preceding lines of code, we are taking the value of the IR proximity sensor and calculating the distance corresponding to it and storing that value in a variable called F1. Once that is done, we are stopping for a brief period of 0.1 seconds using the time.sleep(0.1) function. Thereafter, we are taking the reading from the same sensor again and storing the value in a variable called F2. Why are we doing this? We have already understood that in the previous chapters.

```
F0_final = F1-F2
```

Once the value of F1 and F0 is acquired, we will calculate the difference to find out whether someone has passed through it or not. If no one has passed, then the reading will almost be the same and the difference will not be considerable. However, if a person does pass, then the reading will be considerable and that value will be stored in a variable called F0_final.

```
if F0 > 10 :
    Time0 =  time.time()
```

If the value of the F0 or the difference in distance between the first and the second reading is more than 10 centimeters, then the if condition will be true. Once true, it will set the value of the Time0 variable as the current value of time. The time.time() function will make a note of the exact time.

```
F_value = adc1.get_last_result()
F1 =    (1.0 / (F_value / 13.15)) - 0.35

time.sleep(0.1)

F_value = adc1.get_last_result()
F2 =    (1.0 / (F_value / 13.15)) - 0.35
```

```
F1_final = F1-F2

if F1 > 10:

    Time1 =  time.time()
```

Now, we'll perform the exact same step for **Sensor 2** as well. There is nothing new to tell here; it's all self explanatory.

```
if Time1 > Time0:

    GPIO.output(LIGHT, GPIO.HIGH)
```

Once all of this is done, we compare `if Time1 > Time0`. Why are we comparing it? Because `Time0` is the time noted for **Sensor 1**. If the person is moving inside, then **Sensor 1** would be the first one to be triggered and then the **Sensor 2** would be triggered. Hence, the time noted would be greater for **Sensor 2** and relatively earlier for **Sensor 1**. If that happens, then we can assume that the person is coming inside. Well, if a person is coming inside, then we simply need to switch the light on, which is exactly what we are doing here.

```
if Time1 < Time0:

    GPIO.output(LIGHT, GPIO.LOW)
```

Similarly, when a person is going out, the first sensor to be triggered would be **Sensor 2**, thereafter **Sensor 1** will be triggered. Making the time noted for `Time1` earlier than `Time2`; hence, whenever this condition is true, we will know that the person is moving out of the room and the lights can be switched off.

Go ahead and mount it near the door and see how it reacts. I'm sure this will be way better than what we had done through PIR. Have fun with it and try to find any flaws that it might have.

Perfecting motion

Were you able to find any flaws in the previous code? They are not hard to find; the code works brilliantly when it's only a single person in the room. If this is installed somewhere where multiple people are coming and going, then it might be challenging. This is because whenever a person moves outside, the light will be turned off.

So now that the problem is evident, it's time to make the code even more better. To do this, the hardware will remain exactly the same; we simply need to make the code smarter. Let's see how we can do that:

```python
import GPIO library
    import RPi.GPIO as GPIO
    import time
    import time
    import Adafruit_ADS1x15
    adc0 = Adafruit_ADS1x15.ADS1115()
GAIN = 1
 adc0.start_adc(0, gain=GAIN)
adc1.start_adc(1, gain=GAIN)
GPIO.setmode(GPIO.BCM)
GPIO.setwarnings(False)
PCount = 0
while True:
    F_value = adc0.get_last_result()
    F1 = (1.0 / (F_value / 13.15)) - 0.35
    time.sleep(0.1)
    F_value = adc0.get_last_result()
    F2 = (1.0 / (F_value / 13.15)) - 0.35
    F0_final = F1-F2
    if F0 > 10 :
        Time0 = time.time()
    F_value = adc1.get_last_result()
    F1 = (1.0 / (F_value / 13.15)) - 0.35
    time.sleep(0.1)
    F_value = adc1.get_last_result()
    F2 = (1.0 / (F_value / 13.15)) - 0.35
    F1_final = F1-F2
    if F1 > 10:
        Time1 = time.time()
   if Time1 > Time0:
        PCount = PCount + 1
   if Time1 < Time0:
        PCount = PCount - 1

 if PCount > 0:

        GPIO.output(LIGHT, GPIO.HIGH)
      else if PCount = 0:
        GPIO.output(LIGHT, GPIO.LOW)
```

What we have done is something really basic. We have declared a variable called PCount. This variable is declared to count the number of people who are there inside a room or a home. As you can see in the first few lines of the code, we have declared the value of PCount as 0. We are assuming that once we start this, the number of people inside would be 0.

```
if Time1 > Time0:

    PCount = PCount + 1
```

Whenever the condition if Time1 > Time0: is satisfied, the PCount value is incremented by 1. As we all know, the condition will only be true when a person is walking inside the home.

```
if Time1 < Time0:
    PCount = PCount - 1
```

Similarly, when a person is walking outside, the condition if Time1 < Time0: is true; whenever that happens, the value of PCount is decremented by 1.

```
if PCount > 0:

    GPIO.output(LIGHT, GPIO.HIGH)
```

Now that we have started counting the number of people in the room, we are now applying the condition, which will turn on if the number of PCount is more than 0. Hence, the light will be on for the time when the number of people inside the home is more than 0.

```
else if PCount = 0:

    GPIO.output(LIGHT, GPIO.LOW)
```

In a very similar fashion, the lights will be turned off if the value of PCount or the number of people inside the home gets to 0.

Hence, nailed!

Controlling the intensity

We have controlled a lot of light now. It's time that we control our fans and other air circulation systems. Whenever we talk about fans or any other air circulation devices, then essentially we are talking about motors. As we have learned earlier, motors are simple devices, which can be controlled every easily using a motor driver. But as you know, back then we were controlling DC motors. DC motors are extremely simple devices. But when we talk about our household appliances, then most of these devices will be working on AC or alternating current. I am assuming that you must be aware of what that is and how it is different from DC.

Now that you know that the motors used in our households are working on AC, you must also think about the fact that their control mechanism will be much different to DC motors. You are right, if you thought so. However, the good thing about electronics is, nothing is really difficult or complicated. The basics are pretty much the same. So, let's see how we can control the speed of the motors in AC supply.

As we have seen earlier, we can simply have a PWM signal given to the DC motor and the motor will run at the speed of the average voltage as a result of the PWM signal. Now, you must be thinking that this can be applied to AC as well. The thing is, yes it can be done if you want to control a light or similar devices, which do not have any major change in the characteristics in case the wave form is distorted. However, when we are talking about any other component, then we come across a big problem. The AC wave form looks like this:

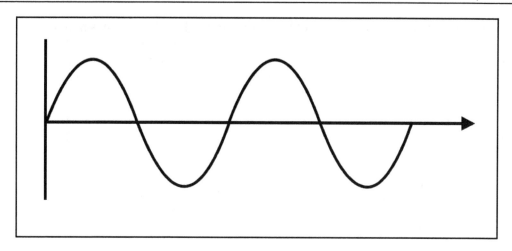

This basically means that the potential is changing periodically. In most of the households, this is 50 times per second. Now, imagine if we have a PWM-controlled device that is switching the circuit that only lets the power supply to pass at certain intervals. Then, the different parts of the sinusoidal waves would be passed on to the final output.

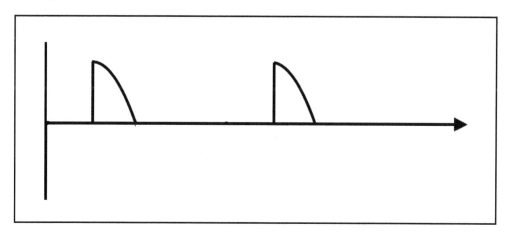

As you can see in the preceding PWM, fortunately the PWM signal has matched with the phase of the AC power; however, due to this, only the positive end of the phase is being transferred to the final output and not the negative end. This will cause a severe problem to our load and there is a very good chance that the appliance that is connected will not work.

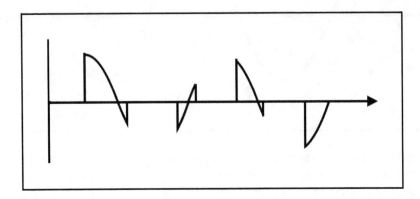

We have another example in which the PWM is random and it lets random parts of the wave pass by. In this, we can clearly see that randomly any part of the wave is being transferred and the positive and negative end voltage is not in sync, which again will be a huge problem. Hence, instead of using PWM, we use something really interesting.

The method that is most commonly used is called **phase fired control**. Sometimes it is also called phase angle control or phase cutting. What it essentially does is, it cuts the wave at certain parts of the phase letting the rest of the wave cross by. Confused? Let me show you here:

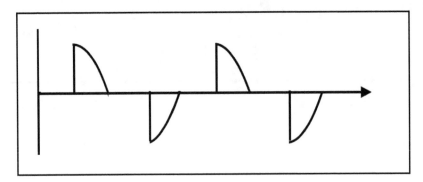

Now, as you can see the phase behind the second half of the AC wave is getting chopped and is not getting passed in the final output. This makes the final output to be only 50% of the overall input. What this technique does is, it maintains the AC nature of the power supply while still being able to reduce the overall resulting voltage. Likewise, as you can see in the next diagram, the wave is getting chopped after 75% of the wave has already passed. This results in the output being relatively lower:

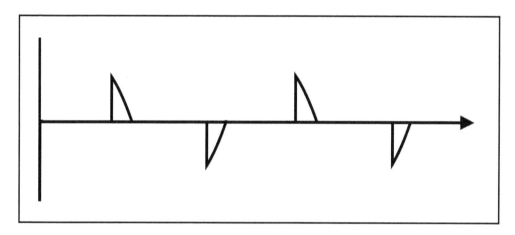

Now you must be asking, how did we actually go ahead and do this? It is done by a relatively complex circuit that detects the phase angle of the wave and then opens or controls a triac, which is a high power bi-directional semiconductor. This leads the power supply to pass or to be stopped at certain phases. We will leave the exact working of this circuit for the next time as it is fairly complex and will not be relevant to this book.

Now coming to the basic point, we know what phase cutting is, we also know that triac is the basic device that lets us do that. But how do we go ahead and do it using Raspberry Pi is the question.

So firstly, we will need an AC-dimmer module. This module already has all the components of phase detection and chopping. So all we need to do is simply control it using simple PWM.

Though I might not have to demonstrate how to connect the circuit or what the code should be, for the sake of understanding, let's connect a light bulb to our Arduino using this module and then control the bulb. Now, the first thing to remember is that the load should be a bulb and not anything else such as an LED light. So go ahead and connect the circuit as shown in the following figure:

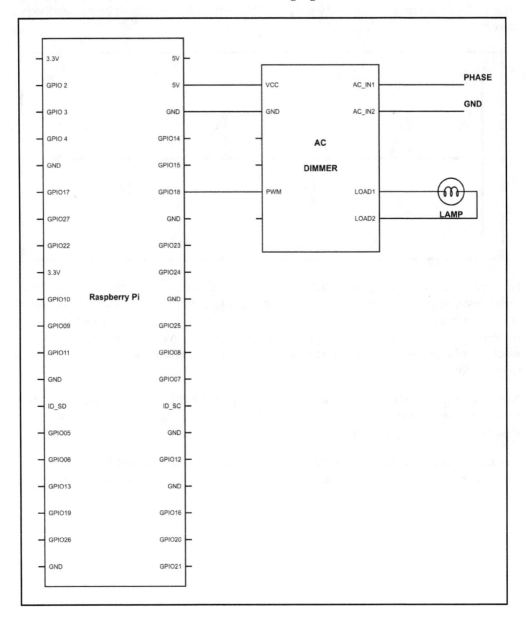

Once this is done, go ahead and upload the following code:

```
import RPi.GPIO as GPIO
import time
GPIO.setmode(GPIO.BCM)
GPIO.setup(18,GPIO.OUT)
I = 0
pwm= GPIO.PWM(18,50)

for I < 100:

    I = I+1
    pwm.start(I)
    time.sleep(0.1)


GPIO.cleanup()}
```

As expected, the attached light will start to glow very faintly first and will increase the intensity gradually until it reaches 100%. That is how simple it is to control such a complex process.

Intelligent temperature control

Now that the basics are done, let's go ahead and build something meaningful using this system. Isn't it difficult to set your air-conditioner to the perfect temperature? No matter what you do, you end up feeling not in the most comfortable spot. This happens due to physiological changes in the body temperature over the course of the day.

When you wake up, your body temperature is relatively low. It is as much as 1° F, which is lower than the normal body temperature. As the day progresses, the body temperature rises until the time you hit the bed. Once you sleep, again your body temperature starts to dip reaching its lowest point around 4:00-6:00 am in the morning. That's the reason why what might feel warm while you go to bed, can be pretty cold when you wake up. Modern air-conditioners have something called a sleep mode. What this does is, it simply increases the temperature through the night. So that you do not feel cold at any point. But then again, how well it works is also a question.

So, now that we know the robotics very well, we will go ahead and make a system of our own that will take care of everything.

In this part, we will connect both the air-conditioner and your fan together so that they can both work in tandem and make you sleep well. Now, before jumping straight into it, I would like you to see the ratings that are mentioned on the relay. As you can see, the relay can handle only 250V and 5 ampere. Now, if you go through the brochure of your air-conditioner, you will easily understand why I am showing all of this to you. The power consumption of the air-conditioner will be much higher than what your relays can handle. So, if you try to run your air conditioner using the normal relays, then you will surely end up blowing the relay. There might be a chance that your appliance will be of a lower current rating than your relay. But with any device that has motors in it just keep in mind that the initial power consumption of that device is much higher than the nominal power consumption. Hence, if your air-conditioner needs 10 ampere nominal, then the starting load may be as much as 15 ampere. You must be thinking, it's not a problem, why don't we just purchase a relay that has a higher rating. Well, correct! That's exactly what we will be doing. But the naming of electronics can be tricky at times. The devices that deal with a higher-power higher-voltage electro-mechanical switching is generally called contractor instead of relay. Technically, they have the same working principal; However, there are construction differences, which at this point would not be our concern. So we will be using a contractor for the air conditioner switching and a dimmer for the fan speed control. Now that this has been cleared up, let's go ahead and attach the hardware as shown in the following diagram:

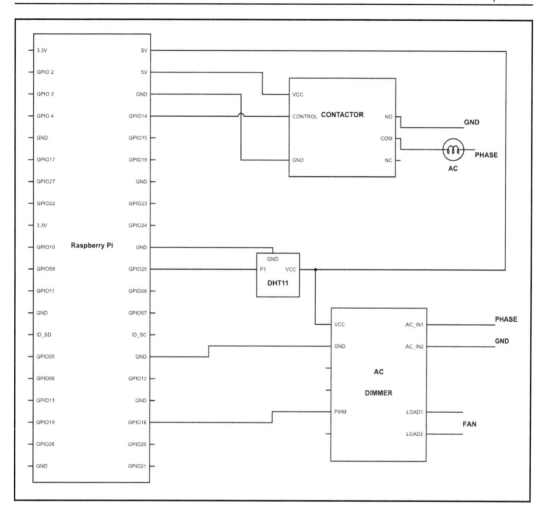

```
import RPi.GPIO as GPIO
import time
import Adafruit_DHT

GPIO.setmode(GPIO.BCM)

FAN = 18
AC = 17

pwm= GPIO.PWM(18,50)
GPIO.setup(FAN,GPIO.OUT)
GPIO.setup(AC, GPIO.OUT)
```

```
while True:

    humidity, temperature = Adafruit_DHT.read_retry(sensor, pin)

    if temperature =>20 && temperature <=30:

        Duty = 50 + ((temperature-25)*10)
        pwm.start(Duty)

    if temperature <22 :

        GPIO.output(AC, GPIO.LOW)

    if temperature >= 24

        GPIO.output(AC, GPIO.HIGH)}
```

The logic used here is pretty basic. Let's see what it is doing:

```
    humidity, temperature = Adafruit_DHT.read_retry(sensor, pin)

    if temperature =>20 && temperature <=30:

        Duty = 50 + ((temperature-25)*10)
        pwm.start(Duty)
```

Here we are taking the value of `humidity` and `temperature`. So far so good, but can we take it a step further and make it even more intelligent? The previous logic must have helped you sleep better, but can we make it just perfect for you?

There are multiple indicators in our body that give us an idea of what the state of the body is. For example, if you are tired, you will probably not be walking very fast or talking very loud. Instead, you would be doing the opposite! Similarly, there are multiple factors that indicate how our sleep cycle is going.

Some of these factors are: body temperature, respiration rate, REM sleep, and body movements. Measuring the exact body temperature or respiration rate and REM sleep is something of a challenge. But when we talk about body movements, I think we have already perfected it. So based on the body movements, we will be sensing how well we are sleeping and what kind of temperature adjustment is needed.

If you notice, whenever someone is sleeping and starts feeling cold, the body will go to a fetal position and will move much less. This happens automatically. However, when a person is comfortable, there are some inevitable movements such as changing sides and movement of arms or legs. This does not happen when a person is feeling cold. So with these movements we can figure out whether a person is feeling cold or not. Now that we have understood the physiological changes of the body, let's try to build a program around it and see what we can achieve.

To do this, firstly, we need to connect the circuit as follows:

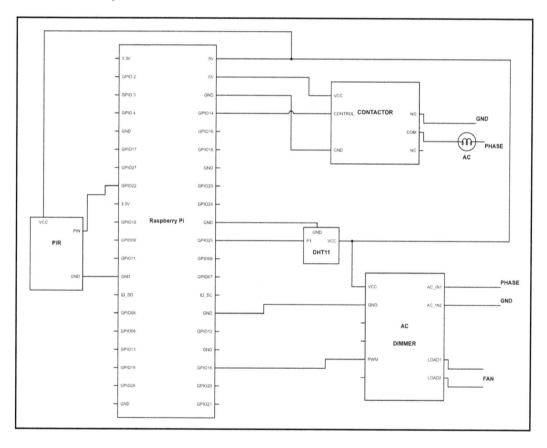

Once this is done, go ahead and write the following code:

```
import RPi.GPIO as GPIO
import time
import Adafruit_DHT

GPIO.setmode(GPIO.BCM)

FAN = 18
AC = 17
PIR = 22
PIN = 11
Sensor = 4

pwm= GPIO.PWM(18,50)
GPIO.setup(FAN,GPIO.OUT)
GPIO.setup(AC, GPIO.OUT)

while True:

    humidity, temperature = Adafruit_DHT.read_retry(sensor, pin)
    H = datetime.datetime.now().strftime('%H')
    M = datetime.datetime.now().strftime('%M')

    if H <= 6 && H <= 22:

        if M <=58 :

            M = datetime.datetime.now().strftime('%M')
            humidity, temperature = Adafruit_DHT.read_retry(sensor,
pin)
            if GPIO.input(PIR) == 0 :
                Movement = Movement + 1
                time.sleep(10)

            if temperature < 28:
                if Movement > 5 :

                    Duty = Duty + 10
                    pwm.start(Duty)
                    Movement = 0

        if M = 59 :

            if Movement = 0 :

                Duty = Duty -10
                pwm.start(Duty)
```

```
        Movement = 0

    if temperature <22 :

        GPIO.output(AC, GPIO.LOW)

    if temperature >= 24 && H <= 6 && H >= 22:

        GPIO.output(AC, GPIO.HIGH)

    if temperature > 27

        pwm.start(100)

for H > 7 && H < 20

    GPIO.output(AC, GPIO.LOW)

if H = 20

    GPIO.output(AC,GPIO.HIGH)


}
```

Let's have a look at what is going on under the hood:

```
    if H <= 6 && H <= 22:

        if M <=58 :

            M = datetime.datetime.now().strftime('%M')
            humidity, temperature = Adafruit_DHT.read_retry(sensor,
    pin)
```

The first thing you will see is that we have a condition: `if H,= 6 && H<= 22:`. This condition will only be true if the time frame is between 10 o'clock in the morning and 6 o'clock in the night. That is because this is the time when we generally sleep. Hence, the logic under this head will only work if it's time to sleep.

The second condition is `if M <= 58`, which will be true only when the time is between 0 and 58 minutes. So when the time is `M = 59`, then this condition will not work. We will see the reason for having this logic.

Thereafter, we are calculating the time and storing the value in a variable called M. We are also calculating the humidity and temperature values and storing it in variables called `temperature` and `humidity`:

```
if GPIO.input(PIR) == 0 :
        Movement = Movement + 1
        time.sleep(10)
```

Now, in this line, we are implementing a condition which will be true if the reading from the PIR is high. That is, there is some motion that will be detected. Whenever this happens, the `Movement` variable will be incremented by 1. Finally, we are using the `time.sleep(10)` function to wait for 10 seconds. This is done as the PIR might be high for a momentary period. In that case, the condition will be true over and over again which in turn will increment the value of `Movement` multiple times.

Our purpose of incrementing the value of `Movement` is to count the number of times the person has moved. Hence, incrementing it multiples times in one single time will defy the objective.

```
if temperature < 28:
        if Movement > 5 :

                Duty = Duty + 10
                pwm.start(Duty)
                Movement = 0
```

Now we have another condition, which says `if temperature < 28`. Not much explanation is needed for when the condition will be true. So whenever the condition is true and if the counted number of `Movement` is more than 5, the value of `Duty` will be incremented by 10. Therefore, we are sending the PWM to the AC dimmer, which in turn will increase the speed of the fan. Finally, we are resetting the value of `Movement` to 0.

So essentially, we are just counting the number of movements. This movement is counted only if the temperature is less than 28° C. If the movement is more than 5, then we will increase the speed of the fan by 10%.

```
if M = 59 :

    if Movement = 0 :

            Duty = Duty -10
            pwm.start(Duty)

    Movement = 0
```

In the previous section, the logic will only work when the time is between 0 and 58, that is, the time in which the counting will happen. When the value of M is 59, then the condition if Movement = 0 will be checked, and if true, then the value of Duty will be decremented by 10. This in turn will reduce the speed of the fan by 10%. Also, once this condition is executed, the value of Movement will be reset to 0. So then a new cycle can start for the next hour.

Now what it basically means is that counting will happen on an hourly basis. If the Movement is more than 5 then immediately the value of the Duty would be increased. However, if that is not the case, then the program will wait until the minute approaches the value of 59 and whenever that happens, it will check whether there is any movement, in which case, the fan speed will be decreased.

```
if temperature <22 :

    GPIO.output(AC, GPIO.LOW)

if temperature >= 24 && H <= 6 && H >= 22:

    GPIO.output(AC, GPIO.HIGH)

if temperature > 27

    pwm.start(100)
```

All of this code is very straightforward. If the temperature is less than 22, then the AC will be switched off. Furthermore, if the temperature is equal to or more than 24, and time is between 10:00 p.m. and 6:00 a.m., then the AC will be turned on. Finally, if the temperature is more than 27, then the fan will be switch on to 100% speed.

```
for H > 7 && H < 20

    GPIO.output(AC, GPIO.LOW)

if H = 20

    GPIO.output(AC,GPIO.HIGH)
```

Finally, we are making sure by using the condition for H > 7 && H <20 that during this time the AC is always switched off. Also, if H = 20, then the AC should be turned on so that the room is cooled before you are ready to sleep.

Adding more

As you would have understood by now, we can control any AC electrical appliances as per our needs. We have understood switching and have also perfected the way we can vary the intensity of light and the speed of fans. But did you notice one thing? Sooner or later as our system gets more and more complex, the number of GPIOs needed will increase. There will come a moment when you will want to have more and more devices connected to your Raspberry Pi; however, you will not be able to do so due to lack of physical ports.

This is a very common situation in electronics. As always, there is a solution for this problem as well. This solution is known as a multiplexer. The basic job of a multiplexer is to multiply the number of ports in any computer system. Now you must be thinking, how is it able to do so?

The concept is extremely simple. Let's first look at the diagram of a multiplexer here:

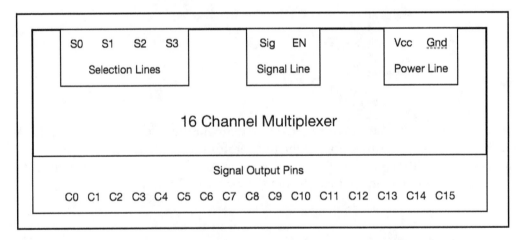

In the preceding diagram, you can see that there are two ends to the multiplexer—one being the signal output lines and the other opposite to it. The first thing we need to understand is that the multiplexer is a bidirectional device, that is, it sends the data from the multiplexer to the connected devices and also vice versa.

Now, firstly, we have the power line, which is pretty basic. It is there to power up the multiplexer itself. Then, we have **Signal Lines**, which have two ports, the **Sig** and **EN**. **EN** stands for enable, which means that until the time **EN** is not high, the data communication will not happen either way. Then we have something called **Sig**. This is the port that is connected to the GPIO of Raspberry Pi for data communication. Next we have the selection line. As you can see, we have four ports for it, namely, **S0**, **S1**, **S2**, and **S3**. The selection lines have a purpose of selecting a particular port that needs to be selected. The following is a table that will clarify what exactly is happening:

S0	S1	S3	S4	Selected output
0	0	0	0	C0
1	0	0	0	C1
0	1	0	0	C2
1	1	0	0	C3
0	0	1	0	C4
1	0	1	0	C5
0	1	1	0	C6
1	1	1	0	C7
0	0	0	1	C8
1	0	0	1	C9
0	1	0	1	C10
1	1	0	1	C11
0	0	1	1	C12
1	0	1	1	C13
0	1	1	1	C14
1	1	1	1	C15

In the preceding table, you can see that by using various logic combinations on the selection lines, various lines can be addressed. Let's say, for example, we have the following sequence on the selection pins—S0 = 1, S1 = 0, S2 = 1, S3 = 1. If this is the input on the selection pins from Raspberry Pi, then the pin number C13 will be selected. This basically means that now C13 can communicate the data to and from the pin **Sig** for the multiplexer. Also, we must remember that the enable pin must be high for the data transfer to happen.

In a similar fashion, we can go ahead and address all the 16 pins of the multiplexer. Hence, if we see it logically, then by using six pins of Raspberry Pi, we can go ahead and utilize 16 GPIOs. Now that we have understood the basics of multiplexing, let's go ahead and try using one of them.

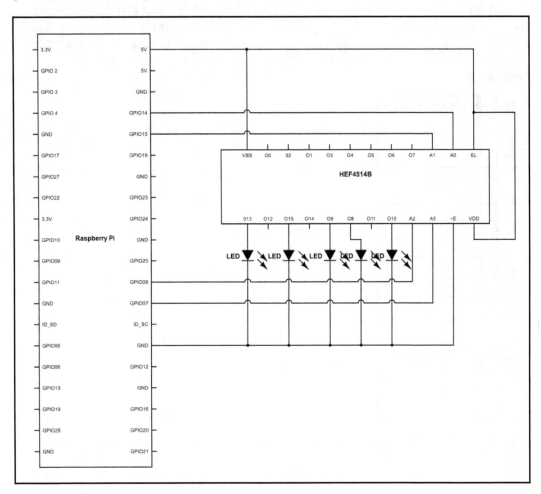

Once the hardware is connected, let's go ahead and upload the following code:

```
import RPi.GPIO as GPIO
import time

GPIO.setmode(GPIO.BCM)
GPIO.setwarnings(False)

S0 = 21
S1 = 22
S2 = 23
S3 = 24

GPIO.setup(S0,GPIO.OUT)
GPIO.setup(S1,GPIO.OUT)
GPIO.setup(S2,GPIO.OUT)

While True:

        GPIO.output(S0,1)
        GPIO.output(S1,0)
        GPIO.output(S2,1)
        GPIO.output(S4,1)

        time.sleep(1)

        GPIO.output(S0,1)
        GPIO.output(S1,1)
        GPIO.output(S2,1)
        GPIO.output(S4,1)

        time.sleep(1)

        GPIO.output(S0,1)
        GPIO.output(S1,0)
        GPIO.output(S2,0)
        GPIO.output(S4,1)

        time.sleep(1)

        'GPIO.output(S0,0)
        GPIO.output(S1,0)
        GPIO.output(S2,0)
        GPIO.output(S4,1)

        time.sleep(1)

        GPIO.output(S0,0)
```

```
GPIO.output(S1,1)
GPIO.output(S2,0)
GPIO.output(S4,1)

time.sleep(1)  }
```

Here, what we are essentially doing is, triggering the selection lines one by one to address every single port where the LED is connected. Whenever that happens, the LED corresponding to it glows. Also, the reason it glows is because the signal port `Sig` is connected to 3.3V of Raspberry Pi. Hence, send a logic high to whichever port it is connected to.

This is one of the basic ways in which the multiplexer works. This can be incredibly useful when we will be using multiple devices and sensors.

Summary

In this chapter, we enabled Jarvis to automate your home appliances under different conditions, also applying various properties to the system. So go on and try many other scenarios under which you can enhance your home automation system.

In the next chapter, we will enable Jarvis IoT, thus controlling the appliances from your mobile phone using Wi-Fi and the internet.

26
Making Jarvis IoT Enabled

There was a time when we used to imagine controlling the world with our fingertips. Now, this imagination has become a reality. With the advent of smartphones, we have been doing stuff which one could have only imagined until a decade back. With mobile phones becoming smart, the industry and businesses have also tried their best to keep up with the disruptive change. However, there is one part that is still lagging behind. Which is that part? Your home!

Think about what you can control in your home using your smartphone? Not many things! There are some devices that can turn on or off a bunch of devices such as your AC. However, the list is exhaustive. So, with all the knowledge gained in the previous chapters and the powerful hardware in our hands, why don't we become the trendsetters and the disrupters and make something that is still just a part of our imagination.

The following topics will be covered in this chapter:

- Basics of **Internet of Things (IoT)**
- **Message Queuing Telemetry Transport (MQTT)** protocol
- Setting up MQTT broker
- Making an IoT-based intrusion detector
- Controlling the home

Basics of IoT

In this chapter, we will be controlling devices in our home using our smartphones, but before doing this, we should understand the basics of this technology. The first topic of this chapter is IoT—the overused jargon in the modern world. It is something that everyone wants to know about but no one does. IoT can be related to a technology, where your refrigerator will tell you what items are low in supply and will order it automatically for you. Poor thing! This technology has some time to invade our houses. But IoT does not mean this alone. IoT is a very wide term, something which can be applied to almost all the places for optimization. So what is IoT then?

Let's break this acronym, **Internet of Things** sometimes also known as cyber physical systems. Now, what is **Things**? Any electronic object that has the ability to collect or receive data without human intervention can be called a thing here. So this thing can be your mobile, a pacemaker, a health monitoring device, and so on. The only *if* is that it should be connected to the internet and has the ability to collect and/or receive data. The second term is **Internet**; the internet refers to the internet, Duh! Now, all of these IoT devices send and receive data from a cloud or a central computer. The reason why it does that is because any IoT device, whether big or small, is considered a resource-constrained environment. That is, the resources such as computing power is much less. This is because the IoT devices have to be simple and cheap. Imagine you have to put IoT sensors on all of the street lights to monitor traffic. If the device costs $500, then it would be impractical to install this kind of device. However, if it could be made for $5-$10, then no one would bat an eye. That's the thing with IoT devices; they are extremely cheap. Now the flip side to this story is that they do not have a lot of computing power. Hence, to balance this equation, instead of computing the raw data on their own processors, they simply send this data to a cloud computing device or perhaps a server where this data is computed and the meaningful result is taken. So, this solves all our problems then. Well, no! The second problem with these devices are that they can be battery operated, use-and-throw devices as well. For example, where temperature sensors are installed all across the forests; in such situations, no one and absolutely no one will go and change the batteries every week. Hence, these devices are made in such a way that they consume little to almost no power, thereby making the programming very tricky.

Now that we have understood the IoT concepts, in this chapter, we'll be making our home IoT enabled. This means, we will be able to receive and collect data from the sensors from our home, see it on our mobile devices, and if needed, we can control the devices using your smartphones as well. There is one thing though, instead of computing it on cloud, we will simply be uploading all of our data onto the cloud and just accessing that data or sending our data to the cloud from where it can be accessed. We will be talking about the cloud computing aspect in a different book as this can be a whole new dimension and will be out of the scope of this book.

The MQTT protocol

MQTT is an ISO-certified protocol and is in use very widely. The interesting thing about this protocol is that it was developed by Andy Stanford and Arlen Nipper in 1999 for monitoring of an oil pipeline through the desert. As you can imagine, in middle of a desert, the protocol they developed had to be energy efficient and bandwidth efficient as well.

How this protocol works is quite interesting. It has a publish-subscribe architecture. This means, it has a central server, which we also call a broker. Any device can register with this broker and publish any meaningful data onto it. Now, the data that is being published should have a topic, for example, air temperature.

These topics are particularly important. Why, you may ask? To the broker, there can be one or many devices that can be connected. With the connection, they also need to subscribe to a topic. Let's say they are subscribed to the topic *Air*-Temperature. Now, whenever any new data comes, it gets published to the subscribed devices.

One important thing to know is that there need not be any request to gain the data from the broker like what we have in HTTP. Rather, whenever the data is received, it will be pushed to the device which is subscribed to that topic. It is very obvious that the TCP protocol will also be up and working during the whole time and the port related to the broker will always be connected for seamless data transmission. However, should there be any break in the data, the broker will buffer all the data and send it to the subscriber whenever the connection is resumed.

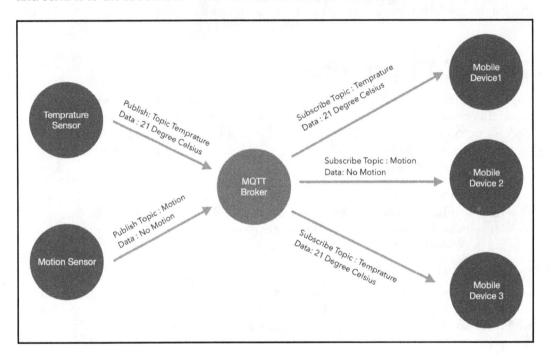

As you can see The motion sensor and the temperature sensors are giving the data to MQTT server by a specific topic namely **Temperature** and **Motion**. Those whose are subscribed to these topics would get the reading from this device. Hence there is no direct communication needed between the actual sensor and the mobile device.

The good thing about this whole architecture is that there can be limitless devices attached with this protocol and there need not be any scalability issues. Also, the protocol is relatively simple and easy to work with even a huge amount of data. Hence, this becomes the preferred protocol for IoT as it provides an easy, scalable, and seamless link between the data producer and the data receivers.

Setting up the MQTT broker

In this topic let's see what we have to do to set up this server. Open up your command line and type in these following lines:

```
sudo apt-get update
sudo apt-get upgrade
```

Once the update and upgrade processes are complete, go ahead and install the following packages:

```
sudo apt-get install mosquitto -y
```

This will install the Mosquitto broker onto your Raspberry Pi. This broker will take care of all the data transfer:

```
sudo apt-get install mosquitto-clients -y
```

Now, this line will install the client packages. As you can imagine, Raspberry Pi in itself will be a client to the broker. Hence, it will take care of the needful.

We have now installed the packages; yes exactly, it was that small. Now, all we need to do is configure the Mosquitto broker. To do this, you need to type in the following command:

```
sudo nano etc/mosquitto/mosquitto.conf
```

Now, this command will open the file where the Mosquitto file configuration is saved. To configure it, you need to get to the end of this file, where you will see the following:

```
include_dir/etc/mosquitto/conf.d
```

Now, you can comment out the the preceding line of code by simply adding # before the lines. Once done then go ahead and add the following lines:

```
allow_anonymous false
```

```
password_file /etc/mosquitto/pwfile
```

```
listener 1883
```

Let's see what we have done here. The `allow_anonymous false` line tells the broker that not everyone can access the data. The next line, `password_file /etc/mosquitto/pwfile` is telling the broker the location of password file, which is located at `/etc/mosquitto/pwfile`. Finally, we will define the port of this broker, which is `1883`, using the `listener 1883` command.

So finally, we have completed setting up the MQTT client in our Raspberry Pi. Now we are ready to go ahead and use it for the IoT-enabled home.

Making an IoT-based intrusion detector

Now that Raspberry Pi is set up and we are ready to make it IoT enabled let's see how we are going to connect the system to the internet and make things work. Firstly, we need to connect Raspberry Pi to the devices, which we want to control using the IoT technology. So go ahead and use the following diagram to make the connection:

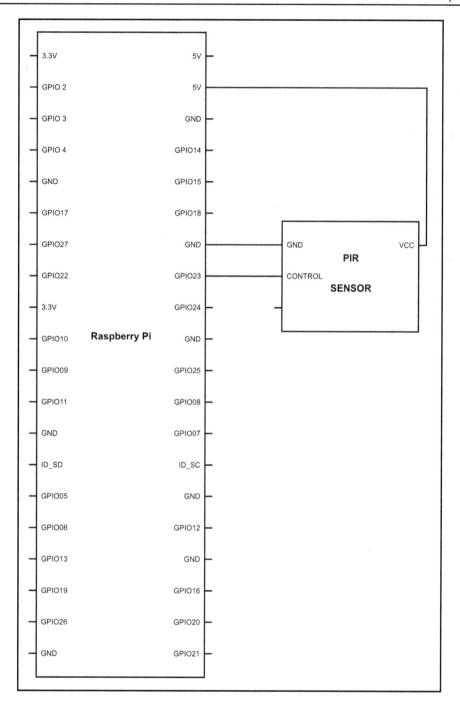

Once you have set up all the components, let's go ahead and upload the following code:

```
import time
import paho.mqtt.client as mqtt
import RPi.gpio as gpio
pir = 23
gpio.setmode(gpio.BCM)
gpio.setup(pir, gpio.IN)
client = mqtt.Client()
broker="broker.hivemq.com"
port = 1883
pub_topic = "IntruderDetector_Home"
def SendData():
  client.publish(pub_topic,"WARNING : SOMEONE DETECTED AT YOUR PLACE")

def on_connect(client, userdata, flag,rc):
  print("connection returned" + str(rc))
  SendData()
while True:
  client.connect(broker,port)
  client.on_connect = on_connect
  if gpio.output(pir) == gpio.HIGH :
    SendData()
  client.loop_forever()
```

This code, unlike the other chunks of code that we have seen so far, will be quite new to you. So I will be explaining every part of it except for a few obvious parts. So, let's see what we have here:

```
import paho.mqtt.client as mqtt
```

In this part, we are importing the `pho.mqtt.client` library as `mqtt`. So whenever this library needs to be accessed, we simply need to use the line `mqtt` instead of the entire name of the library.

```
client = mqtt.Client()
```

We are defining a client using the client method of the `mqtt` library. This can be called using the `client` variable.

```
broker="broker.hivemq.com"
```

So we are defining the broker in our program. For this program, we are using the broker as `broker.hivemq.com`, which is providing us the broker services.

```
port = 1883
```

Now as we have done earlier, we will once again define the port at which the protocol will be working, which in our case is `1883`.

```
pub_topic = "IntuderDetector_Home"
```

Here, we are defining the value of the variable called `pub_topic`, which is `IntruderDetector_Home`. This will be the final topic to which one can subscribe once the code is running.

```
def SendData():
    client.publish(pub.topic, "WARNING : SOMEONE DETECTED AT YOUR
PLACE")
```

Here, we are defining a function called `SendData()`, will publish the data `Warning : SOMEONE DETECTED AT YOUR PLACE` to the broker with the topic which we had declared previously.

```
def on_message(client, userdata, message):

  print('message is : ')
  print(str(message.payload))
```

In this line, we are defining a function named `on_message()`, which will print a value `message is :` followed by whatever the data is. This will be done using the line `print(str(message.payload))`. What this is doing is, it is printing whatever is being passed on in the arguments of the function.

```
def on_connect(client, userdata, flag,rc):

    print("connection returned" + str(rc))
    SendData()
```

In this line, we are defining the `on_connect()` function, which will print the line `connection returned` followed by the value of `rc`. `rc` stands for return code. So, whenever the message is delivered, a code is generated, even if it is not, then the specific code will be returned notifying the error. So, consider this as an acknowledgement. After this is done, the `SendData()` function that we defined earlier will be used to send the data to the broker.

```
client.connect(broker,port)
```

`connect()` is a function of the MQTT library which connects the client to the broker. Doing this is very simple. All we need to do is pass on the arguments of the broker which we want to connect to and the port which would be used. In our case, `broker = broker.hivemq.com` and `port = 1883`. So when we call the function, Raspberry Pi gets connected to our broker.

```
client.on_connect = on_connect
```

This is the heart of the program. What the `client.on_connect` function is doing is that every time Raspberry Pi gets connected to the broker, it starts executing the `on_connect` function defined by us. This in-turn will send the data continuously to the broker after every 5 seconds, exactly the way in which we have defined in the function. This process is also called callback, which makes it event driven. That is, if it is not connected, it will not try to send the data to the broker.

```
if gpio.output(pir) == HIGH :
    sendData()
```

the sendData() function is called when the PIR sensor gets high or whenever the motion is detected the message is sent on the broker with the warning that someone is detected at your place.

```
client.loop_forever()
```

This is my favorite function, especially because of the lovely name it has. As you can expect, the `client.loop_forver()` function will keep looking for any event and whenever it is detected it will trigger the data to be sent to the broker. Now comes the part where we will see this data. For this, we'll have to download the *MyMQTT* app from App Store if you are running iOS or from Playstore if you are running android.

Once you start the app, you will be presented with the preceding screen. You need to fill in the name of the broker URL, which in our case is `broker.hivemq.com`. Then, fill in the port, which in our case is `1883`.

Once this is done, you will see a screen similar to the following:

Simply add the name of the subscription you need, which is `IntruderDetector_Home`. Once done, you'll see the magic!

In the next section, we will be controlling things based on IoT; see you then.

Controlling the home

Finally, using the following diagram, make the connections and upload the following code:

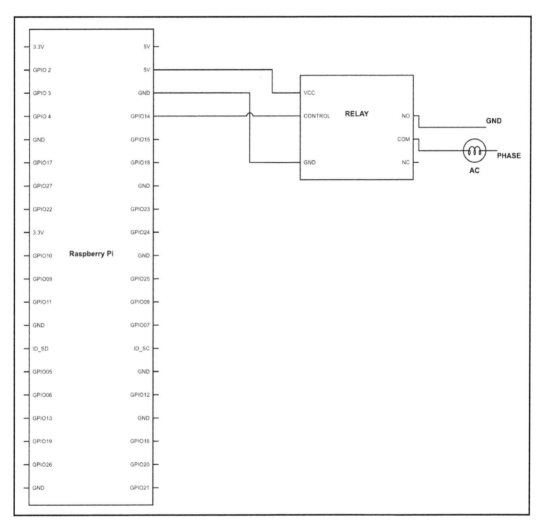

```
import time
import paho.mqtt.client as paho
import RPi.GPIO as GPIO
GPIO.setmode(GPIO.BCM)
GPIO.setup(14,GPIO.OUT)
broker="broker.hivemq.com"
```

```
sub_topic = light/control
client = paho.Client()
def on_message(client, userdata, message):
    print('message is : ')
    print(str(message.payload))
    data = str(message.payload)
    if data == "on":
        GPIO.output(3,GPIO.HIGH)
    elif data == "off":
        GPIO.output(3,GPIO.LOW)

def on_connect(client,userdata, flag, rc):
    print("connection returned" + str(rc))
    client.subscribe(sub_topic)
client.connect(broker,port)
client.on_connect = on_connect
client.on_message=on_message
client.loop_forever()
```

Now, there is not much I need to tell you in this code; it's pretty straightforward. We are sending the data just like we did last time. However, this time we are using a new function. So, let's see what this code is all about:

```
def on_message(client, userdata, message):

        print('message is : ')
        print(str(message.payload))
        data = str(message.payload)

        if data == "on":
            GPIO.output(3,GPIO.HIGH)

        elif data == "off":
            GPIO.output(3,GPIO.LOW)
```

Here we are defining what the `on_message()` function is doing. There are three arguments to the function over which the message would be working on. This includes `client`, which we have already declared previously; `userdata`, which we are not using right now; and finally, `message`, which we will be sending through our smartphones over the internet.

Once you look inside the program, this function will print the message using the lines `print('message is : ')` and `print(str(message.payload))`. Once this is done, the value of `data` will be set as the message sent by the subscriber.

This data will be evaluated by our conditions. If the data is kept `on`, then the GPIO port number 3 will be set to `HIGH`, and if the string is `off`, then the GPIO port number 3 will be set to `LOW`—in simple words, switching your device on or off your device.

```
def on_connect(client,userdata, flag, rc):
    print("connection returned" + str(rc))
    client.subscribe(sub_topic)
```

We have defined the `on_connect()` function previously as well. However, this time it is slightly different. Rather than just printing the connection returned with the value of `rc`, we are also using another function called `client.subscribe(sub_topic)`, which will let us get connected to the broker on the specific topic that we have defined earlier in this program.

```
client.on_message=on_message
```

As we know that the entire algorithm is based on an event-driven system, this `client.on_message` function will keep waiting for a message to be received. Once received, it will then execute the `on_message` function. This will decide whether to turn the appliance on or off.

To use it, just go ahead and send the data based on the topic and it will be received by your Raspberry Pi.

Once received, the decision-making function, on_message(), will decide what data is being received by the MyMQTT app. If the data received is on, then the lights will be turned on. If the data received is off, then the lights will be turned off. It's as simple as that.

Summary

In this chapter, we have understood the basics of IoT and how the MQTT server works. We also made an intruder detection system that will alert you whenever someone is in your home, no matter where you are in the world. Finally, we also created a system to switch on a device in your home using a simple mobile command. In the next chapter, we will let Jarvis enable to let you interact with the system based on your voices.

Giving Voice to Jarvis

27

Ever wondered whether using robots to get our work done is possible? Well yes! Certainly in some high-tech fiction or Marvel movies or even comic books. So, get your seat belt tight and get ready for this amazing chapter where you will actually be implementing what I just mentioned.

This chapter will cover the following topics:

- Basic installation
- Automatic delivery answering machine
- Making an interactive door answering robot
- Making Jarvis understand our voice

Basic installation

There are various ways and methods through which we can control our smart home Jarvis, some of which we have explored earlier such as controlling it through. So, to start with, we need to prepare our system to be able to do speech synthesis; to do that, let's perform the following process.

First, go to the terminal and enter the following command:

```
sudo apt-get install alsa-utils
```

What this will do is install the dependency `alsa-utils`. The `alsa-utils` package contains various utilities that are useful for controlling your sound drivers.

Once this is done, you need to edit the file. To do it, we need to open the file. Use the following command:

```
sudo nano /etc/modules
```

Once that is done, a file will open; at the bottom of that file, you need to add the following line:

```
snd_bcm2835
```

You don't need to get too much into why we are doing it. It's just there to set things up. I can give you an explanation; however, I do not wish to bore you at this exciting moment.

Also, if you are lucky, then sometimes, you might find the line to be already present. If that is the case, then let it be there and don't touch it.

Now, to play the sounds that we need the Jarvis to say, we need an audio player. No, not the one that you have at your home. We are talking about the software that would play it.

To install the player, we need to run the following commands:

```
sudo apt-get install mplayer
```

All right, we are done with audio player; let's see what we have next. Now, again, we need to edit the file of the media player. We will use the same steps to open the file and edit it:

```
sudo nano /etc/mplayer/mplayer.conf
```

This will open the file. As before, simply add the following line:

```
nolirc=yes
```

Finally, we need to give it some voice, so run the following command:

```
sudo apt-get install festvox-rablpc16k
```

This will install a 16 kHz, British, male, voice to Jarvis. We love British accents, don't we?

Perfect. Once we have done all of the steps mentioned previously, we would be good to go. To test the voice, simply connect a USB speaker to the Raspberry Pi and run the following code:

```
import os
from time import sleep
os.system('echo "hello! i am raspberry pi robot"|festival --tts ')
sleep(2)
os.system('echo "how are you?"| festival --tts ')
sleep(2)
os.system('echo "I am having fun."| festival --tts ')
sleep(2)
```

All right then, let's see what we have actually done:

```
import os
```

As you might have figured out, we are importing the library named `os`. This library provides a way of using operating-system-dependent functionality:

```
os.system('echo "Hello from the other side"|festival --tts ')
```

Here, we are using a method called `system()`; what this does is that it executes a shell command. You might be wondering what this is. A shell command is a command used by the user to access the functionality of a system to interact with it. So now that we want to convert our text to voice, we would be providing two arguments to this function. First, what is the text? In our case, it is `Hello from the other side`; the second argument that we have here is `festival --tts`. Now `festival` is a library, and `tts` stands for text to speech conversion. So when we pass it on to the argument, the system will know that the text passed on to the argument has to be converted from text to speech.

And that's it! Yes, that's it. That's all we have to do to make your Raspberry speak.

Automatic delivery answering machine

These days, we all order things online. Yet no matter how automated the process of Amazon is, when talking about 2018, we still have humans delivering the packages to our doorsteps. Sometimes, you want them to know a few things about where to leave the parcel. Now that we are becoming more and more automated, gone are the days when you might leave a note outside your gate. It's time to make something really interesting with our technology. To do that, we hardly need to do anything serious. All we need to do is to wire up the components as shown in the following diagram:

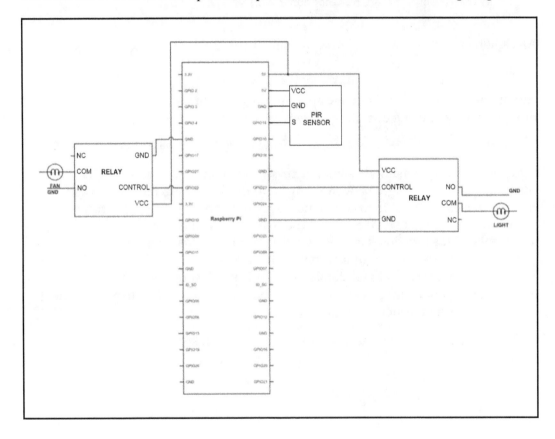

The PIR sensor must be placed so that it gives a logic high whenever there is movement around the gate.

Once that is done, go ahead and upload the following code:

```
import RPi.GPIO as GPIO
import time
Import os
GPIO.setmode(GPIO.BCM)
PIR = 13
GPIO.setup(PIR,GPIO.IN)
while True:

   if GPIO.input(PIR) == 1 :
      os.system('echo "Hello, welcome to my house"|festival --tts ')
      time.sleep(0.2)
      os.system('echo "If you are a delivery agent then please leave
the package here"|festival --tts ')
      time.sleep(0.2)
      os.system('echo "If you are a guest then I'm sorry I have to
leave I will be back after 7pm"|festival --tts ')
      time.sleep(0.2)
      os.system('echo "also Kindly don't step over the grass, its
freshly grown and needs some time"|festival --tts ')
      time.sleep(1)
      os.system('echo "Thank you !"|festival --tts ')
```

Now what we have done is very simple. As soon as the PIR sensor gives a logic high, a certain instruction is spoken. There is no need of an explanation. You can refer to the previous code if you need any clarification.

Making an interactive door – answering robot

In the previous chapter we have used a PIR sensor to sense any human activity, however the problem with the sensor is, that no matter who comes or leaves it would deliver the same message. That basically means that even when you come home after a long day, it would end up asking the same question. Pretty dumb huh?

So in this chapter we would use the previous repository and integrate the vision and the voice together to make an amazing duo. In this, the camera would identify who is on the gate and would recognize if it is a human and a stranger, if so then, it would deliver the message you intend to give. On the other hand if its you then it would simply let you pass with a simple greeting. However if the face is detected but not recognized then it would give a set of instructions to the person standing in-front of the camera.

To implement it all you need to do is to set up a camera on the gate of your door along with the PIR. The PIR is basically to activate the camera. In other words the camera would not get activated till the time no movement is detected. This set up is very straight forward and does not need any GPIO to be used. Simply fix the camera and PIR and upload the following code:

```
import RPi.GPIO as GPIO
import time
Import os
import cv2
import numpy as np
import cv2

faceDetect =
cv2.CascadeClassifier('haarcascade_frontalface_default.xml')
cam = cv2.VideoCapture(0)
rec = cv2.face.LBPHFaceRecognizer_create()
rec.read("recognizer/trainningData.yml")
id = 0

while True:

   GPIO.setmode(GPIO.BCM)
PIR = 13
GPIO.setup(PIR, GPIO.IN)

if GPIO.input(PIR) == 1:
```

```
    ret, img = cam.read()
gray = cv2.cvtColor(img, cv2.COLOR_BGR2GRAY)
faces = faceDetect.detectMultiScale(gray, 1.3, 5)
for (x, y, w, h) in faces:
    cv2.rectangle(img, (x, y), (x + w, y + h), (0, 0, 255), 2)
id, conf = rec.predict(gray[y: y + h, x: x + w])

if id == 1:
    id = "BEN"
os.system('echo "Hello, welcome to the house BEN"|festival --tts ')
time, sleep(0.2)

else :

    os.system('echo "If you are a delivery agent then please leave the
package here"|festival --tts ')
time, sleep(0.2)

os.system('echo "If you are a guest then I'
    m sorry I have to leave I will be back after 7 pm "|festival --tts
')
    time, sleep(0.2)

    os.system('echo "also Kindly don'
        t step over the grass, its freshly grown and needs some time
"|festival --tts ')
        time.sleep(1)

    os.system('echo "Thank you !"|festival --tts ')
cv2.imshow("face", img) if cv2.waitKey(1) == ord('q'):
        break cam.release()

        cv2.destroyAllWindows()

faceDetect =
cv2.CascadeClassifier('haarcascade_frontalface_default.xml')
```

In the preceding code, we are creating a cascade classifier using the method
`CascadeClassifier` so that faces can be detected by the camera.

```
cam = cv2.VideoCapture(0)
rec = cv2.face.LBPHFaceRecognizer_create()
```

In the preceding code, we are reading the frames from the camera using
`VideoCapture(0)` method of `cv2`. Also, the face recognizer is being created to
recognize a particular face.

```
    ret, img = cam.read()
```

Now read the data from the camera using `cam.read()` as done in the previous code.

```
gray = cv2.cvtColor(img,cv2.COLOR_BGR2GRAY)
faces = faceDetect.detectMultiScale(gray,1.3,5)
```

The images are converted into gray color. Then, `faceDetect.detectMultiScale()` will be using the gray color-converted images.

```
for (x,y,w,h) in faces:
    cv2.rectangle(img, (x,y), (x+w, y+h), (0,0,255), 2)
    id, conf = rec.predict(gray[y:y+h, x:x+w])
    if id==1:
        id = "BEN"
        os.system('echo "Hello, welcome to my house BEN"|festival --
tts ')
        time, sleep(0.2)
```

As the face is detected, the part of the image containing the face will be converted into gray and passed to a predict function. This method will tell if the face is known or not, it also returns the ID if the face is identified. Suppose the person is BEN, then Jarvis would say `Hello, welcome to my house BEN`. Now BEN can tell the Jarvis to turn on the lights, and the Jarvis would respond as the wake word Jarvis gets activated. And if the person is not recognized, then maybe it was a delivery boy. Then, the following commands get executed:

```
os.system('echo "If you are a delivery agent then please leave the
package here"|festival --tts ')
time, sleep(0.2)

os.system('echo "If you are a guest then I'm sorry I have to leave I
will be back after 7pm"|festival --tts ')
 time, sleep(0.2)

os.system('echo "also Kindly don't step over the grass, its freshly
grown and needs some time"|festival --tts ')
time.sleep(1)

os.system('echo "Thank you !"|festival --tts ')
```

Making Jarvis understand our voice

Voice is an essence of communication. It helps us transfer huge amounts of data in a very short period of time. It is certainly faster and easier than typing. Hence, more and more companies are working toward making systems that understands human voice and language and work according to them. It is certainly not easy because of the huge variations that are present in the language; however, we have come a considerable distance. So without much time, let's make our system get ready to recognize our voice.

So here, we would be using an API from Google Voice. As you may know, Google is really good at understanding what you say. Like, very literally. So it makes sense to use their API. Now, the way it works is very simple. We capture the voice, and we convert it into the text. Then, we compare if the text is similar to something we have defined in the configuration file. If it matches with anything, the bash command associated with it will be executed.

First, we need to check whether the microphone is connected. To do that, run the following command:

```
lsusb
```

This command will show you a list of devices connected on USB. If you see yours on the list, then thumbs up, you are on the right track. Otherwise, try finding it with the connection or maybe try another hardware.

We also need to set the recording volume to high. To do this, go ahead and type the following command on the serial:

```
alsamixer
```

Now once the GUI pops on to the screen, toggle the volume using the arrow keys.

It's best to hear the sound recorded by yourself rather than directly giving it down to the Raspberry. To do that first, we need to record our voice, so we need to run the following command:

```
arecord -l
```

This will check whether the webcam is on the list. Then, write the following command to record:

```
arecord -D plughw:1,0 First.wav
```

The sound will be recorded with the following name, `First.wav`.

Now we would also like to listen to what we just recorded. The simple way to do that is by typing the following command:

```
aplay test.wav
```

Check whether the voice is correct. If not, then you are free to make any adjustments to the system.

Once we are done with checking the sound and the microphone, it's time to install the real software for the job. There are simple ways with which you can do it. The following is a list of commands that you need to run:

```
wget -- no-check-certificate "http://goo.gl/KrwrBa" -O
PiAUISuite.tar.gz

tar -xvzf PiAUISuite.tar.gz

cd PiAUISuite/Install/

sudo ./InstallAUISuite.sh
```

Now when you run this, very interesting things will start to happen. It will start to ask you various questions. Some of them will be straightforward. You can use your right mind to give the answers to it in the form of yes or no. Others could be very technical. As these questions might change over time, there seems to be no need to explicitly mention the answers that you need to fill, but as a general rule of thumb—Give it a yes unless it's something you really want to say no to.

Perfect then, we have installed the software. Now before you go any further in that software, let's go ahead and write the following programs:

```
import RPi.GPIO as GPIO
import time
import os
GPIO.setmode(GPIO.BCM)
LIGHT = 2
GPIO.setup(LIGHT,GPIO.OUT)
GPIO.output(LIGHT, GPIO.HIGH)
os.system('echo "LIGHTS TURNED ON "|festival --tts')
```

Whenever this program runs, the light that is connected on PIN number 2 will be turned on. Also, it will read out LIGHTS TURNED ON. Save this file with the name lighton.py:

```
import RPi.GPIO as GPIO
import time
import os
GPIO.setmode(GPIO.BCM)
LIGHT = 23
GPIO.setup(LIGHT,GPIO.OUT)
GPIO.output(LIGHT, GPIO.LOW)
os.system('echo "LIGHTS TURNED OFF "|festival --tts')
```

Similarly, in this program, the light would be turned off and it would read out LIGHTS TURNED OFF. Save it by the name lightoff.py:

```
import RPi.GPIO as GPIO
import time
Import os
GPIO.setmode(GPIO.BCM)
FAN = 22
GPIO.setup(FAN,GPIO.OUT)
GPIO.output(LIGHT, GPIO.HIGH)
os.system('echo "FAN TURNED ON "|festival --tts')
```

Now we are doing the same thing for the fan as well. In this one, the fan will be switched on; save it with the name fanon.py:

```
import RPi.GPIO as GPIO
import time
Import os
GPIO.setmode(GPIO.BCM)
FAN = 22
GPIO.setup(FAN,GPIO.OUT)
GPIO.output(LIGHT, GPIO.LOW)os.system('echo "FAN TURNED OFF "|festival
--tts')
```

I don't need to explain the same thing for this do I? As you will have guessed, save it with the name fanoff.py.

All right! When all of this is done, then type the following command to check whether the software is installed properly:

```
voicecommand -c
```

Raspberry Pi responds to the wake word `pi`; let's change it to `jarvis`. All these changes can be made after opening the configuration file using the following command:

```
voicecommand -e.
```

In that file, enter the commands of your own. Here, let's add the following code:

```
LIGHT_ON

LIGHT_OFF

FAN_ON

FAN_OFF
```

Now for each command, define the action. The action would be to run the Python file that contains the code for switching the lights and fan on or off. The code is basic and simple to understand. Add the following to the file:

```
LIGHT ON = sudo python lighton.py

LIGHT OFF = sudo python lightoff.py

FAN ON = sudo python fanon.py

FAN OFF = sudo python fanoff.py
```

Now, let's see what we have done. Whenever you say *Jarvis, light on*, it will convert your speed to text, compare it with the program that it has to run corresponding to it and will do whatever is there in the program. Hence, in this program, whenever we say *Light on*, the lights will be turned on and similarly for the rest of the commands as well. Remember to make it listen to what you are saying. You would have to say the word, *Jarvis*, which will make it attentive to the commands and ready to listen.

Summary

In this chapter, we understood how to interact and make the Jarvis work according to our needs. If this chapter was about verbal communication, then the next chapter is about gesture recognition where, using advanced capacitive techniques, you will be able to control your automation system just by waving at it.

Gesture Recognition 28

Since the beginning of time, humans have communicated with each other using gestures, even before there wasn't any formal language. Hand gestures were the primary way of communication, and it is also evident in the ancient sculptures found all across the world that the signs have been a successful way of transferring a huge amount of data in a very efficient way, sometimes, even more efficient than language itself.

Gestures are natural, and they can occur as a reflex to a certain situation. It also happens subconsciously even without our knowing. So, it becomes an ideal way of communication with various devices. However, the question remains, how?

We can be sure that if we are talking about gestures, then we would surely have to do a lot of programming to identify the gestures in the videos; furthermore, it would require a huge amount of processing power to make it happen as well. Hence, it is out of the question. We can build some basic gesture-recognition system using an array of proximity sensors. However, the range of gestures recognized would be very limited, and the overall ports being used would be multiple fold.

Hence, we need to find a solution that is easy to work with and does not cost more than what it would deliver.

This chapter will be covering the following topics:

- Electric field sensing
- Using the Flick HAT
- Gesture recognition-based automation

Electric field sensing

Near-field sensing is a very interesting field of sensing. Be prepared for some interesting stuff. If you are feeling a little sleepy, or if you are lacking attention, then get some coffee because the working principle of this system is going to be a little new.

Whenever there is a charge, there is an associated electrical field that comes along with it. These charges propagate through the space and go around an object. When that happens, the electric field associated with it has a specific characteristic. This characteristic will be the same till the time the environment around it is empty.

For the gesture-recognition board that we are using, the field that would be sensed around it is only for about a few centimeters, so anything beyond that point can be disregarded. If there is nothing in that vicinity, then we can safely assume that the pattern of electric field being sensed would be unchanged. However, whenever an object such as our hand comes in the vicinity, then these waves are distorted. The distortion is directly linked to the position of the object and its position. With this distortion, we can sense where the finger is, and with constant sensing, we see what kind of motion is being performed. The board in question looks like this:

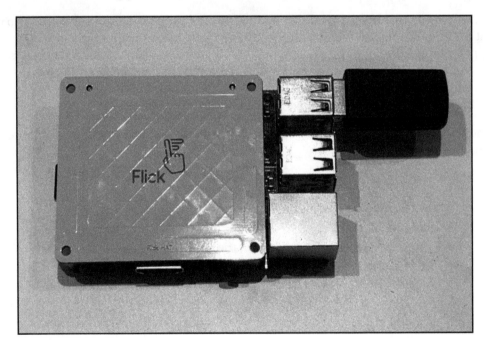

The central criss-crossed area on the board is the transmitter and on the extreme sides are rectangular structures that are four in number. These are the sensing elements. These sense the pattern of waves in the space. Based on it, they can derive what are the x, y, and z coordinates of the object. This is powered by a chip named MGC 3130. This does all the computation and delivers the raw reading to the user, regarding the coordinates.

Using the Flick HAT

Flick HAT comes in the form of a shield, which you can simply plug into your Raspberry Pi and start using. However, once you do that, you will not be left with any GPIO pins. Hence, to save ourselves from that problem, we will be connecting it using male-to-female wires. This will give us access to the other GPIO pins and then we can have fun.

So, go ahead and connect it as follows. The following is a pin diagram of the Flick board:

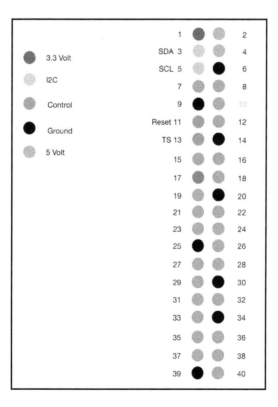

Thereafter, make the connections as follows:

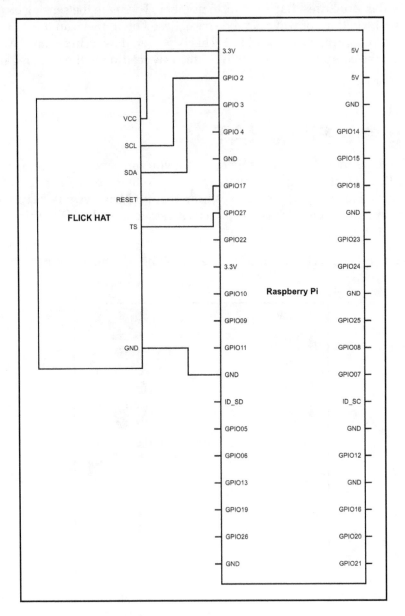

Once the connection is done, simply upload this code and see what happens:

```
import signal
import flicklib
import time
def message(value):
    print value
@flicklib.move()
def move(x, y, z):
    global xyztxt
    xyztxt = '{:5.3f} {:5.3f} {:5.3f}'.format(x,y,z)
@flicklib.flick()
def flick(start,finish):
    global flicktxt
    flicktxt = 'FLICK-' + start[0].upper() + finish[0].upper()
    message(flicktxt)
def main():
    global xyztxt
    global flicktxt
    xyztxt = ''
    flicktxt = ''
    flickcount = 0
    while True:

    xyztxt = ''
    if len(flicktxt) > 0 and flickcount < 5:
        flickcount += 1
    else:
        flicktxt = ''
        flickcount = 0
main()
```

Now once you have uploaded the code, lets go ahead and understand what this code is actually doing.

We are using a library called `import flicklib` this is provided by the manufacturer of this board. The functions of this library would be used all over in this chapter for communicating with the flick board and getting the data

```
def message(value):
    print value
```

Here, we are defining a function named `message(value)` what this would do is simply print whatever value would be passed on to the function in the argument:

```
@flicklib.move()
```

This has a special concept of decorators. By definition, a decorator is a function that takes another function and extends the behavior of the latter function without explicitly modifying it. In the preceding line of code, we are declaring that it is a decorator `@`.

This has a special job: dynamically defines any function in a program. What this means in plain English is that the function defined using this methodology can work differently depending on how the user defines it.

The function `move()` will further be complimented by the function, which is getting defined after it. These kind of functions are named nested functions. That is functions inside a function:

```
def move(x, y, z):
    global xyztxt
    xyztxt = '{:5.3f} {:5.3f} {:5.3f}'.format(x,y,z)
```

Here, we are defining a function named `move()`, which has arguments as `x`, `y`, and `z`. Inside the function, we have defined a global variable named `xyztxt`; now, the value of `xyztxt` would be in a form of five digit, with a decimal after three places. How did we know that? As you can see, we are using a function named `format()`. What this function does is format the values of a given variable according to the way the user has requested it for. We have declared here the value as `{:5.3f}`. `:5` represents that it would be of five digits, and `3f` represents that the decimal places would be after three digits. Hence, the format would be `xxx.xx`:

```
def flick(start,finish):
    global flicktxt
    flicktxt = 'FLICK-' + start[0].upper() + finish[0].upper()
    message(flicktxt)
```

Here, we have defined a function named `flick(start, finish)`. It has two arguments: `start` and `finish`. Using the line `flicktxt = 'FLICK-' + start[0].upper() + finish[0].upper()`, this is slicing the characters as recognized by the gesture board. If a south–north swipe is detected, then the start will get south and finish is north. Now we are only using the first characters of the words:

```
global xyztxt
global flicktxt
```

We are again defining the variables named `xyztxt` and `flicktxt` globally. Earlier, what we have done is that we have defined it in the function. Hence, it is important for us to define it in the main program:

```
if len(flicktxt) > 0 and flickcount < 5:
        flickcount += 1
else:
        flicktxt = ''
        flickcount = 0
```

The `flicktxt` variable would get a value corresponding to the gesture when the gesture is detected. In case there is no gesture then `flicktxt` would be left empty. A variable named `flickcount` will count how many times its swiped. If the values are out of the range specified then the `flicktxt` would be cleared to empty string using the line `flicktxt = ''` and `flickcount` would be made 0.

The final output of this would be a text given to user providing in which direction the hand is flicked.

Gesture recognition-based automation

Now we have interfaced the connections as per the following diagram:

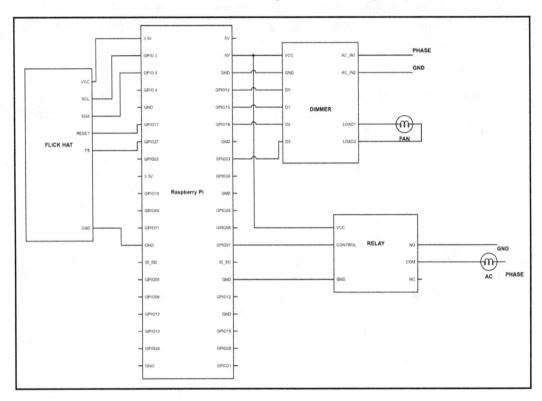

Let's go ahead and upload the following code:

```
import signal
import flicklib
import time
import RPi.GPIO as GPIO
GIPO.setmode(GPIO.BCM)
GPIO.setup(light, GPIO.OUT)
GPIO.setup(fan, GPIO.OUT)
pwm = GPIO.PWM(fan, 100)
def message(value):
    print value
@flicklib.move()
def move(x, y, z):
    global xyztxt
    xyztxt = '{:5.3f} {:5.3f} {:5.3f}'.format(x,y,z)
```

```
@flicklib.flick()
def flick(start,finish):
    global flicktxt
    flicktxt = 'FLICK-' + start[0].upper() + finish[0].upper()
    message(flicktxt)
def main():
    global xyztxt
    global flicktxt
    xyztxt = ''
    flicktxt = ''
    flickcount = 0
    dc_inc = 0
    dc_dec = 0
while True:
  pwm.start(0)
  xyztxt = ' '
  if len(flicktxt) > 0 and flickcount < 5:
    flickcount += 1
  else:
    flicktxt = ''

flickcount = 0
if flicktxt =="FLICK-WE":
  GPIO.output(light,GPIO.LOW)
if flicktxt =="FLICK-EW":
  GPIO.output(light,GPIO.HIGH)
if flicktxt =="FLICK-SN":
  if dc_inc < 100:
    dc_inc = dc_inc + 10
    pwm.changeDutyCycle(dc_inc)

else:
  Dc_inc = 10
  if flicktxt =="FLICK-NS":
    if dc_inc >0:
    dc_dec = dc_dec - 10
    pwm.changeDutyCycle(dc_dec)
main()
```

The program is in addition to the program we have done before, as always we have some added functionality of using the data being received by the flick gesture board and using it to switch on or switch off the lights.

Like the previous program, we are taking in the gestures over the board in the form of the directions of swipes, and using a simple condition to switch off the lights, or switch them on. So, let's see what are the additions:

```
if flicktxt =="FLICK-WE":

    GPIO.output(light,GPIO.LOW)
```

The first condition is simple. We are comparing the value of `flicktxt` to a given variable, which in our case is `FLICK-WE`, wherein `WE` stands for **west** to **east**. So when we flick from west to east, or in other words, when we flick from left to right, the lights would be switched off:

```
if flicktxt =="FLICK-EW":
    GPIO.output(light,GPIO.HIGH)
```

As before, we are again taking in a variable named `FLICK-EW`, which stands for flick from east to west. What it does is whenever we flick our hand from east to west, or from right to left, the lights will be switched on:

```
if flicktxt =="FLICK-SN":
    if dc_inc <= 100:
        dc_inc = dc_inc + 20
        pwm.changeDutyCycle(dc_inc)
```

Now we have put a dimmer along with a fan to control the speed of the fan as well; hence, we will have to give it a PWM corresponding to the speed that we want to drive it. Now whenever the user will flick his hand from south to north or from down to up. The condition `if dc_inc <100` will check whether the value of the `dc_inc` is less than or equal to `100` or not. If it is, then it will increment the value of the `dc_inc` by 20 values. Using the function `ChangeDutyCycle()`, we are providing the different duty cycle to the dimmer; hence, changing the overall speed of the fan. Every time you swipe up the value of the fan, it will increase by 20%:

```
else:
    Dc_inc = 10
    if flicktxt =="FLICK-NS":
    if dc_inc >0:
    dc_dec = dc_dec - 10
    pwm.changeDutyCycle(dc_dec)
```

Summary

In this chapter, we are were able to understand the concept of how gesture recognition works via electric field detection. We also understood how easy it is to use a gesture-controlled board and control the home using gestures. We will cover the machine learning part in the next chapter.

29
Machine Learning

Robots and computers from its primitive days to even right now are being programmed to do a set of activities. These activities can be very large. Hence, to develop complex programs, there is a need for a lot of software engineers who work day and night to achieve a certain functionality. This is workable when the problem is well defined. But what about situations when the problem is also way complex?

Learning is something that has made us humans what we are. Our experiences molded us to adapt to situations in a better and a more efficient way. Every time we do something, we know more. This makes us better at doing that task over a period of time. It is said practice makes a man perfect, and it is learning through doing things again and again that makes us better.

However, let us step back and define what learning is? I would like to quote Google here according to it, *It is a knowledge acquired through study, experience or being taught.* So, learning is basically a way of acquiring information from our surroundings to understand a process and its nature.

Now, you must be thinking, wait a minute, haven't we made our system learn a lot of vision data in previous chapters when we were making the guard robot. You would be absolutely correct to think so. However, the learning can be done in different ways. What may work for one kind of problem can be futile for some other kind of problem. Hence, there are various types of learning algorithms and their principles. In this chapter, we will be focusing on an algorithm named **k-nearest neighbor**. It's named the **lazy algorithm**. I love this algorithm personally for classification. Why? Because technically there is no training phase. How?

k-nearest neighbor is actually a smart algorithm. Rather than computing a regression of data provided and do a lot of mathematics calculations, it simply takes a structured data from the dataset provided. Whenever there is new data that has come in for prediction, then it simply searches the closest *k* match of the data provided by the user to the database based on its classification given. So, in this chapter, we will learn how this algorithm will work and how we can use it to make our home smart.

We will cover the following topics in this chapter:

- Making a dataset
- Prediction using dataset
- Making your home learn
- Home learning and automation

Making a dataset

We would now have to make a dummy dataset so that the machine learning algorithm can predict based on that data what should be done.

To make a dataset, we need to understand what data is being considered. In this chapter, we will be making a machine learning algorithm based on time and the temperature to predict whether the fan should be on or off. Hence, there are at least two things that should be provided by us to the system one being `Temperature`, and the other would be `Time` so that the prediction can take place. But one thing to remember is that we are talking about a supervised learning algorithm, so to train the model, we need to also give the outcome of `Temperature` and `Time` onto the state of the fan. Here, the state of the fan would be either on or off. Hence, we can depict it using `0` or `1`. Now let's go ahead and make a dataset by ourselves.

Now, to make a dataset, you simply have to open Microsoft Excel and start writing the dataset as follows:

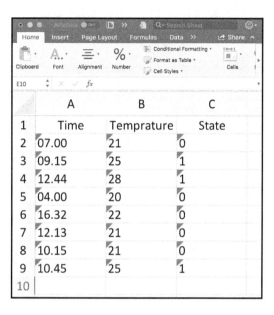

It is always better to have a dataset of more than 20 sets of data. Also, its important that the data has a distinct characteristic and its not random data. For example, in the preceding case, you can see that at 12.44 when the temperature is 28, the fan will be on; however, at the same time, when the time is 12.13 and temperature is 21, then the fan is off.

Once you have created a dataset, then you must save it with the name dataset in the CSV format. There may be some users who would not use a Microsoft Excel, in which case you can write the data with the same format in text editor and finally save it in the CSV format.

Once you have the dataset.csv files, then you must go ahead and copy them into the place where you will be saving the upcoming code. Once you are done, then we can move on to the next step.

Remember that the better the quality of data, the better the learning process. So you may take some time and carefully craft your dataset so that it does make sense.

Predicting using a dataset

Without much talking, let's take a look at the following code:

```python
import numpy as np
import pandas as pd
from sklearn.neighbors import KNeighborsClassifier

knn = KNeighborsClassifier(n_neighbors=5)
data = pd.read_csv('dataset.csv')

x = np.array(data[['Time', 'Temp']])
y = np.array(data[['State']]).ravel()

knn.fit(x,y)

time = raw_input("Enter time")
temp = raw_input("Enter temp")

data =. []

data.append(float(time))
data.append(float(temp))

a = knn.predict([data])

print(a[0])}
```

So, let's see what we are doing here:

```python
import numpy as np
```

We are importing numpy to our program; this helps us handle lists and matrices:

```python
import pandas as pd
```

Here, we are importing a library named pandas; this helps us read files in comma-separated values or in other words, CSV files. We will be using CSV files to store our data and access it for learning process:

```python
from sklearn.neighbors import KNeighborsClassifier
```

Here, we are importing `KneighborsClassifier` from the library `sklearn`. `sklearn` itself is a huge library; hence, we are importing only a part of it as we will not be using all of it in this program:

```
knn = KNeighborsClassifier(n_neighbors=5)
```

Here, we are giving value to variable `knn` wherein the value would be `KNeighborsClassifer(n_neighbors =5)`; what this means is that it is using the `KneighborsClassifer()` function with the argument as `n_neighbors=5`. This argument tells the `KneighborsClassifer` function that we will be having five neighbors in the algorithm. Further to this using this declaration, the whole function can be called using `knn`:

```
data = pd.read_csv('dataset.csv')
```

Here, we are providing value to a variable called `data` and the value passed is `pd.read_csv('dataset.csv')`; what this means is that whenever `data` is called, then a `pd.read_csv()` function from the `pandas` library will be called. The purpose of this function is to read data from the CSV files. Here, the argument passed is `dataset.csv`; hence, it is indicating which data would be read by the function. In our case, it will read from a file name: `dataset.csv`:

```
x = np.array(data[['Time', 'Temp']])
```

In the following line, we are passing value to the variable x, and the value being passed is `np.array(data[['Time, 'Temp']])`. Now the `np.array` function to make an array through the `numpy` library. This array will store the data by the name of `Time` and `Temp`:

```
y = np.array(data[['State']]).ravel()
```

Just like the previous time, we are storing `State` in an array made through the `numpy` library `.ravel()` function at the end would transpose the array. This is done so that the mathematical functions can be done between two arrays—x and y:

```
knn.fit(x,y)
```

In this small line, we are using the function from the `knn` library called `fit()` what it is doing is fitting the model using the x as the primary data and y as the output resultant data:

```
time = raw_input("Enter time")
temp = raw_input("Enter temp")
```

In this line, we are requesting the data from the user. In the first line, we will be printing `Enter time` and thereafter wait for user to enter the time. After user has entered the time, it will be stored in the variable named `time`. Once that is done, then it would move on to the next line; the code and it would print `Enter temp` once that is prompted to the user it would wait for data to be collected. Once data is fetched by the user, it will store that data in the variable called `temp`:

```
data =. []
```

Here, we are making an empty list by the name of `data`; this list will be used for calculating the resultant state of the output. As all the machine learning algorithm is working in list data type. Hence, the input must be given for decision in the form of a list itself:

```
data.append(float(time))
data.append(float(temp))
```

Here, we are adding data to the list that we just created with the name `data`. First, `time` will be added, followed by `temp`:

```
a = knn.predict([data])
```

Once that is done, a function named `predict` from the `knn` algorithm will be used to predict the output based on the list provided with the name of `data`. The output of the prediction algorithm is fetched to a variable by the name a:

```
print(a[0])
```

Finally, once the prediction is done, then we would read the value of a and remember that all the data I/O is happening in the form of lists. Hence, the data output given by the prediction algorithm would also be in the list format. Hence, we are printing the first element of the list.

This output will predict which state will be of the fan according to the dataset given by the user. So, go ahead and give a temperature and a time and let the system predict the outcome for you. See if it works fine or not. If it doesn't, then try adding some more datasets to the CSV files or see whether the values in the dataset actually make any sense. I am sure that you end up with a wonderful predictive system.

Making your home learn

Once this constitution is done, go ahead and wire it up, as shown here:

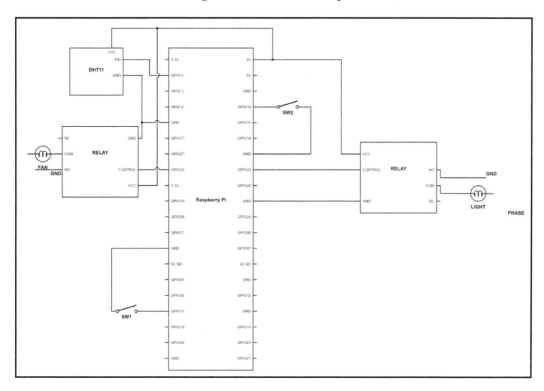

Once that is set, it is time for us to write the following code on to our Raspberry Pi:

```
import Adafruit_DHT
import datetime
import RPi.GPIO as GPIO
import time
import numpy as np
import pandas as pd
import Adafruit_DHT
from sklearn.neighbors import KNeighborsClassifier

GPIO.setmode(GPIO.BCM)
GPIO.setwarnings(False)

fan = 22
light = 23
sw1 = 13
```

```
    sw2 = 14

GPIO.setup(led1,GPIO.OUT)
GPIO.setup(led2,GPIO.OUT)
GPIO.setup(sw1,GPIO.IN)
GPIO.setup(sw2,GPIO.IN)

sensor = 11
pin = 2


f = open("dataset.csv","a+")
count = 0
while count < 50:

 data = ""

 H = datetime.datetime.now().strftime('%H')
 M = datetime.datetime.now().strftime('%M')

 data = str(H)+"."+str(M)
 humidity,temperature = Adafruit_DHT.read_retry(sensor,pin)
 data = data + "," + str(temperature)

prev_state = state

 if (GPIO.input(sw1) == 0) and (GPIO.input(sw2) == 0):
     state = 0
     GPIO.output(light,GPIO.LOW)
     GPIO.output(fan,GPIO.LOW)

 elif (GPIO.input(sw1) == 0) and (GPIO.input(sw2) == 1):
     state = 1
     GPIO.output(light,GPIO.HIGH)
     GPIO.output(fan,GPIO.LOW)

 elif (GPIO.input(sw1) == 1) and (GPIO.input(sw2) == 0):
    state = 2
     GPIO.output(light,GPIO.LOW)
     GPIO.output(fan,GPIO.HIGH)

 elif (GPIO.input(sw1) == 1) and (GPIO.input(sw2) == 1):
    state = 3
     GPIO.output(light,GPIO.HIGH)
     GPIO.output(fan,GPIO.HIGH)

 data = ","+str(state)
```

```
if prev_state =! state:

        f.write(data)
        count = count+1


    f.close()
```

Now, let's see what we have done here:

```
f = open("dataset.csv","a+")
```

In this line of the code, we have assigned the value `open("dataset.csv", "a+")` to the variable `f`. Thereafter, the `open()` function will open the file that is passed on to its argument, which in our case is `dataset.csv`; the argument `a+` stands for appending the value at the end of the CSV file. Hence, what this line will do is to open the file `dataset.csv` and add a value that we will pass later on:

```
data = ""
```

We are declaring an empty string by the name of `data`:

```
data = str(H)+"."+str(M)
```

We are adding values of hours and minutes to the string, separated by a dot in between for differentiation. Hence, the data will look like `HH.MM`:

```
humidity,temperature = Adafruit_DHT.read_retry(sensor,pin)
```

We are using this line to read the humidity and temperature reading from the DHT 11 sensor and the values that would be passed on to the variables `humidity` and `temperature`:

```
data = data + "," + str(temperature)
```

Once the data is read, we are adding temperature to the variable `data` as well. Hence, now the data would look like this `HH.MM` and `TT.TT`:

```
if (GPIO.input(sw1) == 0) and (GPIO.input(sw2) == 0):
state = 0
elif (GPIO.input(sw1) == 0) and (GPIO.input(sw2) == 1):
state = 1
elif (GPIO.input(sw1) == 1) and (GPIO.input(sw2) == 0):
state = 2
elif (GPIO.input(sw1) == 1) and (GPIO.input(sw2) == 1):
state = 3
```

Here, we have defined different types of states which are corresponding to the switch combinations. The table for it is as follows:

Switch 1	Switch 2	State
0	0	0
0	1	1
1	0	2
1	1	3

Hence, by the value of state, we can understand which switch would be turned on and which would be turned off:

```
data = ","+str(state)
```

Finally, the value of state is also added to the variable named `data`. Now, finally, the data would look like `HH.MM`, `TT.TT`, and `S`:

```
f.write(data)
```

Now, using the `write()` function, we are writing the value of data to the file that we have already defined by the value `f` earlier.

Hence, with every single switch on or off, the data would be collected, and the value would be recorded with the time stamp in that file. This data can then be used to predict the state of the home at any given time without any intervention:

```
if prev_state =! state:

    f.write(data)
    count = count+1
```

Here, we are comparing the state with the `prev_state` as you can see in our program. The previous state is calculated at the start of our program. So, if there is any change in the state of the system, then the value of `prev_state` and `state` would be different. This will lead to the `if` statement to be true. When that happens, the data would be written onto our file using the `write()` function. The argument passed is the value that needs to be written. Finally, the value of count is increased by 1.

Once this is left running for a few hours or may be days, then it would collect some really useful data regarding your switching pattern of the lights and fan. Thereafter, this data can be fetched to the previous program wherein it would be able to to take its own decision based on the time and temperature.

Home learning and automation

Now that in the previous section we have understood how the learning works, it's time to use this concept to make a robot that will automatically understand how we function and make decisions. Based on our decisions, the system will judge what should be done. But this time, rather than giving a set of data by the user, let's make this program create the data for itself. Once the data seems sufficient for itself to function. So, without much explanation, let's get right into it:

```
import Adafruit_DHT
import datetime
import RPi.GPIO as GPIO
import time
import numpy as np
import pandas as pd
from sklearn.neighbors import KNeighborsClassifier

GPIO.setmode(GPIO.BCM)
GPIO.setwarnings(False)

light = 22
fan = 23
sw1 = 13
sw2 = 14

GPIO.setup(light,GPIO.OUT)
GPIO.setup(fan,GPIO.OUT)
GPIO.setup(sw1,GPIO.IN)
GPIO.setup(sw2,GPIO.IN)
```

```
sensor = 11
pin = 2


f = open("dataset.csv","a+")
count = 0

while count < 200:

        data = ""

        H = datetime.datetime.now().strftime('%H')
        M = datetime.datetime.now().strftime('%M')

        data = str(H)+"."+str(M)
        humidity,temperature = Adafruit_DHT.read_retry(sensor,pin)
        data = data + "," + str(temperature)

prev_state = state

  if (GPIO.input(sw1) == 0) and (GPIO.input(sw2) == 0):
      state = 0
      GPIO.output(light,GPIO.LOW)
      GPIO.output(fan,GPIO.LOW)

  elif (GPIO.input(sw1) == 0) and (GPIO.input(sw2) == 1):
      state = 1
      GPIO.output(light,GPIO.HIGH)
      GPIO.output(fan,GPIO.LOW)

  elif (GPIO.input(sw1) == 1) and (GPIO.input(sw2) == 0):
     state = 2
       GPIO.output(light,GPIO.LOW)
       GPIO.output(fan,GPIO.HIGH)

  elif (GPIO.input(sw1) == 1) and (GPIO.input(sw2) == 1):
     state = 3
       GPIO.output(light,GPIO.HIGH)
       GPIO.output(fan,GPIO.HIGH)

  data = ","+str(state)

  if prev_state =! state:

      f.write(data)
      count = count+1
```

```
Test_set = []
knn = KNeighborsClassifier(n_neighbors=5)
data = pd.read_csv('dataset.csv')

X = np.array(data[['Time', 'Temp']])
y = np.array(data[['State']]).ravel()

knn.fit(X,y)

While Count > 200:

    time = ""

    H = datetime.datetime.now().strftime('%H')
    M = datetime.datetime.now().strftime('%M')

    time = float(str(H)+"."+str(M))

    humidity, temperature = Adafruit_DHT.read_retry(sensor, pin)


 temp = int(temperature)
 test_set.append(time)
 test_set.append(temp)

 a = knn.predict([test_set]])
 Out = a[0]

 If out == 0:
 GPIO.output(light,GPIO.LOW)
 GPIO.output(fan,GPIO.LOW)

 If out == 1:
 GPIO.output(light,GPIO.LOW)
 GPIO.output(fan,GPIO.HIGH)

 If out == 2:
 GPIO.output(light,GPIO.HIGH)
 GPIO.output(fan,GPIO.LOW)

 If out == 3:
 GPIO.output(light,GPIO.HIGH)
 GPIO.output(fan,GPIO.HIGH)
```

Now let's see what we have done here. In this program, the first part of the program inside the condition `while count < 200:` is exactly the same as what we have done in the last code. So, it is just doing the things according to the user, and at the same time, it's taking in the values from the users to understand their working behavior:

```
while count > 200:
```

Thereafter, we have the second part of the code that will start to execute when the count is beyond `200` that is inside the preceding loop:

```
time = ""
```

In this line, we are forming an empty string by the name of time where we would be storing the value of time:

```
H = datetime.datetime.now().strftime('%H')
M = datetime.datetime.now().strftime('%M')
```

We are storing the values of time into the variable named `H` and `M`:

```
time = float(str(H)+"."+str(M))
```

We are now storing the value of time in the string `time`. This would include both hours and minutes:

```
temp = int(temperature)
```

For the sake of ease of calculations and reducing the computing load on the system, we are reducing the size of the temperature variable . We are doing it by removing the decimal places. To do that `TT.TT`; we are simply eliminating the decimal point and converting it into integer. This is done by the function named `int()`. The value of temperature in `int` will be stored in the variable named `temp`:

```
test_set.append(time)
test_set.append(temp)
```

Here, we are adding the value of the time and the temperature to a list named `test_set` if you look in the program, then you will see the declaration of an empty set in the mid of the program. So, now this `test_set` has the value of `time` and `temp`, which can be further used by the prediction algorithm to predict the state:

```
a = knn.predict([[test_set]])
```

Using the simple function named `predict()` from the `knn` function, we can predict the value of the state. All we need to do is to pass on the data or `test_set` list over to the predict function. The output of this function will be a list that will be stored in a variable named `a`:

```
Out = a[0]
```

The value of `Out` will be set to the first element of the list `a`:

```
If out == 0:
GPIO.output(light,GPIO.LOW)
GPIO.output(fan,GPIO.LOW)

If out == 1:
GPIO.output(light,GPIO.LOW)
GPIO.output(fan,GPIO.HIGH)

If out == 2:
GPIO.output(light,GPIO.HIGH)
GPIO.output(fan,GPIO.LOW)

If out == 3:
GPIO.output(light,GPIO.HIGH)
GPIO.output(fan,GPIO.HIGH)
```

Using the preceding code block, we are able to switch on the light and fans selectively based on the state predicted by the algorithm. Hence, using this, the program would be able to automatically predict and switch on or off the light and the fans without your intervention.

Summary

In this chapter, we understood how machine learning works even without learning. We understood how datasets can be provided, and we can create a new dataset using the existing system. Finally, we understood how the system can work seamlessly to collect data, learn from that data, and finally, provide the input.

Making a Robotic Arm

30

Finally, we are where most of us have wanted to be since the start of this book. Making a robotic arm! In this chapter, we will learn the concepts behind the working of a robotic arm. Undoubtedly, we will also be making a robotic arm for our personal use as well that can do limitless things for us.

Basics of a robotic arm

If you see a human body, then one of the most distinctive parts that makes us able to be different than most other species is the arm. It is the part of the body that we use to do most of the work.

The human arm is a very complex mechanism of joints and muscles that work in tandem to give it the dexterity that we know it for. Take an example of our shoulder joint. If you pay attention, then you will notice that it has the ability to move up and down, right and left, and even rotate on its own axis, and all this while it just has one single joint, which we know as a ball joint.

When we talk about a robotic arm on a robot, we are undoubtedly talking about a complex arrangement of actuators with the body, otherwise known as a chassis, to get the desired motion in a three-dimensional space.

Now, let's understand some of the basic parts of any robotic arm. The first parts are the actuators. We can use motors to control the robotic arm; however, as we have studied earlier, using the motors we have used before will not be the ideal solution for it as it cannot hold its position neither does it have a feedback mechanism. So we are left with only one option, that is, to use servo motors. As we know, they have a handful of torque and have the ability to know where it is and to hold its position for as long as we want.

The second part of the robot is the chassis, that is, the part that holds all the motors together and provides structural support to the robot. This has to be made in such a way that it provides motion in all the desirable axis to any given joint. This is important as a single servo can only provide motion in one single axis. However, there are multiple places in which complex arrangement can be used to make the robot traverse in multiple axes. Also, the chassis should be rigid, which is extremely important. As we all know, all the material on this planet have certain level of flexibility. Also, the construction of the material depends on how noncompliant the material would be. This serves a very important purpose of repeatability.

Now, what is repeatability? As you might have seen in industries or any manufacturing units, the robots are installed and they do the same task over and over again. This is possible as the robots are programmed to perform a specific set of functions under specific circumstances. Now, let's say that the chassis of the robot is not rigid. In such a case, even if the servos are 100% precise and get to the exact same position over and over again, still the robot may actually differ from its actual goal position. This happens as there may be some flexibility in the chassis, which is why the final position may differ. Hence, a right chassis is a must. It becomes even more important when we are talking about large robots, as even the slightest of deformation can lead to a very large change in the final position of the arm.

One very common terminology which we use while talking about the robot arm is the end effector. This is basically the end of the robot arm, which will be doing all the final work for us. End effector in the case of a real human arm can be considered the hand. This is at the top of the arm and all the movement of the arm is basically to articulate the position of the hand in a three-dimensional space. Also, it is the hand that picks up the objects or does the necessary physical action. Hence, the term end effector.

Now, as the robotic arm is moving in a three dimensional space, it becomes a real big problem to define the axis in which the motion is happening. Hence, instead of using the axis to define the motion, we generally use the type of motion being performed, which gives us a realistic idea of what the motion is and in which axis it may be on. To analyze the motion, we use the concept of **Yaw Pitch and Roll (YPR)**.

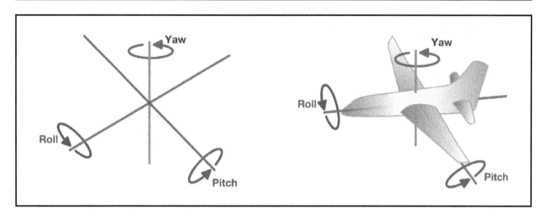

The preceding diagram will clear most of the doubts about YPR. This concept is generally used in aircrafts; however, it is an essential part of a robotic hand as well. So, as you can see from the preceding figure, when the nose of the plane goes up or down, it will be considered as pitch movement. Similarly, if the aircraft changes the heading, then the **Yaw** can be considered to change accordingly—the **Yaw** is nothing but the movement of aircraft in the *y* axis. Finally, we have something called **Roll**. It is used to understand the angel of rotation. As you can see, all these three entities are independent to each other and chasing any of it will not have any effect on the other. This concept is also useful as no matter what the orientation of the aircraft is, the YPR would still be unchanged and very much understandable. Hence, we take this concept straight from the aircraft directly to our robots.

Finally, how can we forget about the processing unit? It is the unit that commands all the actuators and does the coordination and the decision making. This processing unit in our case is Raspberry Pi, which will command all the actuators. All of these preceding components make up a robotic arm.

Degrees of freedom

Not every robotic arm is the same. They have different load ratings, that is, the maximum load that the end effector can take, the speed and reach, that is, how far the end effector can reach. However, one very important part of a robotic arm is the number of motors it has. So, for every axis, you need at least one motor to make the robot traverse in that axis. For example, a human arm has three-dimensional freedom in the shoulder joint. Hence, to mimic that joint, you will need a motor for every axis, that is, a minimum of three motors are required for the arm to move in all the three axis, independently. Similarly, when we talk about the elbow joint of our hand, it can only traverse in two dimensions. That is the closing and opening of the arm and the finally the rotation of the arm—the elbow does not move in the third dimension. Hence, to replicate its motion, we need at least two motors, so that we an move the robot in the w axis.

From what we have understood so far, we can safely assume that the more the number of motors, the more dexterous the robot would also be. This is mostly the case; however, you may use multiple motors to make the robot turn in a single axis itself. In such a scenario, the basic concept of counting the number of actuators to determine the dexterity of the robot will not work. So how do we determine how dexterous the robot is?

We have a concept called **degrees of freedom** (**DOF**). If I go by the standard definition, then I can be very sure that you will be left confused as to what it actually means. If you are not convinced, then try finding out on Google yourself. A DOF, in very simple and plain English, is a joint that can independently move on any given axis. So, for example, if we are talking about a shoulder joint, then we have movement in all the three axis. Hence, the degrees of freedom would be three. Now, let's take into consideration the elbow joint of our arm. As it can only move in pitch and roll, hence there are two DOFs that we end up with. If we connect the shoulder joint with the elbow joint, then the DOF will be added up and the whole system would be called to have six DOFs. Keep in mind that this definition is a very simplified one. There are multiple complexities that you will encounter should you choose to dig deeper.

Now, most of the robotic arms that you will encounter would be having close to six DOFs. Though you may say that it is less than what human arms have, in practicality, it does most of the work and obviously having less DOFs means less number of motors leading to lower cost and obviously lower complexity in programming. Hence, we try to use as few DOFs as possible.

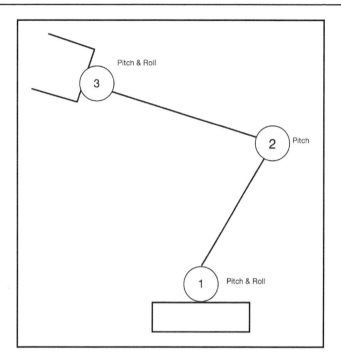

Now, in the preceding diagram, you can see a typical robotic arm which has six DOFs. The base actuator marked by number **1** gives the freedom of rolling and altering the pitch. The elbow actuators marked by number **2** add only one DOF of the pitch to the robot. Furthermore, joint number **3** is has the ability to travel in **Pitch & Roll**. Finally, we have the end actuator as the gripper here; the gripper in itself has one DOF. So, cumulatively, we can say that the robot is a six-DOF robot.

Power house

There is one unit that we have been using in all our projects, but I want to emphasize on it in this chapter. This unit is the power unit. The reason we are talking about it is because in this chapter we will be controlling multiple servos. When we are talking about multiple servos, naturally we will be talking about a lot of power consumption. In the robot arm, we have six servo motors. Now, depending upon the make and model of the motor, the power consumption will vary. But keeping yourself on a safer side and assuming every servo's power consumption to be around 1 amp would be a good idea. Most of the power supply you would be using might not be able to give you this much of burst current. So what should we do?

We can take the easy approach of taking a higher power output. But, instead, we can take the unconventional route. We can have a battery that can deliver this much of power when needed. But, the question is, will any battery solve our purpose? Obviously, the answer would be no.

There are multiple types of batteries that exist. These batteries can be distinguished based on the following parameters:

- Voltage
- Capacity
- Power to weight ratio
- Maximum charge and discharge rate
- Chemical composition

These are covered in detail in the upcoming subsections.

Voltage

Voltage is the overall potential difference that the battery can create. Every battery has a specific voltage that it delivers. One thing to remember is that this voltage will vary slightly based on the charge condition of the battery. That is, when a 12V battery is fully charged, it may be giving an output of 12.6V. However, when it gets fully discharged, it may reach up to 11.4V. So, what battery voltage means is the nominal voltage that the battery would be providing.

Capacity

Now, the second parameter is the capacity. Generally, when you buy a battery, you will see its capacity in **milliampere hour (mAh)** or in **ampere hours (Ah)**. This is a very simple term. Let me explain this term to you using an example. Let's say you have a battery with a capacity of 5 Ah. Now, if I draw 5 amperes continuously for 1 hour, then the battery will be completely discharged. On the contrary, if I draw 10 amperes continuously, then the battery will be discharged in half an hour. With this, we can also derive the overall power that the battery has using the following simple formula: *Overall Power in Watts = Nominal Voltage of Battery x Overall battery capacity of battery in amperes*

Hence, if you have a battery of 12V, which has a capacity of 10 Ah, then the overall capacity in watts will be 120 watts.

Power-to-weight ratio

Weight plays a very crucial role in robotics and if we increase the weight of the robot, then the force required to move it can exponentially go up. Hence, the concept of power to weight ratio comes into play. We always prefer a battery, which is extremely lightweight and delivers a large sum of power in respect to the weight. The equation for the power-to-weight ratio can be defined as follows: *Power to weight ratio in watt hour/kg = Maximum Power in watts / Overall weight of battery in kg.*

Now, let's say a battery is providing a power of 500 watts and the weight is 5 kg, then the power to weight ratio will be 100 Wh/kg. The higher the power to weight ratio, the better the battery is.

Maximum charge and discharge rate

This is perhaps one of the most crucial parts of the battery. Often the batteries are capable of running the robot for a span of 1 hour. However, the power consumption of robots is not constant. Let's say for 90% of the time, our robotic arm is consuming 2 amperes of power, so the battery capacity is of 2 Ah. However, at some points of time during the operation, the robot needs all the motors to work on peak power. The peak power consumption of the robot is around 6 amperes. Now, the question is, will the battery of 2 Ah be able to provide 6 amperes power to the robot?

This is a very practical challenge. You may say, it is better to go with a battery that is much bigger than a 2 Ah battery. But, as you know, it will increase the weight phenomenally. So what's the solution?

There is something called peak discharge current. This is denoted by C rating. So, if our battery is of 1 C rating then a 2 Ah battery will only be able to give us a maximum of 2 Ah of power supply at any given time. However, if the battery is of 10 C rating, then it should be able to provide a burst power supply of up to 20 amperes. These days, you can find batteries that can give a burst power supply of up to 100 C or even more. The reason we have this is because the peak power consumption of robots can be exponentially higher than their constant power consumption. If, at any point, the battery is not able to pull ample amount of power, then the robot would behave erroneously and can even shut down.

The second part of this story is the charge rating. This is the maximum charge current that you can provide to the battery. It is also denoted by the same C rating. So, if the C rating is 0.5, then you can provide a max of 1 ampere of charge to a 2 Ah battery.

In other words, the fastest you can charge a battery would be in 2 hours.

Chemical composition

There are different types of batteries that you can find on the market these are broadly segregated by their chemical composition. All of these batteries have their own pros and cons. Hence, we cannot say that one is better than the other. It is always a trade-off between various factors. The following is a list of batteries you can find on the market along with their pros and cons:

Battery	Peak power output	Power-to-weight ratio	Price
Wet cell	Low	Extremely low	Cheapest
Nickel metal hydride	Medium	Low	Cheap
Lithium ion	High	Good	High
Lithium polymer	Extremely high	Extremely good	Extremely high

As you can see from this table, the peak power output is something which we highly want and so is the good power-to-weight ratio; hence, spending a good amount of money on a lithium polymer battery makes sense.

These batteries, at a minimum, have a 20 C rating with a power-to-weight ratio around five times higher than the normal wet cell batteries. However, they can be up to 10 times more expensive than the normal wet cell batteries.

Now we know which batteries to choose for those higher current requirements. A lithium polymer battery of 11.1V and 2200 mAh will not cost you more than $20 and will provide you with immense power that you may never need. So, we have the power supply issue sorted. Now it's time to go ahead and make the robotic hand operational.

Finding the limits

The robotic arm kit is a fairly easy one to procure from eBay or Amazon. This is not very difficult to assemble and will require a few hours to prepare. Some of the robotic arm kits might not ship with servo motors, in which case, you may have to order it separately. I would say go for the kit that comes bundled with the servos, as there can be compatibility issues if you choose to order servos separately.

As you know, these servos will work using PWM and it's not hard to control them either. So, let's go straight onto it and see what we can do. Once you have assembled the robotic arm kit, connect the wires of the servos as follows:

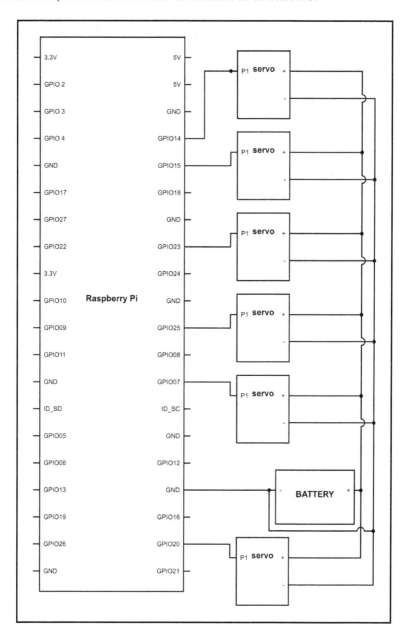

Now, firstly, we need to know what are the maximum physical limits of every single servo connected on our robot. There are various techniques to do that. The very basic one is to measure it physically. This method can be good but you won't be able to ever utilize the full potential of the servo motor as you would be having some degree of error in measuring. Hence, the value you put in the servo will be slightly less than what you think it can go to. The second method is by manually feeding the data and finding out the exact angle. So, let's go ahead with the second way of doing things and upload the following code:

```
import RPi.GPIO as GPIO
import time

GPIO.setmode(GPIO.BCM)
GPIO.setup(14,GPIO.OUT)
GPIO.setup(16,GPIO.OUT)
GPIO.setup(18,GPIO.OUT)
GPIO.setup(20,GPIO.OUT)
GPIO.setup(21,GPIO.OUT)
GPIO.setup(22,GPIO.OUT)


GPIO.setwarnings(False)

pwm1 = GPIO.PWM(14, 50)
pwm2 = GPIO.PWM(16, 50)
pwm3 = GPIO.PWM(18, 50)
pwm4 = GPIO.PWM(20, 50)
pwm5 = GPIO.PWM(21, 50)
pwm6 = GPIO.PWM(22, 50)

pwm1.start(0)
pwm2.start(0)
pwm3.start(0)
pwm4.start(0)
pwm5.start(0)
pwm6.start(0)

def cvt_angle(angle):
    dc = float(angle/90) + 0.5
    return dc

while 1:

  j = input('select servo')

  if j == 1:
```

```
    i = input('select value to rotate')
    pwm1.ChangeDutyCycle(cvt_angle(i))
    time.sleep(2)
    pwm1.ChangeDutyCycle(cvt_angle(90))

elif j ==2:

    i = input('select value to rotate')
    pwm2.ChangeDutyCycle(cvt_angle(i))
    time.sleep(2)
    pwm2.ChangeDutyCycle(cvt_angle(90))


elif j ==3:

    i = input('select value to rotate')
    pwm3.ChangeDutyCycle(cvt_angle(i))
    time.sleep(2)
    pwm3.ChangeDutyCycle(cvt_angle(90))

elif j ==4:

    i = input('select value to rotate')
    pwm4.ChangeDutyCycle(cvt_angle(i))
    time.sleep(2)
    pwm4.ChangeDutyCycle(cvt_angle(90))

elif j ==5:

    i = input('select value to rotate')
    pwm5.ChangeDutyCycle(cvt_angle(i))
    time.sleep(2)
    pwm5.ChangeDutyCycle(cvt_angle(90))

elif j ==6:

    i = input('select value to rotate')
    pwm6.ChangeDutyCycle(cvt_angle(i))
    time.sleep(2)
    pwm6.ChangeDutyCycle(cvt_angle(90)) }
```

Now, let's see what this code is doing. This code may look pretty elaborate, but what it is doing is extremely simple.

```
    j = input('select servo from 1-6')
```

Using the preceding line of code, we are printing the statement for the user `select servo from 1-6`. When the user enters a value of the servo, this value gets stored in a variable `j`:

```
if j == 1:

    i = input('select value to rotate')
    pwm1.ChangeDutyCycle(cvt_angle(i))
    time.sleep(2)
    pwm1.ChangeDutyCycle(cvt_angle(90))
```

This `if` condition here checks for the value of `j`. If in this line, `j=1`, then it will run the code corresponding to the servo number 1. Inside this code, the first line will print `select value to rotate`. Once this is done, the program will then wait for user input. Once the user inputs any value, then it will be stored in a variable called `I`. Thereafter, using the `cvt_angle(i)` function, the value which the user has input into the system will be converted to its corresponding duty cycle value. This duty cycle value will be fetched to the `pwm1.ChangeDutyCycle()` argument thereby giving the robot that very certain angle in the particular joint that you want. Due to the `time.sleep(2)` function, the servo will wait to go over to the next line. Thereafter, we are using the line `pwm1.ChangeDutyCycle(cvt_angle(90))`, which will bring it back to 90 degrees.

You may ask, why are we doing this? This is for a very important reason. Let's say you have given it a command to go beyond its physical limit. If that's the case, then the servo will keep on trying to move in that direction no matter what. However, due to the physical constrain, it will not be able to go ahead. Once this happens, then, within a few seconds, you will see blue smoke coming out of your servo indicating its death. The problem is that making such type of errors is very easy and the loss is quite noticeable. Hence, to prevent this, we quickly bring it back to the central position where it does not have any possibility of burning up.

Now, as per the preceding code, the same is done for servos 1-6 through the robot. Now that you know what is happening, it's time to take a pen and a paper and start giving servos the angular values. Do remember that the final goal of this code is to find out the maximum limits. So, let's start doing it starting from 90 degrees onwards. Give it a value on either side and not down until which value you can take it. Make a list on a paper as we will require it for our next code.

Making the robot safe

In the previous part of the chapter, with our multiple attempts, we have been able to find the maximum positions for each of the servos. Now it's time to use these values. In this chapter, we will be programming the servos for what its absolute maximums are. In this program, we will make sure that servos will never need to travel even a degree beyond the defined parameters on both the sides. If the user gives a value beyond it, then it will simply choose to ignore the user inputs instead of causing self damage.

So, let's see how to get it done. There are some parts of this program, where the numeric values have been bold. These are the values that you need to replace with the values which we have noted in the previous section of this chapter. For example, for servo 1, the values noted down are 23 and 170 as the maximum values for either side. Hence, the change in the code will be from if a[0] < 160 and a[0] > 30 to if a[0] < 170 and a[0] > 23. Similarly, for every servo, the same procedure has to be followed:

```
import RPi.GPIO as GPIO
import time

GPIO.setmode(GPIO.BCM)
GPIO.setup(14,GPIO.OUT)
GPIO.setup(16,GPIO.OUT)
GPIO.setup(18,GPIO.OUT)
GPIO.setup(20,GPIO.OUT)
GPIO.setup(21,GPIO.OUT)
GPIO.setup(22,GPIO.OUT)


GPIO.setwarnings(False)

pwm1 = GPIO.PWM(14, 50)
pwm2 = GPIO.PWM(16, 50)
pwm3 = GPIO.PWM(18, 50)
pwm4 = GPIO.PWM(20, 50)
pwm5 = GPIO.PWM(21, 50)
pwm6 = GPIO.PWM(22, 50)

pwm1.start(cvt_angle(90))
pwm2.start(cvt_angle(90))
pwm3.start(cvt_angle(90))
pwm4.start(cvt_angle(90))
pwm5.start(cvt_angle(90))
pwm6.start(cvt_angle(90))
```

```
def cvt_angle(angle):
    dc = float(angle/90) + 0.5
    return dc

while True:

    a = raw_input("enter a list of 6 values")
    if a[0] < 160 and  a[0] > 30:
        pwm1.ChangeDutyCycle(cvt_angle(a[0]))

    if a[1] < 160 and  a[1] > 30:
        pwm2.ChangeDutyCycle(cvt)angle(a[1]))

    if a[0] < 160 and  a[0] > 30:
        pwm3.ChangeDutyCycle(cvt_angle(a[2]))

    if a[0] < 160 and  a[0] > 30:
        pwm4.ChangeDutyCycle(cvt_angle(a[3]))

    if a[0] < 160 and  a[0] > 30:
        pwm5.ChangeDutyCycle(cvt_angle(a[4]))

    if a[0] < 160 and  a[0] > 30:
        pwm6.ChangeDutyCycle(cvt_angle(a[5]))}
```

Now, in this code, we have done something very rudimentary. You can safely say that all we have done is put the `ChangeDutyCycle()` function inside an `if` statement. This `if` statement will govern whether the servo will move or stay still in its own position. To some, it may seem very naive to have this program in a special section. But, trust me, it is not. This statement will now be used as a part of every program from here on. All the code written for the movement of the servos will have to check the final values going to the servos through this `if` statement; hence, a basic visualization of code is extremely necessary.

Now that the explanation is done, it's time for you to give different commands and see whether they are working within the safe working limits.

Programming multiple frames

In the previous chapter, we have learned the basics of how to make sure that the robot is working under safe limits. In this chapter, we will be looking at how a robot can be made to do different activities at a click of a button, instead of typing the values one by one.

To do this, we will need to understand some advanced concepts of motion. Whenever you watch any video or play any video games, then you must have come across the term **frames per second (FPS)**. If you haven't heard this term, then let me explain it for you. Every video made right now is actually made by still images. These still images are captured by cameras that click 25-30 times in a second. When these images are played back on the screen at the same rate at which they are captured, it forms a smooth video.

Similarly, in robots, we do have the concept of frames. These frames, however, are not images but instead multiple steps that the robot has to follow to achieve a specific motion. In a simple robotic program, there could be simply two frames, that is, the initial frame and the final frame. These two frames will correspond to the initial position or the final position.

However, in the real world, this is not always possible, as whenever the robot goes directly from the initial position to the final position, it tends a specific path with a specific curvature. However, there can be obstacles in that path or this path would not be desired as the path that needs to be followed could be a different one. Hence, we need frames. These frames not only define the robot's motion from the initial position to the final position, but also break down the transition from these two positions into multiple steps making the robot follow the desired path.

This can be referred as frame programming, which we will cover in this chapter. One thing to keep in mind is that more the number of frames, smoother will be the functioning of the robot. Do you remember the CCTV footage we saw? We could say it's not smooth and has a lot of jerkiness. This is due to the low frame rate of the CCTV camera. Instead of working on 30 FPS, they work on 15 FPS. This is done to reduce the storage space of the video. However, if you see the latest videos, there are some games and videos with much higher frame rate than normal. Some of our latest camera works on 60 FPS, making the video even smoother and enjoyable to watch. The same will be the case with the robot. The more the number of frames, the smoother and controlled the motion would be. However, make sure you don't go into overkill.

Now, to move from one position to another, we will have to put the values of the angles of every single servos in the very beginning. Once fetched, it will automatically start to execute these values one by one. To do this, go ahead and write the following code:

```
import RPi.GPIO as GPIO
import time

GPIO.setmode(GPIO.BCM)
```

```
GPIO.setup(14,GPIO.OUT)
GPIO.setup(16,GPIO.OUT)
GPIO.setup(18,GPIO.OUT)
GPIO.setup(20,GPIO.OUT)
GPIO.setup(21,GPIO.OUT)
GPIO.setup(22,GPIO.OUT)


GPIO.setwarnings(False)

pwm1 = GPIO.PWM(14, 50)
pwm2 = GPIO.PWM(16, 50)
pwm3 = GPIO.PWM(18, 50)
pwm4 = GPIO.PWM(20, 50)
pwm5 = GPIO.PWM(21, 50)
pwm6 = GPIO.PWM(22, 50)

pwm1.start(0)
pwm2.start(0)
pwm3.start(0)
pwm4.start(0)
pwm5.start(0)
pwm6.start(0)

def cvt_angle(angle):
    dc = float(angle/90) + 0.5
    return dc

prev0 = 90
prev1 = 90
prev2 = 90
prev3 = 90
prev4 = 90
prev5 = 90

while True:

    a = raw_input("enter a list of 6 values for motor 1")
    b = raw_input("enter a list of 6 values for motor 2")
    c = raw_input("enter a list of 6 values for motor 3")
    d = raw_input("enter a list of 6 values for motor 4")
    e = raw_input("enter a list of 6 values for motor 5")
    f = raw_input("enter a list of 6 values for motor 6")


    for i in range(6):

        if a[i] > 10 and a[i]< 180 :
```

```
        pwm1.ChangeDutyCycle(cvt_angle(a[i]))

if b[i] > 10 and b[i] < 180:
        pwm2.ChangeDutyCycle(cvt_angle(b[i]))

if c[i] > 10 and c[i] < 180:
        pwm3.ChangeDutyCycle(cvt_angle(c[i]))

if d[i] > 10 and d[i] < 180:
        pwm4.ChangeDutyCycle(cvt_angle(d[i]))

if e[i] > 10 and e[i] < 180:
        pwm5.ChangeDutyCycle(cvt_angle(e[i]))

if f[i] > 10 and f[i] < 180:
        pwm6.ChangeDutyCycle(cvt_angle(f[i]))
```

In this program, you can see that we have replicated the previous program with some very minor changes. So, let's see what these changes are:

```
a = raw_input("enter a list of 6 values for motor 1")
b = raw_input("enter a list of 6 values for motor 2")
c = raw_input("enter a list of 6 values for motor 3")
d = raw_input("enter a list of 6 values for motor 4")
e = raw_input("enter a list of 6 values for motor 5")
f = raw_input("enter a list of 6 values for motor 6")
```

Here, we are taking the input values for each servo and storing it in a different list. For servo 1, the list a will be used; similarly, b will be used for servo 2, and so on until f. In the preceding lines of code, the robot will prompt the user to fill in the six frame values for motor 1. Then, it will ask six values for motor 2 and similarly until motor 6:

```
for i in range(6):
```

The entire program for giving PWM to the servo is concentrated in this for loop. This loop will check the value of i and increment it every time. The value of i will start from 1 and the loop will run and increment the value of i until it reaches 6.

```
        if a[i] > 10 and a[i]< 180 :
            pwm1.ChangeDutyCycle(cvt_angle(a[i]))
```

In this line of the program, the value contained in the list is headed based on the value of 1. So, for the first time it will read the value of a[1], which will correspond to the first value of the list a[]. This value should be between the safe working limits, hence the if loop. If it is within safe working limits, then the program in the if condition will work, else it won't. Inside the if loop, we have a simple statement: pwm1.ChangeDutyCycle(cvt_angle(a[I])). This will simply take the value of a[1] and convert it into the corresponding PWM value and fetch it to the ChangeDutyCycle() function, which will change the PWM for servo 1.

A similar program is made for the rest of the servos as well going on from servo 1 to servo 6. Hence, all of these will read the values of their corresponding list one by one and change the angle of the servo the way the user has programmed it. Furthermore, as the loop gets executed, the value of i will increase, hence making the program read the different values fetched in the list. Every value of the servo in the list will correspond to a different frame, hence parsing the robot through it.

So go ahead and have some fun making your robot do some awesome moves. Just take care that you be gentle to it!

Speed control

It's amazing to have made a robotic arm so easily, and with just a bit of code, we are now able to control it the way we want. However, there is one problem you might have noticed, that is, the robot is moving the way we want but not at the speed at which we want it to move. This is a very common problem while using the digital PWM-based servos.

These servos do not have a built-in speed control. Their control system is programmed to move the servo as fast as they can to reach the goal position. Hence, to control the speed, we will have to play with the program itself and give it a smooth linear progression.

The speed control can be done through a few different techniques. So, without much talking, let's go and see the code. Before you write it, read it and go through the code once and then see the following explanation to it. Thereafter, you will have a better idea of what we are doing. This will make writing the code faster and easier. So, let's take a look at it:

```
import RPi.GPIO as GPIO
import time

GPIO.setmode(GPIO.BCM)
GPIO.setup(14,GPIO.OUT)
GPIO.setup(16,GPIO.OUT)
GPIO.setup(18,GPIO.OUT)
GPIO.setup(20,GPIO.OUT)
GPIO.setup(21,GPIO.OUT)
GPIO.setup(22,GPIO.OUT)


GPIO.setwarnings(False)

pwm1 = GPIO.PWM(14, 50)
pwm2 = GPIO.PWM(16, 50)
pwm3 = GPIO.PWM(18, 50)
pwm4 = GPIO.PWM(20, 50)
pwm5 = GPIO.PWM(21, 50)
pwm6 = GPIO.PWM(22, 50)

pwm1.start(0)
pwm2.start(0)
pwm3.start(0)
pwm4.start(0)
pwm5.start(0)
pwm6.start(0)

def cvt_angle(angle):
    dc = float(angle/90) + 0.5
    return dc

prev0 = 90
prev1 = 90
prev2 = 90
prev3 = 90
prev4 = 90
prev5 = 90

pwm1.ChangeDutyCycle(cvt_angle(prev0))
pwm2.ChangeDutyCycle(cvt_angle(prev1))
```

```
pwm3.ChangeDutyCycle(cvt_angle(prev2))
pwm4.ChangeDutyCycle(cvt_angle(prev3))
pwm5.ChangeDutyCycle(cvt_angle(prev4))
pwm6.ChangeDutyCycle(cvt_angle(prev5))


while True:

 a = raw_input("enter a list of 6 values for motor 1")
 b = raw_input("enter a list of 6 values for motor 2")
 c = raw_input("enter a list of 6 values for motor 3")
 d = raw_input("enter a list of 6 values for motor 4")
 e = raw_input("enter a list of 6 values for motor 5")
 f = raw_input("enter a list of 6 values for motor 6")

    speed = raw_input("enter one of the following speed 0.1, 0.2, 0.5,
1")


 for i in range(6):

   while prev0 =! a[i] and prev1 =! b[i] and prev2 =! c[i] and prev3
=! d[i] and prev4 =! e[i] and prev 5 =! f[i]

    if a[i] > 10 and a[i]< 180 :

        if prev0 > a[i]
           prev0 = prev0 - speed

         if prev0 < a[i]
            prev0 = prev0 + speed

         if prev0 = a[i]
            prev0 = prev0

        pwm1.ChangeDutyCycle(cvt_angle(prev0))


    if b[i] > 10 and b[i] < 180:

        if prev2 > b[i]
           prev2 = prev2 - speed

         if prev2 < b[i]
            prev2 = prev2 + speed

         if prev2 = b[i]
```

```
            prev2 = prev2

        pwm2.ChangeDutyCycle(cvt_angle(b[i]))


    if c[i] > 10 and c[i] < 180:

        if prev3 > c[i]
            prev3 = prev3 - speed

        if prev3 < c[i]
            prev3 = prev3 + speed

        if prev3 = c[i]
            prev3 = prev3

        pwm3.ChangeDutyCycle(cvt_angle(c[i]))



    if d[i] > 10 and d[i] < 180:

        if prev4 > d[i]
            prev4 = prev4 - speed

        if prev4 < d[i]
            prev4 = prev4 + speed

        if prev4 = d[i]
            prev4 = prev4

    pwm4.ChangeDutyCycle(cvt_angle(d[i]))



  if e[i] > 10 and e[i] < 180:
        if prev5 > e[i]
            prev5 = prev5 - speed

        if prev0 < e[i]
            prev5 = prev5 + speed

        if prev5 = e[i]
            prev5 = prev5

    pwm5.ChangeDutyCycle(cvt_angle(e[i]))
```

```
    if f[i] > 10 and f[i] < 180:

        if prev6 > f[i]
            prev6 = prev6 - speed

        if prev6 < f[i]
            prev6 = prev6 + speed

        if prev6 = f[i]
            prev6 = prev6

    pwm6.ChangeDutyCycle(cvt_angle(f[i]))


 flag = 0
```

In this program, there are quite a few things. We should go through them one by one to have an understanding of it. So, let's see what we are doing:

```
prev0 = 90
prev1 = 90
prev2 = 90
prev3 = 90
prev4 = 90
prev5 = 90
```

Here, we have defined six new variables with the name `prev0` to `prev5` and all of them have been allowed a value of `90`. The term `prev` here stands for previous, so this will be there to indicate the previous value.

```
        while prev0 =! a[i] and prev1 =! b[i] and prev2 =! c[i] and
prev3 =! d[i]    and prev4 =! e[i] and prev 5 =! f[i]
```

After the code line `for i in range 6`, we have the preceding line of code, which is basically checking the value of `a[i]` with `prev0`. Similarly, it is checking the values of `b[i]` with `prev1` and so on. Until the time all of these are not true the `while` loop will be true and will loop the program inside it until the condition is not false. That is, all the `prev` values are exactly equal to the values of the corresponding values of the list.

Again, this may seem a little odd to you, but, trust me, it will be quite useful, which we will see in a while:

```
    if a[i] > 10 and a[i]< 180 :

        if prev0 > a[i]
            prev0 = prev0 - speed
```

```
if prev0 < a[i]
    prev0 = prev0 + speed

if prev0 = a[i]
    prev0 = prev0

pwm1.ChangeDutyCycle(cvt_angle(prev0))
```

Now, here comes the real deal. This is the main program that will control the speed of the servo. In this, the first line is simple; it will check whether the value given to it is valid, that is, between the safe limits. Once that is done, it will then check whether the value of a[Ii] is less than or greater than the previous value. If it is greater than a[i], then it will take in the previous value and decrement it with the speed specified by the user. If it is less than the value of a[i], then it will increment the previous value with the speed specified.

So, if you look at it, the code is simply incrementing or decrementing the previous value every time the while loop is running. Now, the while loop will run until the value of prev is equal to the corresponding list value. That is, the loop will keep incrementing the value until it reaches the specified position.

Hence, lower the value of the speed, lower will be the increments every single time, thereby slowing down the speed all together.

This is the same process which will happen for all other servos as well. It may sound very complicated, but it is not! Programming is easy and will continue to remain easy each time you break it down into small pieces and understand them one by one!

Summary

In this chapter, we have understood the basics of robotic arm, its power source, and its programming. With a very simple program, we were able to find out the limits of the servos and then apply these limits to make sure the servo did not damage itself. We got a basic idea of what frames are and did some programming based on frames. Finally, we also went ahead and controlled the speed of the servo using our very own program on a basic level.

Other Books You May Enjoy

If you enjoyed this book, you may be interested in these other books by Packt:

Build Supercomputers with Raspberry Pi 3
Carlos R. Morrison

ISBN: 978-1-78728-258-2

- Understand the concept of the Message Passing Interface (MPI)
- Understand node networking
- Configure nodes so that they can communicate with each other via the network
  switch
- Build a Raspberry Pi3 supercomputer
- Test the supercluster
- Use the supercomputer to calculate MPI π codes
- Learn various practical supercomputer applications

ROS Robotics Projects

Lentin Joseph

ISBN: 978-1-78355-471-3

- Create your own self-driving car using ROS
- Build an intelligent robotic application using deep learning and ROS
- Master 3D object recognition
- Control a robot using virtual reality and ROS
- Build your own AI chatter-bot using ROS
- Get to know all about the autonomous navigation of robots using ROS
- Understand face detection and tracking using ROS
- Get to grips with teleoperating robots using hand gestures
- Build ROS-based applications using Matlab and Android
- Build interactive applications using TurtleBot

Leave a review - let other readers know what you think

Please share your thoughts on this book with others by leaving a review on the site that you bought it from. If you purchased the book from Amazon, please leave us an honest review on this book's Amazon page. This is vital so that other potential readers can see and use your unbiased opinion to make purchasing decisions, we can understand what our customers think about our products, and our authors can see your feedback on the title that they have worked with Packt to create. It will only take a few minutes of your time, but is valuable to other potential customers, our authors, and Packt. Thank you!

Index

R

Printed in the USA
CPSIA information can be obtained
at www.ICGtesting.com
CBHW040857201223
2695CB00005B/16

9 781838 555795